Vedalakṣaṇa Texts: Search and Analysis

Samīkṣikā Series
No. 11

General Editor
V. VENKATARAMANA REDDY

The Samīkṣikā Series is aimed at compiling the papers presented by the various scholars during the seminars organized by the National Mission for Manuscripts. The seminars provide an interactive forum for scholars to present to a large audience, ideas related to the knowledge contained in India's textual heritage.

In keeping with the title, the Samīkṣikā (research) Series is concerned with research papers of distinguished scholars and specialists in different intellectual disciplines of India.

Vedalakṣaṇa Texts: Search and Analysis

Editor

Nabanarayan Bandyopadhyay

National Mission for Manuscripts

Dev Publishers & Distributors

Published by:
National Mission for Manuscripts
11, Man Singh Road
New Delhi-110 001
Phone: 91 11 2307 3387
E-mail: directornamami@nic.in
Website: www.namami.nic.in

and Co-published by:
Dev Publishers & Distributors
2nd Floor, Prakash Deep,
22, Delhi Medical Association Road,
Darya Ganj,
New Delhi-110002
Phone: 011-43572647
E-mail: devbooks@hotmail.com
Website: www.devbooks.co.in

ISBN 81-904029-6-X (Series)
ISBN 978-93-80829-40-1 (Vol. XI)
First published 2017

Price : ₹ 600

Contents

Foreword

The National Mission for Manuscripts organizes national level seminars in different academic institutions all over India to promote research and interest in Indian knowledge systems with particular emphasis on manuscripts. The present Samikshika series brings forth the research papers on Vedalakṣaṇa texts as were presented by the scholars in the seminar "Vedalakṣaṇa Texts: Search and Analysis" organized at School of Vedic Studies, Rabindra Bharati University, Kolkata.

The Lakṣaṇa-granthas of Vedas deal with phonetics, grammar, anukramanis, modes of recitation etc. These are of ancillary nature and come under Vedāṅga, Śikṣā is considered to be the most important among them.

Śikṣā is the science of phonetics under which syllabication of sound (*varṇa*), accent (*svara*), sound measurement (mātrā, place of articulation (*prayatna*), etc. are elaborately explained. In Vedic period, lot of importance was given to the correct pronunciation of the mantras at the time of their utterance.

Under Śikṣā Vedāṅga, come two types of compositions, viz. Prātiśākhya and Śikṣā. Prātiśākhyas are the first treatises under Śikṣā Vedāṅga dealing with the phonetic pecularities of all the śākhās of a praticular Veda. Śikṣā-texts, too, are related to particular recentions of the Vedas but these texts are posterior to the Prātiśākhyas. These texts are mostly found in Kārikā-form leaving some which are written in the

Sūtra-form. All Veda-lakṣaṇa texts render their help to understand the Vedas in true perspective.

There are a lot of manuscripts related to Vedalakṣaṇas which have not been critically edited till date. Young scholars need to be encouraged to delve into those manuscripts in order to bring fourth the underlying implications of Vedic texts.

The Mission acknowledges the contribution of Prof. Nabanarayan Bandyopadhyay, Director, School of Vedic Studies, Rabindra Bharti University, Kolkata. The organisation of the seminar and publication of this volume wouldn't have been possible without his sincere cooperation. The Mission also thanks Dev Publishers & Distributors for bringing out this volume.

I do hope that the topics dealt with in this volume would help the readers to acquire knowledge of this genre of Vedic literature.

V. Venkataramana Reddy
Director,
National Mission for Manuscripts

New Delhi
Akshaya Tritya, 2017

Introduction

It is not generally realized that the texts on Veda-lakṣaṇa (mainly extant in South Indian Vedic tradition) contain an abundance of valuable material of Vedic studies relating to Phonetics. The Lakṣaṇa-granthas or texts which dilate upon the characteristics and the special features of Vedic texts are generally termed Veda-lakṣaṇa. They are of ancillary nature and generally regarded as a component of the Vedāṅga. Veda-lakṣaṇa texts can be classified into four categories: (a) works (mainly Śikṣā and Prātiākhya) on Vedic phonetics, phonology, grammar (also designated as 'Nomenclative Grammatical Works', according to Surya-kanta), etc., (b) works on Anukramaṇis, (c) works containing lists of words having peculiar characteristics in the Vedic texts, and d) works dealing mainly with modes of recitation, There are a large number of important texts, very few of which are available in print. An account of them can be trailed from various descriptive catalogues of manuscripts largely published from many institutes of South India and a voluminous work entitled *Vedalakṣaṇa: Vedic Ancillary Literature: A Descriptive Bibliography* by K. Parameswara Aithal, (Franz Verlag Stuttgart, 1991, an Indian reprint also published from MLBD, Delhi). It would be appropriate to focus our attention on these works concerning different aspects of Vedic learning. The practice of reciting the Vedas in the traditional manner is becoming fast extinct yet there has been in recent years a growing interest in the study of the oral and exegetic tradition of Vedic recitation amongst a select section of people.

The printed editions, with only a few exceptions, are either edited in a very uncritical manner, or contain a great deal of confusion regarding the authorship, titles, extent of the texts, etc. The unsatisfactory state of the printed editions on Lakṣaṇas is more evident from various publications which are full of errors due to mixing together of texts in the basic manuscript etc. or do contain the extraneous portions.

As we all know, there are two different aspects of the system of learning of the Vedas traditionally – the *svādhyaya* and the *prayoga.* Though a study of these aspects relate mainly to the recitation of the Vedas of one's own *śākhā,* yet the study of the history of grammatical traditions in India as well as different branches of manuscriptology are bound to come with all their importance, thus adding an interdisciplinary essence to the matter as far as possible.

As a growing interest has been found in recent years in the study of the oral tradition of Vedic recitation it seems appropriate to undertake the study and research on these types of texts. The purpose and significance of preparing text-critical edition of the hitherto unpublished Lakṣaṇa texts along with their critical analysis and translation is to attract due attention to this particular branch of Vedic studies which unfortunately appears to have dwindled to the point of extinction despite efforts made by great scholars interested in this particular field more than a century ago.

The significance lies mainly in the history of the study of Indian grammatical and linguistic traditions which begins with the Śikṣā and the Prātiśākhya. Though they contain instructions on pronunciation, intonation, euphonic changes of sounds in word combinations, elongation of vowels etc, the holistic manner of recitation of the Saṃhitās is not itself actual works of grammar still they deal with subjects which belong to grammar and linguistics.

They bear the testimony of the fact that the texts of the Saṃhitās have been preserved without any change throughout all these centuries since the time of the

Prātiśākhya, the Ṛgveda Prātiśākhya being the oldest text book of Vedic phonetics. And the fact that the practice of different modes of recitation or the method of instruction is emphatically necessary for the proper understanding and transmission of any kind of Vedic text, hence the effort to undertake the proposed study. In order to retrieve this hallowed heritage and bringing to light this invaluable treasure of source material as of the Veda-lakṣaṇa texts, serious integrated efforts have to be put in to avoid the inevitable extinction of the quintessence of ancient Indian learning and thought.

The methodological and didactic aspect of Vedic text tradition is yet to be thoroughly and systematically investigated in modern Vedic scholarship and research. A recent study reveals that there are about 200 Śikśā treatises which have not so far received that amount of serious attention of the scholars which they deserve. Very few of them have come out only in the form of popular editions, not in critically edited shape. Although the importance of the *padapāṭha* i.e. word-for-word-recitation, has been recognized, we know that it has neither been systematically studied or researched upon, nor there is a proper edition as it is recited by traditional pundits. To elicit the views of scholars in this field, a 3-day National Seminar on 'Veda-lakṣaṇa Texts: Search and Analysis' was organized by the School of Vedic Studies, Rabindra Bharati University, under the auspices of the National Mission for Manuscripts, New Delhi, which was dedicated to the sacred memory of Swami Vivekananda on his sesquicentennial birth anniversary.

The inaugural session had very distinguished and special personalities as Prof. Karunasindhu Das, former Vice-Chancellor, Rabindra Bharati University as the inaugurator who being a grammarian and philosopher himself, explained the Veda-lakṣaṇa texts with all their technicalities. It was always been a rare experience listening to Prof. T.N. Dharmadhikari, former Director, Vaidika Samshodhana Mandala, who while delivering the keynote address deliberated on most difficult and technically complicated issues on Vedic studies and especially this time he illuminated the audience with demonstration of certain varieties of accents and pronunciation of Vedic *svara*-s of typical type. The session was blessed by the presence of Swami Sarvapriyananda, Acharya, Probationers' Traning College at Belur Math who while delivering his address as the Special Guest brought forth Swami Vivekananda's thoughts on the Vedas and Upanishads and thus initiated the discussion of his multifaceted personality. Prof. Ratna Basu, Dept. of Sanskrit, Calcutta University and Cordinator, Calcutta University Manuscript Resource Centre and Manuscript Conservation Centre, addressed the audience as the Guest of Honour about its aim and activities thereby bringing in the context of text-editing, the highly technical academic exercise involving manuscripts. The brief presidential address by Prof. Chinmoy Guha, Vice-Chancellor of the University, was full of words of encouragement and wishes for its success. He congratulated the School for the concern they keep for the cause of caring and preservation of the ancient Indian wisdom in their every academic effort.

It was very satisfying and encouraging at the same time to note that a large number of research papers were presented during the academic sessions of the seminar besides the key note and the valedictory address. The distinguished outstation scholars included, to name a few, Prof. B.B. Chaubey, former Director, VVBIS & IS, Professor Emeritus, Panjab University, Paper on 'Importance of Editing Vedic Lakṣaṇa-texts with special reference to Stobhānusaṃhāra'; Prof. Sitanath Dey, former Professor, Tripura University, 'The Importance of Studying Prātiśākhyas with special reference to the Vājasaneyi Prātiśākhya'; Prof. S. Sudarshan Sharma, Vice-Chancellor, Sri Venkateswar Vedic University, Tirupati; Prof. Dipak Bhattacharya, former Professor, Dept. of Sanskrit, Pali and Prakrit, Visva-Bharati University, 'Lakṣaṇa granthas in Solving Exegetical Problems of the Atharvaveda'; Dr. C.M. Neelakandhan, Dept. of Sanskrit

Sahitya, Sree Sankaracharya University, Kaladi, 'Veda-lakṣaṇa Texts and Tradition of Kerala'; Dr. P. Ramanujan, Associate Director, IHG, CDAC, Bangalore, 'A Computer–based Manuscript (Palm-leaf) Editor'; Prof. Manjula Devi, Dept. of Sanskrit, Gauhati University, 'Some Observations on the Context of Vedādhyayana i.e., the Study of the Veda in the Prātiśākhyas'; Dr. Nirmala R. Kulkarni, Research Scientist, CASS, Pune University, 'Sabdabrahmavilāsa: An Unpublished Commentary on the Taittirīya Prātiśākhya'; Prof. Bhagyalata Pataskar, Director, Vaidika Samshodhana Mandala, Pune, 'Māṇḍukī Śikṣā, the only Śikṣā belonging to the Atharvavedic Tradition'; Dr. Shri Krishanḥ Sharma, Professor and Ex-Director, Institute of Sanskrit and Indological Studies, Kurukshetra University, '*Pāriśikṣāyāḥ Viśleṣaṇātmakaḥ Paricayaḥ*'; Prof. Radhamadhab Dash, Head, P.G. Dept. of Sanskrit, Utkal University, Bhubaneswar 'Ṛk-Prātiśākhya and Pāṇini or Saṁhitā', etc.

Among the local scholars who participated as resource persons were, to mention a few, Prof. Satya Ranjan Banerjee, former Professor of Linguistics, Calcutta University 'Phonetic Studies in Ancient India'; Prof. Bhabani Prasad Bhattacharya, former Professor of Sanskrit Jadavpur University, 'Nature of Vivṛtti as revealed in Śikṣās and Prātiśākhyas'; Prof. Ratna Basu, Dept. of Sanskrit, Calcutta University, 'Pāṇinīyaśikṣā and Science of Logopaedie'; Prof. Didhiti Biswas, Dept. of Sanskrit, Calcutta University, 'Some Observations on Nāradīyaśikṣā'; Dr. Chhaya Bhattacharya, 'Technical Terms found in the Prātiśākhyas, with special reference to Sound Vibrations'; Prof. Pradyot Kumar Datta, Dept. of Sanskrit, Jadavpur University, 'Emergence of Vedalakṣaṇa Ponetic Text of Sāmaprāliśākhya'; Dr. Mau Dasgupta, Dept. of Sanskrit, Calcutta University, 'In Search of the lost Māṇḍukeya Tradition: A Phonetic Reference at the Ṛkprātiśākhya'; Dr. Indrani Kar, Associate Professor, Dept. of Sanskrit, Scottish Church College, Kolkata, 'Accent in the Ṛkprātiśākhyas: A Study'; Dr. Subhra Ghosh,

'Treatment of the Two Alphabetic Sounds 'ṛ' and 'ḷ' in Sanskrit Phonology'; Prof. Taraknath Adhikari, Dept. of Sanskrit, Rabindra Bharati University, 'Lakṣaṇagranthas of the Atharvaveda and their Importance'; Dr. Parboty Chakraborty, Associate Professor, Dept. of Sanskrit, Rabindra Bharati University, 'The Nature of Anunāsika : Phonetic and Grammatical Speculations'; Dr. Ashok Kumar Mahata, Assistant Professor, Rishi Bankim College, Naihati, 'The Concept of mātrā in the Vājasaneyi Prātiśākhya with special reference to the quantity of *avagraha*'; Dr. Bhaskarnath Bhattacharya, Associate Professor of the School, Rabindra Bharati University, 'Vedalakṣaṇa –how does it establish the magnanimity of the Sāmaveda'; Dr. Soma Basu, Associate Professor of the School, 'Euphonic Combination in the Ṛkprātiśākhya: A Brief Study', etc.

The valedictory session was chaired by Prof. B. B. Chaubey, former Director, VVBIS & IS, Professor Emeritus, Panjab University and the valedictory address was delivered by Prof. Samiran Chandra Chakrabarti, former director of the School and former Emeritus Fellow, UGC, who explained in detail the technicalities of the Lakṣaṇa texts of the different Vedas. It is gratifying to note that we are going to publish maximum number of papers presented at the mentioned seminar in this volume. Very few of them could not be collected from the learned resource persons despite our best efforts. One research scholar, however, Shri Subhendu Manna by name, submitted his paper on 'Upasarga in Sanskrit Language' for publication and myself added a paper on 'Sandhikarikā: An Unpublished Lakṣaṇa Text' relating to the topic of the seminar. I express my sincere thankfulness and gratitude to the distinguished scholars who contributed papers and participated in the deliberations of the seminar. I am grateful to the authorities of National Mission for Manuscripts, New Delhi, for kindly sponsoring the Seminar and undertaking this work of publication. A lot of thanks and appreciation are due to Dr Sanghamitra Basu, Coordinator of Research and Publication of National Mission for Manuscripts for actively assisting me in the process of editing and printing of this volume. Without her encouraging efforts it would not possibly see the light of the day. I shall be failing in my duty if I do not express my heartfelt thanks to the members of the School, specially to Professor Samiran Chandra Chakrabarti, Dr Bhaskarnath Bhattacharyya, Dr Soma Basu and the then Project Assitants who had extended their helping hands in respect of successful organization of the seminar and the related matters of publication. Messrs Dev Publishers & Distributors have also very satisfactorily done the job of printing of this volume. At the end, I also crave for indulgence of the readers for any error inadvertently crept in. Every suggestion for future improvement of this volume will be greatly appreciated. Hope, the present volume will regenerate interest in doing study and research on ancillary Vedic texts among promising scholars.

// bhadraiṣāṃ lakṣmīrnihitādhi vāci //

NABANARAYAN BANDYOPADHYAY
Professor and Director
School of Vedic Studies
Rabindra Bharati University, Kolkata

Key to Transliteration

VOWELS

अ a	आ ā	इ i	ई ī	उ u	ऊ ū
(but)	(palm)	(it)	(beet)	(put)	(pool)
ऋ ṛ	ए e	ऐ ai	ओ o	औ au	
(rhythm)	(play)	(air)	(toe)	(loud)	

CONSONANTS

Guttural	क ka	ख* kha	ग ga	घ gha	ङ ṅa
	(skate)	(blockhead)	(gate)	(ghost)	(sing)
Palatal	च ca	छ cha	ज ja	झ jha	ञ ña
	(chunk)	(catchhim)	(john)	(hedgehog)	(bunch)
Cerebral	ट ṭa	ठ* ṭha	ड/ड़ ḍa	ढ*/ढ़ ḍha	ण* ṇa
	(start)	(anthill)	(dart)	(godhead)	(under)
Dental	त ta	थ tha	द da	ध dha	न na
	(path)	(thunder)	(that)	(breathe)	(numb)
Labial	प pa	फ* pha	ब ba	भ bha	म ma
	(spin)	(philosophy)	(bin)	(abhor)	(much)
Semi-vowels	य ya	र ra	ल la	व va	
	(young)	(drama)	(luck)	(vile)	
Sibilants	श śa	ष ṣa	स sa	ह ha	
	(shove)	(bushel)	(so)	(hum)	
Others	क्ष kṣa	त्र tra	ज्ञ jña	ळ* l	ऋ* ṝ
	(*kṣātriya*)	(*triśūla*)	(*jñānī*)	(play)	

अं *(—) ṁ* or *ṃ amusūra* (nasalisation of preceding vowel) like *saṁskṛti/or soṃskṛti*

अः *visarga* = *ḥ* (aspiration of preceding vowel like (*prātaḥ*)

ऽ *Avagraha* consonant #' consonant (like-*imé vasthitā*)

Anusvāra at the end of a line is presented by m (म्) and not *ṁ*

*No exact English equivalents for these letters.

1

VEDALAKṢAṆA TEXTS: KEYNOTE ADDRESS

T.N. DHARMADHIKARI

Respected authorities of the School of Vedic Studies, Rabindra Bharati University, distinguished scholars of the Vedas, Śāstras and Sanskrit and allied languages—

Let me first very heartily congratulate the School of Vedic Studies and all its authorities for arranging a three-day national seminar on the Veda-lakṣaṇa texts, Search and Analysis; and inviting the profound scholars from every corner of this country to participate and present their studied views on the topic of this seminar, and also inviting me to deliver a keynote address.

Tradition recommends—ब्राह्मणेन निष्कारणं षडङ्गो वेदोऽध्येयो ज्ञेयश्च। i.e., a Brahmin should study the Veda with its six aṅgas without intention to accomplish any worldly benefits.

Mahābhāṣya of Patañjali also recommends studying the Vedic texts with their ancillary texts. Caraṇa Vyūha also has counted the number of the Vedic schools and their ancillary texts.

Śabaraswāmi also referred to the Vedic schools occasionally. शिक्षा कल्पो व्याकरणं निरुक्तं छन्दो ज्योतिषम् are the six aṅgas of the Vedas. प्रातिशाख्य also forms the ancillary literature of the Vedas.

Along with other reasons of differences in ritualistic details, the differences in pronunciation of some consonants, sandhis, formations of words, different traditions and customs may have given rise to the formation of different schools of Vedic literature.

The differences in the ritualistic details have been noted by the different Śrauta sūtras and the differences of phonetic pronunciations have been noted by the Prātiśākhyas and Śikṣā literature.

Pāṇini-Śikṣā notes the pronunciations of a lady from सौराष्ट्र i.e., यथा सौराष्ट्रिका नारी तक्रँ इत्यभिभाषते। एवं रङ्गाः प्रयोक्तव्याः। खे अराँ इव खेदया। (पा शिक्षा 26) i.e,, a lady in Saurāṣṭra pronounces तक्रँ instead of तक्रम् thus the रङ्गाऽ be pronounced with 'म' or 'न' at the end of a word as nasalised; i.e. instead of pronouncing simple 'म' and 'न' at the end of the word, it should be nasalised. To illustrate, one should recite खे अराँ इव for खे अरान् इव (*ṚV* 8.77.3)

Even today in some states the people pronounce 'ह' for 'श' or स. Thus while giving blessings they pronounce हतायुर्भव for शतायुर्भव. Hence one should not accept blessings from such persons.

Ṛk-Prātiśākhya explicitly states—संहिता पदप्रकृतिः पदानाम् (2.1). The commentator comments—पदानि प्रकृतिभूतानि यस्याः संहितायाः— This confirms the view that originally Padas existed and thereafter Saṁhitā was arranged on the basis of the Padas.

Prātiśākhya literature is the time-old science dealing with the euphonic analysis of the first literature of the world viz., the Vedas which have been handed down to us mainly in four schools–viz., the *Ṛgveda, Yajurveda, Sāmaveda* and the *Atharvaveda* which are again known in several versions. Thus the Ṛgveda is known in Śaunaka and Śaṁkhyāyana schools. The Yajurveda is mainly divided into two streams–Kṛṣṇa and Śukla. Kṛṣṇa Yajurveda is found in Kaṭha, Kapiṣṭhala, Maitrāyani and Taittirīya. Kaṭha, Kapiṣṭhala and Maitrāyaṇi form the sub-schools of the Carakas.

The Sāmaveda school has been retained in Kauthuma, Jaiminīya and Rāṇāyanīya while the Atharvaveda is known in Śaunaka and Paippalāda.

Pāṇini Śikṣā also recommends to pronounce the syllables in such a way that they should not be forcibly bitten by teeth, nor they should be allowed to fall down carelessly. Just as a tigress carries her cub with her teeth not hurting it with her teeth nor allowing it to fall down from her mouth, the syllables be pronounced like that.

Prātiśākhya texts deal with the euphonic analysis of the world's first literature, viz. the Vedas which are the time-old heritage of the world.

The Vedic schools are enumerated in the Carana Vyūha and are also referred to in the older literature like the Mahābhāṣya of Patañjali. Cp. पस्पशाह्निक :

> **एकशतमध्वर्युशाखाः सहस्रवर्त्मा सामवेदः**
> **एकविंशतिधा बाह्वृचं नवधाथर्वणो वेदः।**

No wonder that the Mīmāṃṣā text like Śabara's bhāṣya on Jaimini referred to them. Out of these Vedic schools, very few now exist in oral tradition. Some of them are found in manuscript form only.

Between the existing schools of the Vedas, there are differences in case of certain pronunciations and performances of rituals. The topics of pronunciations are clearly noted in Śikṣās and Prātiśākhyas and those in ritual performances in the Śrauta sūtras of the particular sūtras of the Vedas.

Prātiśākhyas embody valuable results of linguistic speculations. The main object of the Ṛg Prātiśākhya is to show how the Pada text is to be turned into Saṁhitā text. It gives directions for preservation and proper pronunciations and recitation of the words of Saṁhitā. It lays down general euphonic rules, points to particular phonetic informations regarding the rules governing the construction of metres. Thus the consonant 'ड' is pronounced as 'ळ' if it appears between two vowels. Cp. अज्मध्यस्थ-डकारस्य ळकारं बह्वृचा जगुः . . . etc. this tendency has been observed by the वाजसनेयिप्रतिशाख्य 4.146 डढौ ळळ्हावेकेषाम्। This tendency of एकेषाम् refers to the Ṛgvedic school since its Prātiśākhya also observes तस्मिन् ळह्ळ-जिह्वामूलीय-उध्मानीय-नासिक्या न सन्ति माध्यन्दिनानाम् (8.39), i.e., the pronunciation of ळह्ळ-जिह्वामूलीय, उपध्मानीय and नासिक्य are absent in the माध्यन्दिन school.

The Vājasaneyi Prātiśākhya 4.57 (एजत्योजोरेकेषाम्) observes that according to some schools, the word एजति and ओज, appearing after 'अ' or 'आ' show *sandhi.* Thus the *sandhi* of 'न' and 'एजति' would be नेजति, that of 'सह' and 'ओज:' would be सहोज: However this view of एकेषाम् refers to Kāṇva school. उवट on this sūtra explains एकेषां किम्? माध्यन्दिनादीनां मा भूदिति, तथा-तन्नैजति (VS 40.5) सहौज: (VS. 36.1).

In the माध्यन्दिन school of the Śukla Yajurveda, the स्पर्श consonant appearing after विसर्ग, not followed by a vowel, is doubly pronounced. To illustrate: विष्णो: क्क्रम: (12.5) नीलङ्गो: क्क्रिमि: (24.30), सवितु: प्प्रसुव (9.1), युञ्ज्जान: प्प्रथमम् (11.1)etc. विसर्जनीया द्वयञ्ज्जनपर:, Vājasaneyi Prātiśākhya (4.107) has noted this unique pronunciation. अनन्ताचार्य comments इदं तु माध्यन्दिनविषयम्।

VājaS. reads 'विष्णवेते (5.16) कृशानवेते (4.2) etc. This sandhi has been noted by Vāja Prāti (4.128) न वकारस्य असंस्थाने एकेषाम्। अनन्ताचार्य here comments—पञ्चदशसु शाखासु आद्यायां काण्वशाखायां नायं विधि:।

Thus उवट and अनन्ताचार्य try to distinguish the readings of Kāṇva from those of the Vājasaneyi Mādhyandina School.

Taittirīya Saṁhitā 4.7.5 reads त्रपुश्च मे which is rendered as त्रपु। च। मे in its Padapātha. MaiS. 2.11.5 however reads त्रपु च मे i.e., without insertion of श between त्रपु and च। TaiPrāti. 5.4 त्रपु मिथुपूर्वश्शकारश्चपर: has noted this insertion of श in the Taittirīya school.

As it is well known, the pronounciations ज for य and ख for ष at certain situations are found in VājaS., e.g.

इखे त्वोर्जे त्वा (1.1) for इषे त्वोर्जे त्वा (TaiS. 1.1.1),

जज्ञेन जज्ञं (VājaS. 31.16) for यज्ञेन यज्ञं in ṚV. (1.164.50) and TaiS. (3.5.11)

Vāja Prāti 4.167 ख्याते: खयौ कशौ गार्ग्य: tells that in the root ख्या, there appears the combination of ख् and य. But गार्ग्य recomends to pronounce क and श in ख्या. Thus, VājaS, reads विक्शाया चक्षुषा (VājaS. 11.20), Gārgya recommends to pronounce विख्याया चक्षुषा. The view of Gārgya according to the commentators is related to Caraka School.

Cp. अनन्ताचार्य-ख्याधातो: क्शापत्तिश्च चरकाचार्याणां मते भवति। वाजसनेयिनां तु यथास्थितिरेव।

Cp. also उवट-ख्याते: क्शापत्ति: उक्ता-एते चरकाणाम्। इतरेषां माध्यन्दिनानां न।

Consequently the instances of क्शा for ख्या are found in the Maitrāyaṇi School. To illustrate–अन्वग्निरुषसामग्रमक्शत् (MaiS. 1.8.9) वि नाकमक्शत् (MaiS. 2.7.8), स्वर्गस्य लोकस्य अनुक्शात्यै (MaiS. 4.8.9); etc.

MaiS. shows few other phonological unique instances of Sandhi also. Thus, MaiS. reads—कर्मणा आप्यायध्वम् for कर्माणा आप्या यध्वम् (1.1.1) जयन्ता इति (2.5.2), वसिष्ठा ऋषि: (2.7.19), भारद्वाजा ऋषि: (2.7.19) etc.

I have shown these differences by way of illustrations only. These different traditions of phonological pronunciation may have been effected due to local influences also.

Regarding the use of different forms, Patañjali in his Mahābhāṣya (Paspaśā) under the caption of सर्वे देशान्तरे, has remarked—एतस्मिन्नतिमहति शब्दस्य प्रयोगविषये ते ते शब्दा: तत्र तत्र नियतविषया दृश्यन्ते। तद्यथा शवतिर्गतिकर्मा कम्बोजेष्वेव भाषितो भवति, विकारमार्या भाषन्ते इति। etc.

Let me now turn to illustrate few differences in the ritual

traditions because occassionally the euphonic part is related to rituals also.

In the new moon-sacrifice, according to the Vājasaneyi School, three oblations are enjoined for a Sacrificer who is not entitled to offer sānnāyya, ie. mixture of curd and milk.

They are—(1) a cake baked on eight potsherds to Agni, (2) Ājya offering for Agnīṣomau or for Viṣṇu, and (3) a cake baked on twelve potsherds to Indrāgnī. For those not belonging to Vājasaneyī school or the Śāṅkhāyana school, the Ājya–oblation to Agnīṣomau or to Viṣṇu is not prescribed. Cp. ĀpaŚS. 2.19.12, stating—आज्यहविः उपांशुयाजः पौर्णमास्यमेव भवति अग्नीषोमीयः प्राजापत्यो वा।

However, Āpastamba further recommeds a Kāmya rite for one who desires to prosper.

Further the Sacrificers of one school prefer to offer the daily Agnihotra rite before sunrise, and those belonging to other schools, after sunrise.

Jaiminīya Sūtra 2.4, 8 in its prima facie view states that if the similar rituals are mentioned in different recensional texts, they should be regarded as different from each other, because of differences in name, in form, in particular details; because of repetition, deprecation, incapacity, declaration of completion, expiatory rites and fulfilment of distinct purposes (नामरूपधर्मविशेषपुनरुक्तिनिन्दासमाप्तिवचनप्रायश्चित्तानर्थदर्शनाच्च शाखान्तरेषु कर्मभेदः स्यात्।) etc. True, that the Siddhāntin holds that the ritual acts mentioned in several recensional texts be regarded as one and the same. But the *Pūrva-pakṣa* appears to give the account for the rise of different recensions of Vedic schools. Jaimini should have read कर्मभेदात् शाखान्तरं स्यात् instead of शाखान्तरेषु कर्मभेदः स्यात्।

Śabara commenting on this *Sūtra* gives some intersting different traditional details, while studying the portions of different recensions. Thus he states–कारीरीवाक्यान्यधीयानाः तैत्तिरीया भूमौ भोजनमाचरन्ति अपरे शाखिनो नाचरन्ति। तथा अग्निमधीयानाः केचिदुपाध्यायस्य उदकुम्भानाहरन्ति अपरे न। अश्वमेधमधीयानाः केचिदश्वस्य घासमाहरन्ति अपरे

न। 'The followers of the Taittirīya school, seated on the ground, take their food while they are studying the portions of Kārīrī iṣṭi, those belonging to other recensions do not do so.

Thus, while studying the Agni section, the followers of some recensions fetch jars full of water for their teachers, while those of other recensions do not do so. Similarly while studying the Aśvamedha, some fetch grass for the horses, while others do not do so.

Probably these differences in traditions of phonologies, rituals, and minor customs may have given rise to the different recensions of the sub-schools of the Vedas. Like Prātiśākhya, Pāṇini also refers to the phonetic aspects related to Vedas.

(1) Thus Pāṇini sūtra 1.2.34 यज्ञकर्मणि अजपन्यूङ्खसामसु observes that in the performance of sacrifice the *mantras* are recited in एकश्रुति i.e, in monotone without reference to accents, excepting those related to *japa, nyūṅkha* and *Sāmans*. I would concentrate here on the recitation of *nyūṅkha* only.

Ait Br. 21.3 refers to न्यूङ्ख to be recited on the fourth day of द्वादशाह-'यत् चतुर्थमहः न्यूङ्खन्ति' etc. ĀśvaŚS 7.11.1.5 further explains चतुर्थेऽहनि प्रातरनुवाके प्रतिपदि अर्धर्चाद्योः न्यूङ्खः। द्वितीयं स्वरमोकारं त्रिमात्रमुदात्तं त्रिः। तस्य तस्य चोपरिष्टात् अपरिमितान् पञ्च वा अर्धौकारान् अनुदात्तान्। उत्तमस्य तु त्रीन्। पूर्वमक्षरं निहन्यते न्यूङ्ख्यमाने।

According to this *sūtra* the न्यूङ्ख style appears in the first Ṛk of the प्रातरनुवाक of the fourth day of द्वादशाह. The ऋक् is as follows—

आपो रेवतीः क्षयथा हि वस्वः क्रतुं च भद्रं बिभृथामृतं च।

रायश्च स्थ स्वपत्यस्य पत्नीः सरस्वती तद्गृणते वयो धात्।। ṚV. 10.30.12

न्यूङ्ख has to be recited at the second vowels of the first and the second half of this verse. Thus ओ in आपो should be recited thrice, with three *mātrās,* and with *udātta* accent. After the first and second of these three ओ३ vowels, short ओ with अनुदात्त accent should be recited five times. After the third ओ३ vowel, short ओ with अनुदात्त should be recited thrice. The verse with such ओ vowels should be,

आपोइ ओ ओ ओ ओ ओ ओ३ ओ ओ ओ ओ ओ।
ओ३ ओ ओ ओ ओ रेवती: क्षयथा हि वस्व: क्रतुं च भद्रं बिभृथामृतं च।
रायो३ ओ ओ ओ ओ ओ / ओ३ ओ ओ ओ ओ ओ ओ।
ओ३ ओ ओ ओ श्च स्थ: स्थ: स्वपत्यस्य पत्नी: सरस्वती
तद् गृणते वयोधो३ म्। (ĀśvaŚS 1.11.7)

The Pāṇini-sūtra 1.2.34 यज्ञकर्मण्यजपन्यूङ्खसामसु clearly suggests that Pāṇini may have before him the हौत्र performances of even द्वादशाह sacrifice as explained by the text of ĀśvaŚS. as quoted above. Cp. also KātyŚS. 1.8.19 एकश्रुति दूरात् संबुद्धौ यज्ञकर्मणि, सुब्रह्मण्यासामजपन्यूङ्खयाजमानवर्जम्।

(2) According to Pāṇini 8.2.89 प्रणवष्टे: the टि (i.e. अचोऽन्त्यादि टि) is substituted by प्रणव i.e. ओ or ओम्। Probably this primarily refers to the continuous recital (संततं) of the *sāmidhenī* verses, with ओ substituted at the end of each *sāmidhenī* verse. ĀśvaŚS. 1.2.7 'ता एकश्रुति संततमनुब्रूयात्' describes that the *sāmidhenī* verses be recited in monotone and with continuity (संततम्), संततम् in this *sūtra* is further explained as स्वरादिमृगन्तरमोकारं त्रिमात्रं मकारान्तं कृत्वा, उत्तरस्या अधर्चेऽवस्येत् तत् संततम् (ĀśvaŚS, 1.2.10). Thus, the end (of the verse) beginning with its last vowel (स्वरादि-ऋगन्त, i.e. टि) should be substituted by ओ or ओम् and the verse be joined with the next verse. The pause be at each hemistich.

To illustrate—

प्र वो वाजो अभिद्यवो हविष्मन्तो घृताच्या।
देवान् जिगाति सुम्नयोम् अग्न आयाहि वीयते गृणानो हव्यदातये।
नि होता सत्सि बर्हिषोम् तं त्वा समिद्भिरङ्गिरो घृतेन वर्धयामसि।
बृहच्छोचा यविष्टयोम् सनः पृथु श्रवाय्यमच्छा देव विवाससि।
बृहदग्ने सुवीर्योम् ईळेन्यो नमस्यस्तिरस्तमांसि दर्शत: etc.

(3) Pāṇini *sūtras* 8.2.88–92 refer to *Yajñakarma.* Pāṇini

8.2.88 'ये यज्ञकर्मणि' enjoins that ये in the performance of a sacrifice becomes *pluta*. This ये forms a part of ये३ यजामहे which is technically called आगूः and which is augmented to every *Yājyā* verse (excepting those related to *anuyājas)*.

According to Pāṇini *sūtra* 8.2.90 याज्यान्तः, the concluding part of *Yājyā* (beginning with its vowel, i.e., टि) is prolated E.G. (समिधो अग्न आज्यस्य) वियन्तू३ (वौ३ षट्) (तनूनपादग्न आज्यस्य) (वौ षट्) Cp. (TaiBr. 3.4.4) etc.

Pāṇini 8.2.91 'ब्रूहि प्रेष्य श्रौषड्वौषड् आवहानामादेः' enjoins that in *Yajña Karma,* the initial vowels in ब्रूहि प्रेष्य श्रौषड् वोषड् and आवह are protracted. Their recitation therefore will be as follows— अग्नयेऽनुब्रू३हि अग्नये प्रे३ष्य। अस्तु श्रौ३षट्। वौ३षट्। अग्निमा३वह। । etc.

The injuctons given by above Pāṇini *sūtra* (8.2.88, 90, 92) are mostly covered by ĀśvaŚS. 1.5.4–8, आगूः याज्यादिः अनुयाजवर्जम्। ये३ यजामह इत्यागूः। वषट्कारोऽन्त्यः सर्वत्र। तयोः (आगूवषट्कारयोः) आदी प्लावयेत् याज्यान्तं च। .etc Vide also ĀśvaŚS. 1.4.13 श्रो३णनिति औकारं प्लावयन्। ĀśvaŚS. 1.3.6 आ३वह इत्यावाहयति आदि प्लावयन्।

Thus, e.g. the recitation of a *yājyā* (at first Prayāja) shall be ये३ यजामहे-समिधो अग्न आज्यस्य व्यन्तू३ वौ३षट्।

(4) ĀśvaŚS 1.5.6 उच्चैस्तरां व्रलीयान् याज्यायाः। speaks of the specially accented nature (उच्चैस्तरां) of वौ३षट् following the *yāiyā*. This appears to have been explained by Pāṇini 1.2.35 उच्चैस्तरां वा वषट्कारः।

Pāṇini had before him the entire हौत्र of यज्ञकर्म।

(5) Pāṇini 1.2.37, 38 न सुब्रह्मण्यायां स्वरितस्य तूदात्तः। and देवब्रह्मणोरनुदात्तः clearly refer to the *nigada* called सुब्रह्मण्या to be recited in a *Soma*-sacrifice. According to AitBr. 26.3 सोमे राजनि क्रीते सुब्रह्मण्यामाह्वयन्ति and Śat Br. 3.3.4.17, Subrahmaṇyā is be recited even after the purchase of *Soma*. In the performance of soma-sacrifice, it is rccited after each morning *upasad*. The सुब्रह्मण्या निगद as found in ṢaḍviBr. is as follows:

ṢaḍviBr. (1.1.2) सुब्रह्मण्यो३म् सुब्रह्मण्यो३म्। इन्द्रआगच्छ हरिव आगच्छ,

मेधातिथेमेंष वृषणश्वस्य मेने गौरावस्तकन्दिन् अहल्यायै जार कौशिकब्राह्मण गौतमब्रुवाण त्र्यहे सुत्यामागच्छ मघवन्, देवा ब्रह्माणः आगच्छत आगच्छत आगच्छत।

सुब्रह्मण्याख्ये निगदे–'यज्ञकर्मणि इति' 'विभाषा' छन्दसिं इति आप्ता एकश्रुतिर्न स्याद् स्वरितस्य तूदात्तात्।

The Pāṇini *sūtra* 'न सुब्रह्मण्यायां, सवरितस्य तूदात्तः।' (1.2.37) prohibits the एकश्रुति recitation in सुब्रह्मण्या and renders the स्वरित to उदात्त, e.g. the vowel ओ in सुब्रह्मण्यों, which is स्वरित as per Pāṇini 6.1.185 तित्स्वरितम् is rendered उदात्त by (न सुब्रह्मण्यायां स्वरितस्य तूदात्तः। Pāṇini 1.2.37)

Similarly in इन्द्र आगच्छ, इन्द्र being vocative is आद्युदात्त according to Pāṇini 6.4.198 आमन्त्रितस्य च Naturally न्द्र in इन्द्र is अनुदात्त which becomes स्वरित by Pāṇini 8.4.66 उदात्तादनुदात्तस्य स्वरितः This स्वरित, viz. 'न्द्र' in इन्द्र is again rendered उदात्त by Pāṇini 1.2.37 न सुब्रह्मण्यायां स्वरितस्य तूदात्तः, Making इन्द्र with two उदात्त accents.

देवा ब्रह्माणः appearing in this *nigada* are vocatives and have their first vowels (accented i.e. उदात्त, vide 6.1.198) The*anudāttas* following *udātta* are changed into स्वरित according to Pāṇini 8.4.66 उदात्तादनुदात्तस्य स्वरितः This स्वरित again, if subjected to the earlier *sūtra* viz., (न सुब्रह्मण्यां) स्वरितस्य तूदात्तः may become उदात्त. The *sūtra* देवब्रह्मणोरनुदात्तः (Pāṇini 1.2.38) prohibits the process of changing this स्वरित into उदात्त and again renders that स्वरित into अनुदात्त.

From this minute observation of Pāṇini, it will be clear that Pāṇini had before him, the entire *nigada* of Subrahmanya as recited by सुब्रह्मण्य priest in the performance of a *Soma*-sacrifice, and that Pāṇini was quite aware of minute details of औद्गात्र also.

It is often said that the Vedic Literature is an inexhaustible treasure for researches.

Since it is unanimously accepted that the Vedas are the

first literature survived from the hoary past, it consequently follows that, the Vedic language has to be regarded as the oldest survived language of the world.

Vedic language has its own pecularities, which differenciate it from the later classical Sanskrit language. Pāṇini had therefore referred to them as *Chandasi* and *Bhāṣāyām*.

The Vedic language can again be divided into sub-sections, viz. Ṛgvedic, Yajurvedic or Brāhmanic and Upaniṣadic. Though they have some common features, they show their distinct peculiarities also.

Since the earlier Vedic literature belongs to Indo-Iranian group, its language and ritual have extensive similarity with that of Avestan Literature.

It is again interesting to note that even though Ṛgeveda is the oldest literary work of the world, it is skillfully composed in metres like Gāyatrī, Anuṣṭubh, Triṣṭubh, Jagatī, Śakvarī etc., which are measured in quarters and in syllables.

Most of the living Vedic literature has retained its accents also. Thanks to the Khaṇḍikopādhyāyas, who very meticulously handed over this literature, along with their accents, to their disciples. Cp. Patañjali on Pāṇini 1.1.1 *Udāttasya sthānē anudattaṁ brute, Khaṇḍikopādhyāyaḥ tasmai śiṣyāya capeṭikāṁ dadāti*, i.e. the Khaṇḍikopādhyāyas used to slap on the cheek of a disciple, who would recite Anudātta for Udātta. It is needless to elucidate that the accents, at times, fix the meaning of the vedic words.

Phonetics, morphological, syntaxical and lexical peculiarities also distinguish the Vedic language from the Classical one. Different Vedic schools also show different peculiarities.

To illustrate a few:

In the Ṛgveda *ḍa* changes to *ḷa*, if it is posed between two vowels (Cp. *ajmadhyasthaḍakārasya ḷakāram bahvṛcā jaguḥ*) e.g. *Agnimīḷe* (Ṛ.V. 1.1.1) is pronounced for *Agnimīḍe*.

Similarly *ḍha* changes to *ḷḥa,* e.g. *dṛḷhāvradanta vīlitā* (RV. 2.24.3) for *dṛḍhāvradanta vīḍitā.*

In Vājasaneyī *Y* changes to *J* and *Ṣ* to *Kh.* e.g. *jajñena jajñam* (VājaS. 31.16) *Svasti naḥ pūkhā viśvavedāḥ* (VājaṢ. 25.19), for *Yajñena yajñam* and *Svasti naḥ pūṣā viśvavedāḥ* respectively. Kāṇva belonging to the same Śukla Yajurveda does not show these peculiarities.'

Taittirīya Prātiśākhya (14.9) *aghoṣād ūṣmaṇaḥ paraḥ prathomo'bhinidhānaḥ sparśaparāt tasya sasthānaḥ* (After a surd aspirant followed by mute is inserted a first mute of the same position with the latter as *abhinidhāna*[1]- W.D. Whitney) According to this rule *ayasmayaṁ vi kṛta* (Tais. 4.2.5) has to be recited as *ayaspmayaṁ vi kṛta,* But this tradition appears to have been lost. Present reciters of TaiS. do not follow this tradition.

Pāṇini's sūtra *ayasmayādīni chandasi* (1.4.120) recomends *ayasmaya* and not *ayaspmaya in chandas* instead of *ayomaya* in *laukika.*

Change of *khy* to *kṣ* is quite regular in the MaiS. Thus we meet with Prakṣāya for Prakhyāya (MaiS. 1.9.8) etc.

On the other hand Ṛgveda Prātiśākhya 1.6.55 *kṣātau khakāra yakārau eke,* optionally recommends *Kh* and *Y* in the root *Kṣā.* Thus according to this tradition one should recite *praty agnir uṣasām agram akṣat,* in place of *praty aganir uṣasām agram akhyat* (ṚV 34.13.1) But this Ṛgvedic tradition of *akṣat* for *akhyat* appears to have been lost.

Sindhūrahinā, (ṚV. 10.1.1.1.9); *Dasyūn̐rekaḥ* (ṚV. 6.18.3) are the Ṛgvedic instances, where final *na* is changed to *anunāsika* and *ra,* when followed by a vowel or semi-vowel. Its *Padapāṭha* is *Sindhūn* + *ahinā,* and *dasyūn* + *ekaḥ.* This peculiarity is observed in TaiS. and MaiS. also. CP *ṛtūr anyo* (MaiS, 4.12.2), *kratūr anyo* (MaiS. 3.11.10) etc. The classical literature has lost this type of *Sandhi.*

In MaiS. *ta* before the initial *śa* is regularly changed *ña,* instead of to *ca,* and the initial *śa* is not changed to *ca.*

Thus *ut śrayasva* is recited as *uñśrayasva*; *tat śakeyam* is changed to *tañśakeyam* and *tat śrayasva* is changed to *tañśrayasva.* etc.

However, that final *na* followed by *ja* is not changed to *ña* in the MaiS. Eg. *tiṣṭhan juhoti* (1.20.18), *dēvān jigāti* (1.6.1) etc.

VājaS. (40.5) reads *tannaijati* being a *Sandhi* of *tat na ejati,* while KāṇvaS. (40.5) reads *tannejati* being *Sandhi* of *(tat) na ejati,* Two sub-schools of the same *Śukla Yajurveda* show this difference in *Sandhi.*

TaiPrāti. 5.4 has noted the tendency of TaiS. wherein the words *trapu* and *mithu* if followed by *ca, śa* is inserted before *ca.* e.g. *trapuśca* (TaiS. 4.7.5) and *mithuś carantam* (TaiS. 4.7.15). MaiS. however reads *trapu ca* (2.11.5) and *mithu carantam* (3.16.5).

A peculiar Sandhi of *tu* + *vai* as *tvai* is observed in TaiS. (2.5.4), TaiBr. (1.4.10) and also in MaiS. (1.6.13). Taittirīya Prātiśākhya 5.13 *tu nu pūrba udāttayor vakāraḥ* has taken note of this pecularity. Bhatta Bhaskara, commenting on TaiBr. 1.4.10 (*esa ha tvai*) remarks—'*tor antyalopas' chāndasaḥ.*'

In MaiS. the final *e* followed by an initial vowel is changed to *ā*. Thus *karmaṇe āpyāyadhvam* is recited as *karmaṇā āpyāyadhvam* (MaiS. 1.1.11). Similarly in *ārabhe ā* is changed to *ārabhā ā* (MaiS. 1.2.2)

Sāṁhitika dīrgha or hrasva is also common feature of phonetics in Vedic Literature, e.g. *pibā* (VājaS. 26.4), *śrudhī* (VājaS. 21.1), *aśītama* (VājaS. 2.70) are rendered as *pibā, śrudhī* and *aśītama* in their respective *padapāṭha.* However, in KāṇvaS. *aśītama* is regarded as *prakṛti-dīrgha* and not rendered as *aśītama* in its *padapāṭha.* The comentator of VājaPrāti. has noted this peculiarity (in the *Padapaṭha*) of Kāṇvas, saying-*kāṇvānām idam prakṛti-dīrgham, padapāṭhē' pi hrasvābhāvāt* (VājaPrāti. 3.129)

In some of the Vedic schools, the final *na* following *ā* and followed by a vowel is changed to *anunāsika.* E.g. *sargā̐ iva* (ṚV 8.35.20), *mahā̐ indro* (ṚV.6.19.1); *ajrā̐ ṛju*

(ṚV.4.1.17) *devahūtamā̐ aśvān* (ṚV. 8.75.1) etc.

nṝn patibhyaḥ is pronounced as *nṝ̐ṣ patibhyaḥ* (MaiS. 4.13.2) and *nṝn pāhi* is rendered as *nṝ̐ṣ pāhi* (MaiS. 2.3.11) Thus the final *na* is nasalised and *ṣa* is inserted after the nasal. Cp. Pāṇini 8.3.10 *nṝ̐n pe.*

Thus having shown few phonetic peculiarities, by way of illustration, let me note some morphological peculiarities. The peculiar morphological forms like *devāsaḥ, devebhiḥ, tmanā,* (for *ātmanā*), *kṛpā* for *kṛpayā, guhā* for *guhāyām, ātman* and *mūrdhan* for *ātmani* and *mūrdhani, vaiśvadevīḥ* (Nom. Plu.) for *vaiśvadevyaḥ, patnīḥ* for *patnyaḥ, juhvam* for *juhūm,* the contracted forms like *havyā* for *havyāni, viśvā* for *viśvāni* are common and are very well known morphological peculiarities in the Vedic texts.

Pronoun forms like *āvam,* for *āvām, yuvam* for *yuvām, asme for asmai, asakau* for *asau* are also very common in the Vedas. In TaiBr. 2.4.3.7 *āvām* (*gamema)* appears to have been used for *vayam.*

In MaiS. (3.2.5) the dual form *caturdaśe,* stands for thirteen and fourteen (*dvādaśa māsaḥ samvatsaraḥ atha ya ete caturdaśe ahorātre* etc.). *Daśame* (MaiS. 3.9.3) is also a dual form referring to ninth and tenth (*aṣṭa āśrayaḥ brahmaṇī daśame ātmaikādaśaḥ).*

Vedic literature has retained the present first person plural forms like *namasyāmasi* (MaiS. 2.2.6), *dīpayāmasi* (MaiS. 2.2.6), *vadāmasi* (ṚV. 6.21.6), *parigṛhṇāmasi* (MaiS. 1.6.1), *paśyāmasi* (ṚV. 1.152.4) etc.

The infinitive forms like *nirmṛjaḥ* (MaiS. 2.5.1) *sampṛcaḥ.* (MaiS. 4.9.1) *vipṛcaḥ* (MaiS. 1.1.10); *gṛbhaḥ* (MaiS. 4.13.7); *vinetoḥ* (MaiS. 2.5.1) *veditoḥ* (MaiS. 1.6.6) *prajanitoḥ* are peculiar morphological forms in the Vedic literature.

The gerund forms like *snātvī* (MaiS. 3.1.10), *hitvī* (ṚV. 2.28.6) *kṛtvi* (ṚV. 2.28.6) *yuktvāya* ṚV 10-93-19) *kṛtvāya, hitvāya* (ṚV 10-14.8) are also unique Vedic forms not found in classical literature.

The verbal forms like *hinotana* (ṚV. 10.30.7), *sunotana* and *dadhātana* (ṚV.6.34.1); *mamattana* (ṚV. 10.179.1) *brabhītana* (ṚV 8.66.15)*jujuṣṭana* (ṚV. 4.3.67), *yuyotana* (ṚV. 8.18.10) *bibhītana* (ṚV. 8.66.15) etc. are the imperative second person form with the extended ending in *tana*. *acucyavītana* appears to be a past perfect, found in ṚV.I.37.12 and also in MaiS. 4.11.4.

Vindāsai bravātai, sandhātai etc. are the unique subjunctive forms.

Vyaśnavai, dātavai, drogdhavai, atyetavai, sartavai etc. are the dative infinitives; while *dṛśe, gṛhe, sartave* are also dative infinitives. *atiṣṭigham, atighātam* are the peculiar accusative infinitives.

These are some unique examples of morpholological forms appearing only in Vedic literature but lost in the classical Sanskrit language.

Thus Vedic language is very much rich in the verbal forms, noun-forms, pronoun-forms, *kṛt* and even *taddhita* forms also.

Vedic language shows some peculiarities of syntax also.

Frequently the *upasargas* are separated from the verbs by insertion of few words, e.g. *Parā hi me vimanyavaḥ patanti vasya iṣṭaye,* (RV. I.25.4), wherein the *upasarga,* viz. *parā* has to be construed with *patanti.*

If the *upasarga* is repeated, it attracts the principal verb, e.g. *Pra tam indra naśīmahi gomantam aśvinam. Pra brahma pūrvacittaye,* (ṚV. 8.6.9), the second *Pra* is also construed with *naśīmahi.*

The genitive and dative cases, at times, appear to be irregular. One often comes across the remarks like *caturthyarthe ṣaṣṭhī* or *ṣaṣṭhyarthe caturthī* in the commentaries.

The use of instrumental case indicating time, in *barhiṣā vai pūrṇamāse vratam upayanti vatsair amāvāsyāyām* (MaiS. 1.4.5), i.e. at the full moon sacrifice they enter upon a vow at the time of fetching the sacrificial grass, and at the new moon day, at the time of separating calves from their mothers, is very note-worthy.

Similarly in *marudbhyaḥ krīdibhyaḥ sākam raśmibhiḥ saptakapālam* (MaiS. 1.10.1), i.e. at the time of the appearance of first rays of sun, they offer a cake baked on seven potsherds to *Krīḍin Maruts,* and also in *sākam raśmibhih pracaranti* (MaiS. 1.10.16), i.e. at the time of the appearance of the first rays of sun, they offer oblations. The use of instrumental case indicates time.

In classical Sanskrit, as is observed by Pāṇini I.4.5 *akathitaṃ ca,* both the principal and auxiliary objects related to the root *brū,* take accusative. But in *rāṣṭrīyāya brāhmaṇam brūyāt* (MaiS. 2.4.2) or, in *tasyai vā etam somo jīvagrāham prābravīt* (MaiS. 3.7.8) the auxiliary objects *rāṣṭrīyāya* and *tasyai* are in dative.

A strange construction *'tām bṛhaspatiś ca anvaitām'* (MaiS. 2.2.4) where, *anvaitām* is dual verb and for the dual subject, the particle *ca* makes us understand an additional noun, viz. Indra standing with Bṛhaspati.

In *agniś ca viṣṇo tapa uttamam mahaḥ* (TaiBr.2.4.3), Agni is in nominative and *Viṣṇo* in vocative. To bring them in juxtaposition, *Sāyaṇa* comments *he viṣṇo tvaṃ ca agniś ca ubhau—'* etc. Here also *tvam* is understood by force of *ca.*

With these few illustrations, one may conceive that the Vedic language is, at places, very unique in syntax, compared to classical one.

Now turning to ritual and philosophy, even according to the tradition, the Vedas are divided into two *kāṇḍas,* viz. *karma-kāṇḍa* and *jñāna-kāṇḍa.*

Tradition states that the Vedas consists of Mantra and Brāhmaṇa portions and that the Brāhmāṇas include the Āraṇyakas and Upaniṣads also. Generally the Mantras i.e., the Saṁhitās and Brāhmaṇas and partly the Āraṇyakas deal with *Pūrvakāṇḍa* and the Upaniṣads are regarded as Uttarakāṇḍa. However this division also cannot be treated as watertight one, since in the Ṛgveda, are included some philosophical *Sūktas* like *Nāsadīya, Puruṣa Sūkta,* and *Īśopaniṣad* forms the last chapter of the *Śukla Yajurveda* (both

Kāṇva and *Mādyandina*), while Chāndogya Upaniṣad deals with the utilising of the *Sāmans* and their nature.

Rituals, according to the tradition are divided into four sections, viz. *nitya, naimittika kāmya,* and *niṣiddha.*

Sāyaṇācārya in the introduction to the TaiS. remarks—*vedas tāvat kāṇḍadvayātmakaḥ tatra pūrvasmin kāṇḍe nitya-naimittika-kāmya-niṣiddharūpam caturvidham karma pratipāditam . . . uttarakāṇḍe brahmopadeśaḥbrahmoprāptiśca iti ubhayam pratipādyate.*

The sacrifice is another name of *Dharma,* according to the Mīmāṁsakas. Jaimini composed his first *sūtra* as *'athāto dharma-jijñāsā'* and explained the sacrificial institutions, in the following twelve chapters.

Nitya and *Naimitttika* sacrifices are regarded as obligatory. They are not performed with a desire to achieve personal material gains. They are performed to avoid the obstacles which may have occured due to their non-performances. *Sāyaṇa* says—*'Nitya naimittikānuṣṭhānād akaraṇe pratyavāya-rūpam aniṣṭam parihriyate.'* Even if these sacrificial actions would yield any material fruit to the sacrificer, they are deemed as secondary, i.e., *ānuṣaṇgika.* ĀpaDs. 1.7.3 states that, the mango-tree is planted for its sweet fruit, but the shadow and fragrance are also derived. Thus when *Dharma* is performed, its secondary fruit also follows. (*tad yathā āmre phalārthe nimitte chāyā gaṇdha iti anūtpadyante evam dharmam upacaryamāṇam arthāh anūtpadyante.*

The sacrifices like *Darśa* and *Pūrṇamāsa, Agnihotra etc.* are regarded as *nitya.* They are to be performed by the sacrificer till his death. (Cp. *Yāvajjīvam agnihotram juhoti*) etc.

The *Naimittika* sacrifices are enjoined by the *Śrutis,* at some auspicious or inauspicious occassions related to the sacrificer, e.g. if a son is born to the sacrificer, he should offer a cake to Viśvānara. *Vaiśvānaram dvādaśa-kapālam nirvapet putre jāte* (TaiS. 2.2.5); or if the house of a scrificer catches fire, he should offer a cake baked on eight potsherds to *Kṣāmavat* Agni Cp. *Yasya gṛhān dahati agnaye kṣāmavate puroḍāśam nirvapet* (TaiS. 2.2.2).

Principally *nitya* and *namittika* sacrifices purify the intelligence and mind of the sacrificer and create in him the urge for inner perception of Brāhman (Cp. Sāyaṇa *'na kevalam nitya-naimittikābhyām ānuṣaṅgika-svarga-prāptiḥ, kintu dhīśuddhyā vividiṣotpādana-dvārā brahmajñāna- hetutvam api tayor asti,* Introduction to TaiS.).

According to pre-Śaṅkarācārya *view, Karma,* i.e. the sacrifice and *Jñāna,* jointly lead to salvation. Just as a bird cannot fly only with one of its two wings; a *sādhaka* cannot achieve salvation with only one wing of the Vedas.

Śaṅkarācārya however proposes an acute contradiction between *Karma* (i.e., sacrifice) and *Jñāna.* But the contradiction is on the level of *'Saha-avasthāna'* (co-existence) only. That is say, one cannot undertake practising *karma* and *Jñāna* simultaneously. Secondly, *karma* can never lead one to salvation, It is only *Jñāna* that is competent to lead one to salvation and *karma* would only be an *upāya*–the means to crcate *jñānaniṣṭhā* in the *Sādhaka. Karma*–the sacrifice only makes the Sacrificer fit for aehieving *Brahmavidyā.* But once the effect in the form of *jñānaniṣṭhā* is produced, the *karma* ceases to exist. Then *jñānaniṣṭhā,* thus produced by *karma,* independent and irrespective of *karma* leads one to liberation. Thus *karma* is the *upāya* of *jñāna* which is *upeya.*

Kāmya sacrifices are those which are prescribed for fulfilling the sacrificer's desires, e.g. *y'olam prajāyai san prajām na vindate, aindrāgnam ekādasa-kapālam nirvapet* (TaiS. 2.1.1. It may be noted that only *kāmya* sacrifices, (and not the *nitya* and the *narmittika* sacrifices) are condemned by the Muṇḍakopaniṣad (*plavā hyete aḍṛḍhāḥ yajñarūpāḥ,* 1.2.7) and Bhagavadgītā—2.42-*yām imāṁ puṣpitāṁ vācaṁ pravadantyavipaścitaḥ,* etc.)

Niṣiddha sacrifices amounting to *abhicāra* fall under the *tāmasa* category. Vedas do not enjoy them, but only refer to them so that they may be avoided, since its performance leads to *hiṁsā* and consequently to hell.

To these four categories, one more type of sacrifice, viz. *Prāyaścittas* be added. According to Jaimini and Śabara *Prāyaścittas* are of two kinds—some are enjoined for mending the lapses and the others are prescribed as a part of sacrificial performances to be performed under certain contingencies, (cp. *Prāyaścittāni dviprakārakāṇi, kānicit vaiguṇyasya pramādād āpatitasya samādhānārthāni, kānicit nimitta karmāṅgāṇi,* MīmāSū, Śābara 12.3.6)

KātyŚS.1.2.1–2 defines the sacrifice as *'yajñam vyākhyāsyāmaḥ dravyaṁ devatā tyāgaḥ i.e.* the offering of oblations to the deities means a sacrifice. This definition is not free from defects. The sacrificial ritual has a well-knit procedure and the sacrificial acts are associated with the recitation of *mantras.*

Yogī Aurobindo in his guide to Upaniṣads (P. 104) observed 'The whole process of the Universe in its very nature is sacrifice'. He appears to refer to the Cosmic Sacrifice ever rotating in the Universe created by Prajāpati. The Puruṣasūkta to certain extent represents this Cosmic Sacrifice, wherein, the Cosmic Puruṣa was the victim, Vasanta (Spring) was the ājya, Grīṣma (Summer) was the enkindling stick and Śarad (Autum), the offering, (*yat puruṣeṇa haviṣā deva yajñam atanvata. vasanto' syāsīd ājyam grīṣma idhmaḥ sarad haviḥ)*

Sāyaṇa, commenting on this verse, states–*'etāvatā sṛṣṭipratipādakasūktabhāgārthaḥ saṅgṛhītaḥ*

The Ṛgvedic Verses 10.130.1 and 2 are also significant in this respect.

yo yajño viśvatas tantubhis tata
ekaśatam devakarmebhir āyataḥ/
ime vayanti pitaro ya āyayuḥ
pra vayāpa vaye' tyāsate tate//
and *pumān enam tanuta utkṛṇatti/* etc.

Sāyaṇa Comments—*tantubhiḥ vidyudādibhūtaiḥ yaḥ sargātmakaḥ yajñaḥ viśvatastataḥ* etc. *Pumām puruṣaḥ ādipuruṣaḥ enam yajñam tanute vistārayati sṛṣṭavān ityarthaḥ.*

Let us first deal with time. Agnihotra is offered at the sunrise and sunset. *Darśa* and *Pūrṇamāsa* sacrifices are offered on the Pratipad, i.e., the joints of each fortnight. In fact on Amāvāsyā day the moon, otherwise called Soma is entered into the Sun, i.e. Agni. This is a cosmic sacrifice. Parvans of the Cāturmāsya are performed at the joints of seasons. The Soma sacrifice is performed at the joint of two consequent years, especially in Vasanta. Ayana sacrifices are offered during the tenure of one full year.

Time is regarded as the divine wheel and it takes one full year for its single rotation. A period of one year is often identified with Prajāpati. Cp. ŚatBr. 11.1.6.12–13 *sa aikṣata Prajāpatiḥ imam vā ātmanaḥ pratimām asṛkṣi yat saṁvatsaram iti. tasmā āhuḥ prajāpatiḥ saṁvatsara iti.*

Turning to the aspect of space, *bhūḥ*, *bhuvaḥ* and *svaḥ*– are termed as *vyāhṛtis* and are also known as *lokas,* otherwise called as *Pṛthivī, Antarikṣa* and *Dyauḥ.*

TaiS. and TaiBr. state that the sacrifice finds support in *Dyauḥ* and Pṛthivī, (*dyāvāpṛthivyor.* TaiS. 2.6.9)

Dyāvāpṛthivī are regarded as the universal parents. *Dyauḥ* is a bull and *Pṛthivī,* the cow which further form a *mithuna* and lead to *Prajanana,* the creation.

TaiBr. 1.1.3 in the context of depositing the fires, narrates a tale, viz. *Dyauḥ* and *Pṛthivī* were once closely joined together. But they had to get separated, so that the creatures could find space to move. But while separating from each other, they, due to their intense love, said to each other, let our best parts, worthy of sacrifice be exchanged. The *Dyauḥ* placed its best part on the earth, that become salty soil.

The *Pṛthivī* gave her best part to *Dyauḥ.* That become the black spot on the moon. Therefore in the *Agnyādhāna* rite the Adhvaryu places the salty soil in the pit of the Āhavanīya, being the best portion of *dyu-loka* and while doing so he contemplates upon the black spot of the moon, the best portion of the *Pṛthivī-loka* . Threby he sets up the fire on the best substances of both. Thus a sacrifice has a direct bearing with space, the *lokas.*

The KāṭhS. 3.6 states—*Saha vā ime agnes tanvaḥiyam odanapacanaḥ, antarikṣam gārhapatyaḥ dyauḥ āhavanīyaḥ.* Thus the three fires represent the three *lokas.*

The sacrifice through time and space, is not only related to cosmos but also to *prajanana.* The KāṭhS 6.7 states—*prajananaṁ vā etat agnihotraṁ, sṛṣṭir vā etat yat agnihotram.*

According to TaiS. 1.5.9, sacrifice is creative. The sacrificer offers the oblation in the fire. The oblation is like the seed sprinkled in the female womb from which a similar but a fresh sprout takes birth. Agni is as if the womb and Soma the seed. It is Tvaṣṭṛ who modifies the seed. As many modifications of the seed as Tvaṣṭṛ makes, in so many shapes does it become fruitful, (TaiS. 1.5.9—*Agnihotraṁ juhōti yad eva yajamānasya svam tasyaitad retaḥ siñcati prajanane, prajananaṁ hi vā agniḥ . . . tvaṣṭā rūpāni vikaroti).* This statement again speaks of the comic sacrifice.

Thus the entire manifestation of the universe is conceived through time and space and through *prajanana.* It therefore appears that the cosmic prototypes were thought to be manipulated by ritual operations. Hence the performances of rituals may be treated as instruments to comprehend the ever active creation and its origin—the creator, i.e. Prajāpati, the ultimate eternal Truth.

Eventually let me refer to another aspect of the rituals. Chāndogya Upaniṣad remarks that the mind is nurished with the subtle part of food (*annam aśitam tredhā vidhīyate . . yo' ṇiṣṭhaḥ tan manaḥ,* Chāndo U.6-5-1) Naturally the subtle part of that food, which is consecreated under the sacred precept of offering to the deities with a sense of gratitude and a concept of *tyāga,* would, when consumed, form the sanctified, pure and accomplished mind.

The actions arise from the mind. The purified mind only can give rise to purified actions, which are lifted to the higher divine plane. *Śivasaṅkalpa sūkta* (VājaS. 34) cherishes that the mind, without which no action is possible, should invoke the pious intentions. The food left after offering oblations in the ritual, is named as *amṛta*, or in later period as *prasāda*.

Consuming this *prasāda* of ritual, thus illustrates–*tena tyaktena bhuñjīthāḥ*, of the Īśopaniṣad.

Thus for purifing the action, the Sacrifice is cherished to purify its roots, viz. the mind, and while purifying the mind, it purifies its *upādāna kāraṇa*, viz. the food. Sacrifice, thus purifies the cause to purify the effect. Therein is reflected the wisdom of *Ṛṣīs* who fabricated the frame of the sacrificc.

Action is inevitable. It binds a person in the cycles of births, deaths and rebirths. Sacrifice, as stated above makes the mind and actions emerging out of it pure, and renders that very action a force for liberation. Naturally the sacrificial actions are thought to be *Śreṣṭhatama karma*.

There are still more aspects of Vedic sacrifices, which I cannot elucidate in the short time, specified for me. I would only say that Sacrificial rites are not awfully empty.

Fritz Stahll, in his *Ritual and Mantras* (P. 365-Para 3) said 'with respect to human sciences of Ritual and Grammar the Indian contributions have not been outstanding but unique.'

The importance of Prātiśākhya is great as much as they reveal valuable results of linguistics and euphonic speculations.

The main object of the Ṛg Prātiśākhya is to show how the pada text formed into Saṁhitā text. It gives special instructions for proper pronunciation and proper presentation of the words of Saṁhitā.

It lays down general euphonic rules, points out peculiar phonetic peculiarities and gives information regarding metrical rules.

This key note address is neither very extenstive, nor very important. It is only a key to unlock the topic.

After all, I know भगवद्गिरामवसरप्रदानाय वचांसि नः। पूर्वरङ्गप्रसङ्गाय नाटकीयस्य वस्तुनः।

2

IMPORTANCE OF EDITING VEDIC LAKṢAṆA-TEXTS WITH SPECIAL REFERENCE TO STOBHĀNUSAṀHĀRA

B.B. Chaubey

In the history of the development of different branches of Vedic literature, after compilation of the *Saṁhitā*-texts in various recensions, to preserve the texts of respective *Śākhās*, there came a period when different *Saṁhitās* of the Vedas began to be preserved in oral tradition from generation to generation, or from teachers (*Gurus*) to students (*Śiṣyas*). In this period various modes of recitation developed not only different from one Veda to other Vedas but from one *Śākhā* to other *Śākhās* of the same Veda also. Among six *Vedāṅgas*, viz. *Śikṣā*, *Vyākaraṇa*, *Nirukta*, *Chanda*, *Kalpa* and *Jyotiṣa*, the former two were related to phonetics and grammar. Under *Śikṣā-Vedāṅga* two types of literature, viz, *Śikṣā* and *Prātiśākhya*, dealing with phonetics including modes of pronunciation in respective *Śākhās* were composed by later Ācāryas. Again keeping in view of some specific features of pronunciation against the general rules of the grammar of Vedic language that followed in different *Śākhāsaṁhitās Lakṣaṇa-granthas* were composed by some later Ācāryas. A huge number of literature was produced under this title, and these were continued to be preserved by later generation of Ācāryas. Their commentaries were also written by Ācāryas, which were preserved in form of manuscripts. Very little attention was given by the modern scholars to edit them. For a long time they remained unnoticed in various Manuscript-collections. Many texts of this genre are found referred to in the commentaries of Vedic texts which are still unpublished. Moreover, in the Manuscript-collections there are huge number of manuscripts which have mis-nomenclatures of the texts, and some are without any title of the text. Shri K. Parameshvara Aithal has prepared a comprehensive Bibliography of all *Lakṣaṇa-granthas* written in various Indian scripts and which were deposited in different Manuscript-collections and mentioned in various catalogues. The first edition of this text was published by the South Asia Institute of Hidelbeg University as volume no. 143 (of the series Beitraege Zur Suedasienforchung through Franz Steiner, Velag, Stuttgart, Germany) in 1993, and later on its reprint was also published from Motilal Banarsidass. Aithal has given information about 1619 titles of such *Veda-lakṣaṇa* texts which are deposited at Manuscript-collections or which have been referred to in some other commentatry texts. He has also given a full information about how many manuscripts of that text are available in different collections and whether that text has been published so far or not.

Being a student of Vedas, after doing my Ph.D on the 'Treatment of Nature in the Ṛgveda.' I was interested in continuing my research in the field of the special branch of *Lakṣaṇa-granthas.* In those days Macdonel's 'Vedic Reader for students' and Peterson's 'Selections from Ṛgveda' were taught in B.A. and M.A. courses respectively. Dr. Sidheshvar Bhattacarya the then Head of Deptment. of Sanskrit inspired me to prepare a new selection for both B.A. and M.A. courses. On his inspiration I prepared the *New Vedic Selection.* In the Appendix of that text I had dealt with in brief the accentuation system of all Vedic texts. While dealing with accentuation system of the *Śatapatha Brāhmaṇa,* I had followed the popular prevalent views of modem Western scholors like Whitney, Macdonel, etc. It was in 1967 my revered Guru Pt. N. Kantanath Shastri Telang, the then Reader in the Deptartment of Sanskrit, B.H.U., drew my attention to the problem of accentuation system of the *Śatapatha Brāhmaṇa.* He did not say anything to me, but he asked me "are you sure about the accent system of *ŚB.* as given in the *New Vedic Selection,* based on western scholors?" This querry inspired me to do further research on the problem. I worked hard and prepared a paper 'शतपथब्राह्मण की स्वर प्रक्रिया' (Accentuation system of the *Śatapatha Brāhmaṇa*) which I presented in the Vedic Section of All India Oriental Conference, held at Varanasi in 1968, under the Sectional presidentship of Dr. C.G. Kashikar. My paper was based on the *Bhāṣika-sūtra* of Kātyāyana, a *Lakṣaṇa-grantha,* which was not critically edited at that time. A great controversy on my propositions particularly on the change of *Udātta* into *Anūdātta,* that of *Anūdātta* and *Svarita* into *Udātta* and the absence of all types of *Svaritas* and lastly the existence of more than one *Udātta* in a word, arose among the Vedic scholars participating in the Session. The traditional scholars of Varanasi, however, supported my view. Paṇḍit Yudhisthir Mimansak was of the view that *Bhāṣikasūtra* was not an authentic text. Thereafter, I concentrated upon bringing out a critical edition of the *Bhāṣikasūtra* with the commentary of Mahāsvāmin and Ananta Bhaṭṭa on the basis of eight manuscripts and three popular editions. After a lot of hard work I completed my critical edition in October 1974. Thereafter, I wrote a paper entitled 'Authenticity of the *Bhāṣikasūtra,* and presented it to the All India Oriental Conference in its 27th Session, held at Kurukeshtra in December 1974. That paper was adjudged as the best paper for the award of Dr. V. Raghavan prize in Vedic Section, and the same was published in the proceedings of AIOC, 27th Session, Kurukshetra, Dec. I974. My critical edition of the *Bhāṣikasūtra* was published from Hoshiarpur, under Panjab University Indological Series-No. 4. Aithal has referred to this edition of the *Bhāśikasūtra* in his Descriptive

Bibliography of his *Vedalakṣaṇa* (p. 485).

The research work done in the field of *Lakṣaṇa-granthas* is very meagre. As long as the living-tradition existed, there were scholars who could know and impart the knowledge. But today it is very difficult to understand those texts. It is the responsibilities of the Vedic scholars working in various Vedic Research Institutes to undertake such texts for their critical editions. In spite of being engaged since 1975 in bringing out the critical editions of many unknown texts of *Vādhūla* tradition, I am still interested in editing of Vedic *Lakṣaṇa-granthas.* I have in my mind to bring out a critical edition of the *Stobhānusaṁhāra* an important text dealing with *Stobhas* used in chanting of the *sāmans.*

Stobha is a technical term used for uttering of certain additional syllables not found in the *Sāmayoni Ṛks,* but used at the time of chanting of that *Ṛks.* The texts related to *Sāmayoni Ṛks* deal with the nature, types and methods of chanting them. Though the word *stobha* is found in the *ṚV* itself, but there it has no restricted meaning as found in the later technical *Sāma*-literature. However, we can see the germ of later *stobha*-chanting in the *ṚV* itself. In a *Ṛk* there is a reference to 'सुष्टुभा गण' and 'ऋक्वता गण' which refer to two groups of syllables, one, an addional syllable and the other, a group of syllables in *Ṛks* in relation to *svaras.*[1]

Stobhas are not only in form of additional syllables, but they also consist of some additional words, not found in *Yoni Ṛk,* but uttered at the time of chanting of the *sāman,* Such *sāmans,* based on additional words, are called *Anarcasāma* (अनर्चसाम) or *Staubhika* (स्तौभिक) The number of such *Anarca-sāmans,* found in the *Āraṇyagāna* is 132. Here a question may arise when a *sāman* is chanted on the basis of a *YoniṚk,* and it is given name after that *Ṛk,* then why such *sāmans,* chanted without *YoniṚk,* are called *sāman.* The answer is these *Anarca* or *Staubhika sāmans* are also chanted on the melodies of the *sāman* which is originally based on *YoniṚk,* *Sāman* is melody, it may be based on a *YoniṚk* or without

YoniṚk, only based on some syllables. The numbers of such *sāmans* are 1 in *Grāmegeyagāna*, 26 in *Āraṇyagāna* and 5 in *Ūhagāna*. This has been mentioned by Pt. Rāmanātha Dixit in his edition of *Ūhagāna* and *Ūhyagāna* (Intro. p. 43).

Pada, Pāda, and *Ardharca* are the units of a *Ṛk*, but in the *Sāma*-chanting *parvan* is the smallest unit of a *Sāman*. It may be pointed out that there is no such fixed rule regarding the number of words or syllables in a *parvan*. A *parvan* may comprise of 2, 3 or 4 syllables or more. Some *parvans* are also found in which the number of syllable is only 1 as in पू (ग्रा 2.8.75.I) ; वा (2.7.72.2), etc. There are certain *parvans* which have no word from *YoniṚk* only *stobha* is there as in होऽ३ (ग्रा. 4.4.144.2); एऽ३ (ग्रा 4.4.151.1), etc.

The *Saṁhitopaniṣad Brāhmaṇa, Puśpasūtra,* and *Sāmatantra* make mention of many types of *Vikāras*, occurring in the chanting of *sāmans* on the base of *YoniṚk*. These *Vikāras* are also known as *Bhāvas*. These *Vikāras* or *Bhāvas* are of different types. *Saṁhitapaniṣad Brāhmaṇa* refers to 18 types of *Vikāras* under which *stobha* is also mentioned. The *Puśpasūtra* refers to 20 types of *Vikāras* and *Sāmatantra* refers to 34 types of *Vikāras*. In the *Saṁhitopaniṣad Brāhmaṇa stobha* is defined as 'सर्वत्रगताः स्तोभाः सर्वत्रनिवृत्ताः सर्वत्रप्रवृत्ताः'[2] (*Saṁhitop Brā*. 2.3.). Interpreting the *sūtra*, Sāyaṇa holds that सर्वत्रगताः means such syllables, which are not found in the *Ārcika Saṁhitā*, but they are found everywhere in *Sāma*-chanting. Sāyaṇa on the authority of *Stobhānusaṁhāra* also holds that at the time of study (अध्ययनविधौ) they are put at the beginning and at the end; at the time of chanting of *YoniṚk* these are taken from there:

आद्यन्तदर्शनं स्तोभो विधागीतेषु सामसु।
पादेपादेऽनुसंहार्यः सोपायो निधने भवेत्॥ (स्तोभानु, 1.1)

According to Jaimini such syllables which are additional

to the *YoniṚk.,* but chanted at the time of singing are called *Stobha.*[3] Mādhavācārya, commenting on *Jaiminisūtra,* also holds the same view in his *Jaimini-Nyāyamālāvistāra.* The syllables or words in *YoniṚk.,* are uttered in as per short (ह्रस्व) long (दीर्घ) and prolated (बृहद्) character of the syllables following the rules of pronunciation of such sounds. But in the chanting of a *sāman* more time is required and for this purpose additional syllables, having no meaning at all, are used for the accomplishment of the chanting. Such sounds are called *stobha.*[4] The *Stobhānusaṃhāra* also expresses the same thing—

ऋचो यदधिकं किञ्चित् द्विरुक्तं वाऽपि दृश्यते।
स्तोभत्वं तस्य मन्यन्त ऋषयः शास्त्रचिन्तकाः॥(*Stobh.* 1.16)

According to *Akṣaratantra, stobhas* are of two types, *viz.,* (i) meaningful (*sārthaka*) and (2) meaningless (*nirarthaka). Sārthaka stobhas* are those *stobhas* which are in form of *padas* (words) having their meanings, *e.g.* नृम्णे, निधीमहि, अनिष्टपतिः, etc. These are called *stobha,* only because of the fact that these are not found in the *YoniṚk,* but only used at the time of chanting of *sāmans.* They form the art of the chanting only, not of the *Ṛk* It may be pointed out that some *sāmans* have been named only on the basis of such meaningful *stobhas,* e.g. भ्राजसाम, शुक्रसाम etc. The *sāman* chanted on *Yoni Ṛk* अग्न आयूँ षि पवसे' (साम. 627) is as under : भ्राजा। भ्राजाऽ३१३। वाऽ२। अग्न आयूँषि पवसे॥ आसुवोर्जमिषञ्च नः। आरे वाधस्व दुच्छुनाम्॥ भ्राजा। भ्राजाऽ313। बाऽ2। ए। भ्राज। (आ. 6.1.255). This *sāman* is called भ्राजसाम because of being chanted on the word भ्राज twice in the first अर्धर्च and thrice in the second अर्धर्च, even though it does not occur in the *Yoni Ṛk.*

The second type of *stobhas* are those *stobhas* which are in form of additional syllables or *padas* having no meaning at all, but employed at the time of chanting : e.g. ए इ उ हाउ औहोयि औहोवा etc., The *sāma*-chanting only on the basis of such *stobhas* are of three types viz.,

(i) छन्नसाम—'*Channa*' menans 'covered.' The *sāman,* chanted only on such meaningless syllables or *padas* from beginning (प्रस्ताव) to end (निधन) are called छन्नसाम. They have no base of any *YoniṚk.*[5] It may be pointed out that such *sāmans* are very few in number in गानसंहिता. However, both types of छन्न *sāman* based on meaningless syllables or meaningful words are found in the गानसंहिता e.g. पातीऽ२: (त्रि:) दिव: आ।। पातीऽ२। (त्रि:) अन्तरिक्षा। स्या। पातीऽ२ (त्रि:) पार्थिवा। स्या। पातीऽ२: (त्रि:) अपामोषधी। नाम्। पातीऽ२ (त्रि:) –(आर. 1.3.39). This is the example of सार्थक छन्नसाम. Another example of छन्नसाम based on meaningless *stobhas* is हाउ (त्रि:)। ऊऽ२ (त्रि:)। हाऊऽ२ (त्रि:)। इयाहाउ (द्वि:)। इयाऽ३ हाउ। वाऽ३ इदस्थिइडा ऽ२३४५.

(ii) लेशसाम–That type of *sāman* which is based on syllables of *YoniṚk* along with both meaningful as well as meaningless *stobhas* in its chanting, is called लेशसाम.

In some *sāmans, stobhas* are chanted along with one or more than one *stobhas,* or sometimes along with each *pada* or that with a *pāda,* लेशसाम is of two types पदस्तोभ and पादस्तोभ.

Again each of पदस्तोभ and पादस्तोभ is further divided into two typeअन्वयी स्तोभ and अनुषंगी स्तोभ.[6]

अन्वयी-स्तोभ is that *stobha* which is chanted before the पद or पाद e.g.

हो। होइ। अक्रान्तसमुद्र: प्रथमेविध:। मान्।
हो। होइ। जनयन्प्रजा भुवनस्यगो। पा:।
हो। होइ। वृषा पवित्रे अधिसानो ऽ2 अ। व्या इ।
हो। हो। बृहत्सोमोऽ२ वावृधे स्वानोर अ। द्रा।

औऽ३ होवा हाउवा ऽ३। एऽ३। स्वानो अ। द्रीऽ२३४५ छ (ग्रा. 15.6.529)

अनुषंगी स्तोभ is that *stobha* which is chanted after पद or पाद,

e.g.—

सधायस्ताऽ३इ। ए। दिवोनराऽ३ः। ए। धियामार्ताऽ३। ए। स्यशमता ऽ३ः। ए।। उताइसबृ ऽ३। ए। हतो दिवाऽ३ः। द्विषो अँ्हाऽ३ः। नातरति। इडाऽ२३ भाऽ३४३। ओऽ२३४५इ। डा।

Here ए स्तोम after each *pada* of the *Ṛk.*

Similarly *stobha* is chanted at the end of a *pāda.* e.g.

आनो मित्रा वरुणाऽ३। औहोवाऽ२३४। घृतैर्गव्यूतिमुक्षताऽ३म्। औहोवाऽ३। माध्वारजाऽ२ सिस्ऽ३। औहोवा। क्रतू। इडाऽ२३ भाऽ२.३। ओऽ२३४५ इडा.

Here औहोवा *stobha* comes at the end of each *pāda.* Pt. Vidyādhara in the Introduction of his commentary on *KātŚS,* keeping in view of the syllable, *pada* and *Vākya-stobhas,* refers to their three groups *viz.*, वर्णस्तोभ, पदस्तोभ and वाक्यस्तोभ. The *stobhas* consisting of only sylables for chanting, are called वर्णस्तोभ e.g. अ इ ए उ औ etc. The *stobha* in which a group of syllables is presented in a *pada*-form are called पदस्तोभ e.g. हाइ हाउ, etc. The words चन्द्र, सूर्य, भ्राज, with some meaning, chanted in a *sāman* without their being occurring in the *YoniṚk.* are also called पदस्तोभ. The *stobhas,* which are used denoting some meaning or emotions, are called वाक्यस्तोभ. According to Pt. Vidyādhara, the वाक्यस्तोभ are of nine kinds,[7] viz., अशस्ति, स्तुति, संख्यान, प्रलय, परिदेवन, प्रैष, अन्वेषण, सृष्टि and आख्यान. These *stobhas* has been defined in the *stobhānusaṁhāra.* These *stobhas* are indicative of different emotions like hatred, laudation, repent, order, legends, etc.

It may be pointed out that these *stobhas,* though described as additional syllables having no meaning, but it cannot be said that they are meaningless. They are part and parcel of the *Sāma*-chanting. In the sacrifices they were used to please the gods. They were like instruments for pleasing the gods while being chanted on *YoniṚk.* The word स्तोभ derived from स्तुभ 'to eulogies' itself indicates its importance for pleasing the gods. These *stobhas* beautify the *Sāmasvaras.* These cannot be removed from chanting. The *Chāndogyopaniṣad* describes them as a part and parcel of the *sāma*-chanting associating them with various deities. There it has been specifically stated that one who knows the *stobhas,* verily he attains the power of speech (*Vāk*) and becomes abundant in eatables. Moreover, the author of the *Chāndogyopaniṣad* visualised this world in हाउ *stobha,* the wind in हाइ *stobha,* the moon in अथ *stobha,* the Self in इह-*stobha,* Agni in इ-*stobha,* Āditya in ऊ-*stobha, Nihava* in ए-*stobha,* the Viśvedevā in औहोयि-*stobha,* and Prajāpati in हि-*stobha* without which no *Sāma* starts in the sacrifice.[8] The *Sāmavidhāna Brāhmaṇa,* takes the *Stobhas* as the hair of the body of the *Sāmans.*[9] *Stobha* is differnt from *Varṇavikāra.* The former consists of syllables or a set of syllables, which generally do not exist in the *mantras* (*Ṛk*) and are added to them for felicity and beauty during the chanting of *Sāmans,* whereas the latter embodies only modification/change of syllables/letters already existing in the *mantras* (*Ṛks*)

From the above description of the *Stobhas* their importance in chanting of *sāmans* is crystal clear. From *Saṁhitā* literature to the Upaniṣadic literature *stobhas* have been regarded as most important constitutent of *sāma*-chanting.

Here I would also like to point out that the texts dealing with *Stobhas* have not been critically edited so far. P.Aithala has given a list of following five texts dealing with *Stobhas*—

1. *Stobha-gatāgata* (स्तोभगतागत) under No. 1508
2. *Stobha-pada* (स्तोभपद) under No. 1509
3. *Stobha-pada-lakṣaṇa* (स्तोभपदलक्षण) under No. 1510
4. *Stobha-bhāṣya* (स्तोभभाष्य) of Bhaṭṭa Śobhākara under No. 1511
5. *Stobhānusaṁhāra* (स्तोभानुसंहार) under No. 1512

Out of the above five texts only *Stobha bhāṣya* of Bhaṭṭa Śobhākara has been edited by Mayura Ramanth Dikshita together with Akṣaratantra (with commentary of Satyavrata

Samashramī) and published from Sir C.P. Ramaswami Iyer Foundation, Madras, 1984.

The manuscript of *Stobhānusaṁhāra*, as mentined by Aithal, are deposited at many Centres. One manuscript of *Stobhānusaṁhāra* is deposited at the Asiatic Society, Kolkata, under the title *Stobhānus-aṁhārakārikā*. MS No. 1955 under Indian Museum collection.

The *Stobhānukārikā* is divided into three *Paṭalas* consisting of 44 (16+10+18) *Kārikās*.

The text begins with the *Kārikā*—

आद्यन्तदर्शनस्तोभो विधागीतेषु सामसु।
पादेपादेऽनुसंहार्यः सोपायो निधने भवेत्॥

and ends with the *Kārikā*—

ऋचो यदधिकं किञ्चिद् द्विरुक्तं वाऽपि दृश्यते।
स्तोभत्वं तस्य मन्यन्त ऋषयः शास्त्रचिन्तकाः॥

Here, I would also like to point out that a text of *Akṣaratantra* ascribed to Audvraji, dealing with the *stobhas* was edited with the commentary of Satyavrata Samashrami by Dr. S.K. Sharma and the text was published in hand-written form in 1993. He had presented a copy of the same to me with request to revise it. I went through the text and revised it very carefully. Now I am happy to say that the revised text has been published from Nirmal Book Agency, Kurukṣetra in 2010. While revising that text I felt a necessity of writing a commentary on it explaining the technical terms with apt examples on the *Vṛtti* of Samashrami as it was printed in that text. The complete text of commentary in English, prepared by myself has also been published.

References

1. स सुष्टुभा स ऋक्वता गणेन बलं रुरोज फलिगं रवेण–ऋ. 4.50.5;
   स सुष्टुभा स्तुभा सप्त विप्रैः स्वरेण अद्रिं स्वर्यो नवग्वैः– ऋ 1.62.4
2. आर्चिकसंहितायाः सर्वत्र निवृत्ताः सन्तः अत्र गानविधौ सर्वत्र प्रवृत्ताः—Sāyaṇa on *Saṁhitop Br.* 2.3
3. अधिकं च विवर्णं च जैमिनिः स्तोभशब्दत्वात्—*JMS* 9-2-29
4. प्रकृतार्थानन्वितं कालक्षेपमात्रहेतुं शब्दराशिं स्तोभ इत्याचक्षते—Sāyaṇa on *Sāmavedabhāsyabhumikā.*
5. केषुचित् सामसु ऋक्पदधर्मा अपि प्रस्तावादारभ्य निधनावसानं यावत् स्तोभपदविशेषैरेव भवन्ति—Sāyaṇa on *SaṁhitopBr.* 2.3
6. अन्वयी चानुषंगी च द्वौ स्तोभावनुकीर्तितौ।
   अन्वयी तु पदादौ स्यादनुषंगी पदात्परः।। (*Stobh.* 1.3)
7. स च स्तोभः त्रिविधः-वर्णस्तोभः, पदस्तोभः वाक्यस्तोभश्चेति। तत्र वर्णस्तोभः इकारादिः, पदस्तोभो हाइ, हाउ आदिः। वाक्यस्तोभो नवविधः-अशस्तिः, स्तुतिः, संख्यानम्, प्रलयः, परिदेवनम्, प्रैषः अन्वेषणम्, सृष्टिः आख्यानमिति। एतेषां लखणादिकं स्तोभग्रन्थादवगन्तव्यम्। उक्तैः कारणैः परिवर्त्तितौ मन्त्रसमुदायो गानम्। गानसंहिता-गेय, ऊह, ऊह्य, आरण्यकभेदैश्चतुर्द्धा—Vidyadhara on *KāŚS* Intro. p. 21.
8. अयं वाव लोको हाउकारो वायुर्हाइकारश्चन्द्रमा अथकारः आत्मा-इहकारोऽग्निरीकारः। आदित्य ऊकारो निहव एकारो विश्वेदेवा औहोयिकारः प्रजापतिर्हिंकारः प्राणः स्वरोऽन्नं या वाग्विराट्।। अनिरुक्तस्त्रयोदश स्तोभः सञ्चरो हुंकारः।। छा० उ. 1.13. 1-3.
9. तस्य ह वा एतस्य साम्न ऋगेवास्थीनि, स्वरो मांसानि स्तोभा लोमानि—*Sāmavidhāna Br.*1.1.10.

3

LAKṢAṆAGRANTHAS IN SOLVING EXEGETICAL PROBLEMS OF THE ATHARVAVEDA

DIPAK BHATTACHARYA

The ancillary Vedic texts on Phonetics called Veda-lakṣaṇa are usually granthas including *Śikṣās* and *Prātiśākhyas.* However, the Atharvapariśiṣṭa counts both the Pañcapaṭalikā and the Bṛhatsarvānukramaṇikā apart from the Śaunakīyacaturadhyāyikā, Atharvaprātiśākhya (AVP) and the Dantyoṣṭhavidhi. The former two works are on the arrangement and contents of the Atharvaveda (AV) that is to say Anukramaṇikās. Against this it will be unfair to limit *Lakṣaṇagranthas* to phonetic treatises only. *lakṣaṇa* means mark and here defining mark. Anything may be a defining mark of a Vedic text—its ritual, its pronunciation, its arrangement. Going by that any ancillary work dealing with a particular Veda will be its *laksaṇagrantha.* Usually we term them Vedāṅga. But Anukramaṇīs and other Pariśiṣṭas will be additionally covered by *Lakṣaṇagranthas.*

Two Pariśiṣṭas of the AV.—the Pañcapaṭalikā and the Bṛhatsarvānaukramaṇī have not been studied very well but they are very important. I shall give one or two examples of how they help. Moreover, I will try to speak on the concept of Prātisaṁhitas introduced by Surya Kanta to replace Prātiśākhya.

There is an enigmatic hymn in the Atharvaveda Śaunakīya occurring as AVŚ 19.23. It is not a heavily worded hymn but consists of small Yajus like sentences. But both Whitney and

Sāyaṇa were baffled by the hymn. Just see the hymn.

Ātharvaṇā́nām caturṛcébhyaḥ svā́hā//1// pañcaṛcébhyaḥ svā́hā//2// ṣaḍṛcébhyaḥ (mss. *ṣaḍaṛcébhyaḥ;* GB (*ṣaḍarcān*) *svā́hā//3// saptaṛcébhyaḥ sváhā//4// aṣṭaṛcébhyaḥ svā́hā//5// navaṛcébhyaḥ svā́hā//6/ daśaṛcébhyaḥ//7// ekādaśaṛcébhyaḥ svā́hā//8 dvādaśaṛcébhyaḥ svā́hā//9// trayodaśaṛcébhyaḥ svā́hā//10// caturdaśaṛcébhyaḥ svā́hā//11// pañcadaśaṛcébhyaḥ svā́hā//12// soḍaśaṛcébhyaḥ svā́hā//13// saptadaśaṛṛcébhyaḥ svā́hā//14// aṣṭādaśaṛcébhyaḥ svāha//15// ekonaviṃśatiḥ svā́hā//16// viṃśatiḥ svā́hā//17// mahatkāṇḍāya svā́yā//18// tṛcébhyaḥ svā́hā//19// ekaṛcébhyaḥ svā́hā//20//kṣudrébhyaḥ svā́hā//21// ekānṛcébhyah svā́hā//22//rohitébhyaḥ svā́hā//23// sūryābhyāṃ svā́hā//24// vrātyā́bhyāṃ svā́hā//25// prājāpatyā́bhyāṃ svā́hā//26// viṣāsahyā́i svā́hā//27// mangalikébhyaḥ svā́hā// 28// brāmā́ṇe svā́hā// 29//*

It is the Paippalāda-Saṁhitā (PS) and two of the five lakṣaṇagranthas of the AV—the Pañcapaṭalikā and Bṛhatsarvānukramaṇī that solved the problem for me. But one may see how it baffled two great scholars of the Atharvaveḍa.

Whitney translates

1. To them of four verses of the Ātharvaṇas, hail! 2. To them of five verses hail! . . . 15. To them of eighteen verses hail! 16. Nineteen hail! 17. Twenty hail! 18. To the great book hail! 19. To them of three verses hail! 20. To them of one verse hail! 21. To the petty ones hail! 22. To them of half-verses hail! 23. To the ruddy ones (*rohita*), hail! 24. To the two Sūryās, hail! 25. To the two Vrātyas, hail! 26. To the two of Prajāpati, hail! 27. To the Viṣāsahi, hail! 28. To the of good omen, hail! 29. To the brahman, hail!

Unfortunately Sāyaṇa could not clarify anything. He misled us by stating *atra caturṛcādidaśarcāntaiḥ śabdaiḥ* (1–7) *tṛcādyekarcāntaiḥ* (19–20) *śabdaiś ca tattat saṃjñakāḥ atharvākhyā ṛṣayaḥ pratipādyante. ekādaśādiviṃśatyantaiḥ śabdair ātharvaṇā ārṣeyāḥ pratipādyante.*

That means vss. 1 to 7 and 19-20 define the Atharvan sage while 8 to 17 define the ārṣeyas of the Atharvan. What does that mean? He cites evidence from the Gopatha which describes the creation of ten Atharvans and ten Ātharvaṇa ārṣeyas. But since this makes nine verses for his ten Atharvans, Sāyaṇa invents a new verse *dvyṛcebhyaḥ svāhā.* Then he reads Mahākāṇda for Mahatkāṇda of vs 18 and thinks that it means the whole Atharvaveda and its seer. So far on the first 20 vss. He goes on to state that *kṣudrebhyaḥ* (Vs. 21) means yajuḥ mantras; invents another verse *paryāyikebhyaḥ svāhā* which, he thinks means the Paryāya hymns of kāṇdas 8-11. *Ekānṛcebhyaḥ* (vs. 22) is interpreted as *ardharcavācaka* 'meaning halfverse.' Whitney accepts this hideous invention.

Only five verses that is 19.23.23–27 meant for Rohita, Sūryā, Vrātya, Prajāpati and beginning viṣāsahi are correctly understood by Sāyaṇa as meaning Kāṇḍas 13. But Sāyaṇa fails with vs. 28 *maṅgalikebhyaḥ svāhā* on which there is no comment. *Brahmaṇe svāhā* is said to mean the AV. and its seer.

Barring five verses which mean kāṇḍas 13 to 17 of the AVŚ. and the last verse meaning the whole of the Atharvaveda, Sāyaṇa not only fails but is misleading. Sāyaṇa could identify these six kāṇḍas because they have the names of the principal deity at the beginning of the hymn and because the name Brahmaveda was very well-known. So there was no difficulty. As for the other verses I think that the cause of the failure is that he did not have the opportunity to consult the Bṛhatsarvānukramaṇikā (BSA) and the Pañcapaṭalikā (PP).

Whitney too totally failed. He (HOS 8: 93I) only gives the views of Sāyaṇa without attempting to explain the names. Lanman follows Sāyaṇa in identifying kāṇḍas 13–17 in vss. 23–27. On *maṅgalikebhyaḥ svāhā* that is vs. 28 Lanman guesses that this 'from its position ought to signify book xviii.' Lanman makes a guess that *caturṛcebhyaḥ* might mean the verses of the first kāṇḍa because four verses are the norm in

it. Beyond that he is a failure. He thinks that verses 1–15 (caturṛca to aṣṭādaśarca) and 19 and 20 (tṛca and ekarca) cover the tirst seven kāndas. He does not show how. 19–20 *tṛcébhyaḥ svā́hā* and *ekarcébhyaḥ svā́hā* of course cover kāṇdas vi and vii. But how the first fifteen verses can mean the first tive kāṇḍas of the AVŚ. is not known. Laman is better than Whitney and Sāyaṇa but still misleading.
Now let ns see how the Lakṣaṇagranthas help.

For AVŚ. 19.23. 23–28

On Rohita *i.e.* kāṇḍa 13 the text of the Pañcapaṭalikā is somewhat corrupt *ṣaṣṭiḥ, saṭcatvāriṃśat, ṣaḍviṃśati, ṣaṭparyāyaḥ/ etatkāṇḍe rohitānām* (Bhagavaddatta 1914: 14). There is no commentary. The meaning, according to me is, 'There are 60, 46 and 26 hymns and six paryāyas in this kāṇḍa of the Rohitas' The mentioned sequence of 60, 46 and 26 hymns in three anuvākas followed by six paryāyas is found in the 13th kāṇḍa. The Bṛhatsarvānukramaṇikā 8.12 confirms this: *ud ehi vājin iti kāṇḍam . . . rohitādidevatyam.* The identification is no problem now.

Then Saurya (14th) follows in the PP (15), as consisting of 64 and 75 verses. This is true of AVṢ 14 consisting of two anuvākas having the above number of verses. BSA. 9 calls this Sāvitrī-Sūryā and ends the description at 9.3 with *eṣa sauryo vivāha iti.* So there is no problem in identifying this as *sūryābhyām* of AVŚ. 19.23.

The Vrātya (PP.15) is said to have two series of seven and eleven paryāyas. This agrees with the arrangement of the 15th kāṇḍa in the existing editions. BSA. 9.4 states *vrātya āsīd iti kāṇḍam/aṣṭādaśaparyāyā . . . . vrātyadaivatam.*

The Prājāpatya (PP. 16) is said to have two series of four and five paryāyas. This agrees with the 16th kāṇḍa consisting of two anuvākas with the mentioned number of paryāyas. BSA 15.17 has the same name *atisṛṣṭo apām iti prājāpatyasya nava paryāyāḥ.*

For *viṣāsahyai svāhā,* AVŚ. 19.23.27, it is not necessary to consult the ancillary literature for identification, for, the

17th kāṇḍa of the Vulgate begins with *viṣāsahiṃ sahamānam* etc. This kāṇḍa has been mentioned in the Pañcapaṭalikā as consituting of thirty verses. BSA 10.1 begins *viṣāsahim ṛcas triṃśat*/The hymn with *viṣāsahim* has thirty ṛks. This is correct.

As to the hymns to the fathers I am coming to them later.

For the remaining kāṇḍas I first begin with the *caturṛcebhyaḥ svāhā* to show how the anukramaṇīs help in identifying them which Lanman could not correctly do.

BSA. 1.13 *venas tat itiprabhṛtir ākāṇḍaparisamāpteḥ pūrvakāṇḍasya caturṛcaprakṛtir iti/ evam uttarottarakāṇḍeṣu ṣaṣṭhaṃ yāvad ekaikādhikā tāvat sūkteṣv ṛg iti vijānīyāt/*

The presentation is bad perhaps because of text-critical anomaly. Its meaning as I understand is

> "What I shall state will hold good from *venas tat* (2.1) till the end of the kāṇḍa. The previous kāṇḍa's hymns have four ṛks in general. Up to the sixth the number increases by one.

This means kāṇḍa 1 is caturṛca, the second is pañcarca and thus the sixth is navarca. But this is wrong. The sixth has tṛca sūktas, each hymn has three mantras.

In the Pañcapaṭatikā (5), the fifth is called mah at (cf. 19.23.18 *mahatkāṇḍāya svāhā*). The Bṛhat-sarvānukramaṇikā (3.1, Vishva Bandhu 1966: 34. see below) has no special name in any case *pañcamaṃ yāvad* meaning "the number increases by one' up to the fifth kāṇḍa was expected.

Obviously this points to some unknown error having crept into the text tradition. Either the Bṛhatsarvānukramaṇikā should read *pañcamaṃ yāvat* or the received arrangement of the AVŚ. is wrong. That is not impossible. We already know of manipulation with kāṇḍas 19 and 20 in the AVŚ. A better edition of the Bṛhatsarvānukramaṇikā may yield new results with other kāṇḍas too.

It may also be speculated upon if *ṣaṣṭhaṃ yāvad* meant *ṣaṣṭhād rābhya.* In that case the statement should be correct.

For, the sixth consists of three ṛks per verse. The first of four and so on.

For the 5th kāṇḍa *mahatsu ekavarjam* (PP 5) 'In the anuvākas (hymns?) called *mahat* (there are five hymn per anuvāka) barring one.' This agrees with AVŚ 5. For, barring its fourth anuvāka that has six hymns in it, the fifth kāṇḍa has five hymns in each anuvāka. But this also means that the AVŚ 5 is denoted by the term *mahat.* Not so in the AVP that knows it as *aṣṭarca.* Now, the Pañcapaṭalikā knows that the eight-ṛk combination has some significance for the fifth kāṇḍa. It states (2.5; Bhagavadddatta:4) *mahatsu kāṇḍasamavāyo 'ṣṭarcaprabhṛtīnām ākṛitīnām aṣṭādaśebhyaḥ ṣoḍaśavarjam.* 'In the mahat hymns the kāṇḍa-specific combination beginning with eight-ṛk forms (goes) up to eighteen leaving out sixteen.' This is true of the hymns of the filth kāṇḍa in the AVŚ. The PP, then, knows the eight ṛk-combination as the shortest one. That, in spite of this awareness, unlike in the AVP, AVS. 5 is called *mahat* in the Pañcapaṭalikā, might have been an old convention. For, the Bṛhatsarvānukramaṇikā (3.1) does not call it *aṣṭarca* like the AVP. It just states *athaivaṃ vakṣyamāṇamantreṣu sūtraprakṛtiḥ sarṣicchandodaivateṣu avagacchet sarvatreti/* Not quite intelligible without an *iti* before *avagacchet,* this may mean 'Now, one should understand (that) thus (*evaṃ*- better 'this') is the nature of the hymns in the mantras to be stated along with (their) seers, metres and deities everywhere.'

This solves the problem of identification of the AVŚ. mantras which mentioned kāṇḍas up to the fifth and partly up to the sixth.

BSA. 4.1 explicitly identifies the sixth as the Tṛcasūkta. It kāṇḍa, states of AVŚ 6 *athātas tṛcasūktakāṇḍe . . . tṛcasūktaḥ prakṛtiḥ/* This is sufficient.

For the seventh it states *ṛksūktā ekarceṣu:* 'One verse makes a hymn among the *ekarcas.'*

So we get solution of the problem of identification from the BSA. and PP of kāṇḍas 1–7, 13–17 in AVŚ 1923 verses

1, 2, 3, 4 (for kāṇḍas 1–4) 18, 19, 20 (for 5—7), 23, 24, 25, 26, 27 (for 13–17). Now remain the kṣudras, ekānṛcas and the maṅgalikas that is 8–11, 12, and 18.

PP. 5 states on the kṣudras *dvisūktāḥ kṣudreṣu* 'One has two hymns in an anuvāka among the kṣudras.'

This is true of kāṇḍas 8–11 which are meant by *kṣudras* and which largely correspond to AVP. 16. BSA. 6.1 begins with the eighth kāṇḍa with the words *atha kṣudrakāṇḍārtha-sūktamantrāṇām ṛṣidaivatacchandāṃsy ucyante, tato yāvad ekādaśakāṇḍāntam arthasūktaprakṛtiḥ tāvad vihāya paryāyān virāḍ vai prabhṛtīn iti.* It states the validity of the name *kṣudra* up to the end of the eleventh kāṇḍa.

PP on ekānṛca: *anuvākasūktā ekānṛceṣu.* This holds good for AVŚ. 12. *ekānṛca* is the name of AVP. 17.

So the names of all the kāṇḍas excepting thc Maṅgalikas mentioned in the AVŚ 19.23 list are traced with the help of the Lakṣaṇagranthas. The Maṅgalikas are treated blow.

The hymns to the fathers are referred to as *yameṣu vihitā ṛcaḥ* and as consisting of 61, 60, 73 and 89 ṛks in four anuvākas in the Pañcapaṭalikā (ch. 4, Bhagvaddatta 1914: 15). In the Bṛhatsarvānukramaṇikā (10.2) too the eighteenth kāṇḍa is mentioned as *ocitsakhāyam iti caturanuvākaṃ tryaśītid-viśatarcaṃ yamadevatyam.* None mention them as Maṅgalikas. So there is nothing in the two anukramaṇīs to identify these as the verses meant by *maṅgalikébhyaḥ svā́hā* in the 28th mantra of 19, 23. On the other hand they are called Maṅgalikas in the Orissa manuscripts. That means the Śaunakīya hymn knows the Paippalāda tradition which was not known even to the authors of the Pañcapaṭalikā and the Bṛhatsarvānukramaṇikā. This I think is important as I try to show.

As Bloomfield (AV and GB. 1899: 35) has shown, at least the Pañcapaṭalikā is older than the nineteenth and the twentieth kaṇḍa of the AVŚ. Thesc two kāṇḍas have not been mentioned in the Pañcapaṭalikā. The antiquity of the Pañcapaṭalikā is apparent in its name, too. The older tradition was to mention books by the number of their chapters or their divisions. So one gets Daśatayī, Aṣṭādhyāyī, Caturādhyāyikā, Navāhnikī, Tipiṭaka, Aṣṭasāhasrikā and so on. The convention occasionally found place in the middle ages as we still have Caturbhāṇī, Catuḥsūtrī etc. Since the Pañcapaṭalikā is not a medieval Lakṣaṇagrantha it must be old and older than the Bṛhatsarvānukramaṇī.

Now, while an old Lakṣaṇagrantha does not know a Paippalāda convention, a later addition to the AVŚ knows that. What does it mean? It means that the name *maṅgalika* was taken from the Paippalādā-Saṃhitā by the Śaunaka-Saṃhitā. Does it not prove Bloomfield's observation about the structure of the AVŚ. to be true'? Bloomfield (ibid.) held that the last two kāṇḍas were added to the AVŚ. just to make it equal to the AVP. in number of kāṇḍas. The secondary position of of the AVŚ. in the Atharvavedic tradition and the intention of superseding the AVP. by structural manipulation is proved by this.

There is a problem with the name ekānṛca too. The twelfth kāṇḍa is called ekānṛca. This name occurs in the older Anukramaṇī that is the Pañcapaṭalikā[5] but not in the *Bṛhatsarvānukramaṇikā,* one may ask the reason for that.

As far as I can see, the reason is that when the Pañcapaṭalikā was composed the twelfth kāṇḍa was really ekānṛca but later it lost its ekānṛca character. I am showing how.

Ekānṛca-kāṇḍa means *ekaḥ anṛk anuvākaḥ/sūktaṃ yasmin kāṇḍe*[6] the kāṇḍa where there is one hymn or anuvāka that is *anṛk* ie not ṛk but prose.[7] The seventeenth kāṇḍa of the AVP fultils this condition because there is a prose hymn in this kāṇḍa of the AVP. The hymn is AVP. I7.35 dealing with the origin of a rite called Anaḍudvrata. The highly interesting hymn shows how Indra killed Vṛtra through the sacrifice of a bull. This killing is meant to serve as the model for the Anaḍudvrata. But the moral standing of the rite was questioned by a wise sage called Ahīnas Āśvatthī. The censure by Ahīnas Āśvatthi must have worked. For, the hymn and the anaḍudvrata both have been lost from tradition outside the Paippalāda-Saṃhitā. It has a sentence *na tād brāhmaṇaṃ nindāni yād enum aśṛṇot.* The sentence has been wrongly cited in the Kāśikā, Nyāsa, Padamañjarī and by Bhaṭṭoji Dīkṣita. Everywhere the citation is wrong. That means though the sentence was transmitted in the grammatical tradition but since the ritual was lost they did not understand what it meant and only a corrupt version was transmitted. This must have been caused by the unpopularity of the black magic as the hymn describes.

The hymn is not found even in the AVŚ. But I shall show how the Pañcapaṭalikā, the old Lakṣaṇagrantha of the Atharvaveda proves that once this hymn existed in the Śaunakīya Saṃhitā too but had been purposely dropped to free the AVŚ. a part of a cleansing process of freeing the AVŚ. of āṅgirasa elements. I am showing how.

The twelfth kāṇḍa is called ekānṛca according to the Pañcapaṭalikā. But, if the term *ekānṛca* means a kāṇḍa that has only one passage that does not have any ṛk, then how could AVŚ 12, that has dropped the said passage, be called *ekānṛca?* This is a misnomer for the AVŚ. The Pañcapaṭalikā retains the name but the Bṛhatsarvāriukramaṇī drops it. It is easy to infer that at the time of the composition of the Pañcapaṭalikā the AVŚ contained the hymn. Later there was a revision of the AVŚ. Two new kāṇḍas were added and undesirable hymns were dropped from it. It was now with 20 kāṇḍas and bereft of the anaḍudvrata hymn that described a black magic.

But the old Anukramaṇī, the most ancient Lakṣaṇagrantha has retained the name *ekānṛca* hinting at the lost unrevised character of the AVŚ.

We saw three instances of the old Lakṣaṇagrantha Pañcapaṭalika helping us to see the history of the development of the redaction called Śaunakīya Saṃhitā. It helps us understand the enigmatic hymn AVŚ. 19.23 by informing us of the names of the various kāṇdas, which even Sāyaṇa failed to understand, not to speak of Whitney and Lanman. Taking further help of Paippalāda and the Pañcapaṭalika we can also prove that there was a revision of the AVŚ. when some hynms were dropped from it. Thirdly the fact that the Pañcapaṭalikā, the Śaunakīya Caturādhyāyikā and the Kauśikasūtra, the three most ancient Lakṣaṇagranthas of the AV. deal with only 18 kāṇdas of the book we can safely conclude that the original Śaunakīya Saṃhitā consisted of 18 kāṇdas only.

Now I draw scholars' attention to one fact pointed to by Sūrya Kanta.

Sūrya Kanta had a theory according to which there is no Prātiśākhya but only PrātiSaṁhitas. The intention is clear. Prātiśākhyas tell of the pronunciation peculiarities of each recension. But in practice we get the pronunciation of only the Śākala recension of the Ṛgveda, the Mādhyandina recension of the White Yaiurveda and the Taittirīya recension of the Black Yajurveda. These, according to Surya Kanta were valid for all the recensions of these Vedas. Hence since there is no Prātiśākhya for particular recensions they are not Prātiśākhyas but PrātiSaṁhitas. The idea leads to one of a standard Saṁhitā for all the Vedas which grew at a time when 'not a śākhā of a particular Saṃhitā, but a Saṃhitā in general; or to be more particular, that śākhā of a Samhitā, which emerged victorious from the conflict of the warring śākhās, . . . was ultimately adopted by all . . . .' He means that the Śākhās struggled between themselves for supremacy and one won and got the general stamp of Saṁhitā to be followed by the Prātiśākhyas of that Veda. He tried to prove that the Vulgate was not the Śaunakīya Saṁhitā and that it was not related to the Śaunakīya-Caturādhyāyikā. The Caturādhyāyikā, Surya Kanta held, was based on a Śaunakīya-Saṃhitā that had been different from the Vulgate of the Atharvaveda and that had been the Saṃhitā of Sāyaṇa. The Vulgate, on the other hand, Surya Kanta tried to show, was *the Atnarvaveda* that served as the general Saṃhitā for the Atharva-Prātiśākhya.

Assuming that his idea of the competition between different śākhās is true, one may still ask, 'What was then the original śākhā of the Vulgate? 'To this is to be added another question—What was the position of the Vulgate vis-ṣ-vis the Paippalāda-Saṁhita in mainstream Vedic tradition represented by Patañjali and the Nirukta.

There is no report of any other name of the Vulgate apart from Śaunakīya. There are two sources to confirm this recensional affiliation of the Vulgate. One is the statement of Sāyaṇa at the beginning of his Introduction to the first kāṇḍa. Surya Kanta regards this as a statement about another recension on which Sāyaṇa supposedly wrote his commentary. But there is another work, unjustifiedly ignored in Westem studies, testifying to the name Śaunakī for the Vulgate. While stating the currency of different śākhās of the Vedas in different regions Mahidāsa in his commentary on the Caraṇavyūha cites from an unknown work that he calls Mahārṇava to show that north of the Narmadā the Śaunakī was current and south of it the Pippalā. Mahidāsa belonged to the mid-sixteenth century (I613 Abda) of the current era. The statement shows that around that time no other recension of the Atharvaveda was known as current. If, as Surya Kanta would make us believe, Śāyaṇa's Śaunakīyā Śākhā' was not the Vulgate it must have been a prominent recension current at that time. In that case how could its name be missed by Mahidāsa?

The currency of other recensions is known only from earlier works. The Kāśikā (on P.1.3.49) speaks of Maudas imitating Paippalādas, the Kauśika-Sūtra (85.8) of the practice of Devadarśins apart from of Śaunakins. If our Vulgate was any of these recensions Mahidāsa would have informed. Again, Sāyaṇa speaks of four prominent recensions Paippalāda, Śaunakīya, Mauda and Tauda. If his Atharvaveda was not the Śaunakīya it could only have been one of the last two. We can exclude the Mauda too along with the Paippalāda. For, the Maudas read like the Paippalādas. But there is no trace of the transmitted text being the Tauda-Saṃhitā of the Atharvaveda. Our authority is Mahidāsa.

The absurdity of Surya Kanta's thesis will be apparent from the above. One has to admit (1) that Sāyaṇa did not write a commentary on the Saṃhitā text of the Caturādhyāyikā that had only eighteen kāṇḍas and (2) that the Vulgate can only be the Śaunakīya-Saṃhitā and no other text.

But there is another aspect of Surya Kanta's novel thesis that is dealt with below.

There is no text that has not remembered its redactor's or his family's name. This is natural. For, with an oral body of literature the redactor carried supreme importance for the accomplished book. Initially there were *ṛks, sāmans, yajuses* and *ātharvaṇāni, bheṣajāni* or *bhaiṣajyāni* etc., learnt by heart and recited by priests or aspirants, but no collection called Ṛgveda, Sāmaveda etc. Cf. AVP 15.14.1 (AVŚ. 11.6.14) *yajñaṃ brūmo yajamānam ṛcaḥ sāmāni bheṣajā/ yajūṃṣi hotrān* (AVŚ *hotrā*) *brūmas* . . . . Even the Ātharvaṇa mantras were just *ṛks*. Take AVP. 17.8.5 (AVŚ. 10.7.14) *yatra ṛṣayo bhūtakṛta ṛcaḥ sāma yajur mahī/ekarṣir yasminn ārpitāḥ skambhaṃ* . . . Also AVP. 17.9.1 (AVŚ. 10.7.20) *yasmād ṛco apātakṣaṃ (<n) yajur yasmād apālakṣaṃ (-n)/ chandāṃsi yasya lomāni skambhaṃ* . . . Expectedy all the known forms of literary compositions have been mentioned in the AVP descriptions. Then we have to place the AV mantras among *ṛcaḥ* and *yajūṃṣi* of the two verses. So at this time there had been no Ṛgveda and no Atharvaveda but only floating *ṛks and yajuses, bheṣajas, ātharvaṇas* (*brahman* for *bheṣaja* 18.32.3) etc. It is because of the redactors that the books, oral at first, came into being from the same floating *ṛcaḥ, sāman, yajuṃsi, bheṣaja* etc. And their names or the names of their families have been gratefully remembered by posterity. This is not only plausible, the tradition mentioned by Veṅkaṭa-Mādhava agrees with this: *maṇḍalānyṛṣayo dṛṣṭvā sarva eva*

samāgatāḥ vinyāysaṃ dadṛśuḥ paścād iti vṛddhebhya āgamaḥ. So, if we follow Surya Kanta's theory of a redaction without a known name the logical conclusion will be that unlike the other Saṁhitās the Vulgate was a got up post-Vedic redaction and hence its redactor's name is missing.

His idea of the Śaunakīya-Saṁhitā being the general Atharvaveda and that we get Prātisaṁhitas based on general Saṁhitās are thus to be rejected.

4

EMERGENCE OF VEDALAKṢAṆA PHONETIC TEXT OF SĀMAPRĀTIŚĀKHYA

PRADYOT KUMAR DATTA

Sūtra literature dealing with phonetics is at least as old as of the subsidiary Vedic texts to include Śikṣās and Prātiśākhyas. The Sūtras of the auxilliary Vedaṅga Śikṣā are connectively related to Vedic Saṁhitās. Source materials of phonetics are to be in Prātiśākhyas as well as in various phonetic texts. Ancient science and mythology are very much inextricably interrelated. In the history of intellectually traditional texts of rare importance including technical studies on Vedalakṣaṇa begot more awe and wonder. Śikṣā and Prātiśākhya works are thus of highly technical field which led to traditional Indian advancement.

The fourteen Pratyāhāra Sūtras believed to have evolved from the sound of Lord Śiva's percussive instrument for musical apparatus not only consist of all phonemes on Sanskrit language but also arranged them in natural classes to be referred to in the ancient Indian phonetic and grammatical texts. Such sophistication in phonological narration does not exist in any other tradition or in any other part of the world not only especially at the dawn of civilisation in the hoary past prior to Indian research of phonetics. In fact the study of phonology is not seriously considered to be pursued until very present period.

The view of any scholar of India engaged in grammatical studies is finally applicable to many of ancient Indian Śikṣā and Prātiśākhya texts while attempting to analyse

Vedalakṣaṇa texts. Such textual works constitute some of greatest monuments of the human intellect. It is extremely difficult to locate many of Śikṣā texts and their Prātiśākhyas and related other important materials of the great Indian phonetic tradition. Beisdes initial path-breaking contributioins by a few scholars there have been very little work done in that tradition. Scholars may find source of ancient phonetic tradition in search of the roots of Indian grammatical information to follow the great intellectual legacy in a field of bibliographic inquiry and other documents.

The traditional list to enumerate six fold Vedāṅgas assigns a first place to Śikṣā in the science of Phonetics. Various recensions of Vedas are connected with works of ancillary sciences during oldest period of Śikṣā school. There are instructions for the pronunciation, accentuation, euphonic alteration of sounds as mentioned in Śikṣā texts. Śikṣā is a work of great importance for the technical studies of Vedic literature. This is a comprehensive study on Vedic form covering all its delicate shades.

Ancient works on Phonetics are the pioneers in the interpretation of Vedic passages. The prehistory of Sanskrit grammar dates back to Śikṣā works. There is a large number of extant Śikṣās. Out of fifty Śikṣā texts, thirty-one are published in Benaras Edition of 1893; sixteen manuscripts in Madras Government Oriental MSS Library and three manuscripts in Bhandarkar Oriental Research Institute, Poona. Many of these Śikṣās, however, are mere catalogues of certain sounds of Vedas, and contain very little matter of linguistic studies. Even more famous Śikṣās like Bhāradvāja and Siddhānta Śikṣās deal with different sounds in alphabetical order and pronunciation as well to facilitate research work. Nevertheless, even the minor Śikṣās do not differ from several portions of representative Vedāṅga Phonetics themselves, which are mere catalogues of works. Such Śikṣās illustrate the way wherein the earliest Phonetic texts seem to have built up a gradual alteration of materials, general and particular.

Prātiśākhyas are earliest representatives of Vedāṅga Śikṣā to corroborate some recensions of a particular Veda Saṁhitā as M. Winternitz comments on such a Vedāṅga Śikṣā in his treatise '*A History of Indian Literature*', vol. I, pp. 248–49. Many of the Śikṣās consist of a number of valuable and striking phonetic observations connected with the Prātiśākhyas. Sarvasammata Śikṣā, MS. No. 998 of 1905, Madras, is a far different work from the one edited by Otto Franke in 1886. The latter is a short manual of forty-nine verses without having any mention of names of either author or commentator with a very meagre treatment of most difficult points in phonetics viz. accent and quantity. In treatise of Franke's edition such work has more verses having four chapters with an elaborate gloss. The name of author is Keśavācārya while its commentator is Mañci Bhaṭṭa. Franke's commentator, seems to be a separate person, but his commentary does not vary from the point of treatment. Sarvasammata Śikṣā, subject is common and it is acceptable by all phonetic works as the Taittirīya recension.

Introductory verse of each commentary is different. Certain portions of this work are evidently nothing else but elaboration of corresponding portions like Vyāsa Śikṣā. Franke's edition has only two verses on accent, but the Madras Manuscript has thirty-three verses with a fairly copious treatment of accent. Two verses of such edition do not occur amongst these thirty-three verses, but are laid down at the end of the Madras MS, being verses as IV/104–5. This may be true of Franke's edition but not so much of the Madras MS; which comprises some materials hardly to be connected with any other extant Śikṣā i.e. Phonetics.

There are three Śikṣā texts like Nārada, Lomaśī and Gautamī in Sāmaveda. Nārada Śikṣā is one of the oldest and most profound Śikṣā. It states that its object is for the treatment of accents in such Veda. This is corroborated by nature of the text relating to accent and its relation to musical lore with other subjects of Phonetics and so on. The treatise has been attributed to Nārada for its authorship. The Lomaśī Śikṣā makes general but concise observations for doubting. The title of Śikṣā suggests that its author is a person named Lomaś. This Śikṣā is a work on Phonetics. A manuscript of the then Jātakapaddhati ascribed to Madras. manuscripts, catalogue, 1913 enumerates a list of teachers where Gargya and Romaśa along with Vyāsa, Vasiṣṭha, etc. have been mentioned. This Śikṣā was attributed to the same person as either Romaśa or Lomaśa. Such names of the author are identical to be called Lomaśī or Romaśī after Romaśā, the goddess of speech referred to as the daughter of Bṛhaspati in Bṛhaddevata III/156. Gautamī Śikṣā is ascribed to Gautama.

This Śikṣā text manifests a connected study of vowel and consonant groups. It refers to a Prātiśākhya wherein a consonant group like युङ्ङ्क्ष्क्ष्व is said to occur and such group is to be traced in any of the extant texts. In Bṛhaddevatā there is a description of connotation entitled to the Lomāśī Śikṣā after Romaśā, the goddess of speech is a daughter of Bṛhaspati who is the author of this phonetic text so referred to in two stanzas:

"पञ्चामन्दान्भावयव्यस्य गीता जायापत्योः संप्रवादो द्वृचेन।
संप्रवादं रोमशयेन्द्रराज्ञोरेते ऋचौ मन्यते शाकपूणिः।।
इन्द्रेण जायापत्योश्चेतिहासं द्वृचेऽस्मिन् मन्यते शाकटायनः,
प्रादात् सुतां रोमशां नाम नाम्ना बृहस्पतिर्भावयव्याय राज्ञे।।

—बृहद्देवता. 3/155–156

The contributions as prototypes of Prātiśākhyas were made to the science of Phonetics of the Vedalakṣaṇa Śikṣā texts. The name as Prātiśākhya of each Sūtra form intends for a recension. It deals with a discussion on the aspects of many branches existed in certain Vedas word by word, so-called the Upāṅga as referred to in the commentary of

Tribhāṣyaratna in the Introduction of the Taittirīya Prātiśākhya ascribed to Māhiṣeya, Ātreya and Vāraruca. Then the salient features like phonetics, grammar ect. which assist the study of Vedas as branches for advancement of learning gave rise to many recensions of Vedas to various teachers and their schools or disciples gradually emerged.

The earliest speculations of a Śikṣā nature are to be referred to either in the Taittirīyopaniṣad or in Muṇḍakopaniṣad I/I and I/4-5 as well. There existed around the same time texts or various manuals of Phonetics dealing with alphabets, quantity, pronunciation, accentuation and euphonic rule. It must have been prior to the composition of Prātiśākhya literature. The earlier treatises classified Vedic texts into four forms of speech following carefully the definition of some previous Saṁjñās like technical terms and techniques possibly with an attempt to reduce word and an explanation of their phonetic formation.

Even modern scholars both eastern and western have laid their hands on such works and their contributions have thrown useful insight on various problems dealt with Śikṣā and Prātiśākhya texts in the Vedalakṣaṇa analysis. But Scholars now-a-days try to give an explanation of such texts through modern outlook to bring the wealth of ideas in those compendium. Every Vedic recension is supposed to have a separate Phonetic and Prātiśākhya text. There must have been many Vedalakṣaṇa texts or ancillary Vedic texts on Phonetics affiliated to each branch or Śākhā of each of four Veda Saṁhitā.

Prātiśākhyas are treated as the whole treatise of collective Veda-assistant scriptures like Phonetics, etc. mainly dealing with peculiarities relating to Śikṣā, metre of the speech in various recensions or Śākhās.

The last Sūtra of first chapter for the Vājasaneyi-Prātiśākhya refers to a remarkable stanza which is commented upon by Uvaṭa, a great commentator of same Prātiśākhya. The oldest text book of Śikṣā is Prātiśākhya which contains the rules of instruction for its pronunciation, accentuation, euphonic alteration of the sounds etc.

There are treatises of phonetics mainly dealing with peculiarities relating to grammar of speech in various Vedic recensions and their pronunciation—वृद्धमिदं शास्त्रमन्यानि शास्त्राण्यपेक्ष्य शिक्षाविहितं व्याकरणविहितं चास्मिन् शास्त्र उभयं यतः प्रक्रियत इति हेतोश्च्छिष्याणामेतच्छास्त्रश्राविणां वृद्धिर्भवति। A number of forms may be found in various Vedas of different branches ascribed to different teachers and their schools but not explicable by general norms. They can be explained by taking resort to the Phonetic texts to be applicable in the Prātiśākhyas as found in a remarkable passage तस्मात्तत्तत्समाम्नाये प्रातिशाख्या-विरोधतः कार्यं एवं व्यवस्थाप्यं शिक्षा व्याकरणोदितम् तै. प्रा. प्र. अ. सू? वृत्ति। The Tribhāṣyaratna, a commentary as well as Vaidikābharaṇa of Taittirīya Prātiśākhya relates to Prātiśākhyas in the Vedalakṣaṇa as Upāṅga scriptures as they analyse various features ascribed to the branches of Vedas word by word:

प्रतिपंद चानुपदं छन्दोभाषासमन्वितम्।
मीमांसान्यायतर्कांश्च उपाङ्गानि विदुर्बुधाः।।

Śikṣā means instruction on pronunciation of Vedic words. The science of phonetics has been studied with a great zeal having carried to a perfection. The discovery of such text has created a revolution on the science of Philology. It leads to momentous consciences in the development of thought. The inevitable dialectal peculiarities arise within a language. It was taken as a science in earnest. Satisfactory interpretation of Vedas is a huge task to do full justice while explaining Vedic mantras. Śikṣā then leads to the method of pronouncing letters, vowels and accents for accurate recitation of Vedic verses— शिक्षा नाम स्वरवर्णोच्चारणोपदेशकं शास्त्रम्।

There are sixfold precepts like syllable, accent, mora, pronuncial breath, equality for pronunciation and euphoinc combination as mentioned in the Taittirīyopaniṣad.

Language is the vehicle of thought. It is expressed in sentences. The enunciation of letters is the knowledge of the desired letters. Phonetics are applicable either in isolation or combination. Some sorts of modifications or changes are possible in any sound or in both sounds emerged therein.

They depend upon the nature of changes. The quality of work as produced has won a recognition as well as an honourable mention even in the hands of scientific philologists of their time for the necessity of Phonetic study.

Even a bare Catalogue of the names of Phoneticians both ancient and modern with their valuable works still preserved can amply bear the truth of such assertion. On the basis of calculation there are currently a dozen of different schools of Vedalakṣaṇa text including Śikṣās and Prātiśākhyas of highly technical field of Indian learning which are available only from quotations in separate treatises in original form. The study of the pause of speech is of sufficient importance to be pursued by the usage itself independently from generation to generation. The technical terms used by the so-called Aindra treatise are connected with one other and are simples and more formative. The Prātiśākhya of the Sāmaveda known as Ṛktāntra composed by Śākaṭāyana is also mentioned as Aindra treatise alluded to Pre-Pāṇinian sect. Its author's name is mentioned in the Ṛgveda-Prātiśākhya and the Aṣṭadhyāyī of Pāṇini considers him superior than the authors of other texts like of Śaunaka and other composers.

It is interesting to note how A.C. Burnell arrived to a similar result through an independent study of the Ṛktantra known Vyākaraṇa. He says: "These words belong to the other what I have termed the Aindra school of grammar, and where any of the words in question is used by Pāṇini, it is with a new meaning." He also sums up the whole position in the following words: "All existing Prātiśākhyas are, in their present forms, later than Pāṇini, but some (e.g.—the Ṛkprātiśākhya, etc.); have been but little modified, while the others have suffered more. All, however, belong to a school that existed before Pāṇini invented his system." It does not appear perhaps to be a very recent production because of being possibly composed while Sanskrit was a spoken language to be treated as bhāṣā i.e.—tongue of speech.

Sacred Vedas are most ancient works in the vast range of Indian Aryan Literature. Any interpration of Vedas must have some traditional materials to elucidate varied and various meanings of Vedic hymns. Such materials are supplied by the ancillary limbs of Vedas. In midst of them, Śikṣā as a highly technical Phonetic text may be systematically investicated through its modern outlook for traditional Indian learning. Organs are always concerned for production of any sound. The immovable place of production is called the Sthāna and it is the position of articulation for the system of वर्णोच्चारण।

Then the Sthāna is a place for articulation of syllables. Active one mostly is designated as the Karaṇa as instrument of production. Sound receives its character by contact with organs. There are fivefold organs for pronunciation of letters like अनुप्रदान, संसर्ग, स्थान, करणविन्यय and परिमाण to mean emitted material contact, place of production, instrument of articulation and measurement of letters chronologically as referred to in the Taittirīya Prātiśākhya XXIII/2. Thus the Prātiśākhya as a work of rare importance among the technical studies with its phonetic method must be taught for correct and accurate pronunciation of words of Vedic Literature. The teaching of letters, accents, quantity of syllables, stress, melody and combination of words in continuous recitation are noted in all chapters of Phonetics. The culture of Phonetics had started long ago as a science of languages. The first Vedāṅga Śikṣā or the Prātiśākhya for technical studies of Vedic literature means instruction of pronunciation of Vedic words as mentioned by Śaunaka in his Ṛgveda-Prātiśākhya कृत्स्नं च वेदाङ्गमनिन्द्यमार्षम्—ऋ. प्रा. 24/99

Saṁhitā and Pada are two different systems of pāṭhas to

link their teachings amidst various readings. Such Pāṭhas are the oldest productions of the Śikṣā school. On the basis of commentary of Veṅkaṭamādhava in the Ṛgveda VIII/I/7 three personalities like Śākalya, Yāska and Pāṇini are treated as analysts of pauses. An ascertainment in made for determination of prime meaning of words through the analysis of sounds. Śākalya belonging to the recension of the Ṛgveda is the composer of Padapāṭha. In this connection it may be mentioned that Swami Dayānanda Saraswati, a well-known founder of Ārya Samaja has created a system of separate Padapāṭha by neglecting the rules of Śākalya's Padatype. He also recognised Veda solely as a nature of Saṁhitā part without mentioning other portions of Vedas because of a system of unauthoritative nature of it. All types of Vedas are included in the Saṁhitā part. Certain grammatical and Phonetic norms along with pronunciation of syllables are worthy to be mentioned in the Ṛgveda-Prātiśākhya ascribed to a school regarding variation of those Pāṭhas like उकारश्चेतिकरणेन युक्तो रक्तोऽपृक्तो द्राघितः शाकलेन ऋ. प्रा. 2/75. There are five disciples of Preceptor Śākalya viz. Mudgala, Gokhk̄ula, Vātsya, Śaiśira and Śiśira as recognized in a remarkable line of the Vargadvayavṛtti of Viṣṇumitra i.e.—मुद्गलो गोखूलो वात्स्यः शैशिरः शिशिरस्तथा, पञ्चैते शाकलाः शिष्याः शाखाभेदप्रवर्तकाः. These disciples of the same preceptor are organizers of diverse readings of various recensions of the Ṛgveda. The name of Śākaṭāyana is worth-mentioning both in the Ṛgveda-Prātiśākhya and in the Aṣṭādhyāyī of Pāṇini प्रथमं शाकटायनः ऋ. प्रा. 2 like and त्रिप्रभृतिषु शाकटायनस्य-पा. 2/8/50 respectively.

The Aindra school of Ṛktantra of Śākaṭāyana relating to the Prātiśākhya of the Sāmaveda is alluded to as the recension of such a school itself. The composer of this Prātiśākhya text is earlier among the authors of the Ṛgveda-Prātiśākhya and also of the Aṣṭādhyāyī as referred to in the above-mentioned aphorisms. The name of Vyāḍi, an interpreter of ancient seriptures and then the composer of the book intitled *Saṁgraha* having verses of one lakh is mentioned in the Ṛgveda-Prātiśākhya उभे व्याडिः समस्वरे– ऋ. पा. 3/2 and in the Varttika of Kātyāyana द्रव्याभिधानं व्याडिः so referred to in the norm of Pāṇini I/2/64—ससूपाणामेकशेष एक विभक्तौ Vyāḍi is also maternal uncle of Pāṇini—व्याडिर्नाम पाणिनेर्मातुलः Accordingly it may be ascentained which scripture is earlier and then to fix a comparative priority between two scriptures which is still a desideratum. On the basis of Prātiśākhya such authors are older than Yāska, Pāṇini and so on. There is a long gap between the composition of Prātiśākhyas and that of the Śikṣā texts. The Ṛktantra is also treated as Aindra School of grammar and is earlier than other grammatical texts including Śikṣā texts.

The Prātiśākhyas serve useful purposes in recording the Sūtras and examples in the Kārikās for purposes of special dialected pronunciation and modes of accentuation peculiar to a Vedic recension.

There is a mention of Kāra to treat a letter in the Taittirīya Prātiśākhya in the aphorism वर्णः कारोत्तरो वर्णाख्या–तै प्रा. 2/13 There are so many recensions of Vedas yet to be known by the scholars at the moment through quotations, but no publication has come out regarding this till dates. It is feared that the recensions might have been lost beyond recovery, but it is possible to have a clear idea specially of those lost Śākhās from an intensive study of the references found in the Śikṣās and Prātiśākhyas which are still available.

Works in the Phonetic texts and Prātiśākhyas are very important for the interpretation of Vedic verses. Even modern scholars have found ample sources of data referred to in the Atharvaveda-Prātiśākhya. कृणोत्विति–अ. प्रा. 3/2/8 The intensive and extensive works on Vedalakṣaṇa including interpretation of Śikṣās and Prātiśākhyas should be made if the scholars really intend to interpret Vedic verses with the broad principle of comparative study. Such tasks invariably involve all important chapters on Phonetics, Grammar, Etymology, Philology etc. to attain high appreciation of all scholars both traditional and modern. The texts on Vedalakṣaṇa contain a comparative comprehensive study regarding all features of Vedas on Phonetics and Prātiśākhyas to be helpful for persons in pursuit of Vedic knowledge for critical analysis of a particular area through modern outlook of system.

Even modern scholars without having dogmatic mention follow eastern interpreters and take the advantage of modern resources of scientific analysis for explaining obscure hymns.

The Vedalakṣaṇa texts of Śikṣā and Prātiśākhya are different in nature and Śikṣā is said to be the less authoritative. The Śikṣā Vedalakṣaṇa is called weaker as the deer is weaker than the lion. The Sarvasammata Śikṣā edited by an occidental scholar, Franke refers to such a version as: "शिक्षा च प्रातिशाख्यं च विरुध्येते शिक्षैव दुर्बलेत्याहुः सिंहस्यैव मृगी यथा" The numerous statements on Phonetic matter are to be found in grammatical works. The subjects of the Śikṣā are worth-mentioning in the Śikṣādhyāya. The Śikṣās may supply teaching of the Prātiśākhyas in many cases, but on the other hand they are less related to a particular Veda with some exceptions. Prātiśākhyas are based on an early Śikṣā as referred to in the Taittirīya Āraṇyaka VII/11/I. The extant texts of the latter seem to be of later date than the former in the *Muṇḍakopaniṣad* I/4-5.

The most important of texts is sometmes claimed to be the original Śikṣā and in consequence goes back to a very early date of the Phonetic text. The Ṛktāntra of Śakaṭāyana is alluded to a Prātiśākhya of the Sāmaveda. Hence the Ṛk means any portion of Vedas as per the grammatical term of the Aindra school appearing from the alphabets at the beginning of collective syllables closely nearest to phonemes for analysis of the word-isolates.

Tantra substitutes syntax of component features within

the sound-unit having no independent existence. The words on their own have no separate existence. Jaimini, the author of Pūrvamīmāṁsāsūtra text termed Dvādaśalakṣaṇī having twelve chapters on this philosophy admits the breath-group corresponding to one line of verse by a norm अर्थैकत्वादेकं वाक्यं साकाङ्क्षं चेद् विभागे स्यात्-जै. सू. पाद। अध्याय 2/ सू 46 for the purpose of word-division. The Prātiśākhya of Sāmaveda does not appear to be a current production because of its being possibly composed when Sanskrit was a spoken language to be treated as bhāṣā or mother tongue when the formation of स्वैरिणी, अक्षौहिणी etc. such words either have the diphthongs by Sandhi or contraction of vowels like hiatus.

Bhāṣā merely indicates grammatical phraseology. It makes more interesting observation of the former letter of *pra* and *apa* to be lengthened before *Vṛ* in a sense of either closing or guarding at a pause like *Prāvṛṇute*, otherwise it is to be shortened like प्रवृणुते ऋत्विजम् as is noted in भाषायां णी परमोः, दीर्घं भाषायां प्रापवृणोतौ संवरणे. The contracted word may remain among either two vowels or consonants, or a consonant and a vowel in a case of pronunciation as an euphonic combination.

The study of Phonetics as a science was taken earnestly and came into existence about the same time for different senses of phonetics dealing with letters, accent, quantity, pronunciation and euphonic norms. The period must have been prior to the production of Prātiśākhya literature. Dr. A.C. Burmell called terms of the Aindra school technically primitive. The terms possibly were made for explanation of the mode of nature through their phonetic pronunciation. The Aindra recension was the oldest school of Sanskrit Phonetics. Such treatise still exists in Prātiśākhya amongst technical studies as source materials of Phonetics. Technical terms used by the Aindra treatise supposed by Ṛktantra are connected with one another and are also more simples being primitive than later terms to represent a school of Phoneticians. The texts of Vedic verses necessitated the emergence of vast phonetic literature called Prātiśākhya.

The Prātiśākhyas are treatises of phonetic text like Ṛktantra mainly dealing with the peculiarities relating to the mode of pronunciation. The norms of Prātiśākhya may be explained by taking resort to as is mentioned here: "अस्य शास्त्रस्य मूलीमूतं व्याकरणं पूर्वशास्त्रमित्युच्यते, तस्मिन् · · · न विधीयते साक्षाच्छिक्षायां तु विधीयते, व्याकरणप्रधानं ह्येतच्छास्त्रम् तस्माद् वैयाकरणेभ्योऽन्ये शिक्षाकारा इहैक इति व्यापदिश्यन्ते" and in other passages. The Phonetic text of Ṛktantra as a separate Prātiśākhya composed by Śākaṭāyana belonging to the Aindra school of the premier branch of grammar which was invented before Pāṇini relates to both Śikṣā i.e. phonetics and Vyākaraṇa equally.

The scheme is supposed to benefit Vedic language properly interpreted with the help of phonetic and grammatical rules. A beginning may be made with extraction of relevant terms from the information brought out from the original source books. For the time being, emphasis can be laid on the textual support of Veda-Saṁhitā and other recensions of Vedas. Work on grammar is a premier Vedāṅga and is considered to be the mouthpiece of Veda for ascertaining the derivation of Vedic terms. It contains the Vedic rules in general bearing a sweet fruit of meaning of Vedas. The phonetics, grammar, accentuation, etc. are found to be essential parts. Knowledge of accents is very essential during the ritual application of Vedic mantras and it became the section of the Vedic portion. Svarādi chapters are partly traced in the phonetics and pronunciation had its influence over all the branches of Vedic literature in general. The rules of grammar are solely devoted to the study and practice of Vedic forms. There is a broad field through all branches of Vedic literature generally regarding the people and method of Vedic studies. A grammatical stamp has accommodated many irregular uses in Vedic dialect and language through the broadbased norms like "बहुलं छन्दसि". Then Vedic language is standardized by a very important and valuable contribution of aphorisms to save it from the unwanted invasion by non-Aryan influence.

Modern scholars both eastern and western have discussed extensively on such works. Their contributions contain very useful insight connected with various rules of Vedic studies to interpret Vedic language. In fact, Pāṇini's work consists of framework of the Vedāṅgas having the sections of Veda related rules of grammar, phonetics and svarādiprakriyā in the sphere of application in all the branches of Vedic literature in general.

The linguistic analysis of Vedic words is the popular practice both in east and in west as its aims to ascertain meaning. A full-fledged discipline of learning the philological study is the scientific approach through the eye of modern scholars. A cursory view is highlighted to the schools of grammar dealing with Vedic texts.

The Vedāṅgas like phonetics, rituals, grammar, etymology, etc. individually ascertain the Vedic forms and formulas used in Vedic mantras. Thus grammar as a premier Vedāṅga determines the meaning of Vedic words by rules of the formation of sounds as revealed in Vedic texts.

In regard to intensive and extensive works on the Vedāṅgas specially on Nirukta, modern philology scholars may intend to find out the proper interpretations of various Vedic sounds with a broad mind. The methodology and the plan are adhered to its relation with the contents. The oldest text book of the Vedāṅgas like Śikṣā, etc. deals with the oldest production of pronunciation of Vedamantras on the whole as well as on various topics viz. sandhi, quantities, accentuation, etc. The origin of the supplementary sciences of Vedas is to be traced in the phonetics, grammar, etymology, etc.

There are some publications covering catalogues, indices of the contents of Veda-Saṁhitā in regard to different items. A glossary occurs to the hymns for collection of rare and obscure words. So the manuscripts of some unpublished

Vedic texts, and collection of books as well as journals are to be noted as tools for extraction of data. The aims are related to the dialectal variations with reference to the zonal words, some sorts of pronunciation, śabdānuśāsana to determine the proper meaning of Vedic sound depending upon the accents. A work on grammatical study was indispensable for correct, exact and accurate study of Vedamantras which regulated the society of ancient India.

The dialectal variation is important for pronunciation of some zonal sounds like Prācya, Pratīcya, Udīcya, etc. It is very important and valuable contribution to regulate some terms like chāndasa, mantra, āgama, ārṣa, vyatyaya, bahula, etc. while using them as the grammatical stamps. The work of technical studies is thus very important so far Vedalakṣaṇa Phonetic texts are concerned.

Bibliography

Allen, W.S., *Phonetics in Ancient India,* Geoffrey Cumberlege, Oxford University Press, London, New York, Toronto, 1953.

Bhattacharya Bishnupada, *Yāska's Nirukta* (The Science of Elymology), Firma K.L., Mukhopadhyay, Calcutta, 1958.

B hattacharya, Dipak, *Indian Etymologists and their Etymologies,* School Vedic Studies, RBU, March, 2002.

Chakraborti, Samiram Chandra, *Proper Names of Persons in Vedic Literature,* School of Vedic Studies, RBU, 2008.

Datta, Pradyot Kumar, *Pāṇini and Prātiśākhya,* Sanskrit Pustak Bhardan, Bidhan Sarani, Calcutta-700006, first published Kolkata, 1994.

—, *Source Materials of Phonetics,* Jadavpur University (DSA) Publication, Sanskrit Pustak Bhandar, Bidhan Sarani, Kolkata, 2004.

Kānta Sūrya, *Atharvaveda-Prātiśākhyam* (with exhaustive notes), Oxford University Press, Lahore, Pubjab, 1939.

—, *Ṛktantram,* ed., Meherchand Lachamandas, Delhi, 1970.

Varma, Siddheshwar, *Criticla Studies in the Phonetic Observations of Indian Grammarians,* Munshiram Monaharlal Publishers, New Delhi, first Indian edn., 1961.

Vidyārthī, Vishva Bandhu, *Atharva-Prātiśākhyam,* Vaidika Āśrama, Lahore, October, 1922.

Whitney, William, *The Atharva-Veda Prātiśākhya or Śaunakīya Caturadhyāyikā* (Text, translation and notes) D, the Chowkhambha Sanskrit Studies, (Series office), vol. XX, Vārā?sī-1 (India), 1923.

5

VEDALAKṢAṆA TEXTS AND TRADITION OF KERALA

C.M. NEELAKANDHAN

The traditional method of learning of the *Ṛgveda* in Kerala involves hard and strict practices to be followed by the students. The students are admitted to the traditional Vedapāṭhaśalā for learning the *Ṛgveda* at Brahmaswam Matham, Trissur, at the age of seven or eight and for four years and they are taught Saṁhitāpāṭha from morning to evening. After that, the students are admitted to school system and they are given facilities to catch on modern education along with the traditional Vedic learning. They learn higher modes of chanting of the *Ṛgveda* like Pada, Krama, Jaṭā and Ratha in the morning, evening and holidays along with school/college education. Among the eight modes of higher levels of chanting of the *Ṛgveda* (Aṣṭavikṛtis), only Jaṭā and Ratha are practiced in Kerala. This system of Vedic education is followed in Brahmaswam Matham, Trissur, in Kerala even now. Earlier, most of the Nampūtiri households had the facilities for Saṁhitāpāṭha and the students used to be admitted to Brahmaswam Matham for higher learning only. Due to the socio-cultural changes that took place in the society, the system of teaching Saṁhitāpāṭha in Nampūtiri households became extinct and Ṛgvedic education is imparted in Brahmaswam Matham, Trissur starting from Saṁhitāpaṭha to the higher modes of chanting. Earlier, Trissur Brahmaswam Matham was devoted only for Ṛgvedic education. Recently, *Yajus* and *Sāma* are also taught there in the traditional way along with ṭhe *Rgveda*.

Thus learning of the priliminary (Saṁhitāpāṭha) and higher levels of chanting of *Ṛgveda* (Pada, Krama, Jaṭā and Ratha) for about twelve to fifteen years, the memorising of the whole text in all modes of chanting need to be preserved. It is a very diflicult task, as one can imagine, to memorise the order of the chanting of more than ten thousand Mantras in different modes following the Svaras. For this, the Ṛgvedic tradition of Kerala has maintained some techniques from ancient days. They are available in Malayalam, the local language of the region as well as in Sanskrit. Most of them are preserved in oral tradition and recently some of them have been printed in local Malayalam script.

An important text of this kind is the commentary on *Śaunakaśikṣā* by K.N.M. Divakaran Namboothiri who was a great scholar in Veda and Vyākaraṇa. The commentary along with the text was published from Mangalodayam Press, Trissur in 1962 which includes the text and Sanskrit commentary, a Preface in English by T.K. Ramachandra Iyer, a Prastāvanā in Sanskrit by the author, an Avatārikā by Peruntarnam Narayanan Namboothiri, a colleague of the author and an Āmukha with detailed explanation of the author in Malayalam. The text is very important for following the Padapāṭhas and Svaras while chanting the *Ṛgveda* in the Kerala style.

Tāṇṭam is a popular work followed in Kerala for the purpose. The word in Malayalam has been derived from the root 'Taṇṭuka' which means 'to cross' or 'to overcome' implying the sense that the text helps to cross the ocean of doubts while chanting the *Ṛgveda* mainly the Padapāṭha. The text *Tāṇṭam* has three main divisions. First is *Paṭṭarutāṇṭam.* The word *'Paṭṭar'* is used in Kerala for the Tamil Brahmins who have migrated and settled here. The word conveys sometimes the sense related to the Brāhmaṇas other than the Nampūtiris, the local inhabitants of the region. The *Paṭṭarutāṇṭam* is written by the scholars Nāgadeva and Śeṣanārāyaṇa as is clear from their statements in the beginning of the text:

> यज्ञनारायणाख्यस्य यज्वनः प्रियसूनुना।
> शमानं साधु सव्याख्यं नागदेवेन निर्मितम्॥
> प्रणम्य गरुडारूढं हरिं नीलाभ्रसन्निभम्।
> शेषनारायणाख्येन लक्षणं क्रियते मया॥

Paṭṭarutāṇṭam includes the topics Śamānam, Vilaṅkhyam, Naparam, Taparam, Avarṇi and Āvarṇi. All these are lists of words (Padas) of the *Ṛgveda* to determine the Padapāṭha wherever doubts may arise regarding the splitting of Padas while its chanting. The work is used in other parts of India also and this is known among the Nampūtiris of Kerala as Paṭṭarutāṇṭam as it is written by non-Kerala scholars.

The other two main divisions of Tāṇṭam are *Malayāḷatāṇṭam* and *Saṁhitātāṇṭam*. The former text is particularly used in Kerala and the latter, a separate text popular in Kerala among the Nampūtiris, is used for clearing the doubts of the Padapāṭha of the Saṁhitā of the *Ṛgveda*. Name of the authors of *Malayālatāṇṭam* and *Samhitātāṇṭam* are not given anywhere in the text. Profound Nampūtiri scholars of the *Ṛgveda* in Kerala might have composed them which were handed down from generation to generation. As a result, many additions and modifications might have happened in the text in course of time as the *Ṛgveda* scholars of Kerala use to create or write new Tāṇṭams of their own using their intellect and genius and which is continuing even now. Many such additions and modifications are not recorded as they are preserved in their memory only. Some remain in the private writings of the scholars which they have received from their Gurus. Tāṇṭams of such kind are collected and printed in Malayalam script and published fiom Panchangam Pustakasala, Kunnamkulam, Trissur

District, in Kollam era 1105 (AD 1930). A serious effort has yet to be done to collect and publish all such Tāṇṭams which are not included in that edition, but are used by the Ṛgvedic scholars.

The book *Tāṇṭam* published in I930 from Panchangam Press, Kunnamkulam, is very old and only rare copies of the same are available now. The letters are not clear in many places and no reprint of the book has come in Malayalam script also after that.

In the 'Malayālatāṇṭam' portion the initial part explaines the Acsandhis, Halasandhis and Svarasandhis of the *Ṛgveda* giving examples wherever doubts may occur while chanting them. The explanation of Sandhis in the portion is given in Malayalam language. In the same way, one or two instances in that text, passages from the *Malayālatāṇṭam* and *Saṁhitatāṇṭam* are also seen explained in Malayalam language.

Tāṇṭam is a unique technique used for the preservation of the *Ṛgveda* chanting in Kerala. Much work needs to be done on the text like adding notes on the signficances of the words listed, tracing the Mantras of the *Ṛgveda* where the words are found and giving an alphabetical index of them, explaining the Sandhis and splitting the words based on Vedic grammar and the combination of Svaras, giving an account of the historical evolution of these methods, tracing the slight differences in the Sandhis, Svaras and modes of chanting among the two groups of Ṛgvedins of Kerala (Trissnr and Tirunavaya Mathas) and those of the other places of lndia, preparing critical edition of each text etc.

Mudrā recitation of the *Ṛgveda* is a unique the practice of which is followed in Kerala. There are some hand gestures (Hastamudrās) showing which the whole of the *Ṛgveda* chanting can be communicated to another scholar who also has the knowledge of such Mudrās. The Mudrās or gestures in the *Ṛgveda* chanting indicate not the meaning of the words like in Tantra worship or in the theatrical art forms like Kūṭyiyāṭṭam and Kathakali in Kerala (as in the case of Mudrās for lotus, cupid etc.), but they indicate the letters at the end of the words (Padas) of the *Ṛgveda*. These Mudrās help to determine the Padapāṭha of the *Ṛgveda* and to memorise it. This practice of Mudrā recitation of the *Ṛgveda* was followed in Kerala from very ancient days. In some Śikṣā texts, there are references to certain Mudrās and hand movements used while the *Ṛgveda* is chanted. But the specific Mudrās used in Kerala tradition are not referred to or defined in any Śikṣā text, as far as our knowledge goes. Such Mudrās are not used for the *Ṛgveda* in other parts of India. No Mudrās of this kind are practiced for *Yajurveda* or *Sāmaveda* in Kerala or in any other part of India, except some movements of the hands according to the Svaras. Dr. K.V. Vasudevan, Reader in the Dept. of Sanskrit at Sreekrishna College, Guruvayoor, Kerala, a scholar of Vedic texts and various Śāstras has recently composed a small work *Bahvṛcahastalakṣaṇadīpikā*, in Sanskrit giving the definitions of the Hastamudrās of the *Ṛgveda* as they are practiced and followed in Kerala. There are about thirty such Mudrās which are defined in the work.

Vedavikṛtivivaraṇam is a small work describing the definition of the eight Vikṛtipāṭhas of the *Ṛgveda* chanting, Jaṭā, Mālā, Śikhā, Rekhā, Dhvaja, Daṇḍa, Ratha and Ghana. Among these, only Jaṭā and Ratha are practiced in Kerala. The text *Vedavikṛtivivaraṇam* is written by a Kerala scholar named Damodaran Namboothirippad. It is in verses describing the definition of each Vikṛti with a detailed Ṭippaṇī by the author himself for each verse. The work was published by Kunnamparamb Sankaran Namboothiri, a desciple of Damodaran Namboothiri, from Kashi in 1955.

Sūktaślokas have nine verses in Sanskrit composed by the famous scholar, philosopher and poet of Kerala, Melputtūr Nārāyaṇabhaṭṭa, author of the famous works like *Nārāyaṇīyam* and *Prakriyāsarvaṣvam*. *Sūktaślokas* contain the explanation of the number of Sūktas and Vargas of the *Ṛgveda* in all the eight Aṣṭakas and each verse from second to nine dedicated to each Aṣṭaka. The first verse is a general introduction to the theme. Thus the number of Sūktas and Vargas of the whole text of the *Ṛgveda* is given in this work. The number of Adhyāyas of each Aṣṭaka is eight which is not noted separately as it is not needed. The Kaṭapayādi method is used for denoting the numbers. So it is very difficult to explain the words of the verses with their meaning, at the same time denoting the numbers according to the Kaṭapayādi system. Moreover, it is generally believed that the verses in the *Sūktaślokas* contain a meaning praising the goddess Devī of Candanakkāvu, the family deity of Melputtūr. The Vedic scholars of Kerala used to interpret the verses in *Sūktaślokas* according to the number they denote. But the explanation of the verses as praising the Goddess Devī has not been attempted by anyone before. Dr. Kompamkulam Vishnu Namboothiri, a good Vyākaraṇa scholar and Reader in the Dept. of Vyakarana, Sree Sankaracharya University of Sanskrit, Regional Centre, Payyannur, has written a commentary on the *Sūktaslśokas* in Sanskrit explaining their meaning related to the number of the Sūktas and Vargas of each Aṣṭaka of the *Ṛgveda* and at the same time, related to the eulogy of Goddess Devī. As one can imagine, this is really a challenging task which only a scholar prfound in the Veda, Vyākaraṇa and Kaṭapayādi system can undertake. Dr. Vishnu Nambootliiri has composed the commentary excellently well. A detailed table of the number of Sūktas and Vargas of each Aṣṭaka as explained in the verses according to the Kaṭapayādi scheme, is also given by Vishnu Namboothiri in his commentary.

There are some other works of this kind like *Trisandhā, Vedapāṭhānadhāyasaṅgraha* and *Sarvānukramaṇīpadya-vivaraṇam* written by K.P. Krishnan Bhattathirippad, a great scholar in Veda and Tantra who belonged to the famous family of Tantrins Kunnathur Paṭiññārēṭattu Mana, Cherpu, Trissur, Kerala. These three works are included in the book

Śrīkṛṣṇacintāmaṇī which contains some other compositions of the author in Sanskrit but related to other topics like Tantra and Prāyaścitta. *Śrīkṛṣṇacintāmaṇī* is published from Mangalodayam Press, Trissur, in 1962. The three above mentioned treatises contained in the work, are related to the preservation techniques of the *Ṛgveda* chanting of Kerala.

Trisandhā is a long-term ritual extending upto eight months when conducted continuously, practiced in Kerala for memorising the chanting of the *Ṛgveda.* The full-time involvement of twenty or more scholars are needed for this. At least five scholars at a time have to chant the Veda without a break from morning to evening. This is conducted in the traditional Svādhyāyas (working days) only.

In Trisandhā, Saṁhitā, Pada and Krama are chanted with Svara. The name Trisandhā is meaningful because all the three styles of chanting (Saṁhitā, Pada and Krama) are combined here. Teaching and learning method is used in this ritual. One recites the Mantras in the place of the teacher and the others repeat them. After each Varga the one who acts as teacher, is changed. Thus all scholars will come in the position of teacher and students in turn. This is the method of the *Ṛgveda* Trisandhā which is explained in the text.

Vedapāṭhānadhyāyasaṅgraha is a small work explaining the holidays (Anadhyāyas) for Vedic learning. According to the tradition, the Anadhyāyas for Vedic learning are calculated based on Lunar calender, not usual Saturdays and Sundays. The holidays for Vedic learning are explained in the text briefly.

Sarvānukramaṇīpadyavivaraṇam is a work describing the contents of *sarvānukramaṇī* of Kātyāyana in 487 verses. The text *Saravānukramarṇī* has been published from Oxford University, London, in 1895 by A.A. Macdonnel with the commentary *Vedārthadīpikā* of Ṣaḍguruśiṣya. The second edition of the text with the same commentary edited by Dr. Vijayapal, was published from Calcutta in 1967.

Sri K.P. Krishnan Bhattathirippad has presented an excellent explanation of *Sarvānukramaṇī* in verses in his *Sarvānukramaṇīpadyavivaraṇam.*

There is an unpublished commentary on *Sarvānukramaṇī* from Kerala by Akkittam Narayanan Namboothiri who belonged to eighteenth century AD. The name of the commentary is *Nārāyaṇīyam.* It is also famous as *Dīpaprabhā.* Akkittam Narayanan Namboothiri was a celebrated scholar of Veda and different Śāstras who is the author of many commentaries on different Vedic texts. The manuscripts/ transcripts of *Nārāyaṇīyam* (*Dīpaprabhā*) commentary are available at Vadakke Matham Brahmaswam, Trissur, Oriental Mss Library, Madras and in the private collections of PazhedathSankaran Namboothiri, Killikurussimangalam, Lakkidi, near Ottappalam in Kerala. The commentary is an exhaustive one giving valuable details of the original text and hence is a worthy contribution to the commentary literature of Vedas.

A recent work that can be included in the group of Tāṇṭam named *Nānābhedaprakāśinī* been written recently by K.M, Vasudevan Namboothiri, one of the foremost *Ṛgveda* scholars of Kerala at present. The letter 'Na' is pronounced in two ways both in ordinary usage and in Vedic chanting. It explains with examples different pronunciation of 'Na' in the chanting of the *Ṛgveda* with the rules that are followed for the difference. It is a small treatise, but it sheds light to the phonetic principles that are governing the pronunciation of the difference in the letter 'Na' as in the example of the word 'Nānā.' A few works related to the preservation techniques of the *Ṛgveda* chanting are being written even now by present scholars of Kerala.

Recently another book has been published from Vedic Studies, Sree Sankaracharya University of Sanskrit, Kalady, Kerala, titled *Preservation Techniques* of the *Ṛgveda Chanting of Kerala* (2010). In that text, all the above mentioned works which are related to the preservation techniques of the

Ṛgveda chanting of Kerala, are included in Devanāgarī script. There may be other works of similar type and a thorough survey can bring them to the fore. Moreover, there are similar texts related to the preservation techniques of the chanting of *Yajurveda* and *Sāmaveda* in Kerala and the collection and edition of which have not been attempted yet by anyone. Critical editions with elaborate notes, introductions and studies of each of these texts will be a valuable contribution to the field of Vedic studies and research. Hopefully young scholars and researchers in the field will take up the matter some day with sincerity, devotion and dedication.

Rituals

There are many rituals which are followed in Kerala to preserve the skill of the Ṛgveda chanting. Among the Vedic rituals, Yāgas are the most important. In Yāgas many hymns of the three Vedas are used and some Mantras are also chanted which are not found in Saṁhitā texts. These may be the Mantras of some recensions which are not traced in Vedas. Besides these Yāgas, there are many other rituals, which are very helpful for the preservation of Vedas. Most of them are regional in practice and those followed in Kerala are explained here.

Murajapam, Vāram, Ottūṭṭ, Trisandhā, Murahomam and Lakṣārcana are the main rituals introduced by ancient scholars for the preservation of Vedas in Kerala. There are some Vedic rituals which are included in the daily duties of Brahmins. Svādhyāya, Sūryanamaskāra and Trīṇi are some of them.

Svādhyāya

Svādhyāya is a daily ritual performed by the Brahmins after completing their primary Vedic education or Saṁhitā course. It is believed that Svādhyāya is a ritual to be practiced strictly by all who have studied the *Ṛgveda*. It is considered as a Brahmayajña. The student has to recite a portion of

Saṁhitā every day till the end of his life. This is done by all Vedic scholars. Ṛgvedic scholars recite one Sūkta or Anuvāka in the Svādhyāya day. For Yajurvedins and Sāmavedins one chapter has to be chanted. Related to the chanting there are many ritual performances which are needed to be followed along with it.

Sūryanamaskāra

This practice is helpful for mental concentration and physical exercise. They chant a certain portion of the related Veda and practice the Sūryanamaskāra. The scholars who belong to the *Ṛgveda* and the Sāmaveda practice Namaskāra for each Ṛk or hymn and Yajurvedic scholars perform five Namaskāras for each Pañcāśat (Collection of fifty Padas or words) which they call Paññādi in local language.

Trīṇi

This is a rare ritual performed by the Vedic scholars. Only a few scholars are able to perform this. Saṁhitā, Padapāṭha and Kramapāṭha are recited in this ritual. This is more fruitful than the other daily rituals like Namaskāra and Svādhyāya so far memorising of Vedic chanting is concerned. The name Trīṇi is meaningful as the three modes of chanting of Veda (Saṁhitā, Pada and Krama) are combined in this. Usually one *Ṛgvedasūkta* is chanted in Trīṇi style one day. So it will take about one thousand days for the complete recitation of the *Ṛgveda* in this style.

There are some rituals which are observed in special occasions. Murajapam, Murahomam, Trisandhā, Ottūṭṭ and Vāram are the examples of such type of rituals.

Murajapam

It is a ritual which is related to special occasions. This is performed in respected Brahmin households as well as in temples. Recitation of the whole Saṁhitā within a certain period is called as Murajapam ('Mura' denotes Saṁhitā and 'Japam' means recitation. Thus 'Murajapam' is the recitation of Saṁhitā of Veda). The Vedic scholar who can chant the whole Saṁhitā with the correct Svara can only participate in the Murajapam. This is performed by a single scholar or a group of scholars. If one scholar devotes five hours a day for this type of chanting, it may be completed within four days. This is done by a group of scholars with more elaborate Svara, repeating the Saṁhitā text in this way many times. In the famous Murajapa festival conducted at Śrī Padmanābhasvāmi temple, Tiruvananthapuram, this ritual used to prolong for fifty-six days. In this festival the Saṁhitā was chanted seven times by each Vedic scholar devoting eight days for the completion of the recital.

Murahomam or Saṁhitāhomam

Saṁhitāhomam is a Vedic ritual practiced by Ṛgvedic scholars only. It is conducted not only in Kerala but in other states of India also. Saṁhitā is chanted with Ṛṣi, Chandas and Devatā and ghee is offered in the fire at the end of every hymn with Svāhākāra. Three Vedic scholars are eligible to participate in this ritual. One priest performs the Homa with the recitation of Mantra, the second one does the Anujapa (reciting along with the former) and the third one is called Brahman who takes care of the whole procedure, not to have any mistake.

Vedalakṣārcanā

This is a new Vedic ritual that was started by Śrī O.M.C. Narayanan Namboothirippa, a great Vedic scholar, the former president of Vatakke Maṭham Brahmasvam (Brahmasvam Maṭham) and the author of *Ṛgveda-bhāṣābhāṣyam.* The frst Vedalakṣārcana was conducted at Brahmasvam Maṭham, Trissur, in the year 1975. At least ten scholars who can chant the whole Saṁhitā are needed for the Vedalakṣārcana. This ritual is commonly practised in temples with all three Vedas.

Trisandhā

This is a long-term ritual. In order to conduct a Trisandhā, about eight months are necessary. There are two types of Trisandhā among Ṛgvedins-Pādasahitā and Padarahitā. In Pādasahitā type of Trisandhā, Padapāṭha is also chanted. Sāmavedins also have Trisandhā. They chant Ṛk, Sāma, and Ūha in Trisandhā. The last Sāmavedic Trisandhā was held before seventy years at Toṭṭattil Mana, Paññal. There is no Sāmavedic scholar alive who had participated in that Trisandhā. The last Trisaudhā of the *Ṛgveda* was conducted at Brahmasvam Maṭham, Trissur during the years 1994–1998, two months each year.

Ottūṭṭu

This is a Vedic ritual conducted by the scholars of Yajurveda. This ritual is like that of Trisandhā. This is conducted every six years at different temples. Saṁhitā, Pada and Koṭṭu are recited in Ottūṭṭu ('Ottu' means Veda, Koṭṭu is an excersise of chanting of *Yajurveda* in Kerala, where four Padas of the Padapāṭha will be chanted by one scholar which will be repeated by others thrice. The word Ottukoṭṭu becomes Ottūṭṭu in colloquial language). Apart from these three, Krama and Śākhā are also included in some places for this ritual. In order to conduct such a ritual minimum thirty-two Svāhyāyas (working days) are essential. Presently this ritual is hardly performed in Kerala.

Vāram

Vāram is considered as a sacred Vedic ritual. This is performed almost during all the rituals mentioned above. During the time of Trisandhā, Vāram is performed on every Ekādaśi day and the days of Anadhyāya (holidays) of each Pakṣa. lt is conducted at temples and in some Brahmin families special occasions.

This ritual is common to all Vedas. Ṛgvedic scholars chant the Kramapāṭha of continuous ten Mantras for Vāram.

According to the scholars belonging to Yajurveda, Vāram is the recitation of Padapāṭha of continuous 250 Padas. Sāmavedic scholars use the Vikṛtipāṭha, Ūha for Vāram. Vedic scholars use a particular method to choose a portion of Veda to chant for Vāram. They use pieces of stones to decide the particular portion of Veda that is to be chanted for Vāram. This method is known as Kallu Vaccu Vāram (Kallu=stone, Vaccu = puting. Thus the term means 'putting stones and deciding a portion of the Veda to be chanted in the ritual of Vāram'). This method is also followed by Tamil Brahmins.

In Kerala, Vāram is used to evaluate the talent of scholars. Munpilirikkal, one of the great examinations in Kaṭavallūr Anyonyam, is a typical example for this kind of Vāram. Mūṭippacca is a Vikṛti of Kerala tradition. This is reverse chanting of Vāram. In Vāram mistake is not allowed at all. If one makes a mistake, he cannot continue the chanting and it is considered as a sin.

There are several other devices for the preservation of Vedas. Vedavikṛtis and some other techniques like Tāṇṭaṃ and Pādakkuttu are important among them.

Vedavikṛtis

Vedavikrtis are one of the important devices followed for the preservation of Vedas. These are eight in number. They are:—

जटा माला शिखा रेखा
ध्वजो दण्डो रथो घनः।
अष्टौ विकृतयः प्रोक्ताः
क्रमपूर्वा मनीषिभिः॥

These Vikṛtipāṭhas help the scholars to reafiirm their knowledge in the chanting of Vedas. These are practiced by Ṛgvedins and Yajurvedins.

In Kerala, Jaṭā and Ratha are popular Vikṛtis among

Ṛgvedins. The famous Vedavikṛti, Daṇḍa is popularly known among Nampūtiris as Ratha. They practice these two Vikṛtis as they consider Jaṭā and Ratha as the basic Vikṛtis.

Vikṛti chantings are performed during the days of Vāram. After the Vāram Vikṛtipāṭha, Jaṭā or Ratha is recited. Nampūtiries adopt particular modes of expansion in Svaras while chanting these Vikṛtipāṭhas which are very distinct from other parts of India. Vikṛtis, especially Ratha is considered as the main scale to evaluate the skill of a Vedic scholar in Kerala. Ghoṣa is another popular Vikṛti practiced by Yajurvedins in Kerala. Ūha and Ūṣāṇi are the famous, Vikṛtis of Samaveda chanting in Kerala as well as in other parts of India. Besides Ūha and Ūṣāṇa, Kerala Sāmavedins introduced a new method of chanting, that is known as Vacanam. lt has many similarities with the Jaṭā style of chanting by Ṛgvedic scholars in Kerala.

Thus there are many textual and ritual methods followed in Kerala for the preservation of the skill of Ṛgvedic recitation.

6

ṚK-PRĀTIŚĀKHYA AND PĀṆINI ON "SAṂHITĀ"

RADHAMADHAB DASH

The Veḍic literature is classified into Saṁhitā, Brāḥmaṇa, Āraṇyaka and Upaniṣad on the basis of the characteristic nature of the type of literature, i.e, hinting both at structural and thematic significance[1] of those classes. Later on, the Vedic literature included the six vedāṅgas[2] *chandas* 'Metrics,' *kalpa* 'Science relating to sacrifice,' *jyotiṣa,* 'Astronomy', *nirukta* 'Etymology,' *śikṣā* 'Phonetics' and *vyākaraṇa* 'Grammar'. The *Vedāṅgas* were composed to take care of the Vedic language and sacrifial science by providing all details of metrical peculiarities of the Vedic composition (*chandas*), pronunciation of Vedic sounds (*śikṣā*), derivation of Vedic words (*vyākaraṇa*), etymology or meaning analysis of the Vedic usages (*nirukta*), and all these are of linguistic nature; and the details of sacrilicial sciences include building typical altars etc. (*kalpa*), and determining the appropriate time for performing different sacrifices (*jyotiṣa*). Besides these Vedāṅgas, there is a class of literature called Prāti-śākhyas connected with various *Pārṣadas* or *Caraṇas* of the Vedas. Normally they deal with the topics of phonetics, grammar and metrics. Hence, they are looked upon as *lakṣaṇa granthas* which are essentially meant to safeguard the Vedic language and literature. *Ṛkprātiśākhya* (*RP*) of Śaunaka connected with the *śākala* recension and its *śaiśirīya* sub-recension of the *Ṛgveda* (*ṚV.*) is the earliest and the most precise of all the Prātiśākhyas. This has been referred to in this study while assessing the significance of morphophonemic combination of the Saṁhitā literature.

In the present study relating to morphophonemic combination in the Saṁhitā literature, it is proposed to highlight the essence of the concept of *Saṁhitā*. It is to be remarked here that the word *Saṁhitā* is a technical term (*Saṁjñā*) used in grammatical science. And it refers to a class of literature comprising the *sūktas,* poems of invocation in praise of different gods and goddesses. This is called *Saṁhita* as the stanzas in every poem are formed of inter-combined or coalesced words inside the mantras. *RP.* lays down that the *padas* are the bases (*prakṛti*) of *Saṁhitā.*[3] Śaunaka, explaining the term, defines that a word final (*padānta*) if combined with the word-initial (*padādi*) without allowing any time-gap of pronunciation, it is called *Saṁhitā.*[4] This is of two types[5]-*ārṣī saṁhitā* and *krama-saṁhitā*. An instance of *ārṣī-saṁhitā* is *ayaṁ devāya janmane (RV* 1.20.1) where the words are only once combined among each other in order of their occurrence from left to right The *krama-saṁhitā* refers to the *kramapāṭha* such as in the instances *parjanyāya pra. pra gāyata. gāyata divaḥ.* (*ṚV.* 7.102.1) where every word is combined twice, i.e., once with the preceding word, and once with the following word except the first and last words of the mantra. However, in the *Saṁhitā,* the gaps occurring between two vowels present a linguistic phenomenon called as *vivṛti.*[6] 'hiatus'. The mantra-lines such as *nu itthā te pūrvathā ca (ṚV.* 1.123.4) containing a gap between *u* of *nu* and *i* of *itthā* is designated as *vivṛti.* Had this gap been closed, it would have been *nuitthā* by kṣaipra[7] variety of sandhi. It is also prescribed that the gap created due to pronunciation of two vowels may be measured in term of *mātrā.* This *vivṛti* or gap between word-final vowel and word initial vowel is of the same *mātrā* of *svarabhakti* optionally[8] or may be more. Thus *vivṛti* (gap between two vowels) may be of three types : (i) 1/4th of a *mātrā* if both the vowels are short as in *pra ṛbhubhyaḥ* (*Ṛ*V. 4.33.1), (ii) 1/2 of a *mātrā* if one of the vowels is long as in nū *itthā te* (*Ṛ*V. 1.132.4) and (iii) 3/4th of a *mātrā* if both the vowels are long as in *tā ī vardhanti* (*Ṛ*V. 1.155.3). It is clear now that closing the gap betwen two sounds occurring in word final (of the preceding word) and word-initial (of the following word) is *Saṁhitā*. *Aitareya Āraṇyaka* 3.1.5 elaborates the nature of *Saṁhitā* in the following manner: *pūrvamevākṣaraṁ pūrvarūpam uttaram uttararūpam yo' vakāśaḥ pūrvarūpottararūpe antareṇa yena sandhir vivarttayati yena svarā' svaraṁ vijānāti mātrā' mātraṁ vibhajate sā saṁhiteti*. It emphasizes three aspects of *Saṁhitā* such as (i) Morphophonemic combination occurs in a gap (*avakāśa*) created by both preceding and following letters, (ii) performing the action of combination in that gap, and (iii) knowledge of accentual phenomena and the length of the resulting sound of the combination. The same idea is also conveyed when Pāṇini defines Saṁhitā as *paraḥ sannikarṣaḥ saṁhitā* (*P*. 1.4.109). *Siddhāntakaumudi* explains *para sannikarṣaḥ* as *atiśayitaḥ sannidhiḥ*[9] closer adjescence.' This closer adjacence is again explained as *ardhamātrādhika-kālavyavadhānābhāva* 'absence of a gap of more than half of a *mātrā* since half a *mātrā* is a recognizable length of the gap and a gap of the length of less than that is not cognizable.[10] Now it will be plausible to say that a type of Vedic literature is designated as Saṁhitā because the technical device *saṁhitā* or *sandhi* 'morhophonemic combination' is the essence of such literature. No Vedic sentence is available where the component morphological structures (Vedic words) are left uncombined. There is no question of optionality of making sandhi in Vedic mantra. Vedic lenguage is different from non-Vedic Sanskrit language from this point of view also. In non-Vedic Sanskrit sentence, the combining of two words is subject to the desire of the speaker.[11] One may use the sentence *agnim iḍe purohitam* in non-Vedic Sanskrit. On the other hand, the adjacent word final and word initial will be chanted combinedly for all the words found in the mantra, then only it will be a correct Vedic mantra or sentence. Hence the act of morphophonemic combination is very fundamental a consideration of Vedic Saṁhitā literature.

The *Saṁhitā* occupies so much importance in the Vedic langauge that the *Taittirīya Upaniṣad (Tai.U.)* eulogizes the mystic quality of *Saṁhitopāsanā* which is termed as *saṁhitopaniṣad.*[12] *RP.* also refers to this Upaniṣad in part in the introductory verse. The purpose of this mystification is disclosed by Sāyana in his commentary on *Aitareya Āraṇyaka* (*Ai Ā*. 3.1.1) where he speaks of these categories of recipients[13] of learning (*Vidyādhikārī*). They are the excellent (*uttama*), mediocre (*madhyama*) and the ordinary (*adhamas*). The excellent are the ones who are in the highest level of experience, who being completely detached from the wordly affairs, concentrate on the liberation of self from the bondage of nescience (*ajñāna*) and for whom is instructed the texts like *ātmā vā idam eka evāgra āsīt* (*AiĀ* 2.4.1) The second veriety, consisting of mediocre ones, practise *prāṇa-vidyā* and have the desire of only gradual liberation through the agency of hiraṇyagarbha for whom is referred the texts like *uktham uktam (AiĀ.* 2.1.2). The third variety of recipient neither aspires for Brahmavidyā nor Prāṇavidyā but desires to obtain wealth and worldly pleasures and go for Saṁhitopāsanā. The details of their *upāsanā* are available in the third chapter of *Ai Ā*. There is much of Arthavāda or hyperbolic praises here in support of the Saṁhitopāsanā.

The *Saṁhitopaniṣad* referred to above from *TaiU.* mystifies *Saṁhitā* or euphonic combination by prescribing for the sādhakas to have five viewpoints: *loka, joti, vidyā prajā* and *śarīra*. From the point of view of *loka* 'region,' one is to conceive the presence of earth in the preceding sound, heaven in the following sound, sky in the joining link and air in the linking process. This is considered as *adhilaukika-*

dṛṣṭi on *Saṁkitā.* From the point of view of *jyoti* 'source of light,' the sādhaka should concentrate in the preceding word-final as fire, the following word-initial as sun, water as joining link and lightining as helping process of the linkage. This is considered as *adhilaukika-dṛṣṭi* on *Saṁhitā.* From the point of view of *jyoti* 'source of light,' the sādhaka should concentrate in the preceding word-final as fire, the following word-intial as sun, water as joining link and lightining as helping process of the linkage. This is considered as *adhijyautiṣa-dṛṣṭi* on *Saṁhitā.* From the point of view of *vidyā* 'acquisition of learning,' the preceding sound be considered as if the preceptor, the following sound as the ward, the knowlege as link and the instruction as the linkage or process of linking. This is the *adhividyādṛṣṭi* on *Saṁhitā.* From the point of view of *prajā* or progeny the preceding sound be considered as mother, the following as father, the progeny as the link and giving birth (*prajanana)* is instrument of such link. This is the *adhipraja-dṛṣṭi* on *Saṁhitā.* From the point of view of *śarīra* or body the sādhaka is to identify the preceding sound with the lower jaw of the mouth, the following sound with the upper jaw, speech as link and tongue as intrument of such linkage. This is the *ādhyātmikadṛṣṭi* on *Saṁhitā.* One who knows all this mystery of Saṁhitopāsanā is said to be bestowed upon with children, domestic animals, lustre. food and good living conditions of the earth.

Śaunaka is also impressed by this mysterious version of eulogizing the role of *Saṁhitā* and he refers of *ādhibhautika* (same as *ādhilaukika)* or *adhidaivika-dṛṣṭi* in *RP.* in verse no. 7.2.[14] This version quoted slightly in different manner from *Ai Ā.* 3.1.1.[15] alludes to the difference of opinion between the two scholars Māṇḍukeya and Mākṣavya and the solution given by Āgastya on the nature of Saṁhitopāsanā. When Māṇḍukeya considers *vāyu* 'air' as link (*Saṁhitā*) between *pṛrthvī* and *dyaus,* Mākṣavya considers *ākāśa* 'sky' as the link. However, the son of Agasti (Āgastya) considers both sky and air equally important from upāsanā point of view though by saying sky, the air is automatically included in it, but the vice versa i.e., *vāyu* will not include *ākāśa*. hence Māṇḍukeya's opinion appears refuted but for the *siddhānta* of Āgastya.

In *RP*. verse 1.3[16] Śaunaka also refers to *adhyātma-dṛṣṭi* on Saṁhitopāsanā by way of presenting a dialogue between Śūravīra and his son with regard to the order of action between speech and mind. For Śūravīra, speech preceeds, mind follows and vital breath (*prāṇa*) acts as the connecting link between the two while his son says the reverse, but there is no controversy regarding *prāṇa* to be considered as *Saṁhitā* or the connecting link. Now the phenomenon of morphophonemic combination be viewed from point of view of the inner essence as stated above. In the combined structure *agnimīle*, the preceding word-final '*m*' be conceived as speech (*vāk*) and the following word-initial '*ī*' mind (*manas*) (according to Śūravīra) or vice verse (according to his son). From the viewpoint of upāsanā both the opinions are equally powerful but from factual viewpoint the son's hypothesis is practical.

Similarly in verse 1.4 of *RP*. it is said that food, heaven and the both are obtained by practising respectively the Saṁhitāpāṭha, Padapāḍha and Kramapāṭha.[17] The mystification and metaphysics of morphophonemic combination is strengthened when Śaunaka enjoins that *prāṇaḥ ṣakāro yacca balaṁ ṇakāraḥ (RP*. 1.5*)* "cerebral '*ṣ*' is the vital air, and cerebral '*ṇ*' is the strength of morphophonemic combination."[18] Sāyaṇa clarifies the purpose of saying so in the following manner. The twenty-five contact consonants (*k* to *m*) heve been divided into five classses, and the middle class (*ṭ* class) contains *ṇ* sound and one needs to take care to pronounce this *ṇ* in the morphophonemic structure to strengthen the quality of *Saṁhitā*. The '*ṣ*', a product of dental '*s*' in the *Saṁhitā* structure, is also in the middle position among the three sibilants *s, ṣ* and *ś* and figuratively it is the *prāṇa* or vital air. One, who bears vital air and strength, is said to be a living being. As is said in the *AiĀ*. 3.2.6 —*sa yo hetau ṇakāra-ṣakārāu anusaṁhitam ṛco veda sabalāṁ sprāṇāṁ vedāyuṣyamiti vidyāt.* In Padapāṭha, *padas* are in their original form and accent, but in Saṁhitāpāṭha they undergo varieties of changes and the dental sounds, particularly '*s*' and '*n,*' get changed into their respective cerebral counterparts. The preceptor by way of answering to the query of the disciple emphatically instructs that the latter while chanting a Saṁhitā should take care of the pronunciation of *ṇakāra* and *ṣakāra* as is evident from the dialogue between the preceptor and disciple-*sa yadi cikitset saṇakāraṁ bravāṇī3 aṇakārā3 iti saṇakāram eva brūyāt. saṣakāraṁ bṛavāṇī3 aṣakārā3 iti saṣakāram eva brūyāt* (*AiĀ*. 3.2.6) Sāyaṇa commenting on this context further explains that as in all sacrificial operations, the oblation designated as *sviṣṭakṛt homa* is obligatorily perfomed, so also in all Saṁhitopāsanā the *upāsaka* should take proper care to pronounce the above two cerebral sounds[19] without fail.

The mystic discourse on Saṁhitopāsanā quoted from *Ai. Ā*, third chapter, by Śaunaka in *RP.* further enjoins that one should have the upāsanā of *Saṁhitā* in the form of *Vāṇi* or speech. It is the combination of *vāk* in the form of *rathantara-sāma* and *prāṇa* in the form of *Bṛhatsāma* according to the scholar Tārkṣya as referred to in *AiĀ*. 3.1.6.[20] The scholar Kauṇṭharavya[21] designates *Avarāparā saṁhitā* to a chain of metaphysical combinations according to which vāk becomes connected with prāṇa, prāṇa with pavamāna-vāyu, pavamāna with viśvedevās, viśvedevās with svarga and svarga with Brahman. Pañcālakaṇḍa, another ācārya, professes that *vāk* or *vāṇī* is, in fact, *Saṁhita* because the recital of the Vedas is done only by *vāṇī*. The different Vedic metres are articulated by *vāṇī* and finally *vāṇī* befriends all and subjugates all.[22] When *Saṁhitā* is recited, *vāṇī* predomintes and *prāṇa* or vital force is infused in it.

When there is no action of speech organ, speech remains in *prāṇa*. Hence. *vāk* or speech is the most appropriate instrument of Saṁhitopāsanā. This is why *vāk* is mystified as mother and *prāṇa* as the son,[23] and this idea is conveyed through the text of *RP*. in its sūtra 1.6: *vāk-prāṇayoryaśca homaḥ parasparam.*

3.0 From the above discussion, it is clear tht *Saṁhitā* or morphophonemic combination is the essence of *Saṁhitā*-literature. The Prātiśākhyas devote much of their discussion in the niceties of correctly forming these combination patterns and specific names are also given to them to distinguish among themselves. Neither these names (*saṁjñās*) nor the elaborate treatment available there on this topic is found in Pāṇini's grammar. As *Saṁhitā* is not a very serious or emotional question for non-Vedic language, Pāṇini, in his scheme, though refers to all the major. verieties of combination-patterns, has not been very much specific as in the Prātiśākhyas. The Sandhi-prakaraṇa comprising five secitions is popular as Pañca-sandhi-prakaraṇa in *Siddhāntakaumudī* the famous *prakriyā* work in Pāṇinian system. They are *ac-sandhi* 'vowel-vowel combination, *hal-sandhi* 'consonant-consonant combination,' *visarga-sandhi* 'combination with a *visarga,*' *svādisandhi* 'combination in the process of declension of nominal forms.' and finally *prakṛti-bhāva-sandhi* 'combination without any change of the original form.' The *ac-sandhi* etc. are the generic names only. But in *RP*. each individual combinantion coming under all the above generic categories has been given a specific designaion.

RP classifies morphophonemic combination into four generic categories:[24] (i) vowel-vowel combination, (ii) vowel-consonant combination, (iii) consonant-vowel combination, and (iv) consonant-consonant combination. The generic names *visarga-sandhi* and *prakṛtibhāva sandhi* of Pāṇinian system are included within consonant-consonant combination and vowel-vowel combination respectively in *RP*.

An humble attempt is made in the following pages to have an assessment of vowel-vowel combination types as seen in the Vedic *Saṁhitā* literature and presecribed in *RP* Simultaneously their parallels have been traced in Pāṇinian system.

3.1 *Praśliṣṭa-sandhi*

This sandhi refers to the phonomena covered by what are known as *savarṇa-dīrgha-sandhi,*[25] *guṇa-sandhi*[26] and *vṛddhi-sandhi*[27] in Pāṇinian system. (i) The *savarṇa-dīrgha* operation is spoken exactly in the same manner in *RP.* as in Pāṇini-that if vowel homogeneous to he preceding *samānākṣara* (*a, ā, r, ṛ, i, ī, u,* and *ū*) follows as in the *Ṛkpāda-aśvājani (aśva + ajani) pracetasaḥ* (*RV.* 6.75.13), *sadyo jajñāno vi himiddha* (*hi + īm + iddhaḥ*) etc. both will coalescc into one long letter of the same vowel. [28] (ii) If *i/ī* follow *a/ā* there will be an *e* in place of the both.[29] For example *endra (ā + indra) sānasiṁ rayim (RV.* 1.81) supplies the instance of this type of *praśliṣṭa-sandhi,* if *u/ū* follow *a/ā* there will be a common *o* for both[30] as in *etāyāmopa* (*ā+ ita + ayāma + upa*) *gavyata indram (RV.* 1.33.9) These two phenomena are covered by *guṇa-sandhi* of Pāṇini : (iii) if *e/ai* follow *a/ā* there will be a common *ai* in place of the both as in *ainaṁ* (*ā+ enam*) *devāsaḥ* (*RV.* 1.123.1); if *o/au* follow *a/ā* there will be a common *au* in place of the both as in *yatrauṣadhīḥ (yatra + oṣadhīḥ) samagmata (RV.* 10.97.6). These two phenomena.[31]exactly correspond to the *vṛddhisandhi* of Pāṇini. For Pāṇini's three sūtras, Śaunaka spares six sūtras to explain *praśliṣṭa-sandhi* (*RP.* 2.15-20). This is called *praśliṣṭa* because of very closely sticking together of the two vowels there. The combination gives the impression of an insparable sound.

3.2 *Kṣaipra-sandhi*

This variety of vowel combination corresponds to *yaṇ-sandhi*[32] of Pāṇinian system where non-velar *samānākṣaras,* i.e., i.ī. & *u,ū* change respectively into *y* and *v* provided they are followed by vowels other than the vowles homogenous to the preceding one (i.e. except *i, ī* and *u, ū* res-pectively).[33]

The examples are the Vedic citations such as *abhyārṣeyam* (abhi + *ārṣeyam*) *jamadagnivanna* (*RV.* 9.97.51) *adhīnnvatra* (*adhi + it + nu + atra*) *saptatiṁ ca sapta ca (RV.* 10.93.15) etc. It is to be noted that here the following vowels remain unchanged and the change into *y/v* occurs of the preceding vowels only.[34] As here, the vowels, *i,u* and ṛ very readily change (*kṣipratayā saha*) into *y,v* and *r*, this sandhi is called *kṣaipra.*

3.3 Padavṛtti-sandhi

(i) Along with the preceding *visarjanīya* not originated from a *repha,* the preceding long velar vowel *'ā'* will change into *ā* if it is followed by a vowel–short or long.[35] In other words, in the combination *āḥ* + any vowel (short/long), *āḥ* final will be replaced by a long *ā.* This combination is seen in the Vedic citations like *yā oṣadhīḥ* (*yāḥ* + *oṣadhīḥ) somarājñī (RV.* 10.97.8). When *Śaunaka* directly transforms *āḥ* into *ā,* Pāṇini justifies this tranformation by a relatively longer formation procedure. This is because of the intricacies of ordering technique of the sūtras in view of their strength in terms of *paranitya-antaraṅga* and *apavāda* nature. This goes like *yāḥ* + *oṣadhīḥ* > *yās* + *oṣadhīḥ* (by P. 8.3.34): *visarjanīyasya saḥ)* > *yār oṣadhīḥ* (by P. 8.2.66 *sa sajuṣo ruḥ) / yāy* + *oṣadhīḥ* (by P. 8.3.17 *bhobhogoagho-apūrvasya yo śi)* > *yā oṣadhīḥ* by (P. 8.3.19: *lopaḥ śākalyaya).* No further combination resulting in a common *au* by P. 6.1.88 in place of *a* + *o* is possible due to the *asiddhatva* of the preceding sūtra P. 8.3.19 which causes the dropping of *y.*

(ii) Morphophonemic combination designated as *Padavṛtti-sandhi* is to be extended to the phenomena where *ai/au* final becomes *ā* being followed by a vowel[36] as seen in the instance like *sūryāya panthām anvetavā u (anvetavai + u) (RV.* 1.24.8) and *ubhā u (ubhau + u) nūnam (RV.* 10.106.1) For Pāṇini, these combination-structures can be derived by dropping *y* of *ay* and *v* of *av* which were respectively availed in the places of *ai* and *au* final being followed by a vowel. To be more elaborate, according to Pāṇini, *anvetavaiv* + *u* will result in *anveṭavāy* + *u* and *ubhau* + *u* will result in *ubhāv* + *u* by P. 6.1.78: *eco' yavāyāvaḥ* and y final and *v* final of both the structures will drop by P. 8.3.19 : *lopaḥ śākalyasya.* This variety of combination though not seen used in *Ṛgveda,* making such provision by Śaunaka leads to *dharma* 'merit' as says Uvaṭa.[37] The significance of this designation of *Padavṛtti* is self explanatory as there still remains a *vivṛti* 'hiatus' between the two vowels even after the combination has taken place of the two padas. *Padavṛtti* may be an abbreviation of *Padavivṛtti.*[38]

3.4 *Udgrāha-sandhi*

(i) A *visarjanīya* originated not from *repha* along with the pereceding short vowel *a* (i.e., aḥ) will change into *a* being follwed by any vowel—short or long.[39] This morphophonemic structure can be seen in the *Ṛk ya indra (yaḥ + indra) somapātamaḥ* (*RV.* 8.12.1) But the components of the mantra such as *antaḥ icchanti* will lead to the combination *antaricchanti (RV* 8.72.3) since this *visarjanīya* is originated from *repha.* The structure *ya indra* can be developed exactly in the same way as demonstrated above in case of *yā oṣadhīḥ* from *yāḥ. oṣadhḥḥ* under *Padavṛtti sandhi* in Pāṇini an way.

(ii) Similarly, *e/o* final will result in *a* being combined with a vowel short or long.[40] This can be demonstrated from the mantra *agna indra (agne + indra) varuṇa mitra devāḥ* (*RV* 5.46.2) and *vāya ukthebhir (vāyo + ukthebhir) jarate* (*RV* 1.22.2) Both these morphophonemic structures can be developed in Pāṇinian way exactly in the process shown above under *Padavṛtti-sandhi* (3.3.ii).

3.5 *Udgrāha-padavṛtti-sandhi*

This morphophonemic structure is just a variation of Udgrāha type of combination. Here if the following vowel is long and the other conditions remain the same as in *Udgrāha*, it will be called *Udgrāhapadavṛtti*.[41] The instance of this type is *ka īṣate tujyate (kaḥ + īṣate)* (*RV*. 1.84.17).

3.6 *Udgrāhavat-sandhi*

This euphonic structure arises from the phonemic situation where two velar vowels *a/ā* final followed by *ṛ* initial will result in the replacement of *a/ā* final by *a*[42] as seen in the mantra-*pra ṛbhubhyo dūtamiva (pra + ṛhubhyaḥ) (RV*. 4.33.1) and *āprusāyan madhuna ṛtasya (āprusāyan madhunā + ṛtasya) (RV*. 10.68.4). It is called *Udgrāhavat* or like *Udgrāha* because as *a gets replaced for elo* in *udgrāha, a/ā* also gets replaced by *a* before *ṛ*. In Pāṇini's system *upa + ṛcchati* will give *upā-rcchati* and *pra + ṛcchati* will give *prārcchati* by P. 6.1.91: *Upasargād ṛti dhātau: pra + ṛṣabhīyati* will give optionally a *vṛddhi* form according to *Āpiśali* as *prārṣabhīyatī* and *prarṣabhīyati* by P. 6.1.92: *vā supy āpiśaleḥ* and *a* and *ā followed* by *ṛ* normally give *ar* and *ār* combination respectively in non-vedic Sanskrit like *parama + ṛtaḥ > paramartaḥ* and *brahmā + ṛṣiḥ > brahmarṣiḥ* by P. 6.1.87 *ād guṇaḥ* along P. 1.1.51: *uraṇ raparaḥ*. However, optional *Prakṛtibhāva* is seen as in *brahma ṛṣiḥ* developed from *brahmā ṛṣiḥ* (shortening of the *ā of brahmā* into *brahma* by P. 6.1.127 : *iko'savarṇe śākalyasya hrasvaḥ* (only optionally) and this shortened final vowel *a* will remain unchanged being followed by the *ṛ* beginning word *ṛṣiḥ* by the sūtra of P.6.1.128; *ṛty akaḥ [prakṛtyā]*

3.7 *Bhugna-sandhi*

A morphophonemic phenomenon where *v* gets augmented after *a* and *ā* which are originated from *o and au* labial (*oṣṭhayoni*) when non-labial vowels (other than *u, o, au)*[43] follow as in the mantras *vāyavāyāhi darśata (RV*. 1.2.1) where *vāyo + āyāhi> vāyo + āyāhi > vāyav + āyāhi* is the combination-process: *ṛtena mitrāvaruṇāv ṛtāvṛdhāv ṛtāspṛśā (RV* 1.2.8) where *mitrāvaruṇau + ṛtāvṛdhau > mitrāvaruṇā +*

ṛtāvṛdhau > *mitrāvaruṇāvṛtāvṛdhau* is the process of combination. These phenomena are covered by the very popular sūtra of Pāṇini *eco'yavāyāvaḥ* (P. 6.1.78) which alone replaces *ay. av, āy* and *āv* in place of, *e, o, ai* and *au* word-final directly when any vowel follows. This augmentation of a *v* sound after *a/ā* final and before non-labial word initial vowel is called *Bhugna*. Hence this combination is called *Bhugna-sandhi.*[44]

3.8 *Prācya-padavṛtti and Pañcāla-padavṛtti combinations*[45]

These morphophonemic phenomena are related to *Udgrāha* type and are only the re-designation of the same. In the *Udgrāha* combination when *e/o* final remains unchanged being followed by *a*, the phonemic structure consisting of *e* + *a* out of it, is called *Prācyapadavṛtti* and the remaining *o* + *a* (both these two) will be designated as *Pañcāla-padavṛtti* type of combination. In *Pañcālapadavṛtti,* the preceding vowel must be a labial one without mattering whether it was originally labial *o* or a result of short *a* and the following *visarjanīya* taken together when the following sound is a vowel. The mantras like *te agrepā ṛbhavo mandasānā* (*RV* 4.34.10) *where te agrepā* presents a combination-structure called *Prācya-padavṛtti: purolāśṁ yo 'smai (RV.* 8.31.2) and *pro ayāsīd indur indrasya (RV* 9.86.16) present combination-structures called *Pañcāla-padavṛtti.* From the examples cited above for *Pañcāla-padavṛtti,* in the former, i.e., *yo 'smai, 'o'* is developed from *yaḥ* + *asmai* but in the latter case–*proayāsid,* the *'o'* is original one.

3.9 *Abhinihita-sandhi*[46]

(i) This combination-structure allows coalescing of *ṛkpāda* initial *a* with *e, o* word final (both original *o* and also with the *o* developed from *a* and *visarjanīya*). The following *a*-initial gets lost bccause of its submerging in the preceding vowel. This combination is widely seen in vedic mantras. Instances of this structural pattern are noticed in the mantras like *sugaṁ tatte tāvakebhyo rathebhyo' gne* (*rathebhyo + agne* < *rathebhyaḥ + agne) RV.* 1.94.11) *dadhāṣi ratnaṁ draviṇaṁ ca dāśuṣe' gne (dāśuṣe + agne)* (*RV.* 1.94.14) *atrā cinno madho pito' ram (pito + aram) (RV.* 1.187.7) and so on. The *abhinidhāna* or coalescing is due only when the line of the mantra starting with an *a* vowel follows the *e/o* final. Inside the mantra, if such occasions like *e/o + a* arise, there is no *abhinidhāna.* For counter examples, *cikitvāṁso acetasaṁ nayanti (cikitvāṁso + acetasaṁ* with no change) (*RV.* 7.60.7) or *āre asme ca śṛṇvate (āre + asme* with no change) shows the non-application of the rule because in both these cases the following *a* is not in the beginning of a *ṛk-* line. It is inside the line.

In the non-Vedic Sanskrit, this type of combination is frequently seen. Pāṇini provides this combination to occur by the rule *eṅaḥ padāntād ati* (P. 6.1.109) which is known as *pūrvarūpa-sandhi.* In the non-Vedic Sanskrit, the unchanged structures (*prakṛtibhāva*) i.e., *e-a* and *o-a* are not normally seen as in the counter examples cited above. The counter examples are justified as *Prācyapadavṛtti* (*e + a* unchanged) and *Pañcāla-padvṛtti* (*o + a* unchanged) types of combination.

(ii) Inside the *pāda,* also there is coalescing of word-initial a with preceding word-final e/o provided the following *a* is a light (*laghu)* letter and the same is followed by a light syllable (*laghu akṣara*) with either *y* or *v* as the beginning sound,[47] for example *yamaicchāmma manasā so 'yam āgāt (so + ayam* < *saḥ + ayam)* (*RV.* 10.53.1), *yaste manyo 'vidhadvajra manyo + avidhat) (RV.* 10.83.1), and *te 'vadan prathamāḥ* (te + avadan) (*RV.* 10.109.1), This principle will not work if the following a is heavy as in *vrataiḥ sīkṣanto avratam,* (the initial *a* of *avaratam* is heavy or *guru*) (*RV.* 6.14.3); or if the following syllable beginning with *y/v* is heavy as in *druho nido mitramabo avadyāt* (the syllable *va* is heavy due to its occurrence before the conjunct consonant *dy* (*ā*) in *avadyāt*)[48]

(iii) Inside the *pāda,* also there appears coalescing of word-initial *a* with word-final *e/o* preceding, if the same *a is* fallowed by a light syllable starting with letters other than *y* or *v*[49] and the word finals *e/o* are preceded by the combinantion *āv* (from *āvaḥ).* It is seen in the xample like *tam atra gāvo 'bhitoṅ navantaḥ (gāvo + abhitaḥ) (RV* 5.30.10). But the mantra portion *ā gāvo agman* (*RV.* 6.28.1) does not allow coalescing of *a* (heavy due to the following conjunct consonant) with *o* final.

Thus, Śaunaka goes on counting exceptional cases (*apavādas*) where *abhinidhāna* is seen in the *RV.* The scope of this paper does not permit to enumerate them one by one. Pāṇini in his Vedic rules 6.1.11 *prakṛtyāntaḥ pādam avyapare* (examples : *upaprayanto adhvaram, sujāte aśvasūnṛte)* and 6.1.116) *avyād-avadyād-avakramur-avrata-ayamavantv-avasyuṣu ca* (example: *vasubhir no avyāt* etc.) provide the cases which are not covered by *anabhidhāna* or they are in unchanged structure. The counter examples, however, show the *anabhidhāna. RP.* is very elaborate[50] in counting every individual case of *anabhidhāna* and also in the cases not covered by it whereas Pāṇini's apporach is only illustrative.

4. Resume

The Present study is an attempt to refersh our memory regarding the concept of *Saṁhitā* or Morphophonemic combination in the context of Vedic Saṁhitā literature in general and vowel combination in particular. The following points have been discussed in this paper.

(i) the *Vedāṅgas* including the *Prātiśākhyas* are immensly valued as they are indispensable aids to interpret Vedic literature;

(ii) Saṁhitā is not only a typical secition of Vedic literature, it is also a teachnical term further classified into several varicties;

(iii) Definition of *Saṁhitā* according to Vedic texts such as *Aitareya Āraṇyaka* and also according to Pāṇini;

(iv) The metaphysical interpretation and mystification of *Saṁhitā* as seen in *Aitareya Āraṇyaka* in the name of *Saṁhitopaniṣad;*

(v) Śaunaka's highlighting of the mysterious *Saṁhitopāsana* in *Ṛkprātiśākhya* and its purpose;

(vi) Classification of Morphophonemic combination patterns both by Pāṇini in his grammer and Śaunaka in *Ṛkprātiśākya;*

(vii) Treatment of vowel-vowel combination by Śaunaka keeping in view its available types in the *Ṛgveda;* and

(viii) The vowel-vowel combination named as *praśliṣṭa, kṣaipra, padavṛtti, udgrāha, udgrāhavat, bhugna, prācya-padavṛtti, pañcālapadvaṛtti* and *abhinihita* types are discussed along with their counterparts of Pāṇinian system.

References

1. The modifier 'structural' refers to linguistic significance including the semantic analysis and 'thematic' refers to the institution of sacrifice and other details, which are linguistic in nature.
2. Cp. *Pāṇinīyaśikṣā* where the *Vedāṅgas* are compared with the different organs of a human being.
   chandaḥ pādau tu vedasya hastau kalpo' tha paṭhyate/ jyotiṣām ayaṇaṃ cakṣur niruktam śrotram ucyate// śikṣā ghrāṇaṁ tu vedasya mukhaṁ vyākaraṇaṁ smṛtam/ tasmāt sāṅgam adhītyeva brahmaloke mahīyate//
3. *See RP* 2.1
   Saṁhitā padaprakṛtiḥ (saṁhitādhikāra begins from this *sūtra).*
4. Ibid., *padāntān padādibhiḥ sandadhad eti yat sā kālāvyavāyena RP* 2.2
5. Ibid., see *Uvaṭa-bhāṣya* on 2.2
6. See *RP* 2.3 *svarāntaraṁ tu vivṛtiḥ. Yājñavalkya-śikṣā* 94 prescribes *vivṛti* in the same way: *dvayos tu svarayor madhye sandhir yatra na dṛśyate/ vivṛtis tatra viṣeyā ya īśeti nidarśnam//* quoted in p. 129 of *RP*, Ed., Virendra Kumar Varma (1970). Banaras Hindu University.
7. *RP*. 2.21 *samānākṣaram antaḥsthāṁ svām akaṇṭhyaṁ svarodayam* and 2.23 *te kṣaiprāḥ prākṛtodayāḥ.*
8. *RP* 2.4. *sā vā svarabhakti-kālā,* 2.33 *drāghīyasī sārdhamātrā* 2.34. *itare ca,* 2.35 *ardhonānyā.*
9. See *Sidhānta-kaumudī with Bālamanoramā* comm. ed. by Pt.

Gopalasastri Nene (1969), Varanasi : Chowkhamba Sanskrit series Offices, p. 28.

10. Ibid., *sannikarṣaḥ sāmṣpyam, ardhamātrādhikakālv-yavadhānābhāvaḥ, ardhamātrākāla-vyavadhānasya avarjanṣyatvāt.*
11. Cp. *saṁhitaikapade nityā nityā dhātūpasargayoḥ/ nityā samāse vākye tu sā vivakṣām apekṣate//*
12. *Tai U.,* 1.3.1-6 : *athātaḥ saṁhitāyā upaniṣdaṁ vyākyāsyāmaḥ. pañcasv adhikaraṇeṣu adhilokamadhijyotiṣam-adhividyam-adhiprajam-adhyātmam. tā mahāsaṁhitā cakṣate. athādhilokam. pṛthivī pūrvarpam. dyaur uttararūpam. ākāśaḥ sandhiḥ. vāyuḥ sandhānam ityadhilokam. athādhijyotiṣam agniḥ pūrvarūpam. ādityaḥ uttara-rūpam. āpam. āpaḥ sandhiḥ. vidyutaḥ sandhānam. ityadhijyautiṣam. athādhividyam. ācāryaḥ pūrvarūpam. vidyā sandhiḥ pravacanaṁ sandhānam ity adhgividyam. athādhiprajam mātā pūrvarūpam. pitottararūpam. prajā sandhiḥ. prajanaṁ sandhānam. ity adhiprajam. athādhyātmam. adharā hanuḥ pūrvarpam uttarā hanur uttararūpam. vāk sandhiḥ jihvā sandhānam,. ityadhyātmam. itīmā mahāsaṁhitāḥ. ya evam etā mahāsa+hitā veda sandhṣyate prajayā paśsubhir brahmavarcasenā 'nnādyena suvargyeṇa lokena.*
13. See *RP* (*paṭalas* 1-4) (Hindi comm.), ed. B.B. chaube (1986), Varanasi: Bharatiya Vidya Prakashan, p. 8
14. See *māṇḍukeyaḥ saṁhitām vāyum āha tathākāśaṁ cāsya mākṣavaya eva/ samānatām anile cāmbare ca matvāgastyo' vipariharāṁ tadeva// RP.* p. 4
15. See *athātaḥ saṁhitāyā ypaniṣat. pṛthivī pūrvarūpaṁ dyaur uttararūpam vāyuḥ saṁhitieti māṇḍukeyaḥ. ākāśaḥ saṁhitetyasya mākṣavyo vedayāñcakre. sa hāviparihṛto mene na me'sya putreṇa samagād iti. samāne vai tatpārahṛto mena ityāgastyaḥ samānaṁ hyetad bhavati vāyu cākāśaś ceti. ityadhidaivatam.*
16. *adhyāmaklptau śūravṣaḥ sutuś ca vāṅmanasayar vivadanty ānupūrvye/*
17. *sandher vivartanaṁ nirbhujaṁ vadanti śauddhākṣa-roccāraṇaṁ ca pratṛṇṇam/ ubhayaṁ vyāptam ubhayam antareṇa tathā kāmā anna-nākobhayākhyāḥ//*

    Note: *nirbhuja* = *saṁhitāpāṭha, pratṛṇṇ* = *padapāṭha, ubhayamantareṇa* = *kramapāṭha, nirdiṣṭau bhujasadṛau pūrvottara-śabdau yasmin saṁhitārūpa uccāraṇe tad uccāraṇam nirbhujam, yaddhi sandhiṁ vivartayati tan nirbhujasya rūpam (Ai Ā* 3.1.3); and Sāyaṇa explains *pratṇṇa as vicchedarṣupa-hiṁsāvācinā pratṛṇṇa-śabdena vicchinnaṁ padam abhidhīyate* on *Ai Ā* 3.1.3.
18. Cp. *Ai Ā* 3.2.6 *tasyai vā etasyai saṁhitāyai ṇakāro balaṁ ṣakāraḥ prāṇa ātmā,* it is also said-*ya ūṣmānaḥ sa prāṇaḥ* (*Ai Ā* 2.2.4).
19. See *RP,* and Chaubey, op. cit., pp. 16–18 for all details.
20. See *Ai Ā* 3.1.6 *bṛhadrathantarayo rūpeṇa saṁhitā saṁdhīyata iti tārkṣyaḥ.*

vāg via rathantaṛasya rūpaṁ prāṇo bṛhata ubhābhyām u khalu saṁhitā saṁdhīyate vācā ca prāṇena ca.

20. See Ai Ā 3.1.6. *bṛhadrathantarayo ṛpeṇa saṁhitā saṁdhīyata iti tārkṣyaḥ. vāg vai ruthantarasya rūpaṁ prāṇo bṛhata ubhābhyām u khalu saṁhitā saṁdhīyate vācā ca prāṇena ca.*
21. See *Ai Ā* 3.1.6 *vāk prāṇena saṁhiteti kauṇṭharavyaḥ. prāṇaḥ pavamānena pavamāno viśvairdevair viśve degvāḥ svargeṇa lokena svargo loko brahmaṇ saiẓā varāparā saṁhitā.*
22. See *A Ā* 3.1.6 *vāk saṁhiteti pañcālakhaṇḍoḥ. vācā vai vedāḥ sa+dhiyante vācā chandāmsi vācā mitrāṇi saṁdadhati vācā sarvāṇi atho vāg evedaṁ sarvam iti.*
23. See *Ai Ā* 3.1.6 *tad yatraitad adhīte vā bhāṣate vā vāci tadā prāṇo bhavati vāk tadā prāṇaṁ relahyatha yatra tuṣṇīṁ vā bhavati svapiti vā prāṇe tadā vāg bhavati prāṇaxs tadā vācaṁ reliha tāv anyonyaṁ rīlaho vāg vai mātā prāṇaḥ putraḥ.*
24. See *Uvaṭa-bhāṣya* on *RP*, *paṭala*-IV *catvāraḥ saṁdhayaḥ, tad yathā pṣurve svarāḥ vyañjanāny uttarāṇy anulomā anvakṣara-saṁdhayaḥ. pūrvāṇi vyaṣjanāny uttare svarāḥ pratilomā anvakṣara-saṁdhayaḥ. svarasaṁdhiṣu praśleṣādy aneka-prakāra uktaḥ idānīṁ pariśiṣṭo vyañjana-saṁdhir ucyate-*

    The vowel-consonant *sandhi* is designated as *anulomā anvakṣara-sandhi* prescribed under the sūtra *eṣa sya s ca svarāś ca pūrve bhavanti vyaañjanam uttaraṁ yadaibhyaḥ. te' nvakṣara-sandhayo' nulomāḥ RP* 2.8 and the consonantvowel *sandhi* is designated as *partilomā anvakṣarasandhi* by the rule : *pratilomāstu viparyaye ta eva-RP2.9.*
25. Cp. *akaḥ savarṇe dīghaḥ [ekaḥ parayaḥ] (*6 1.101).
26. Cp. *ād guṇaḥ [aci, ekaḥ pūrva-parayoḥ/* (6.1.87)
27. Cp. *vṛddhir eci [āt, ekaḥ pūrva-parayoḥ]* (6.1.88)
28. *samānākṣare sasthāne dīrgham ekam ubhe svaram (RP.* 2.15).
29. *ikārodaya ek ram akāraḥ sodayaḥ* (*RP.* 2.16)
30. *tathā ukārodaya okāram* (*RP.* 2.17).
31. *pareṣv aikāram ojayoḥ* (*RP.* 2.18), *aukāraṁ yugṁayoḥ (RP.* 2.19) and *ete praśliṣṭā nāma sandhayaḥ* (*RP.* 2.20)
32. Cp. *iko yaṁ aci [saṁhitāyām]* (P. 6.1.77).
33. *samānākṣaram antaḥsthāṁ svām akaṇṭhyaṁ, svarodayam (RP.* 2.21) and *na samānākṣare sve sve (RP.* 2.22).
34. *te kṣaiprāḥ prākṛtodayāḥ* (*RP.* 2.23).
35. *visarjanīyo riphito dīrghapūrvaḥ svarodaya ākāram (RP.* 2.24)
36. *uttamau ca dvau svarau* (*RP* 2.25) & *tā padav+ttayaḥ* (*RP.* 2.26)
37. See Uvaṭa on *RP.* 2.26 *atra yābhiḥ saṁjñābhiḥ śāstrakṛd vyavaharati tāvatyaḥ sva-vyavahārāthāḥ. yābhir vyavahāro nāsti tāsāṁ jñāne dharmaḥ phalam.*
38. See *RP.* (*paṭalas* 1-4), Ed. B.B. Chaube, op. cit., p. 139

39. *hrasvapūrvas tu so 'kāram* (*RP*. 2.27)
40. *pṣurvau compottamāt svarau (RP*. 2.28) and *ta udgrāhāḥ (RP* 2.29)
41. *dīrghaparā udgrāhapadavṛttayaḥ (RP*. 2.30)
42. *ṛkāra udaye kaṇṭhyāvakāraṁ tadudgrāhavat (RP*. 2.32).
43. *oṣṭhyayonyor bhugnam anoṣṭhye vakāro trāntarāgamaḥ (RP*. 2.31).
44. See *RP*., B.B. Chaube, op. cit., p. 142.
45. *udgāhāṇāṁ pūrvarūpāṇy akāre prakṛtyā dve o bhavaty ekamādyam/ prācya-pañcāla-padavṛttayas tāḥ pañcālām oṣṭhyapūrā bhavanti// (RP* 2.33)
46. *athābhinihitaḥ sandhir etaiḥ prākṛta-vaikṛtaiḥ/ ekībhavati pādādir akāras te' tra sandhijāḥ//* (*RP*. 2.34).
47. *antaḥpādam akārāc cet saṁhiāyāṁ laghor laghu/ yaikārādyakṣaraṁ paraṁ vakārādyapi vā bhavet//* (*RP*. 2.35).
48. Cp. *sañyoge guru [hrasvaḥ]* (p.1.4.11).
49. *anyādyapi tathāyuktam āvontopahitāt sataḥ* (*RP*. 2.36).
50. See *RP*. 2.37-81 for details.

7

MĀṆḌŪKĪ ŚIKṢĀ

BHAGYALATA PATASKAR

This is the only Śikṣā belonging to the Atharvaveda tradition. It is available in the printed form in the *Śikṣā Saṃgraha* ed. by Yugal Kishor Vyas and published in Benaras Sanskrit series in 1893. The same is published in the *Śikṣāsāragraha* ed. by Ramprasad Tripathi and published by Sampurnanand Sanskrit Vishvavidyalaya, Varanasi in 1989. The text of the Māṇḍūkī Śikṣā (MŚ) is also separately published under the title *'Atharvavedīyā Māṇḍūkī Śikṣā: Bhūmikā Pariśiṣṭa Tathā Sūciyon Sahita'* (in Hindi) by Dayananda Mahavidyalaya Sanskrit Grantha Mala, Lahore in 1921 ed. by Bhagavaddatta.

As it is discussed by Pt. Bhagavaddatta the manuscript (ms) of the MŚ was first available from a Pancholi Brahmin from Gujarat. Another ms. is also undated and there is no special mention of the scribe. However Pt. Bhagavaddatta arrives at the conclusion 'yah lag-ghag 250 varśa purānā hyan' (p-2) (in Hindi). He has quoted the beginning where it is mentioned *'Oṃ namo brahmavedāya.'* This ms. also belongs to the Brahmin from Gujarat.

The third ms. mentioned by him is from Maharashtra and belongs to some 'gore iti upanāmaka Bhāskarabhattasyedaṃ pustakaṃ khalu.'

The Kashi edition of Pt. Yugal Kishor Vyas gives following note at the end of the MŚ . . . *tato Vārāṇaseya-rāmabhaṭṭa-*

vāstavya-gurjaradeśīya pañcolyupādhi-dhāriṇo'tharvavedīya-śaunakaśākhīyādhyayanādhyāpanaśālinaḥ Śrīmajjayadeva-śarmahastapaṅkajān-māṇḍūkī. . . .

The pañcolis of Gujarat belong to *Atharvaveda*. Hence the śikṣā is stamped with *Atharvavedīyā Māṇḍūkī Śikṣā.*

There are 16 adhyāya-s in this śikṣā and total number of the śikṣā is 178 or with one repeated is 179.

According to the Siddheshwar Varma the time of this śikṣā is fifth century AD.

About Māṇḍūka

The present śikṣā twice mentions this name Māṇḍūka as follows—In 2.3 it says:

prathamāvantimau caiva varttante chandasi svarāḥ/
trayo madhyā nivarttante maṇḍūkasya mataṃ yathā //

In 16.16 it says:

maṇḍūkena kṛtāṃ sikṣāṃ viduṣāṃ buddhidīpinīm/
yo hi tattvena jānāti brahmalokaṃ sa gacchatīti //

One has to collect several references from different sources to reconstruct the history of MŚ.

Pāṇini Sūtra 4.1.119 prescribes the suffix *ḍhak* and *aṇ* to the word Maṇḍūka (cf. *ḍhak ca maṇḍūkāt*) in the sense tasyāpatyam, his offspring. Thus the son of Māṇḍūka is Māṇḍūkeya and also Māṇḍūka. The rule also avails of the suffix *iñ* on the basis of *anuvṛtti* (of *vā*) and the alternative form for son of Maṇḍuka is Māṇḍūki. This gives rough idea that some Maṇḍūka might have been the renowned person whose descendents were known/recognized by his name.

Pāṇini Sūtra 4.1.19 describes feminine suffix *spha* to the word Māṇḍūka. cf. *'kaurovyamāṇḍūkābhyāṃ ca.'*

Going back to the Vedic literature the person Māṇḍūkeya is mentioned by the *Aitareya Āraṇyaka* 3.15 *iti ha smāha hrasvo*

Māṇḍūkeyaḥ, thus said short junior Māṇḍūkīya. The *Śatapatha Brāhmaṇa* mentions Māṇḍūkiputra as one of the teachers. The *Ṛgvedaprātiśākhya* and the *Atharvapariśiṣṭa* refer to one Māṇḍūkeya (*Māṇḍūkeyasya sarveṣu praśliṣṭesu tathā smaret/ Ṛ.P.*—200) (*Māṇḍūkeyaṃ tarpayāmi* 43.4.46). The name of the sage Māṇḍūkya intimately related to the Upaniṣad perhaps has the stem Māṇḍūka, it seems. According to *Atharvapariśiṣṭa* 49.1.6 (*Māṇḍūkeyāśca*) the Māṇḍūka-s are the followers of the Maṇḍūka school.

Thus Māṇḍūka seems to be very celebrated personality in the Vedic time, which is known as the śākhāpravartaka–revealer of the Vedic recention. Initially his name is associated with *Ṛgveda*, so is known from the *Aitareya Āraṇyaka*, *Ṛgvedaprātiśākhya* and *Atharvapariśiṣṭa*. My conjecture is the descendants of Maṇḍūka are Māṇḍūkeya, Maṇḍūka and Māṇḍūkī. Out of these the Māṇḍūkeyas might have associated to the *Ṛgveda Śākhā* and Maṇḍūka-s might have been further associated with *Atharvaveda*. Considering the mixed characteristic of the Śikṣā, I think it might have been composed by some Maṇḍūka i.e. one actually related to *Atharvaveda* tradition, however in order to give authenticity and sanctity he has mentioned *maṇḍūkasya matam* or *maṇḍūkena kṛtā*.

It will not be out of context if I mention opinion of Vedic scholar Shridhar Vyankatesh Ketkar who in his Vedavidyā Khaṇḍa of Mahārāṣṭrīya Jñānakoṣa says that *Atharvaveda* itself is the collection of the things that are not directly related to Śrautadharma: (p. 169 column 1). This statement is significant in case of the present Śikṣā, because it is the collection or compilation of several issues related to Vedādhyayana and Vedic recitation.

It also contains some points related to the recitation of *Śūkla-Yajurveda* and *Sāmaveda* without giving any textual examples.

In the paradigm of the śikṣā-s we find that some śikṣā-s is exclusively related to some Veda, e.g. *Yājñavalkya-śikṣā* to

Śukla-Yajurveda, Bhāradvāja-śikṣīā to *Taittirīya Śākhā, Nāradīya–śikṣā* to *Sāmaveda,* and some bear very general characteristic, e.g. *Pāṇinīya-śikṣā.* The *Māṇḍūkī-śikṣā* though is known as *Atharvavedīyā,* shows very general feature dealing with very common topics such as mode of recitation, discipline of recitation, accent, *kampa* etc. Therefore content wise it belongs to the general class.

I would like to submit my humble opinion in this regard here. This śikṣā seems to be later crafted/composed text by somebody belonging to *Atharvaveda* tradition. In order to add one text to the literary complex of the *Atharvaveda,* the person composed it borrowing heavily from *Yājñavalkya-śikṣā* and *Nāradīya-śikṣā* and little from *Pāṇinīya-śikṣā.* In order to give weightage to the work he might have added as many subjects as he could. Since the *Atharvaveda* recitation doesn't have any special, distinct feature of recitation, there was hardly any scope to reflect and comment on it. I sincerely maintain that this śikṣā was composed not to help or facilitate the oral tradition of *Atharvaveda* or not to make the documentation of the oral tradition of the *Atharvaveda* but to save and strengthen it by adding one big text to its complex, lest it might become weaker; since the *Atharvaveda* mantra-(s) have no direct access in the *Śrautayajña*-(s).

Thus I would like to put forth my conjectures about this śikṣā as follows—

The present śikṣā belongs to that time, when the *Atharvaveda* oral tradition might have lost its nuance and distinction

An idea behind the composition seems that a work on Vedic recitation and Vedādhyayana in general, added to its literary complex may strengthen its position.

A scholar belonging to the *Atharvaveda* tradition then but did have some linkage with *Ṛgveda* tradition might have composed it.

Hereafter I will submit the analysis of the text in detail:

The Māṇḍūkī-śikṣā (MŚ) has heavily borrowed from the *Yājñavalkya-śikṣā* (YŚ) and *Nāradīya-śikṣā* (NŚ). From YŚ it has borrowed 67 verses and from NŚ it has borrowed 66 verses. Out of these 39 verses are common to YŚ and NŚ.

Excluding this portion one can trace out the exclusive MŚ observations about recitation. Few can exemplify this point:

1. After enumerating the Sāmavedic-svara-(s) the Śikṣā says:

prathamāvantimau caiva varttante chandasi svarāḥ/
trayo madhyā nivarttante maṇḍūkasya mataṃ yathā //2.3

The first two are *ṣaḍja* and *ṛṣabha* and last two are *dhaivata* and *niṣāda* (cf. 1.8). Further he says that the second *ṛṣabha* one is called *svarita*. The sixth one i.e. *dhaivata* is called *pracita*. The *niśāda* (the last 7th one) is *ucca* i.e. *udātta* and the first one i.e. *ṣaḍja* is *nīca* i.e. *anudātta*. What he means to say that in the chandas recitation only these four svara-(s) i.e. accents viz *udātta, anudātta, svarita* and *pracaya* are found which correspond to four musical notes (*niṣāda, ṣadju, ṛṣabha* and *dhaivata* respectively). The remaining three (i.e. *gāndhāra, madhyama* and *pañcama*) have no scope in Vedic recitation. In fact according to *traisvarya* concept, *pracaya* is not the distinct *svara*. It is even not distinctly heard, even in *Ṛgveda* recitation, certainly not in *Atharvaveda*. Although there is no audible distinction between *udātta* and *pracaya*, the hand movements have maintained this distinction. The accents are indicated by touching particular points on the palm, e.g. the *ṣaḍja* on the *anāmikā*, i.e. ring finger. This kārikā about the *hastasvara* is borrowed from NŚ. The NŚ gives the interrelation between three Vedic accents and the musical notes, viz.

udātte niṣāda-gāndhārāvanudātta ṛṣabha-dhaivatau/
svaritaprabhavā hyete ṣadjamadhyama-pañcamāḥ //
(NŚ— 1.8.8)

I just want to share with you that does the Maṇḍūka knows any such tradition where *pracaya* was distinctly pronounced? Anyhow relating the stress accent with the musical is novel idea of Maṇḍūka.

However it should be noted that in 6.1 the MŚ says—

svara uccaḥ svaro nīcaḥ svaraḥ svarita eva tu/
svarapradhānaṃ traisvaryyamāhurakṣaracintakāḥ//

One more observation found is *nāsikāyāstu pūrveṇa hastaṃ saṃcālayet budhaḥ* (2.13) meaning the hand movements should be in front of the nose. The feature we don't find in the Maharashtriya pronunciation. However in Keralite Ṛgvediya recitation, the hand movements are free, little uplifted. The NŚ I.6.13

(nāsikāyās tu pūrveṇa hastaṃ gokarṇavad dharet /
nibeśya dṛṣṭiṃ hastāgre śāstrārtham anucintayet//)

mentions this position of hand i.e. nāsikāyā sammukha.

The common topics of the śikṣā such as points of articulation, efforts of articulation, three *vṛttis, vivṛttis* (i.e. articulation of non-sandhi situation, non-sandhi phenomenon), *svarabhakti, svara-sandhi, saṃhitā* to *pada* conversion, general do's and don'ts of the Vedic recitation etc. are dealt with by this śikṣā. However the arrangement of the topics is not well arranged but bit complex and haphazard, e.g. the second adhyāya and the fourth ones deal with the *hastasvara.* The general tips or guidelines for Vedic recitation recurringly occur e.g. in first, third, twelfth, fifteenth and sixteenth adhyāyas.

The complex character of this śikṣā can be noticed from its discussing the Sāmavedic recitation as well as Śukla-yajurvedic recitation to considerable extent, e.g. the MŚ 2.1, 2 describes the hastāṅguśṭhayojana as follows:

bāhyāṅguṣṭhaṃ tu kruṣṭaṃ syād aṅguṣṭhe madhyamaḥ svaraḥ/
prādeśnyāṃ tu gāndhāro madhyamāyāṃ tu pañcamaḥ/ 2.1
anāmikāyāṃ ṣadjas tu kaniṣṭhāyāṃ tu dhaivataḥ/
tasyādhastāt tu yo' nyaḥ nyān niṣāda iti taṃ viduḥ //2.2

It is almost copied in toto from NŚ.

aṅguṣṭhasyottame kruṣṭo'ṅguṣṭhe tu prathamaḥ svarah/
prādeśinyāṃ tu gāndhāro ṛṣabhas tad anantaram// 1.7.3
anāmikāyāṃ ṣadjas tu kaniṣṭhāyāṃ tu dhaivataḥ/
tasyā' dhastāc ca yā' nyā tu niṣādaṃ tatra vinyaset // 1.7.4

The points mentioned by both these śikṣā-(s) are same i.e. *bāhyāṅguṣṭha* (NŚ—*aṅguṣṭhasyottame*), *aṅguṣṭha, prādeśinī, madhyamā* (NŚ—*tad anantaram*), *anāmikā, kaniṣṭhikā* and *tasyādhastāt.* The technical terms used for the musical notes are *kruṣṭam, madhyamaḥ* (NŚ—*prathama*), *gāndhāra, pañcama* (NŚ—*ṛṣabḥā*), *ṣaḍja, dhaibata* and *niṣāda.*

What is madhyama (*aṅguṣṭhe madhyamaḥ svaraḥ/* MŚ. 2.1) in *laukikagāna* is *prathama* in Sāmāgāna (hence the NŚ. *hy-aṅguṣṭhe prathamaḥ svaraḥ*). However the difference between the statements madhymāyāṃ tu pañcamaḥ of MŚ and *ṛṣabhas tad anantaram* of MŚ. is not satisfactorily justifiable.

To stress the inter-relation between MŚ and YŚ, here is the passage about

hastasvara—mānte muṣṭyākṛtiṃ kuryāt takārānte viśleṣayet/
nakhasya dakṣiṇe pārśve nakārāntaṃ niveddyet //4.10
kaṭāntāyos tu kartavyamaṅgulyagraprakuñcanam/
ṅaṇanāte tathaiva syāt pānte tvaṅgulipīḍanam//4.11
ūrdhvakṣepāpi yā mātrā adhaḥ kṣepāpi yā bhavet/
ekaikām utsṛjed dhīraḥ pracite lūbhayaṃ tathā//4.12
hrasvānusvārakaraṇe tvaṅguṣṭhāgraprakuñcanam/
dīrghe tu sūrayaḥ prāhuḥ prādeśinyāḥ prasāraṇam//4.13

The same topic from YŚ is as follows:

muṣṭyākṛtir makāre syān nakāre tu nakhagrahaḥ//1.61
kakārānte ṭkārānte ṅaṇe tarjanikāṃ namet/
pañcāṅgulaṃ pakāre ca takāre kuṇḍalākṛtiḥ//1.62
ūrddhakṣepāc ca yoṣmā syād adhaḥkṣepāc ca yā bhavet/
ekaikām utsṛjed dhīraḥ svarite tubhayaṃ kṣipet // 1.63

The YŚ further goes on giving several such details. However the MŚ covers only these many points, such as the position of the fingers or the posture of the palm while pronouncing the consonant *m n, k, t, ṅ, ṇ, p, t*–when they occur at the end of the *pada,* and the *visarga* when it is preceded by the *udātta, anudātta* and the *svarita* vowels. However there are two points regarding which the MŚ differs from YŚ. The YŚ says that the sound *t* be associated with *kuṇḍalākṛti mūdrā* i.e. half circular shape of a palm, whereas MŚ says *muṣṭim viśleṣayet.* One should release the feast which may not be exactly kuṇḍalākṛti, where YŚ says *tarjanikāṃ* namet (one should bend the forefinger, the MŚ just mentions *aṅgulyagraprakuñcanam*–bending the tip of a finger. YŚ says that to indicate *'n'* one should touch the nail with the finger. The MŚ adds the detail that the right side of the nail be touched. The examples can be multiplied. But the *Atharvaveda* tradition does not show the *hastasvara* as it is described by the MŚ. It is far away from *saptasvara* recitation. Then what is the significance of its recording different *hastasvara* than YŚ? Is it that this śikṣā is familiar with the tradition that is slightly different from the YŚ tradition? Now I will quote few verses from MŚ which I find extremely difficult to understand. e.g.

svaritānāmanahrādamudāttānāmatāḍanam/
anudāttamanādhiṣṭhaṃ śaṣasānāmaromaśam// 5.4

The verse that precedes is *yadudāttam udāttam yad yatsvaritaṃ tat pade bhavati nīcam/yan nīcaṃ nīcam eva tad yat pracayasthaṃ tad api nīcam//* It is clear that the śikṣā is talking about Saṃhitā to Pada change. However the present verse renders no compatible meaning:

svaritāvadhṛta udātte paras tripūrvo vikramocyute/
svaritāvadhṛta udātte pādaḥ syāt sa hi vikramaḥ // 5.8

is one more verse occurring in the context of *Saṃhitā* to *Pada* relation. Considering the style of the MŚ following observations can be put forth:

With the exception of few verses, the MŚ is composed in the Anuṣṭup metre. Few are in Āryā metre. However irregularity in composition is found considerably.
Here is one more example:

nanu dhārayed dhrtam upasparśam upodāttaṃ nipātayet/
ekākṣare patanaṃ na ca dhṛtam uccārayet svare vāpi //5.9

The *mātrāsaṃkhyā* is irregular viz. 16-13-13-15.

svaritprabhavaṃ pracitāt svaritaṁ vidyata udāttaṃ vā/
anudāttam eva tad vidyādyadṛtaṃ ca tad viddhi yat pracitam//
5.6

The text gives *svaritprabhavam* instead of *svaritaprabhavam.* The rectified version disturbs *mātrāsaṃkhyā.*

svaritātparāṇi yāni syur anudāttāni kānicit/
sarvāṇi pracayaṃ yānti hyupodāttaṃ na vidyate //5.7

The number of syllables in first quarter is 9.

Somewhat unfamiliar form śikṣuka is found used thrice 1.6, 14.10 and 22.15.

After this brief note about the contents of the text I would like to discuss the period of the text. The chronological arrangement of all the śikṣā-(s) and the Lakṣanagrantha-(s) is a desideratum. My study reveals that there is a bulk of

10-15 verses which are occurred in almost 90 percent of the śikṣā texts. More than that is shared by a fair number of the texts (e.g. yathā saurāṣṭrikā nāri. . ., mantra hīnaḥ. . . , hastāt bhraśṭaḥ. . .). At this stage, when the chronological table is not fixed, any statement about the mutual give and take will be subject to re-examination.

The MŚ has drawn heavily from YŚ and NŚ. Although the period of both these śikṣā-(s) is a point of dispute, still the scholars have accepted them that they belong to comparatively older group of the Śikṣā-(s). The detailed treatment of the YŚ and a great informative feature of the NŚ imply that they are talking about the live tradition. I sincerely maintain that the MŚ don't show any such trait of the strong live tradition of the oral recitation. There aren't many examples. I could not find it having any relationship with the Atharvaprātiśākhya-(s). My conjecture is that the present text belongs to that period, when the śrauta practices has got severe set back which might have resulted into weakening of the oral tradition of all the Vedas in general. I find the present śikṣā is some sort of primer or a selection if not pedagogical exactly, which introduces a subject matter of Vedic recitation in general to one, irrespective of one's Vedaśākhā. So to me it seems that the text belongs to the second bulk of śikṣā literature.

The period of the śikṣā-(s) and the Lakṣaṇagrantha-(s) can be divided into three stages. I am not talking about the śikṣā vedāṅga but the today's available śikṣā texts,

(1) The older period—this is the period when the Vedic tradition was strong, well spread and alive.
(2) The later period śikṣā-(s)—this is the period when the oral tradition got severe set back. Hence what was already in practice was to be deliberately documented as a need of the time. I think the śikṣā-(s) that focus on particular special aspect of recitation—such as karma-saṃdhāna.

(3) The śikṣā which exhibit the characteristic of the personal notes e.g. quickening about ba-kāra-va-kāra or galaddṛk or ṛkpāṭhadūṣaṇoddhāra etc. they may fall in still later period.

This is very broad and hypothetical table of the chronology of the śikṣā literature. To fix the period of any given text of the śikṣā, internal and external evidences will only be conclusive.

Incidentally I would like to shed light on the association of the hand movements with the pronunciation i.e. phonetic values added to the hand movements.

Almost all the śikṣā-(s) agrees with the importance of the *hastasañcālana.*

hastahīnaṃ tu yo' dhīte svaravarṇavivarjitam/
ṛgyajuḥsāmabhirddagdho viyonim adhigacchati//
[Pāṇinīya Śiksā (PŚ)—54, YŚ—41]
hastenādhīyamānasya svaravarṇān prayuñjatah/
ṛgyajuḥsāmabhiḥ pūto brahmalokam avāpnuyāt //
(*YŚ*—44)

hastena veda yo' dhīte svara-varṇā' rthasaṃyutam
ṛgyajuḥsāmabhiḥ pūto brahmalokamāhīyate// (*PŚ*—55)

The first prescriptive reference of this is in *Vājasaneyī Prātiśākhya—jātyābhinihitakṣaipraprаśliṣṭāś catvāras tiryag-ghastaṃ kṛtvā pradarśanīyāḥ, pitṛdānavaddhas taṃ kṛtvetyar-thaḥ.*

tiryagghastakaraṇaṃ mādhyandinīyānām eva (1.122)
anudāttaṃ cet pūrvaṃ tiryaṅ nihatya kāṇvasya (1.123)

Thc later Śikṣā-(s) developed this elaborately e.g.

anudātto hṛdi jñeyo mūrdhnyudātta udāhṛtaḥ/

svaritaḥ karṇamūlīyaḥ sarvāsye pracayaḥ smṛtaḥ// (PŚ–48)

This stress on hand movements for *udātta, anudātta* and *svarita* being up, down and in between respectively just seem the physical paraphrase of uccairudāttaḥ, nīcairanudāttaḥ and samāhāraḥ saritaḥ. (Pāṇini Sūtra–1.2.29–31)

In *Yajñakarma, ekaśruti* is prescribed which seems quite obvious on this background. When the hands are engaged in some other activity the *hastasañcālana* is not possible. It goes without saying that pārāyaṇa and for svādhyāya the recitation should be necessarily with *hastasvara.*

Now a question why hastasañcālana is closely related to *adhyayana.*

udāttam ākhyāti bṛṣo' ṅgulīnāṃ pradeśinīmūlaniviṣṭa-mūrdhā/
upāntamadhye svaritaṃ dhṛtaṃ kaniṣṭhikāyām anudāttam eva// (PŚ–43)
udātto bhruvi pātavyaṃ pracayaṃ nāsāgra eva ca/
hṛṭ pradeṣe' nudātttaṃ ca tiryag jātyādikāḥ svarāḥ // (YŚ 51)

Prātiśākhyapradīpaśikṣā

I think the association of the *hastasañcālana* might have been a device to improve the concentration in learning. Not only *hastasañcālana* but the *Cārāyagṇi Śikṣā* has also associated eye movements with the recitation *(dakṣiṇāg-nipātena dṛṣṭiṃ hanyāt kanīyasīṃ/ nāsāgaṇḍabhruboḥ sandhim udāttaviṣaye viduḥ*—Cā. Ś— p. 6 from Rameshwar Prasad Caturvedi, p. 180). Employing the entire body might be helping the child to retain the text in the memory. This point also needs investigation why certain letters only are selected to be presented through *mudrā* (ka, ṭa, ta, pa, ṅa, na, ma). ls the pronunciation of these consonants subject to get affected by regional dialects?

Here is one more point to be discussed. MŚ is the only Śikṣā, traditionally known as the *Atharvavedīyā Śikṣā.* However it doesn't deal with any special phonetic feature exclusively belonging to the *Atharvaveda* or any special mode of the recitation of the text. A query arises why there is no special śikṣā for *Atharvaveda*? I sincerely maintain that the reason lies in its constitution and the role it plays in the Śrauta Yajña. Out of 20 kāṇḍas of the *Atharvaveda*, the entire 20th kāṇḍa heavily drags from *Ṛgveda*. Out of the remaining portion, the 1/6 portion is borrowed from *Ṛgveda*. These being the ṛk-(s) and not the yajus, the general rules of the pronunciation of the *Ṛgveda* can easily account for the *Atharvaveda*.

Though a brahman is supposed to belong to the *Atharvaveda* tradition, he doesn't perform any special karma, where the Atharvaveda mantras are employed. In iṣṭikarma only the Brahman needed. With the severe set back to Śrautakarma, the Śrautayajña-(s) also stopped. This situation might have affected the Atharvaveda oral tradition. Even the *Atharvaveda Saṃhitā* doesn't have aṣṭavikṛtis. This might have been the reason for the Atharvaveda not having its own Śikṣā–(s).

To conclude:

(1) The *Atharvaveda Māṇḍūkī Śikṣā* doesn't shed any light on exclusively *Atharvaveda* recitation.
(2) It being a compilation, belongs to sāmānya śikṣā group and bears the feature of a primary/introductory text.
(3) Hence it belongs to later bulk of the śikṣā and implies the period when Atharvaveda had become weakened.
(4) Because of the constitution of Atharvaveda and its role in Śrautayajña the phonetic speciality might not have developed which might have affected its Śikṣā texts.

8

ŚABDABRAHMAVILĀSA: AN UNPUBLISHED COMMENTARY ON THE TAITTIRĪYA PRĀTIŚĀKHYA

NIRMALA RAVINDRA KULKARNI

The Taittirīya Prātiśākhya (TPr) holds an important position among the Lakṣaṇa texts. It is mainly because it presents a systematic disposal of various concepts either of phonetics or phonology. It is survived with eleven commentaries. Two commentaries on the TPr have been lost, five are published and the remaining ones are waiting to see the light of the day. The present paper takes note of Śabdabrahmavilaśa an incomplete single codex composed by Vīra Rāghava Kavi.

Śabdabrahmavilāsa

(1) Description of the Manuscript

The manuscript lies in the Government Oriental Manuscript Library, Madras (MT 2450, a) and is transcribed in Grantha Script from a Ms of V. Gopalacharya of Villiyambakkam (Chingelpet dist.) It is extended in 30 folios i.e. 60 pages, yet it is incomplete. In 1984 I had personally visited the said library and made a transcript with the help of Pandit S.N. Bhaskar. In the beginning he dictated me the contents and after my return to Pune he transcribed the remaining folios and sent it to me by post. The analysis which I am presenting in this paper is based on the said transcript.

(2) *The Author*

The description of the manuscript in the catalogue gives just one line description of the author as follows: A commentary . . . by Vira Raghava Kavi, son of Laksmi belongs to Desika family of Conjeevaram' i.e. Kanjeevaram. This information is based on the description given by the author himself in the introductory verses.

The verse reads as follows:

Lakṣmīnandana-tāta-deśikakula-kṣīrābdhilabdhodayaḥ/
Yo'tānītavanisutā-priyatamaprītyai prabandhān bahūn/
So'yam śrotriya-vīrarāghavakaviḥ kartum samujjṛmbhate/
Śabdabrahmavilāsam āgamagavi-lakṣmaja-modapradam[1]//

On the basis of this description the following things could be known :

(1) Vīra Rāghava Kavi hailed from a Deśika family.
(2) He was a son of Lakṣmī.
(3) He had composed many texts to please the king. He has neither specified the king nor the texts.
(4) He himself was a Śrotriya, a Brahmin well-versed in Vedas.
(5) He aspired to compose a text called Śabdabrahmavilāśa. He has narrated the importance of the text by using a *rūpaka* of cow. He has compared the Vedic texts with a cow. In general, identification of any cow is done on the basis of the signs—either natural or owner made. These signs are called *'lakṣma'*, e.g. if a particular cow is identified with a white patch on her forehead it will be a *lakṣma,* mark of identification for her. The owner of that cow will recognize her with the help of that particular identification mark. If cows of a particular family are branded with a sign of *svastika, svastika* will be a *lakṣma.* Vīra Rāghava Kavi has compared the Āgama texts with a cow. Each of the Vedic branches

bears special identification marks. To explain his contention with my example, in the Śukla Yajurvedic texts certain words use the phoneme *j*' in place of '*y*.' This is a special feature, *lakṣma* of the said school. Only the scholars acquainted with the recitational or analytical practice will notice these special features as the owner of a cow might have noticed; and they will be pleased to receive the text. Without the knowledge of such signs it is difficult to identify the Vedic branches. Thus, the author has skillfully mentioned the essence of the '*lakṣaṇa*' texts that explain the special characteristic marks, the lakṣmas.

In the next two verses he enlists commentaries of the TPr viz. Ātreya Bhāṣya, Māhiṣeya Bhāṣya, Bhāṣya of Vararuci, Tribhāṣyaratna (TR) based on these three and another commentary which has criticized TR very often i.e. Vaidikābharaṇa (VB) of Gargya Gopāla Yajvan. Thereafter, he gives details of the *uddeśa* i.e. the objectives of his texts.

Objective of the Śabdabrahmavilāsa

According to Vīra Rāghava Kavi the TPr is misinterpreted by the earlier Bhāṣyakāras viz. Tribhāṣyaratnakāra and Gārgya Gopāla Yajvan, author of the Vaidikābharaṇa. He specifies that the Tribhāsyaratnakāra was often condemned by the VB. He wants to interpret it correctly for the pleasure of Vedic scholars.

Ātreyo Māhiṣeyo vararucir api ca prātiśākhyasya cakruḥ/
Vyākhyām bhāsyaṇyamīṣām anuvidadhad atha trīṇi kaścid vipaścit/
Vyātānvīd bhāṣyaratnam tad anupadam avādhīrayat ko'pi dhīraḥ/
Kiñcit Sañcintayāmaḥ sadasad iha vayam vedavinmodavṛdhyai//

The author is confident about his capability of interpreting the text. He confidently says that he aims at the correct interpretation by contesting the interpretations of TR and VB.

Yatra tribhāṣyaratnasya vaidikābharaṇasya ca/
Spardhām badhvā 'tra śuddhārtham addhā nirdhārayāmyaham//

He further specifies that he will raise altogether new doubts, and not in the spirit of simply as opponent, but he will use his entire skill to tear up their views.

Navyam karomi cākṣepah kākṣeyakam ihāsakṛt/
Na tat pratibhaṭāṭopaḥ pāṭanasphuṭapāṭavam//

A Completely New Introduction to the Prātiśākhya Literature:

The introductory verses thereafter give an altogether new introduction to the Prātiśākhya literature. According to Vīra Rāghava Kavi the Vedas were revealed by Brahmā to the world. To protect these texts Hanumān has created the Prātiśākhya type of Lakṣaṇa texts. Out of these the Adhvaryus read the TPr. He has quoted a verse of Agasti to support his claim that the composer of the Prs is Hanumān.[2] The verse is from the Rāmāyaṇa. Indian tradition also includes Hanumān among nine grammarians. To my dismay I could search a book in Google entitled 'The Monkey Grammarian' by Octavio Paz a Nobel Prize winner for literature from Mexico (Paz, 1990). He has printed a photograph of a picture of Hanumān on paper belonging to eighteenth century AD. To mark his scholarship Hanumān has been painted amongst the written passages in that drawing. As has been discussed in the above paragraph, Vīra Rāhava believes that the Pr literature is a composition of Hanumān; he being the son of Vāyu. Ātreya, Māhiṣeya and Vararuci have commented on the text composed by Hanumān. According to the Somayārya and Gārgya Gopāla Yajvan however, the TPr is composed by Ātreya. The same Ātreya also wrote a *svopajña bhāṣya*[3] on it. With this innovative introduction he begins his commentary.

(1) The first sūtra of the TPr is *'atha varṇasamāmnyāyaḥ/*

Vīra Rāghava has focused on refuting the interpretation of the word *'atha'* by the VB. First he has analyzed the exposition of TR. According to a floating maxim the word *'atha'* in general should be employed in the following three contexts: (a) as an auspicious word (*maṅgalārtha*), (b) to denote the sequential position of something (*ānantaryārtha,* (c) as a section heading (*adhikārārtha*).[4] Accordingly Somayārya, the author of the TPr has explained these three purposes behind the employment of the word *atha* by the TPr. However, the VB has taken objection to the interpretation *ānantaryārtha* by quoting a traditional maxim, *'tu, atha, eveti vinivartaka, adhikāraka* and *avadhārakam*' i.e. the particles *tu, atha,* and *eva* refute the earlier view, mark the section heading and stamp the emphasis respectively, Vīra Rāghava questions his objection with hair-splitting arguments and concludes that the word *'atha'* in the first *sūtra* is used only as *maṅgalārtha.* "*Tasmāt athaśabdo anyatra adhikārārtho' pi prathamasūtre maṅgala-mātrārthakaḥ ityeva siddham.*" Thus, in accordance with his objective he has refuted the standpoints of both the commentators.

(2) The second part of the *sūtra* is *'varṇasamāmnāya'*. Both the commentators have interpreted the word *varṇasamāmnāya* to denote the serial order of phonemes beginning with *'a'* and ending in *'svarabhakti.'* Vīra Rāghava holds a strong objection to this interpretation.

"Dvābhyāmapi tābhyāmakarādikramabaddha-
svarabhaktiparyantavarṇasvarūpa
nirupaṇamātraparamidaṁ śāstramityuktam bhavati/
taccānupapannam/ akārādīnāmanirūpaṇāt."

According to him the phonemes *'a'* etc are not cited in the TPr. One cannot know the nature of vowels just on the basis of the statement 'the sixteen from the beginning are vowels.'[5] According to Vīra Rāghava if one interprets the word *'atha'* as *'adhikārārtha'* then absence of list of phonemes will be a lacuna in the structure of the TPr. However, if it is interpreted only as an auspicious word and the word *samāmnāya* if is interpreted as traditionally laid down by the Śikṣāśāstra the difficulty will be solved. To quote himself verbatim, *"ānupūrviviśeṣavibhūṣita varṇagaṇamayam āmnāyam stanandhayam iva jananī prathamam akṣatam rakṣati śikṣā."*

Concluding Remarks

What is explained in this paper is a synopsis of just ten pages. The work extends up to approximately forty pages. On the basis of these ten pages it could be said that the author seems to be well trained not only in Vedic learning, but also in other Śāstras like Nyāya, Mīmāṁsā etc. He seems to have command over Shastric form of explanation. Apparently the text bears a stamp of *vitaṇḍā* type of arguments as seen in texts like *'Khaṇḍanakhaṇḍakhādya.'* However, one has to go through the text very carefully to judge the arguments presented therein. At least today I could not collect any information of the author. On the basis of the available documentation in the printed catalogues the text should be regarded as having a single manuscript. It is possible that the efforts of National Mission Manuscripts may bring to light more manuscript material. Furthermore, one also should peep in the historical context of the text. Some texts could be the results of either academic rivalry or political rivalry. It could be summarized in just one sentence that the Śabdabrahmavilāsa is a unique and worth studying commentary.

References

1. Tr. Vīra-Rāghava Kavi, son of Lakṣmī and (Kumāra?) Tāta, born in

the family of Deśika's, who has composed many texts for the love of the king, the same Śrotriya, well-versed in the Vedic recitation aims at composing Śabdabrahmavilāsa which may give pleasure to those who know the signs of Vedic recitation.

2. *Sītāpatiduto vātātmajah/*
   Nahyasya kaścit sadṛśo'sti śāstre vaiśārade chandagatau tathaiva/
   Sarvāsu vidyāsu tapo vidhane praspandate yam hi guruḥ surāṇām//
3. *Śikṣoktam svamatam āha*' VB, on the TPr. 17.8
4. *'Tu, atha, evaiti vinivartaka' dhikāraka' vadhārakāḥ' iti paribhāṣānurodhāt adhikārārthavam api abhāśiṣṭa*
5. *Śoḍaśāditaḥ svarāḥ/*

9

THE IMPORTANCE OF STUDYING PRĀTIŚĀKHYAS WITH SPECIAL REFERENCE TO THE VĀJASANEYĪ PRĀTIŚĀKHYA

SITANATH DEY

As the Vedas were transmitted in the early days by oral tradition, and not by writing it is but natural that importance of phonetics was indicated right from the beginning. 'Vāc' or personified speech is celebrated in one whole hymn in the Ṛgveda (X-I25), where the deity 'Vāc' describes herself and major portion on the another hymn (Rv. 71) is devoted to the same deity.

The traditional title for Phonetics 'Śikṣā' appears for the first time in the Taittirīya Upaniṣad (1.2) which gives a bare enumeration of the six elements constituting it, namely, 'Varṇa' (individual sound), 'Svara' (accents), 'mātrā' (quantity), 'bala' (organs of pronounciation), 'Sāman' (delivery) and 'Santāna' (euphonic loss). The scope of 'Śikṣā,' one of the six Vedāngas, was restricted in accordance with the aforesaid 'Śikṣādhyāya' of the Tai. Upaniṣad, to the teaching of correct pronunciation of individual sounds, accents etc. relating to chanting of Vedic verses. Almost similar type of the definition of Śikṣā is seen in the observation of celebrated Vedic scholar, M. Winternitz.

'Śikṣā actually means 'instruction,' then in particular instruction in reciting i.e. in correct pronunciation, accentuation etc. of the Saṃhitā texts (H.I. Literature, Vol.-l). The main objective of Śikṣā Vedāṇga was therefore, the maintenance of proper pronunciation and accentuation of Vedic verses. Among the ancient Śikṣās, Yāyñavalkya Śikṣā and Pāniniya Śikṣā are worth mentioning in view of their popularity in dealing with the subject matter aptly. There is interrelation and unity between 'Śikṣā' and 'Prātisākhya' so far as their subject matter is concerned.

It is quite natural that the vast realm of Vedic Saṃhitās were divided into a number of recensions (Śākhās). Every school of these recensions have their own way of dealing with accentuation, pronunciation etc. and hence the different Prātiśākhyas were evolved out of the original Śikṣā Vedānga. Although the title Śikṣā itself came to be applied later to the Prātiśākhyas, we may demarcate the respective spheres of the Śikśās and the Prātiśākhyas thus: As associates of Śiksa Vedanga, the Pratisakhyas too deal with the subjects of Śikṣā. The scope of Śikṣā as told by Sayana is—alphabets, accent and mode of pronunciation of letters.

'वर्णस्वराद्युच्चारणप्रकारो यत्रोपदिश्यते सा शिक्षा' (ऋक् भाष्यभूमिका)

The scope of Prātiśākhya is wider than Śikṣā since it deals with both Śikṣā (Phonetics) and Vyākarana (grammar) as well. In order to indicate the importance of Prātiśākhyas, Uvata, the celebrated vedic commentator says that one cannot claim his right to recite vedic verses properly unless he acquires the skill of recitation through the proper knowledge of Prātiśākhya

"जपादौ नाधिकारोऽस्ति सभ्यक् पाठमजानतः।
प्रातिशाख्यमतो ज्ञेयं सम्यक् पाठस्य सिद्धये॥"

(Uvata bhāṣya on V. P.l.l.)

As already told, due to wider scope of dealing with the subject matter of Śikṣā the extant Prātiśākhya treatises of different Saṃhitās, obviously, became more popular than the Śikṣā Vedāṇga itself and their studies were treated as essential.

The extant Prātiśākhya of the Ṛgveda is the Sākala Prātiśākhya (Ṛgveda Prātiśakhya) of Sāunaka. The Taittirāya Prātiśākhya of the Kṛṣna-yajurveda quotes several caraṇas of this Veda. The extant Prātiśākhya of the Vājasaneyi Saṃhitā or Śuklayajurveda is Vājasaneyi Prātiśākhya of Kātyāyana. The Prātiśākhyas of the Sāmaveda are Sāma Prātiśākhya and Puspasūtra. The Rg. tantra-vyakarana, another prātiśākhya of the Sāmaveda is post Paninian. The Prātiśākhya of the Atharvaveda called the Śaunakiya caturādhyāyikā belongs to Śaunakīya School of the Atharvavedins. Though these Prātiśākhyas are said to be the ancillary of the Śikṣā, yet they are in no way of lesser importance than the Śikṣā. Rather, in the gravity of the contents and volume, Prātiśākhyas definitely enjoy a higher status.

The importance of the phonetic observation of the Prātiśākhya treatises may be highlighted in the following manner :

When the Prātiśākhyas and Panini deal with Phonology and Panini treats of morphology their observations are based on the linguistic phenomena of a living language used by the cultured and educated classes for conversation of literature. For a proper analysis of the gradual evolution of the history of Vedic literature and Sanskrit language at large, the importance of the study of Prātiśākhya treatises are unparallel. Although Prātiśākhyas are associated with Śikṣā Vedāṅga mainly, not the Vyākaraṇa, still amazedly we find the treatment of grammatical analysis to some extent in some of the Prātiśākhyas specially to that of Vājasaneyi. It is generally admitted that the Vedas specially the Ṛgveda is the oldest literary monument of the world. The vast Vedic literature was handed down from time immemorable from generation to generation through oral tradition by means of unique technique of the six Vedangas, specially that of Prātiśākyas which are part and parcel of the Śikśā Vedānga. In the matter of retaining the age-old Vedic lore in non-corrupted manner the unique contribution and importance of Prātiśākhyas should be ever remembered.

The primary aim of the Vājasaneyi Prātiśākhya is to conserve the correct pronunciation of the verses of Vājasaneyi Saṃhitā. The statement made by Kātyāyana, the author of Vājasaneyi Prātiśākhya, about the mode of Vedic learning is very explicit. He also not have much faith on mere reading rather he has emphasized on understanding of the Vedic texts. He wants a reader to clearly understand the faults in the pronunciation of the letters or articulate sounds. He also states carefully the scopes of a study. He believes that unless the reader is familiar with necessary grammatical aspects of Vedic language, Vedic texts cannot be properly understood. Hence for the purpose of proper understanding the purport of a vedic text, the proper knowledge of the phonetical, morphological aspects of the vedic language is essential. Herein lies the importance of intensive study of the Prātiśākhyas, specially that of Vājasaneyi Prātiśākhya for the sake of right pronunciation and for understanding of Vedic lore.

10

A COMPUTER BASED MANUSCRIPT EDITOR

P. Ramanujan

Introduction

Facilities to preserve, study and publish information contained in manuscripts (palm leaf, paper, etc.) with the help of advanced computing tools and technologies are welcome in order to unearth the treasures hidden in them for betterment of mankind.

C–DAC has developed a comprehensive Manuscript Processing Software *Pandu-Lipi Samshodhak* for the purpose.

Background

Having evolved PC-ISCII standards for proper representation of all Sanskrit and Vedic character set in computers, developed an exhaustive knowledgebase of Vedas, Vedāṅgas and Upāṅgas and application programs for the fourteen Vidyāsthānas and tools and utilities like editor, index, search, concordance etc., we now undertake to extend these to the deciphering of manuscripts in scripts like Grantha, Nandinagari, Telugu, Malayalam etc., of Sanskrit/Vedic texts, many of which are not yet published.

It also helps collation of various version/variant forms of texts from different sources for critical editions of such rare, unpublished works in these domains.

Features

The functional modules of the system cover acquisition, formatting, inputting, indexing, creating database, searching, locating, printing, collation and publishing.

The range of texts covered include Shastric texts, Rgveda, Krishna-yajurveda, Sāmaveda, Lakshana granthas, texts in Tamil, a combination of Tamil and Sanskrit, called Manupravala, etc., in a variety of scripts. The sample includes about 50 works, 120 manuscripts, 6 scripts and many domains. There are about 3500 leaves (pages) as images to accompany the PC-ISCII texts.

Two of these texts, viz. Shadvimsati Sutra and Yohi Bhashya, are chosen, for illustration and possible publication of a critical edition with a Sanskrit commentary by the author.

Description of the modules
Acquisition

(a) One typically starts with consulting catalogues, indices, lists, reports, etc., of manuscript collection of desired texts through a number of sources—Bibliographic survey.
(b) Select the ones feasible to obtain from the list (shortlisting). Provide for balanced representation of various regions, script and versions (i.e. with commentaries, with accents etc.)
(c) Acquire copies Xeroxed/scanned/microfilmed.
(d) Convert/export to a single (uniform) format i.e. jpeg in the current case. Factors like clarity, condition of original, resolution of scanning and size of the image files, all influence the choice of common format used.

Formatting

The inputs come in variegated forms, when raw, i.e. from the institutions/library collections. Even cost considerations, since usually copies of manuscripts are charged on per-exposure basis and good-quality multi-folio image files while scanning are perfectly possible. We may have 3, 5 or even 10 folios per scanned image. Here the two sides of the folios are in different files and the job of sequencing the image as per text and separation of folios are involved. Numbering them serially according to the text is done.

An important task here, in the case of manuscript bundles containing different texts, is separation of the texts and folios belonging to multiple texts. They must be present in all the works concerned. Usually, libraries offer separation, if catalogued already.

Inputting

We strongly recommend the entry of the data contained in the manuscripts for the purpose of study, word-split, index, search (phrases), editing and collation. This, of course, requires domain experts who can do the job efficiently. And IHG offers expertise in this endeavour.

We also have another possible source for data entry, which is loading text, if the work in the manuscript is one of available digital texts from our repository. (a list of about 250 texts from all Vidyāsthānas is available. C-DAC Indian Heritage Portal would make this available on the web soon).

Adding commentaries, translations, hyperlinks, annotations for collation etc., are the factors necessitating data-entry. Also transliteration, training in rare scripts etc., is enabled. However, efforts may be launched to develop efficient OCR or speech recognition systems of high quality simultaneously and when these mature, we can minimize data entry needed.

Editing

This step involves aligning the data entered, with the original manuscript, line by line and page by page. This also can be done in an edit-box/window below (or adjacent to) the image of the manuscript or entered through Vedic Editor and inserted into the database. The pages and line boundaries are as before. Adding information for retrieval, hyperlinks etc., can also be done.

Multilingual texts, currently require LEAP-like software for data entry and use in RTF format in the system for further processing. Here ISCII-ISFOC conversions are employed.

Currently Vedic texts of Sāmaveda Gāna require use of only Grantha script and transliteration is not available. Śrautam and Guruparamparā Prabhāva etc. are multilingual samples. These are typed in LEAP and processed through rtf controls.

Creating database

The PC-ISCII text files (*.pci) created by data entry or loading data are to be converted into database format. This is either Microsoft Access or Microsoft FoxPro format covering various fields for facilitating info. retrieval. There is a utility that converts from aci/pci format to db format.

Databases of works, institutions, manuscripts, books etc., are also created and linked in the application list of abbreviations. Scheme of data for reference in these texts etc. are also created as tables.

Searching

This is the crux of the system and helps in providing word or phrase level search (with and without accent-markers) across the database, textwise, and lists the Manuscript ref. nos. where the search string occurs. In future, we can even extend this across texts if need be (this feature is there in our Vedic Editor, wherein a string occurring in any of the 250+ texts are listed as a concordance).

Choice of script, facility to transliterate, and seeing the results in the same manner of alignment as in the manuscript are the useful aspects.

Locating

This refers to locating the search string in the image of

the particular page of the manuscript where it occurs including the line number and location in it. We see the string 'highlighted' in the text window by choosing 'find' in the page and physically looking in the corresponding line and 'location' in it on the image above by selecting view in 'search' mode. The text window is provided with line numbers to facilitate this manual locating in the image.

Printing

Provision to print the texts in database, search results etc., in any script of choice or script of the original etc. so that further reference or insertion into documents can be enabled. Report geneartion kind of printing needs can also be addressed. List of texts, institutions, reference details etc. can be printed.

Collation

From the search function, we can organise the readings of different texts (like 'file compare') across the manuscripts combined with report generators. A scheme for annotating can be devised to assist here. Work will follow to enrich features here.

Publishing

Publication through Desk-top-publishing can be done by exporting to some DTP software and adding embellishments as desired.

Annexure - Dataflow chart of the system
Screen shots of some of the modules
List of texts and detailed List of manuscripts

I do hope the new generation will be successful to carry forward the use of computer to decipher, transliterate and collate the manuscript.

11

IN SEARCH OF THE LOST MĀṆḌUKEYA TRADITION: A PHONETIC REFERENCE IN THE ṚK-PRĀTIŚĀKHYA

MAU DAS GUPTA

J. Gonda: 29 remarks in accordance with L. Renou: 28: 'Already at an early time the contents of the Ṛg-veda—like the other Vedas, . . . —must have been transmitted in, and to a certain extent have developed as, independent traditions of 'branches" (*śākhā*).' The characteristic feature of these *śākhās* or Vedic 'schools' has been elaborated by Gonda: o.c.l.c., 'Tradition has it that this name is given to those 'schools' which possess a recension of the *samhitā* of their own, on contradistinction to the subdivisions called *caraṇa* which are not in possession of such a text.' According to the *Caraṇa-vyūha*, the only comparatively ancient source dealing with the *śākhās*, there were five recensions or schools of the Ṛg-veda: Śākala, Bāṣkala, Āśvalāyana, Śāṅkhāyana and Māṇḍūkeya. According to Macdonell: 51, there was actually no difference between the Āśvalāyana and Śāṅkhāyana schools, the sole distinction between them and the Śākalas having been that the Āśvalāyanas recognized eleven Vālakhilya hymns as canonical, and the Śāṅkhāyanas admitted the same group only diminished by a few verses. That is why the later Puranic tradition does not recognize the Āśvalāyana and Śāṅkhāyana schools and mentions only the three schools of Śākala, Bāṣkala and Māṇḍūkas (cf. *Devī-purāṇa* 107.15). Macdonell (o.c.l.c.) further remarks that if the Māṇḍūkeya tradition ever had a recension of an independent character, all traces of it were lost at an early period in ancient India, for no information of any kind about it has been preserved.

In the critical edition of the Ṛgveda-saṃhitā, C.G. Kashikar: 891 remarks in the preface of his introductory notes on the Khilas of the Ṛg-veda: 'Of these [the five recensions mentioned at the *Caraṇa-vyūha*], the Śākala recension is well known and has come down in a definite form. The other recensions did not differ much from the Śākala recension except an omission or addition of certain hymns or verses within or without the Maṇḍalas and also within or without the hymns, as well as certain changes in the order of hymns or verses. No definite conclusions seem to have been drawn as to the exact nature of these recensions for want of decisive data.

The direction towards the reconstruction of Ṛg-vedic recensions other than the Śākala started taking shape after the discovery of the most important and extensive collection of the Khilas by Prof. Bühler in Kashmir. His description of the same came out as 'Detailed Report of a tour in search of Sanskrit MSS.' in Dr. Phil, J. Scheftelowitz' book titled '*Apokryphen des Ṛg-veda*' published from Bonn in 1906.

At the end of the Khilas in the Kashmir manuscript, some portion of the *Aitareya Āraṇyaka* is placed, which is divided into three adhyāyas, the first two of which form the third Āraṇyaka, some portion of which is called the 'Māṇḍūkeyīya.' Scheftelowitz has suggested that certain of the Khilas represent parts of the Māṇḍūkeya-*saṃhitā,* but Oldenberg and Keith in their respective reviews in 1907 have criticized his theory.

The Prātiśākhyas take account of the phonetic characteristics peculiar to every recension of the concerned Vedas. Thus it is expected that the *Ṛk-prātiśākhya* acted as the repository of the phonetic peculiarities prevailing in all the Ṛg-vedic recensions current at the time of Śaunaka, its author. The name of Māṇḍūkeya occurs only once in the main body of the *Ṛk-prātiśākhya* (3.14). The third *paṭala* (chapter) of this book deals with the accentuation of the Ṛg-vedic mantras. The author broadly follows the School of Śākalya, though he misses not a chance to mention the peculiarities of other Schools. In the course of discussing the emergence of independent *svarita*, four kinds of it have been mentioned there. They are viz. *jātya, abhinihita, kṣaipra* and *praśliṣṭa*. The first of the list is a *svarita* by origin, since it does not come up as a result of any euphonic combination or vowel-sandhi, while the rest are produced when the respective sandhis occur, where the pre-sandhi vowels were *udāta* and *anuddtta* respectively. There too, the *praśleṣa* sandhi (i.e. the euphonic combinations prescribed by the Pāṇinian rules *akaḥ savarṇe dīrghaḥ* 6.1.101, *ād guṇaḥ* 6.1.87 and *vṛddhir eci* 6.1.88) does not always generate a *praśleṣa svarita*. The Śākalya School holds that only the *praśleṣa* between two short *i* vowels produces a *praśliṣṭa svarita*:

ikāmyoś ca praśleṣe kṣaiprābhinihiteṣu ca/
udāttapūrvarūpeṣu śākalyasyaivam ācaret// (ṚP 3.13)

Thus we get *srucīva ghṛtām* (ṚV 10.91.15) where the ultimate *ī* of *srucī* is combined with the initial *i* of *iva,* the former being accented and the latter not, the resultant form is an independent *svarita* termed as *praśliṣṭa*. But on the contrary, according to Māṇḍūkeya, informs Śaunaka, all cases of *praśliṣṭa* sandhi generate *praśliṣṭa svarita* if the accentuations in the pre-sandhi vowels are *udātta* and *anudātta* respectively:

māṇḍukeyasya sarveṣu praśliṣṭeṣu tathā smaret// (ibid 14)

To comment on this *kārikā*, Uvaṭa says: '*māṇḍūkeyasya ācāryasya matena sarveṣu praśliṣṭeṣu tathāsmarat, na tu kuryāt*' (—according to the preceptor Māṇḍūkeya, such is the accentuation in every case of *praśliṣṭa* sandhi, where the first member is *udātta* and the second *anudātta*. But, this custom of Māṇḍūkeya is only to be remembered and not to be practiced.)

The matter can be elaborated with examples

The *saṃhitā*-text being *éndra yāhi hāribhiḥ* (ṚV 8.34.1), the *pada*-text, according to Śākalya, should be like this:

ā/ indra/ y*āhi/ hāri S bhiḥ/*

But, according to Māṇḍūkeya, with the euphonic combination of *ā* and *i* (a case of sandhi by the Pāṇinian rule *ād guṇaḥ*) in the initial word *éndra,* the saṃhitā-text should be read like the following:

endra yāhi hāribhiḥ

Another instance can be taken up where a *praśleṣa* of two i-vowels (one short and the other long, therefore not fulfilling the criterion to produce an independent *svarita*) generates an *udātta* in the usual *saṁhitā*-text:

vī hīm iddho ākhyad ā rodasī (ṚV 10.45.4)

The *pada*-text of the same runs thus:

vī / hi/ īm/ iddhaḥ/ ākhyad/ ā rodasī īti/

But, according to Māṇḍūkeya the *saṃhitā*-text should be pronounced like the following:

vī hīm iddho ākhyad ā rodasī

At ṚP 3.16 (*paraiḥ prathama-bhāvinaḥ*) Śaunaka asserts that the emergence of independent *svaritas* through vowel combinations depends solely on their being *udātta* and *anudātta* in respective order at their pre-sandhi stage. If the order is reverse the resultant form will be an *udātta* as prescribed at ṚP 3.11 (*udāttavatyekībhāva udāttaṃ sandhyam akṣaram*), and not an independent *svarita*, In the commentary of ṚP 3.I6 Uvaṭa elaborates that both the preceptors, viz. Śākalya and Māṇḍūkeya, agree in this matter that the resultant form becomes an *udātta* when the prior member is *anudāta* and latter *udātta* (*parais tūdattair ya ekībhāvās te prathamabhāvinaḥ syuḥ/dvayor apy ācāryayor matenodāttabhārinaḥ syuḥ*).

The name of Māṇḍūkeya is found in the second introductory verse of the *Ṛk-prātiśākhya*. The verse runs thus:

māṇḍūkeyaḥ saṃhitāṃ vāyum āha
tathākāśaṃ cāsya mākṣavya eva/
samānatānile cāmbare ca
matvāgastyo 'viparihāraṃ tad eva//

In these introductory verses, to justify the utility of the study of Prātiśākhya the author tells about the discourse of ancient sages on some tenets of the *Ṛk-prātiśākhya* like *saṃhitā, nirbhuja, pratṛṇṇa* and so on and so forth. Viṣṇumitra, the famous commentator from Campā, remarked in his *Vargadvaya-vṛtti* on the *Ṛk-prātiśākhya,* that the Māṇḍūkeya mentioned in the above verse is none other than the sage Māṇḍūkeya mentioned in the *Aitareya-āraṇyaka* at 3.1.1. In fact, in three consecutive verses constituting the introduction to the *Ṛk-prātiśākhya* the author refers to the discourse on the philosophical significance of *saṃhitā* found at the chapter three of the *Aitareya-āraṇyaka.* The verse quoted above informs that according to Māṇḍūkeya, *saṃhitā* is the wind (*vāyu*), while another preceptor Mākṣavya considers it to be the sky (*ākāśa*). These two views have been equalized by the son of Agastya (Āgastya), since he thinks that both *vāyu* and *ākāśa* can be applied to designate *saṃhitā.* Viṣṇumitra, after the exposition of Sāyaṇa on AĀ 3.1.1, elaborates that it is the philosophical aspect of the symbols like *vāyu* or *ākāśa* that is to be meditated upon and not the actual state of fact, that is why Mākṣavya's contention cannot be considered more adorable than that of Māṇḍūkeya's.

In course of discussing the above-mentioned discourse some more information about Māṇḍūkeya have been related in the said verses, i.e. alternatively called Śūravīra, Māṇḍūkeya had a dispute in spiritual discourse with his son over the priority and posterity of *vāc* (speech) and *manas* (mind): *adhyātmakḷptau śūravīraḥ sutaś ca vāṅmanasayor vivadanty ānupūrvye* (verse no. 4). This comment is again based on the reference found at AĀ 3.1.1, where it is stated that the eldest son of Māṇḍūkeya disagreed with his father on the philosophical symbolization of the two components of sandhi. According to the father—in sandhi of two consecutive letters, the former should be worshipped as speech (*vāc*) and the latter as mind (*manas*). The son, however, preferred to accept the reverse of his father's content since he argued that it is the mind that thinks first and later the speech comes up to express the thought. Here too, the same logic applied to resolve the dispute between Māṇḍūkeya and Mākṣavya, has been used once again: i.e. in context of worshipping the saṁhitā the state of fact is never taken into consideration. The symbols mentioned by the preceptors are to be meditated upon irrespective of their factual existence. Therefore, both the theories propounded by the father and the son are equal, says the Āraṇyaka: '*samānam enayor atra pituś ca putrasya ca.*'

In this way, a long discourse runs through the whole third chapter of the *Aitareya-āraṇyaka*, where among other preceptors of the Vedas, Māṇḍūkeya and Śākalya have been mentioned with prominence. One comes to know from the information provided by the Āraṇyaka that Māṇḍūkeya was a dwarf (*hrasva*) and had several sons, with whom he had philosophical disputes. lt is interesting to note that in *sāmpradāyika* tradition of the Vedic people, inter-school conflict was a common affair, but to witness a conflict between father and sons, of whom the former is a natural preceptor of the latter, is unique.

In conclusion we may suggest that the Māṇḍūkeya mentioned in the AĀ 3.1 may well be considered as the preceptor of the Māṇḍūkeya recension of the Ṛg-veda; since this Āraṇyaka belongs to the Ṛg-veda and the man in question is found engaged in discussion on the philosophical aspects of the *saṃhitā-pāṭha.* The *Ṛk–prātiśākhya* mentions at least one characteristic of that School. It considers that every case of *praśleṣa* sandhi generates *praśliṣṭa svarita* provided the pre-sandhi vowels were respectively accented and unaccented. Despite the fact that their tradition was not in vogue at the time of Śaunaka, to pay tribute to this ancient school, the author of the *Ṛk-prātiśākhya* draws the attention of the learners by saying *'māṇḍūkeyasya sarveṣu praśliṣṭeṣu tathā smaret.'*

Abbreviations

AĀ	Aitareya-āraṇyaka,
RP	Ṛk-prātiśākhya
ṚV	Ṛg-veda]

References

1. Gonda, J. (ed.) (1975) *Vedic Literature* (*Saṁhitās and Brāhmaṇas*). In *A History of Indian Literature,* Vol. I, Fasc. I. Otto Harrassowitz, Wiesbaden.
2. Keith, A.B. (ed.) (I909) *The Aitareya Āraṇyaka.* In *Anecdota Oxoniensia,* reprint I969, Oxford: The University Press.
3. Macdonell, A.A. (1900, 2nd edn. 1925) *A History of Sanskrit Literature,* 3rd Indian edn. 1972, New Delhi: Munshiram Manoharlal.
4. Renou, L. (1947) *Les écoles védiques et la formation du Veda.* In *Êtudes vēdiqueset pāṇinēennes,* vol. 6, Paris.
5. Shastri Talekar, Rahara (ed.) (1959) *Aitareyāraṇyakam* (with the

commentary of Sayana). Poona: Ānandāśrama Press.

6. Sontakke, N.S. and Kashikar, C.G., (eds.) 1933–51. *Ṛgveda-saṃhitā.* Vol. 4. 2nd edn. 1983, Poona: Vaidika Samśodhana Maṇḍala.
7. Verma, Virendra Kumar (ed.) (1970) *Ṛgveda-Prātiśākhya of Śaunaka (along with Uvaṭabhāśya)*, repr., 2007, Delhi: Chaukhamba Sanskrit Pratishthan.

12

UPASARGA IN SANSKRIT LANGUAGE

SUBHENDU MANNA

Introduction:

In the study of Sanskrit language we see Yāska (seventh century BC) has mentioned four divisions of *pada* or word, namely *nāman, ākhyāta upasarga* and *nipāta.*[1] Whereas according to Pāṇini *padas* have two divisions, namely *sub-anta* or *nāman* and *tiṅ-anta* or *ākhyāta.*[2] Bhartṛhari (6th century AD), the great philosopher of Pāṇinian system of Sanskrit grammar, told that sentence is the ultimate part of a language which expresses an indifferent meaning. According to him to understand meaning of a *pada,* separation is imagined between suffix and stem in a *pariniṣṭhita pada* or completely formed word. Comparably to realise meaning of a sentence, there also separation is imagined of words from a complete sentence. Thus Bhartṛhari says—

> *dvidhā kaiś cit padaṃ bhinnaṃ caturdhā pañcadhāpi vā/*
> *apoddhṛtyaiva vākyebhyaḥ prakṛti-pratyayādiva//*[3]

According to few scholars, those imagined *padas* are of two types, i.e. noun *'nāman'* and verb *'ākhyāta'*. If prefixes *'upasarga'* and particles *'nipāta'* are counted separately then words or *padas* will have four divisions. Once more *padas* have five divisions according to them who accept *karma-pravacanīya* as a separate word. Among those divisions of *pada* the term *upasarga* first occurs in Aitareya Brāhmaṇa (XVI/4): *mahānāmnīnām upasargān upasṛjanti.* There *upasarga* means 'addition'.[4] But technically *upasarga* means 'a prefixed word'; cf. *sopasargeṣu nāmasu* (Ṛgveda-Prātiśākhya or ṚP, XVI/38).[5] The derivation of this term is—*upa-sṛj+ ghañ = upasarga.* Here in the derivative word *upa* means 'near' and the root *sṛj* means 'to discharge'. Thus *upasarga* literally means 'discharge near,' then 'addition', then 'addition to the verb'.[6] In Upasargārtha-saṃgraha, an unpublished text, the author Kṛṣṇācārya derives the term *upasarga* as —*pra* etc. a group of words is called *prādi* to which *pra* precedes. The term *prādi* is a *tad-guṇa-saṃvijñāna*[7] Bahuvrīhi compounded word. A word of *prādi* list is called *upasarga* when it is placed near a verbal root.[8] Durga, the commentator of Nirukta (I/I/4), derives *upasarga* as *ākhyātam upa-gṛhyārtha-viśeṣam ime tasyaiva sṛjantīty upasargāḥ.* Skandasvāmin also repeats the same—*upetya nāmākhyātayor arthasya viśeṣṃ sṛjanty utpādayantīty upasargāḥ.*

To define the term *upasarga* Pāṇini has *upasargāḥ kriyā-yoge* (P-I/IV/59). It means the words *pra, parā, apa* etc. are designated as *upasarga* or prefix or preposition when they are in composition with a *kriyā* 'verb'. In Yāska's Nirukta *pra, parā, apa* etc. twenty words are termed as prefix. Those are—*pra, prā, apa, sam, anu, ava, nis, nir, dus, dur, vi, āṅ, ni, adhi, api, ati, su, ut, abhi, prati, pari* and *upa.* In Pāṇinian system of Sanskrit grammar these words are termed as prefix, including *nis* and *dus* (there is *āṅ* instead of Yāska's *ā, a ity arvāg arthe*—Nirukta I/1/5). In brief, this list of words is also called *prādi.* Later grammarians like Vopadeva the author of Mugdhabodha (13th century AD), Padmanābha Datta the author of Supadma (fourteenth century AD), Pandit Ishwar Chandra Vidyasagar the author of Vyākaraṇa Kaumudī (19th century AD), Cidrūpāśrama the author of Dīpa Vyākaraṇa (16th century AD, it's an unpublished text being edited by the present author) and so on have counted twenty prefixes like Yāska. There is a well-known Śloka—

pra-parāpa-sam-anv-ava-nir-dur-abhi-vy-
adhi-sūd-ati-ni-prati-pary-apayaḥ/
upa āṅ iti viṃśatir eṣa sakhe upasarga-
vidhiḥ kathitaḥ kavinā//

(See Gurupada Haldar, p. 345)

In several unpublished short treatises, composed by later Sanskrit grammarians, like Upasargārtha (Manuscript No. G7260), Upasargārtha-saṁgraha. (Manuscript No. G9655), twenty words are termed as prefix. Pāṇini counts *nis* and *dus* only to support his system. Thus Jñānendra Sarasvatī; the author of Tattvabodhinī, a commentary on Siddhānta Kaumudī of Bhaṭṭoji Dīkṣita, explains—*'upasargasyāyatau' iti nir-duror latvam, nilayate, dulayate/niso dusaś ca rutvasyāsiddhatvāl latvabhāvaḥ* (Siddhānta Kaumudī 23. *gatiś ca*). Under the rule *upasargasyāyatau* (SK 2326) Bhaṭṭoji Dīkṣita says—*nis-duso rutvasyāsiddhatvān na latvam/nirayate/durayate/nir-duros tu nilayate dulayate.* According to *upasargasyāyatau* (P. VIII/II/19) when the root *ay* follows, *l* becomes substitute for *r* of a prefix. Thus when *s* of the prefix *dus* and *nis* is changed to *r* by the Pāṇinian rule *sa-sajuṣo ruḥ* (P. VIII/II/66) and when it is followed by the root √ay, *l* should be the substitute of *r*. But there according to *pūrvatrāsiddham* (P. VIII/II/1) the rule *upasargasyāyatau* (P. VIII/II/19) becomes *asiddha* 'invalid'. So *dus-√ay+ta* = *durayate* and *nis-√ay + ta* = *nirayate* these two words are formed. To derive *dulayate* and *nilayate* Pāṇini counts these two words, i.e. *dur* and *nir* in the list of prefix. Thus Vāsudeva Dīkṣita says in his commentary namely Bālamanoramā—*tarhi nilayate dulayate iti katham ity ata āha nir duros tv iti/etad-artham eva prādiṣu sāntayo rephāntayoś ca nirdeśa iti bhāvaḥ* (under SK 2326. *upasargasyāyatau*). The author of Bṛhaddevatā says that according to Śākaṭāyana *accha, śrat* and *antar* also should be termed as prefix as they are also used being connected to verbs. In Upasargārthasaṃgraha of Kṛṣṇācārya and in Laghūpasarga-dīpikā adding *śrat, antar* and *āvir* the number of prefixes has been increased to 25.[9]

In the colophon of the text the author writes—*iti pañca-viṃśati upasargāḥ saṃpūrṇāḥ,* i.e. here the description of 25 prefixes ends.[10] In Taittirīya-Prātiśākhya (TP) *ā, pra, ava, upa, abhi, adhi, prati, pari, vi* and *ni* only these ten words are termed as *upasarga.*[11] The commentator Somayārya says, though in Nirukta, Pāṇinian and other systems of Sanskrit grammar there are twenty or twenty two prefixes but TP has mentioned only ten, as in the Yajur-veda no more prefix is found other than those.[12]

In Sanskrit language prefixes are preplaced to a verbal root.[13] Example from classical Sanskrit—*so' dhy-aiṣṭa vedāṃs-tridaśān ayaṣṭa pitṝn apārīt sam-amaṃsta bandhūn/ vy–ajeṣṭa ṣaḍ-vargam araṃsta nītau samūla-ghātaṃ ny-avadhīd arīṃś ca/ /* (Bhaṭṭi-kāvya 1/2). Here in this Śloka there are several examples of prefixes which precede verbal root. In *adhy-aiṣta adhi* is employed before the verbal root *aiṣṭa.* Prefix *sam* is employed before the verbal root *amaṃsta* in *sam-amaṃsta.* In the *pada vy-ajeṣta* prefix *vi* is preplaced to the verbal root *ajeṣṭa.* In *ny-avadhīd* prefix *ni* is followed by verbal root *avadhīd.* Example from Vedic text–*prati tyaṃ cārum adhvaraṃ gopithāya pra-hūyase/marudbhir agna ā-gahi* (Ṛgveda I/19/1). In this mantra prefix *pra* and *ā* are uttered before verbal roots *hūyase* and *gahi* correspondingly. In Vedic language prefixes are also seen indifferently after the verbal root, as well as before it.[14] E.g. *vāya-indraś ca sunvata āyātam upa niṣkṛtam/ makṣvitthā dhiyā narā* (Ṛgveda 1/2/6) - here in this mantra prefix *upa* is employed after the verbal root *āyātam.* In classical Sanskrit this should be *upāyātam.* One example is - *yāti ni hastinā.*[15] Here prefix *ni* is uttered indifferently after the verb *yāti.*[16] In Vedas prefixes are also seen separated from verbal root by intervening words. E.g. *upa tvāgne dive dive doṣāvastar dhiyā vayam/namo bharanta emasi* (Ṛgveda I/1/7)—here in this mantra *upa-ā-imasi* is a single *pada.* But the prefix *upa* is uttered separately from the verbal root intervening by several words. Here is one more example—*pari pūṣā parastād dhastaṃ dadhātu dakṣiṇam/ punar no naṣṭam ājatu* (Ṛgveda VI/54/10). Prefix *pari* should be connected with the verbal root *dadhātu*. But those are separated by three *padas*.

Accentuation and sound changings of Prefix in Vedic language:

In Vedic language there are several instances where phonetic changes of prefixes are found. Now we may notice those examples by the help of Prātiśākhyas, related to a particular branch of the Vedas. Here is a very little description of phonetic changes of prefixes citing examples from corresponding Saṃhita-texts. Ṛgveda-Prātiśākhya of Śaunaka, Vājasaneyi-Prātiśākhya (VP) of Kātyāyana, Taittirīya-Prātiśākhya (TP), Atharvaveda-Caturadhyāyikā (AC), Ṛk-tantra (ṚT), Aṣṭādhyāyī of Pāṇini, Phiṭ-sūtra etc. have lightened this matter. Paṇini has described accentuation system of prefixes in general. But to know more phonetic changes of prefixes, we should go through Pratiśākhyas, which describe special changes of accentuation of prefixes in a special branch of Veda.

In Ṛgveda-Prātiśākhya Śaunaka says, accent of vowels of all the nine monosyllabic *upasargas* should be acute *'udātta;'* e.g. *prā, ā, nīs, dús* etc., whereas accent of foremost vowel or *svara* will be acute *'udātta'* of rest prefixes except *abhi;* e.g. *párā, ánu, úpa* etc. Final vowel *i* of *abhi,* will be acute accent; i.e. *abhí.*[17]

In Vājasaneyi-Prātiśākhya Kātyayāna has beautifully described the accentuation of prefixes according to the Vājasaneyi-Saṁhitā (VS). When a prefix follows another prefix changes its acute accent to grave accent.[18] E.g. *sam-prá-cyavadhvam úpa samprá-yā́tā́gne pathó devayā́nā́n kṛṇudhvam* (VS-XV/53)—here in this mantra *sam-prá-cyavadhvam* and *sam-prá-yātā́gne* are two suitable examples where *sam* is followed by *pra.* Thus the acute vowel of *sam* changed to grave accent. *upasarga upasarge* (VP- VI/2)—this rule has several exceptions in VS. In *abhi-prehi, upa-sam-prayāta, praty-ā-tanuṣva* and *ā-su-ṣāva* acute vowel of foremost prefix doesn't change its accent to grave.[19] Once more acute vowel of the prefix *ā* and *upa* doesn't become change to grave if acute *pra* follows. E.g. *vaiśvānaró na ūtáya ā́ prá-yātu parāvátaḥ* (VS- VIII/72)—here in this mantra *prá* follows *ā́* but *ā́* doesn't change its accent. One more example—*úpaprā́gācchásanam* (VS- XXIX/23).[20]

According to *nipātā ādy-udāttāḥ* (Phiṭ-sūtra-80), first vowel of *upa* should be acute *'udātta'*. But if side by side a prefix repeats in a mantra, vowel of the later prefix will be grave accent '*anudātta*.'[21] E.g. *úpopénnú magһávan bhúya īnnú te dā́na devásya pṛcyate* (VS-III/34)—here in this mantra *pada úpopénnú* is our example where the prefix *upa* is repeated. Thus acute or *udātta u* of later *upa* changed to grave *anudātta*' Here is one more example—*déva tvaṣṭarbhúri te sāṃ-sam-etu sálakṣmā yádvipurūpambhávāti* (VS-VI/20)—here in this mantra prefix *sam* is repeated. Thus the acute vowel of second *sam* is changed to grave. According to the rule *kṛd-ākhyātayoś codāttayoḥ* (VP-VI/4) if a primary-suffixed *'kṛdanta'* word or a conjugated word follows, of which foremost vowel is acute accent, acute vowel of a prefix will be grave '*anudātta*'. E.g. *agnīṃ svar ābhárantaḥ* (VS-XV/49) or *vi-bhrā́jamānaḥ sarirásya mádhye* (VS-XV/52)—in these two mantras *bhárantaḥ* and *bhrā́jamānaḥ* are *kṛdanta* words which are preceded by *ā* and *vi*. Thus acute vowels of those two prefixes changed to grave. Now example of a prefix, followed by conjugated word of which foremost vowel is acute-accented, is given here. *ye cā́rvate pácanaṃ sam-bháranty uto teṣāṃ abhi-gūrttina invatu* (VS-XXV /29)—here in this mantra conjugated word *bhā́ranti* follows prefix *sam* and its fore most vowel is acute. Thus the acute vowel of *sam* becomes grave-accented. The commentator says where this rule is not followed; prefix would be a separate word or *pada* according to the rule *svarita-varjam ekodāttaṃ padam* (VP-II/1).[22] In VS when an acute-accented word, except *kṛdanta,* follows, vowel of the monosyllabic prefix and of *abhi,* doesn't change its accent if there a vowel euphonic combination *'svara sandhi'* happens. E.g. *abhyāvarttasva pṛthivi yajñena páyasā sahá* (VS-XII/103) - here in this mantra acute-accented word *ā́varttasva* follows *abhi*. Thus *abhi* doesn't change its accent. *yábhir mitrā-varuṇāv abhy-áṣiñcan* (VS-X/1)—here in this mantra acute-accented word *āṣiñcan* follows *abhi*. Thus *abhi* doesn't change its accent. Now an example of monosyllabic prefix is given here which doesn't change its acute accent. *dṛṣṭvā rūpe vyā́karot satyānṛte prajāpatiḥ* (VS-XL/77).[23] In VS prefixes don't change their accent when a few special words follow them. Kātyāyana has the rule—*ā pūta-jātayoḥ* (VP- VI/6). When *pūta* and *jāta* these two *kṛdanta* words follow, acute accent of the prefix *ā* doesn't become changed to grave. E.g. *údīdābhyaḥ śúcir ā́-pūtā emi* (VS-IV/2) and *agnīr bhānúnā rúśatā svánga ā́-jótó viśvā sádmānyaprāḥ* (VS-XII/13). In a mantra of VS when *kṛdanta* words *śrita, atriṇam, bhānavaḥ* and *pacata* follow *adhi, ni, pra* and *prati* correspondingly, vowels of these four prefixes don't become changed to grave.[24] Once more acute vowel of *anu* will not be changed to grave if *ujjeṣam, āvarte, āpanīphaṇat, saniṣyadat, saṃvatam, prayāṇam, sañcarantam, saṃrabhadhvam, prasitim* and *vikramasva* these words follow.[25] E.g. *agnī-ṣómayor újjitim ánū́jjeṣaṃ vā́jasya mā prasavéna próhāmi* (VS II/15).

In Taittirīya-Prātiśākhya, a few euphonic changes, by the influence of prefixes, are noticed. Cerebralisation of dental *s* is described in sixth chapter. A dental *s* is converted into cerebral *ṣ* in an unaccented *pada,* when a prefix or *nis* precedes.[26] In third chapter of eighth book of Aṣṭādhyāyī, Pāṇini has provided thirteen rules corresponding to this.[27] E.g. *aśmann ūrjam iti pari-ṣiñcan* (Taittirīya Saṁhitā or TS V/IV/4), *imaṃ vi-ṣyāmi* (TS-I/II/10), *yajamāne prati-ṣṭhāpayanti* (TS-VI/I/4) etc. In Atharva-veda-Caturadhyāyikā *upasargād dhātoḥ* (AC-II/90) corresponds to this rule of TP. "Thc commentator selects as illustrations these two: *vṛkshaṃ yad gâvaḥ parishasvajānâ anusphuram* (i.2.3: p. *pari-sasvajānāḥ; anusphuram* is an exception to the rule, akin with those detailed in rule 102, below), and *vishitaṃ teieastibilam* (i.3.8 : p *vi-sitam)*. As counter-examples, to show that it is only after a preposition that the initial *s* of a root is regularly converted into *sh,* the commentator fabricates a couple of cases, viz. *dadhi siñcati, madhu siñcati;* the former of them appears also among the counter examples under the corresponding rule of Pāṇini (viii.3.65). The proper exceptions to the rule are detailed below, in rules 102–7.

The Taitti. Pr. (vi 4) has a general rule for the change of an initial *s* after a preposition: the other two Prātiśākhyas rehears the case in detail (R. Pr. v.4–10; V.Pr. iii. 58–70)."[28]

Instead of Pāṇini's rule *upasargād ṛti dhātau* (P-VI/I/91) TP says when *ṛ* follows if a prefix, ending in *a* or *ā,* there *ār* would be substitute of both.[29] E.g. *upārcchati* (TS IV/9), *avārcchati* (TS-II/VI/3), *ṛtavyā upopārttavyā ṛtavyā upa* (TS-V/III/1) etc. Once more in the fourteenth chapter TP has noticed the augmentation of cognate sound when a prefix precedes *cha, khi* and *bhuja.*[30] Commentator Somayārya has given several suitable examples quoting from TS. Like *ā-cchṛṇatti* (TS-V/I/7), *nama ā-kkhidate ca prakkhidate ca* (TS-IV/V/9), *ayakṣmayā pari-bbhuja* (TS-IVN/1).

Expressiveness and Indicativeness of Prefix:

Since very early period there are different views about the meaning of prefix and particles in Sanskrit studies. We get earliest evidence on this contradiction in the Nirukta (seventh century BC) where the author Yāska has mentioned two different views about the meaning of prefix. In Nirukta Yāska quotes two predecessors, Śākaṭāyana & Gārgya. According to Śākaṭāyana, ". . . when prefixes are detached from their fixture, that is, when they are used by themselves, they have no meaning whatever"[31] *(na nirbaddhā upasargā arthān nirāhur iti śākaṭāyanaḥ-* Nirukta I/3). Here Durga in his commentary says that if letters are detached from the words, they become meaningless. Like this, if prefixes are withdrawn from their connection with nouns and verbs and then by those prefix if sentences are formed these sentences would have no meaning *(yathā-varṇānāṃ padād apa-gatānām arthābhidhāna-śaktir nāsti evam eteṣām api nāmākhyāta-viyoge' rthābhidhāna-śaktir nāsti-* Durga under Nirukta 1/3). Thus according to Śākaṭāyana prefix modify the senses of nouns and verbs, but practically they are meaningless. An union of the nouns or verbs, with other senses, owing to circumstances undergoes a change in meaning; a new sense comes to inhere in them; there is a chemical change as it were in the noun or verb itself; prefixes are only signs *(dyotakā bhavanti)* to show that such a material change has taken place. "The Mahābhāṣya also holds this view."[32] Śākaṭāyana found that the prefix or prefixes were always connected either with nouns or with verbs, e.g. *prati-tiṣṭhate,* and in each case there was a certain modification of sense. So he regarded them as empty words.

The second view of Yāska's predecessor, Gārgya who did not deny that the prefix modified the senses of nouns and verbs. He merely went a step farther than Śākaṭāyana and said that the prefixes are *padas (padāni)* and as such have their own various *(uccāvaca)* meanings and by those meaning they cause modification in the sense of nouns and verbs. To support his own opinion Gārgya argued that if prefixes are detached from the nouns and the verbs and then if they become meaningless, by those meaningless prefixes no meaning could be modified. Because, if prefixes are meaningless and if any word is formed by those meaningless prefixes, the word also would be meaningless. By those meaningless words formed sentences, formed Vedic mantras also would be meaningless. And by this the whole literature would be meaningless. Thus Durga says in his commentary under Nirukta 1/3, in meaningful words letters also have their own meaning, by which they make meaningful words *(sāmānyā hi varṇeṣv abhidhāna śaktir asty eva)*. Prefixes also being meaningful; by their own meaning they modify the sense of nouns and verbs *(evam upasargā arthavanto 'pi santaḥ svārthābhidhāna-śaktim aneka prakāraṃ vidyamānām api svārthābhidhāna-śakty-ādhāra-bhūte nāmākhyāte pratyāyyābhi-vyañjayeyuḥ-* Durga under Nirukta 1/3). Those who support Śākaṭāyana, they say that like a lamp prefix being meaningless they only can modify the sense of nouns and verbs *(pradīpavad anarthakā upasargāḥ)*. Gārgya refuted their opinion by saying that, along with the power of modifying the sense *(arthābhidhāna śakti)* of nouns and verbs, prefix should also have their own meaning.

Yāska, the author of the Nirukta, accepts the view of Gārgya and mentions the twenty prefixes with their various meanings, e.g. *ā* 'hitherward' *(ā ity arvāg-arthe* Nirukta 1/3), *pra* and *parā* opposite of hitherward *(pra-parety etasya prātilomyam* Nirukta 1/3) and so on.

Bṛhaddevatā accepts the view of Śākaṭāyana and regards prefixes as having meaning of their own[33] *(vivecayanti te hy arthaṃ nāmākhyāta-vibhaktiṣu*—Bṛhaddevatā). In ṚP we see there also Śākaṭāyana's view is accepted by saying that the twenty prefixes are expressive of meaning in combination with nouns and verbs.[34]

How prefix modify the sense of nouns and verbs, now a few examples are given here:

1. *ā ity arvāg-arthe (vartate); ataḥ: o ā-gahi divo vā rocanād adhi* (Ṛgveda - 1/6/9); *ā gahi* = come down. This sense of *á* is accidental; one may come from an underground region in this case *ā* would mean 'up'. *ā* really reverses the sense of the root to which it is prefixed; *gaccha* = go; *ā-gaccha* = come; *naya* = take; ā-naya = bring back.[35]

2. *prātilomyam (ā-hatuḥ athavā ā cakṣāte) ; pra* and *parā* mean the reverses of the sense of ā; they mean 'up', *sudevo adya pra-pated anāvṛt parāvṛt parāvataṃ paramāṃ gantavā u* (Ṛgveda - X/95/14) = today the good king would fly *(patet)* up *(pra)* to go to the highest upper region *(paravatam)* never to return *(anāvrt); parāvat* = an upper region. *parā me yanti hdītayaḥ* (Ṛgveda I/25/16) = my prayers go up *(parā)*.[36]

In Pāṇini's system when *pra, parā* etc. *(prādayaḥ)*

connected with verbs then they are called prefix (P. I/IV/59). But being detached from verbs themselves have no meaning and then they are called particles *(nipātāḥ,* P. II/IV/56). Kātyāyana has the Vārttika (under P. I/III/1*) kriyā-viśeṣaka upasargaḥ.* Under P/II/I/1 Patañjali, the Great Commentator of Pāṇini says: 'such is the nature of *upasargas* that where a word denoting action (i.e. verb) is used, they express the special character of the action.'[37]

Under the Vārttika *kriyā-viśeṣkaka upasargaḥ* (P. I/3/1/7) Patañjali appears to accept the view of Śākatāyana and holds that *upasargas* merely make explicit what was implicit in the root itself (*pacatīti kriyā gamyate tāṃ pro viśinaṣṭi . . .evam ihāpi tiṣṭhatir eva vraji-kriyām āha, tiṣṭhatir eva vraji-kriyāyā nivṛttim)* Mahābhāṣya under the Vārttika I/III/I/7).

Philosophical discourses on grammar like Vākyapadīya of Bhartṛhari, Parama Laghu-mañjūṣa of Nāgeśabhaṭṭa and Vaiyākaraṇa Bhūṣaṇa-sāra of Kauṇḍabhaṭṭa may lighten this topic. European scholars like F. MaxMüllar, A.A. Macdonell, Renou, Bloomfield, M.R. Kale and others contribute to the analysis of the role played by particles including prefixes.

According to Naiyāyikas prefix only can modify the senses of verbs, practically they have no meaning. But except prefix (*prādi*) particles have their own meanings.[38] Like grammarians they also accept, when *pra, parā* etc. (*prādayaḥ*) connected with verbs they are called prefix '*upasarga*'. They become meaningless being detached from verbs *'kriyā'*. Grammarians refuted their view by saying that there is no reason to distinguish between prefix and particles. Grammarians say *anu-bhūyate ity anena sākṣāt-kriyate ity asya samatvāt/ nāmārtha-dhātv-arthayor bhedena sākṣād anvayābhāvān nipātārtha dhātv-arthayor anvayasyai vāsambhavāt/ nipātārtha-phalāśrayatve 'pi dhātv-arthānvayaṃ vinā karmatvānu-papatteś ca.*[39]

In Kaumāra of Śarvavarman (first/second century AD) we see this idea represented by the commentator Durgā Siṁha under the rule *dhātos to'ntaḥ pānubandhe.* There says—at first verb combines to *sādhana* 'activity' and then to prefix.[40] Why grammarians say that when *prādi* connects to a verb they become *dyotaka* 'indicative'? Durgā Siṃha, the commentator of Mugdhabodha replies—*kevala dhātor anekārthatve avaśya-vaktavye upasarga-pūrvvakatvenānyārtho 'pi dhātor eva kalpyate lāghavāt/ dhātūnām anekārthatvam upasargāṇām apy anekārthatvam iti vidhi-dvaya-kalpane gauravaṃ syād iti/ evaṃ 'sambhavaty eka-vākyatve vākya-bhedo na ceṣyata' iti jaimini-sūtrāt.*[41] In Śabda-khaṇḍa of Tattva-cintāmaṇi Gaṅgeśa also says prefixes are not expressive, but they are indicators. And their indicativeness *'dyotakatva'* is a *tātparya-grāhakatva* in a special meaning of verb.[42]

There is a very beautiful well-known stanza in Māgha's Śiśupāla-badha, where "The intoxicating due to drinking brought out in a beautiful manner the amorous gestures of the young women; gestures that had been lying dormant for a long time because there had been no occasion for their manifestation, even as the upasargas bring out the sense latent in the root."[43] Māgha says thus—

santam eva ciram aprakṛtatvād aprakāśitamadidyutadaṅge/
vibhramaṁ madhumadaḥ pramadānāṃ dhātulīnam upasarga ivārtham//
(Śiśupāla-badha: X.15)

Nārāyaṇā, the commentator of Māgha, makes clear under I.25. He says, along with prefix, which meaning is expressed by verbs, this is its own meaning. Prefix only can modify the sense of the verb, they actually have no own meaning.[44]

In the library of The Asiatic Society, Kolkata there are several unpublished texts, preserved in manuscript form, containing the meaning of prefix. In Upasargārtha-saṃgraha the author Kṛṣṇācārya clearly stated that as *upasarga* is a technical term used in accordance with the sense of its constituent parts, i.e. *anvartha saṃjñā,* it requires company with root. Thus when the group of words beginning with *pra,* i.e. *prādi,* becomes connected with verb then they termed as *upasarga* 'prefix.' Actually they are without any significance. They possess a meaning only when used in company with roots which bear an independent sense.[45] After that Kṛṣṇācārya has given meanings of prefixes with suitable examples. E.g.—*parā vadhe gatau darśane ca vikrātābhi-mukhe bhṛśe adhīna-mokṣaṇa-prātilomyakeṣu parā mataḥ//2// vadhe yathā parā-hataḥ gatau yathā parā-gataḥ darśane yathā parā-dṛṣṭaḥ vikrate yathā parā-krāṃtaḥ abhimukhe yathā parā-vṛtaḥ bhṛśe yathā parā-jitaḥ adhīne yathā parādhīnaḥ mokṣaṇe yathā parā-kṛtaḥ tyakta ity arthaḥ prātilomye yathā parāṅmukhaḥ.*[46] In Laghūpasarga-dīpikā the author has shown fifteen meanings of the prefix *pra,* e.g. employment *(niyoge),* separation *(viyoge),* frequent *(bhṛśārthe)* etc.[47] In another unpublished text namely Upasargārtha-saṃgraha of Kṛṣṇācārya gives the different meanings of twenty five prefixes in 19 verses with perhaps his own commentary. The author gives meaning of these three extra prefixes which are not found in Pāṇinian tradition. Those given meanings are—*śrat śraddhādau23 aṃtar madhyādau24 āvir prākāṭyādau25.*[48] This text has a commentary named Upasargārtha-vṛtti composed by the author himself. In the beginning Śloka the author stated himself to be a nephew of Rāmacandrācārya.[49] In Laghūpasarga dīpikā also meanings of these three prefixes have given as -*śrat śraddhāyām āstikāvuddhau śradhadhate/29/ antar madhye tirodhāne ca āvir prāgadye āviṣkaroti,*[50] There in the library of The Asiatic Society, is another manuscript of an unpublished text named Upasargārtha which gives various meanings of twenty prefixes. The manuscript is incomplete and name of the author is not mentioned anywhere. There also thirteen meanings are given of the prefix *pra—athopasargārthā-likhyaṃte/pra-ādi-karmodīrṇa bhṛśārthaiś-varya-saṃbha-viyoga-tṛpti-śuddhi + śakti-śāṃti pūjāgraha-darśaneṣu,*[51] See appendix for the text of Upasargārtha-saṃgraha, where a critical edition is given with an introduction.

Upasarga-varga of Śrī Mahādeva Bhaṭṭācārya, duly edited on the basis of a published (from Ārṣamudrāśālā

Viśākhapaṭṭaṇa 1913) work and on the bais of a manuscript, was published by Amaranātha Pāṇḍeya from Varanasi in 1968.[52] In this treatise, containing 165 verses, the author has told the meanings of several roots with the combination of prefixes.

Upasargārtha-candrikā composed by Charudeva Shastri is completed in five volume which deals with the prefixes in a well-known order, i.e.—

pra-parāpa-sam-anv-ava-nir-dur-vy-āṅ-ny-adhayo'py-atī/
sūd-abhayaś ca pratinā saha pary-upayor api//[53]

Among them first volume deals with *pra* to *sam, second* volume deals with *sam* to *vi,* third volume deals with *vi* to *adhi,* fourth volume deals with *adhi* to *pari* and fifth volume deals with *pari* and *upa.* In the preface of the first volume the author has described his determination to compose such a notable work. He said—"I set myself the task of studying the vast Sanskrit literature, both Vedic and Classical, in my quest of the appropriate uses of the Sanskrit prepositions. I endeavoured to discover their true meanings with the help of the commentaries, wherever available, which I have quoted in this work in extend. But I have not allowed my regard for the old commentators to prevail over my sense of judgement. I have on occasions discarded the meanings offered by them in favour of my suggestions, for which I have invariably given reasons. I have also gone into textual criticism, wherever it was called for."[54] Examples are taken from Saṁhitās, Brāhmaṇas, Gṛhya and Dharma Sūtras, epic literature and also from classical literature. There in these volumes is an internal order—Roots read in the Dhātupāṭha come first and complex roots come next. Then roots with primary suffixes and secondary suffixes are dealt there. The author has mentioned a reason why he followed the sequence.[55]

Using the roots from Kavi-kalpa-druma, a Dhātu-pāṭha of

Vopadeva, in Upasargamaṇḍanam Maṇḍanamantrī has dealt with the meanings of various roots when prefixes are attached to them. About the purpose of the text author says *kavi-kalpa-drume dhātu-pāṭhe'py aprāpyam icchayā/ saṃsargād upasargāṇāṃ dhātv-arthaṃ kathayāmi tam//* (the meaning of roots combined with prefixes, which is not available in the Kavi-kalpa-druma i.e. a Dhātu-pāṭha, is provided here in this treatise; verse no. 6). It has shown around 2350 meanings of prefix-root combination. Upasargamaṇḍanam is edited by Dr. Dhaval Patel, I.A.S., District Development Officer, Rajkot. He says in a brief account of the work duly published in the Bharatiya-vidvatparishat, Google Group "After the introductory part is over, the main text starts (7-338ab). In this section the roots are arranged as per their order in Kavikalpadruma. In rare cases, the order is changed. Kavikalpadruma has a peculiar way of arranging the roots i.e. by the last letter of the root. In a way, it can be called the earliest reverse dictionary in Sanskrit language. Upasargamaṇḍanam has covered अकारान्त to हकारान्त roots in this part. Upasarga-maṇḍanam doesn't attend to सौत्र roots, because they are not supposed to be used in literature, but only in their specific use in the grammar. Therefore, it ends with हकारान्त unlike Kavikalpadruma, which ends in सौत्र roots."[56] Another text i.e. Upasargavṛtti was edited by the same person and was published in the said group in 2011. In this treatise several meanings are told of twenty prefixed with suitable exampes. E.g. "अव।। विज्ञानावलंबने शुद्धीषदर्थव्याप्तिपरिभावियोगेषु। अवेत्ययमुपसर्ग एतेष्वर्थेषु वर्तते। विज्ञाने अवगतोऽर्थः। अवलंबने अवष्टभ्य यष्टिं गच्छति। शुद्धौ अवदात्तं मुखम्। ईषदर्थे अवभुक्तम्। व्याप्तौ अवकीर्णं अवकीर्णं पांशुभिः। परिभेवे अवहसति। वियोगे अवमुक्ता कान्ता।।6।।

The Significance of Prefixes in Philosophical Terminology is a laborious work done by Betty Heimann, where the author has investigated different modes of application of prefixes in terminology of different Indian philosophical schools;

namely Vedānta, Mimāṃsā, Sāṃkhya, Yoga, Nyāya, Vaiśeṣika, Vyākaraṇa, Buddhism and Jainism. The author made a few significant questions in the introduction. He observed that in Sanskrit language it is a remarkable fact that the accumlation of two,[57] or even more,[58] prefixes in a single Sanskrit term, which is observed in no other language to the same degree and strength of expression. "Do these different prefixes corroborate or contradict or merely modify each other? And are the rules of the relation between the different prefixes difinitely fixed? In the course of studying the terms applied in the different philosophical schools one has to take account of this additional problem and to summarize the conclusions at which one arrive."[56] The author's endeavor is to show that choice of prefixes for terminology in different philosophical schools, based upon their basic needs. Thus about the usage of prefix *adhi* in Vedānta Philosophy Heimann says—"The prefix *adhi,* from the above, is accordingly favoured. All actual facts are valued from the transcendental angle, from above. Terms like *adhi-ṣṭhāna* are accepted as a proper expression of the dependency of all worldly thing on a superimposed order which is, at the same time, the basis and the ruling law from above. If, on the other hand, not the transcendental but the human reason superimposes attributes and properties to the objects, then terms formed with the prefix *adhi* are applied which involved a deprecatory meaning. As such *adhy-ā-ropa* means: an erroneous application or superimposition. In the same way *adhy-asya* indicates: a false supposition *(Kā. Up.,* 5, 11, *Comm.).*"[60] In Yoga philosophy *adhi* indicates forward tendency and its result, a kind of progress to a higher view in the term *adhi-ṣṭhāna.* In the term *vi-dhi* of Mīmāṃsā philosophy, the prefix *vi* is applied designating singleness and diversity. At the end of the book author has given a list of terms which treated in his book.

Now we may conclude with the views of modern scholars. Macdonell says, in Sanskrit language the prefixes have to be distinguished in two classes. The first among them comprises the genuine or adverbial prefix. He says—those prefix connected with verbs ". . . are words with a local sense which, primarily used to modify the meaning of verbs, came to be connected independently with the cases governed by the verbs thus modified. They show no signs of derivation from inflexional forms or (except *tirās* and *purās*) forms made with adverbial suffixes."[61] M.R. Kale says - in Sanskrit a preposition is an indeclinable word. Prefix has an independent meaning and they prefixed to verbs and also to their derivatives. "These prefix modify, intensify and sometimes totally alter the senses of roots; *saṃhṛ* 'to contract,' *vihṛ* 'to sport,' *parihṛ* 'to avoid,' etc. Sometimes they are prefixed without any alteration in the sense."[62]

Select Bibliography

1. Aṣṭādhyāyī of Pāṇini, ed. and trans. by Rama Nath Sharma. *The Aṣṭādhyāyī of Pāṇini,* vols. I, II, Munshiram Manoharlal Publishers Pvt. Ltd, Delhi, 2000.
2. Do : Ed. and trans. Sivsa Chandra Vasu. *The Ashṭādhyāyī of Pāṇini,* 8 vols. Indian Press, Allahabad, 1891.
3. Atharva-veda-Prātiśākhya of Śaunaka, ed. and trans., William Dwight Whitney, *The Atharvaveda-Prātiśākīyā or Śaunakīya Caturadhyikā,* third ed. Chowkhamba Sanskrit Series Office, Varanasi, 2002.
4. Chatterjee, Kshitish Chandra, *Technical Terms and Techniques of Sanskrit Grammar,* Sanskrit Pustak Bhandar, Kolkata, 2003.
5. Haldar, Gurupada, *Vyākaraṇa Darṣaner Itihāsa,* [A History of Sanskrit Grammar], vol. I, repr., (in Bengali), Sanskrit Book Depot, Kolkata, 2006.
6. Heimann, Betty, *The Significance of Prefixes in Sanskrit Philosophical Terminology,* first ed. 1951, The Royal Asiatic Society, Retypesetted and printed. D.K. Printworld (P)

Ltd., New Delhi, 2012.

7. Kale, Moreshvara Ramachandra. *A Smaller Sanskrit Grammar for the Use of Schools.* 4th ed, Gopal Narayan & Co. Booksellers & Publishers, Bombay, 1924.
8. Macdonell, A.A., *Vedic Grammar for Students.* 1st Indian ed, Motilal Banarasidass Publishers Private Limited, Delhi 1993.
9. Nirukta of Yāska, ed. with Durga's commentary and Bengali Trns. Brahmachari Medhacaitanya. *Maharṣi-yāska-praṇītam Niruktam.* second ed. Dakshineswar Ramkrishna Sangha, Adyapeeth Balakashram, Kolkata, 2002.
10. Parama Laghu-mañjūṣā of Nāgeśa Bhana, ed. with Sanskrit commentary and Hindi Trans. Lokmani Dahal. *Vaiyākaraṇa-Siddhānta Paramalaghumañjūṣā* Chaukhamba Surabharati Prakashan, Varanasi, 2009.
11. Ṛgveda-Prātiśākhya of Śaunaka, ed. with Uvvaṭabhāṣya and Hindi Trans. Virendrakumar Verma. *Ṛgveda-Prātiśākhya of Śaunaka.* reprt., Chaukhamba Sanskrit Pratishthan, Delhi, 2007.
12. Ṛgveda-Saṁhitā : Ed. F. Max Müller. *The Hymns of the Rig-Veda in the Samhita and Pada Texts,* 2 vols., second ed, Trübner and Co. London, 1877.
13. Shāstrī, Haraprasād. *A Descriptive Catalogue of Sanskrit Manuscripts in the Government Collection,* vol. VI, The Asiatic Society, Kolkata, 2006.
14. Siddhanta Kaumudi of Bhattoji Dikshita : Ed. with Sanskrit commentary Tattvabodhinī and Bengali trans. Binod Lal Sen, *Siddhanta Kaumudi Parisiśiṣtam.* Adi Ayurbed Aushadhalay, Kolkata, 1893 (1300 bangabda).
15. Śuklayajurveda-Prātiśākhyam or Vāsaneyi-Prātiśākhyam of Kātyāyana, ed. with commentaries of Uvaṭa and Ananta Bhaṭṭa and Hindi Trans. Virendrakumar Verma. *Śuklayajurveda-Prātiśākhyam* or *Vājasaneyi-Prātiśākhyam of Kātyāyana* Chaukhamba Sanskrit Pratishthan, Delhi, 2007.

16. Syanyal, Ajodhyanath, *Vaidika Svararahasya.* 2nd ed. Burdwan University, Burdwan, 2009.
17. Taittirīya-Prātiśākhya, ed. with commentary Tribhāṣyaratna and trns. Willian D. Whitney, *The Taittirīya-Prātiśākhya.* repr. first ed. New Haven, 1868, Motilal Banarsidass Publishers Private Limited, Delhi. 1973.
18. Ibid., ed. with Sanskrit commentaries Tribhāṣyaratna and Vaidikābharaṇa. R. Sharma Sastri and K. Rangacarya. *The Taittirīya-Prātiśākhya* rept., Motilal Banarsidass Publishers Private Limited, Delhi, 1985.
19. Upasargārtha-candrikā of Charudev Shastri, *Upasargārtha-candrikā; A Thesaurus of Sanskrit Prepositional Verbs.* Vols. 5 Vol. 1, 2nd ed. 1997; vol II, 1978; vol. III, 1979; vol. IV, 2nd ed. 1997, vol. V. 1982 Bharatiya Vidya Prakashan, Delhi.
20. Upasarga-varga of Śrī Mahādeva Bhaṭṭācārya, ed. Amaranātha Pāṇḍeya. *Upasarga-vargaḥ.* Kaśī Vidyāpīṭha. Varanasi, 1968.
21. Vākyapadīya of Bhartṛhari : Ed. with commentaries of Helājāja and Raghunātha Śarmā. Subrahmanya Ayyar. *Vākyapadīyam,* vol. III, second ed. Sampurnananda Sanskrit University, Varanasi, 1912.
22. Vedantatirtha, N.C. and Chakravarti P.B. *Descriptive Catalogue of Sanskrit Manuscripts of The Asiatic Society (The Indian Museum Collection).* The Asiastic Society, Calcutta, 1973.

Manuscripts:

1. Laghūpasarga-dīpikā. Manuscript No. G 8918, The Asiatic Society, Kolkata.
2. Upasargārtha. Manuscript No. G 7206, The Asiatic Society, Kolkata.
3. Upasargārtha-saṃgraha of Kṛṣṇācārya. Manuscript No. G 7609, The Asiatic Society, Kolkata.
4. Upasargārtha-saṃgraha of Kṛṣṇācārya. Manuscript No.

G 9655, The Asiatic Society, Kolkata.

5. Upanargārthavṛtti of Kṛṣṇacārya, Manuscript No. I.M. 10150, The Asiatic Society, Kolkata.

References

1. *tad yāni catvāri pada-jātāni nāmākhyāte copasara-nipātāś ca* (Yāska's Nirukta-I/1).
2. *sup-tiṅ antaṃ padam* (P-I/IV/14).
3. Vākyapadīya III/I/1.
4. *Technical Terms and Technique of Sanskrit Grammar,* p. 389–99.
5. *A Dictionary of Sanskrit Grammar,* p. 81
6. *Technical Terms and Technique of Sanskrit Grammar,* p. 398.
7. "connection with what is denoted by the constituent members; the word refers to a kind of Bahuvrīhi compound where the object denoted by the compound includes also what is denoted by the constituent members of the compound" (*A Dictionary of Sanskrit Grammar,* p. 168).
8. *prādir upasargaḥ/pra ādir yasya sa prādi tad-giṇa-saṃ viñjāno yaṃ bahuvrīhiḥ/ upa samīpe sajyate uccāryate kriyā vācakasya śabdasyeti upasargaḥ, karmaṇi ghañ (*Upasargārtha-saṃgraha, manuscript No. G 9655, folio-1a, line 1-2).
9. Upasargārtha-saṃgraha, manuscript No. G 7609, folio-2a, line-5 Laghūpasaga-dīpikā manuscript no. G 8918, folio 3a, line 13.
10. Upasargārtha- saṃgraha, manuscript no. G7609, folio-2a, line 6.
11. *ā-prāvopābhy-adhi-prati-pari-vi-nīty upasargāḥ*-Taittirīya Prātiśākhya, I/15.
12. *katham atra sūtra-kṛtā nirargalam upasargā iti-śabdena saṅkucitāḥ? ucyate/ yajurveda-viṣavye etāvanta eveti mantavyam/* (Tribhāṣya-ratna of Somayārya under TP I/15).
13. *te prāg dhātoḥ* (P. I/IV/80).
14. *chandasi pare'pi* (P. I/VI. 81).
15. Reference is taken from *The Aṣṭādhyāyī of Pāṇini,* by Ram Nath Sharma (Vol.-II, p. 289) where real source is not mentioned.
16. The Aṣṭādhyāyī of Pāṇini, ed. Ram Nath Sharma, vol. II, p. 289.
17. *viṃśater upasargāṇām uccā ekākṣarā nva ādy-udāttā daśaiteṣām, antodāttas tv babhīty ayam* (ṚP-XII/22–24).
18. *upasarga upasarge* (VP-VI/2).
19. *abhi-prehy upa-sam-prayāta praty-ā-tanuṣvā-suṣāva* (VP-VI/10) Also see Uvaṭa-Bhāṣya (UB) for more examples.
20. See Uvaṭa-Bhāṣya under *opa prodātte* (VP-VI/9).
21. *āmreḍite cottaraḥ* (VP-VI/3).

22. *yatra cānudāttatvam upasargasya na bhavati tatra pṛhak padatvam api bhavati/ "svarita-varjam ekodāttaṃ padam" (II/1) iti paribhāṣā-balāt*—UB under *kṛd -ākhyātayoś codāttayoḥ* (VP-VI/4).
23. See Uvaṭ-Bhāṣya for more example and illustration under VP-VI/5
24. *adhi-ni-pra-prati-śritātriṇaṃ bhānavaḥ pacateṣu* (VP-VI/7). Also see UB for suitable examples cited from VS.
25. *ujjeṣam-āvarta-āpanīphaṇat-saniṣyadat-saṃvataṃ prayāṇaṃ sañcarantaṃ-saṃrabhadhvaṃ prasitiṃ-vikramasvety eteṣv anu* (VP-VI /7).
26. *upasarga niṣ-pūrvo'nudātte pade* (TP.IV/4).
27. See Aṣṭādhyāyī VIII/III/65–77.
28. Atharva-veda-prātiśākhya, p. 117-118 (William D. Whitney's edition)
29. *upasarga pūrva āram* (TP-X/9).
30. *upasarga-pāthaeṣ'tyāti-dhāma- parama-bhūte-pūrveṣu cha-khi-hbujeṣu ca* (TP-XIV/8).
31. *Yāskha's Nirukta,* vol. 1 p. 228.
32. Ibid.
33. *Technical Terms and Techniues of Sanskrit Grammar,* pp. 401–2
34. *upasargā viṃśatir artha-vācakāḥ sahetarābhyām and kriyā vācakam ākhyātam upasargo viśeṣakṛt*—ṚP—XII/200 and 24.
35. Yāska's Nirukta, vol. 1, p. 229
36. Ibid.
37. *Technical Terms and Techniques of Sanksrit Grammar,* p. 402.
38. *upasargāṇāṃ dyotakatvaṃ tad-itara nipātānāṃ vācaktvam* (Parama Laghu-mañjūṣā, Chapter-Nipātārtha-nirṇaya).
39. *Parama Laghu-mañjūṣā,* p. 170.
40. *pūrvvaṃ dhātuḥ sādhanena yujyate paścād upasargeṇeti nyāyyaḥ pakṣaḥ* (Gurupada Haldar, p. 350)
41. Ibid., p. 349.
42. *uparsagās tu dyotakā na vācakāḥ/ dyotakatvaṃ ca dhātor artha viśeṣe tātparyya-grāhakatvam* (Ibid., p. 349).
43. *Technical Terms and Techniques of Sanskrit Grammar;* p. 403.
44. *dhātūnām upasargeṇa ye 'rthāḥ pratīyante te sarve'pi teṣāṃ svārthā eva/ upasargāṇāṃ punar abhivayañjakatvam* —Nārāyaṇa under Śiśupāla-badha: I. 25.
45. *anvartha saṃñjā-kriyā-saṃbaṃdhaṃ labhate yad uktaṃ yat kriyā-yuktaḥ prādayaḥ tān praty evopasarga saṃñjeti upasargā hi artha-viśeṣasya dyotaka na tu vācakāḥ*—Upasargārtha- saṃgraha, manuscript no. G 9655, folio—1a, line 1–2.
46. Ibid., line 7.
47. *pra ity upasargaḥ pañca-daśasv artheṣu/ niyoge pra-yuktaḥ/1/ viyoge proṣitaḥ/2/ bhṛśārthe pra-vadanti dāyādaḥ /3/* etc.—Laghūpasarga-dīpikā, manuscript no. G8918, folio-1a, line 1–4.
48. Upasargārtha-saṃgraha, manuscript no. G 7609, folio 2a, line 5.

49. *kṛṣṇācāryai rāmacandrācārya bhrātṛ-sutaiḥ kṛtā A Descriptive Catalogue of Sanskrit Manuscripts of The Asiatic Socieyty (The Indian Museum Collection),* compiled by N.C. Vedantatritha and P.B. Chakravarti, p. 154, The Asiatic Society, Calcutta 1973.
50. Laghūpasarga-dīpikā, manuscript no. G8918, folio-3a, line 13.
51. Upasargārthaḥ, manuscript no. G7260, folio-1a, line 1–2.
52. Upasarga-varga Introduction, p. 1.
53. Gurupada Haldar; p. 411
54. Upasargārtha-candrikā; Prefece, p. iii.
55. For more description see Volume III; Preface, p. 5.
56. Source—Bharatiyavidvatparistha, Google Group link: https: // groups.google, com/forum/ #!searchin/bvparishat/upasarga-mandanam/bvparishat/3xuDGwgyoo/h4f9ZJeCVKAJ; date: 21/08/ 2014, time 7.00 am. The book Upasargamaṇḍanam is published in a digitized from and is avaliable here—https://kindle. amazon. com/ work/upasargamandanam-mandanamantri-treatisesanskrit-prefixed -ebook/BOOKK4FB4G/BOOKK4FB4G (present author has seen this on 21th august, 2012 at 7.30 am).
57. E.g.—*abhi-ni-viś,* 'to enter into possession of ; to sit down or be settled in, to occupy'.
58. E.g. *abhy-upā-gam (abhi-upa-ā-gam),* 'to come too.
59. *The Significance of Prefixes in Sanskrit Philosophical Terminology;* Introducation, p. 12.
60. *The Significance of Prefixes in Sanskrit Philosophical Terminology,* p. 15
61. *Vedic Grammar for Students,* p. 208.
62. *A Smaller Sanskrit Grammar for the Use of Schools,* p. 125.

13

TREATMENT OF *MĀTRĀ* IN THE VĀJASANEYI-PRĀTIŚĀKHYA WITH PARTICULAR REFERENCE TO THE QUANTITY OF *AVAGRAHA*

ASHOK KUMAR MAHATA

The six topics connected with Vedic learning and teaching are important in ancient Indian phonetics to prevent the fault in recitation of the Vedic *mantras*. The earliest mention of these instructions in reciting the sacred texts is found in the Taittirīya Upanisad in the following manner: *śīkṣāṃ vyākhyāsyāmaḥ/varṇaḥ svaraḥ mātrā balaṃ sāma santānaḥ/ityuktaḥ śikṣādhyāyaḥ/* (TU, 1.2). These six topics are the letters, accents, quantity of syllables, melody and combination of words in continuous recitation of the *mantras* of the Vedas. Therefore, *mātrā* (quantity of syllables) plays an important role in the correct utterance of the alphabetic sounds.

In Sanskrit grammar and phonetico-grammatical treatises of ancient India, we come across the term *mātrā* which literally means measure, quantity, duration etc. In the Prātiśākhyas and other Vedic ancillary literature, it is used in the sense of length of time in the pronunciation of alphabetic sounds. The vowels are of three kinds according to the duration of their utterance viz. *hrasva* (short), *dīrgha* (long) and *pluta* (prolated). In the Pāṇinīya Śikṣā it is mentioned in the following manner: *hrasvo dīrghaḥ pluta iti kālato niyamā aci* (PS, 11). The values of these three kinds of vowels are stated in the Ṛgveda Prātiśākhya thus:

cāṣastu vadate mātrāṃ dvimātrāṃ vāyaso'vravīt/ śīkhī trimātro vijñeya iti mātrāparigrahaḥ (RP, 13.50)

It conveys, *mātrā* i.e. one mora is of the same value as the cry of the blue jay, two *mātrās* are equivalent to those of the crow and three *mātrās* are of the same duration as those of the peacock.

In the Vājasaneyi-Prātiśākhya, the term *mātrā* denoting mora is defined thus: *amātrasvaro hrasvaḥ mātrā ca* (1.55, 56). A vowel having the duration of the sound 'a' is called *hrasva* (short) and it is termed *mātrā* also. So here *hrasva* and *mātrā* are synonymous. The celebrated commentator Uvaṭa clearly states: *mātrā ca yatra śruyate tatra akārakālo mātrāsvaraḥ pratyetavyaḥ hrasvo mātreti paryāyāvityarthaḥ.* In the same treatise, duration of long and prolated vowels is fixed as two and three moras respectively *dvistāvān dīrghaḥ. plutastriḥ* (VP, 1.57, 58).

In the first chapter of the Ṛgveda Prātiśākhya quantities of short, long and prolated vowels are laid down, *mātrā hrasvah dve dīrghaḥ tisraḥ pluta ucyate svaraḥ* (RP, 1.27, 29, 30). Here quantity of short, long and prolated vowels is stated to be one, two and three moras respectively.

The Taittirīya Prātiśākhya furnishes the same theory regarding the length of the vowels and it includes 'anusvāra', having the same value of a short vowel. *ṛkāraḷkārau hrasvau. akāraśca. tena ca samānakālasvaraḥ. anusvāraśca. dvistāvān dīrghaḥ. triḥ plutaḥ* (TP, I.31-36).

The Atharvaveda Prātiśākhya expresses its view on short and long vowels only. It remains silent on the prolated variety of the vowels. *ekamātro hrasvaḥ dvimātro dīrghaḥ* (AP. I. 59-61)

Now let us discuss about the quantity of *avagraha* as found in the Prātiśākhya and Śikṣā works. In the word *avagraha* there are three components viz. the prefix *ava*, the root *grah* and the suffix *a*. It means *avagṛhyate vicchidya paṭhyate ityavagrahaḥ*. In the Pada-texts of the Vedic *mantras* component parts of a compound are separated. Sometimes separation of the stem and certain suffixes and inflectional terminations are also made there. This separation is called *avagraha* and it is marked by the roman letter *'S'*. So, *avagraha* is a kind of pause in utterance of the Vedic *mantras* in the Pada-text. Before going to discuss the quantity of *avagraha*, let us look at the classification of pause mentioned in the Prātiśākhya and Śikṣā works. In the Kālanirṇaya Śikṣā, rules regarding duration of articulation of sounds are divided into three kinds. These are related to vowels, consonants and pause. Pauses are of four kinds and their duration is also mentioned in the Taittirīya Prātiśākhya. The relevant rule runs thus: *ṛgvirāmaḥ padavirāmo vivṛtti-virāmassamāna-padavivṛtti virāmastrimātro dvimātra ekamatro'rdhamātra ityānupurvyeṇa* (TP, 22.13).

So we find that the names of the categories of the pauses are: verse pause, pada-pause, pause for hiatus and pause for hiatus in the interior of a word. Quantities of these pauses are three moras, two moras, one mora and half a mora respectively.

The Vaidikābharaṇa commentary of Gārgya Gopāla-yajvan on the above rule of the Taittirīya Prātiśākhya throws fresh light on the duration of *avagarha*. It quotes a Śikṣā and agrees with its opinion that *avagraha* is a pause and its value is one mora. *avagrahāntaṿirāmasya tu śikṣāyāṃ viśeṣasmaryate– 'avagrahānāmante ca virāmo mātrikasmṛtah' iti. yathā upāyava ityupa'āyavaḥ.*

We find the view of the Vājasaneyi-Prātiśakhya regarding the quantity of *avagraha* in the following manner: *samāse'vagrho hrasvasamakālaḥ. Avagraha* comes between the two words in a compound and its quantity is equivalent to that of a short vowel. The celebrated commentator Uvaṭa makes the point clear thus: *samāsapade avagraho bhavati. dvayoḥ padayoḥ pṛthaggrahaṇamavagrahaḥ nānāgraha ityarthaḥ. sa ca hrasvasamakālaḥ hrasvākṣaratulyakālaḥ bhavati. yathā ṛksāmābhyāmityṛksāmābhyām. santaranta iti sam' tarantaḥ* (VS, 4.1).

As the Ṛgveda Prātiśākhya is regarded as the oldest Prātiśakhya, we may safely experess that the view of this Prātiśākhya (*mātrā hrasvaḥ tāvadavagrahāntaram,* RP, 1.27 and 28) regarding the quantity of *avagraha* is fully supported by the Vājasaneyi Prātiśākhya (V.1). The Yājñavalkya Śikṣā shows the divergent view on the quantity of *avagraha.* According to it, the quantity of *avagraha* is half a mora. *avagrahe tu kālah syādardhamātrātmako hi saḥ* (Y.S. 1.13). In the commentary Śikṣāvallivivṛti it has been stated in the following manner: *avagraho nāma padapāṭhakāle samastā'samastasya padasya prakṛtipradarśanārthaṃ yo vicchedaḥ saḥ. tatra tu yaḥ kālaḥ sa ardhamātrātmakaḥ syāt. yathā sahasraśīrṣeti sahasra'sirṣā* (S YV, Pada. 31.1) *atra sroccāraṇānte ardhamātrā vilambo vidheya eva.*

According to it, *avagraha* is a pause for hiatus where two components of a compound are divided to show their original forms. Its quantity is fixed to half a mora. It apparently contradicts the theory of the Vājasaneyi-Prātiśākhya, but the commentator of the Yājñavalkya Śikṣā finds nothing wrong in this case and he expresses the opinion that the author of the Vājasaneyi-Prātiśākhya has fixed the quantity of *avagraha* as one mora for normal articulation. But in the Yājñavalkya Śikṣā, determination with regard to duration of *avagraha* as half a mora is laid down for technical purpose and that is why it does not contradict the doctrine of the Vājasaneyi-Prātiśākhya. *nanvatra viṣaye kātyāyanena 'samāse'vagraho hrasvasamakālaḥ'* (VP, 5.1) *iti mātrākālavilamba ukta ato viruddha iti cet, na. tasya svābhāvikamātrādhikāparatvāt. asya ca pāribhāṣika-mātrāvidhānaparatvenā'virodhāt. tenātra 'dvayostu svarayormadhye' (YSVP,* 9) *ityādilakṣitavivṛttivadeva srutirbhavati.*

After going through the views of the Prātiśākhyas and Śikṣā works, it is found that though there is no unanimity among them regarding the exact quantity of *avagraha,* most of them prescribe one mora for it.

14

TREATMENT OF THE TWO ALPHABETIC SOUNDS ṛ AND ḷ IN SANSKRIT PHONOLOGY

Subhra Ghosh

In the Indo-Aryan languages there is a long-drawn confusion between the two vowel sounds ṛ and ḷ ? What constitutes the exact element of these two vowel-sounds ṛ and ḷ? In reply to this question RP (xii 34)[1] says that *r* forms part of ṛ vowel and is found in the middle of it. AP[2] echoes the same view. But neither of the treatises explicity mentions the nature of the remainder of the vowel. However, it has been unanimously accepted by all the treatises that in ṛ there are two constituting particles—one is *r* and another is some vowel-element. Similarly, ḷ consists of two elements— one is *l* and other is some vowel-element.

As regards the place of articulation of these two alphabetic sounds there is divergence of opinion among the different treatises. The RP (1.41) says that both ṛ and ḷ are velar spirant (*jihvāmūlīya*)[3] and they are pronounced from the root of the tongue. Similar opinion can be found in AP (I.20)[4] which refers to ṛ as velar and ḷ as dental. But none of the Prātiśākhyas designates ḷ as being cerebral which is maintained by Pāṇinian system. As regards to ḷ all the Prātiśākhyas except VP[5] maintain ḷ as velar. But the Pāṇinian system recognizes it to be dental. However, it seems that difference between the articulation of the two vowel sounds ṛ and ḷ as maintained by Pāṇini, was not accepted by the later grammarians of his own school. On the commentary of Pāṇini sūtra *tulyāsyaprayatnam savarṇam* (1.1.9) both Patañjali and Kātyāyana point out that these two vowels *ṛ* and *ḷ* are homogeneous vowels, and there must have some similarity between the articulation of *ṛ* and *ḷ*.[6]

In this connection we may refer to an euphonic rule of Pāṇini in which two homogeneous vowels become one long vowel *'akaḥ savarṇe dīrghaḥ'* (6.1.102) So, in the combination *hotṛ* + *ṛkāraḥ* with the help of this rule we get one long *ṛ* and the form become *hotṝkāraḥ*. Similarly, in the combination of *hotṛ* + *ḷkāraḥ* we get, in the place of *ṛ* and *ḷ*, one long-*ḷ* in-as- much as *ḷ* has no long form. So the euphonic combination between *hotṛ* + *ḷkāraḥ* will be *hotṝkāraḥ*.

But both Patañjali and Kātyāyana point out that when ṛ (short) is followed by ṛ (short), the long substitution is optional.[7] So, in the combination of *hotṛ* + *ṛkāraḥ*, we get another form as hotṛkāraḥ. Similarly, when *ṛ* short is followed by *ḷ* short, the long substitution is optional.[8] So, in the combination of *hotṛ* + *ḷkāraḥ*, we get another form as *hotṛkāraḥ*.

Now the question arises whether the single substitute short *ṛ* or short *ḷ* which comes in the combination of hotṛ + ṛkāraḥ and *hoṛt ḷkāraḥ* respectively should really be teated as short. In reply to this question Kāiyaṭa in his commentary Pradīpa points out that the *ṛ* and *ḷ* which comes in place of *ḷ* + *ṛ* and *ṛ* + *ḷ* respectively should be regarded as long, consisting of two morae in this way—

hokṛ+ ṛkāraḥ
> *hotrakāraḥ*[9] [(∂ = ½) ṛ = ½ ∂ (½) = 2 *morae]*

Though these two *r*'s are not visible in ordinary writing device, they are there. They constititute one mora. The two extra-short vowels, one of which precede and another succeed the two *l*'s make one mora. So one mora of two *r*'s and one mora for two vowel elements together make two morea. Though apparently a short *ḷ* is retained as a result of the euphonic combination, it should for all practical purposes be deemed long. Similarly, in the case of *ḷ* there are two *ḷ*'s which may be put down in this way.

hotṛ + *ḷkāraḥ*
hotə//*ə kāraḥ* [(ə = ½), l = ½ *l* = ½ ə (½) = 2 *morae]*

The two *l*'s together make one mora and the two vowel-elements of half a mora each, one preceding and another succeeding the two *l*'s, make one mora. So the single substitute *l* contains in it two morae.

So we can find that both the long *ṝ* and apparently short *ṛ* which come in the combination of *hotṛ* + *ṛkāraḥ* by the rule '*akaḥ savarṇe dīrghaḥ*' and '*ṛ ti savarṇe ṛ vā*' consist of two morae. In the articulation of the vowel *ṛ* which is the combination of *r* and some vowel element there are two different efforts (*prayatna*). The former i.e. *ṛ* needs the effort *īṣatśpṛṣṭa* for its articulation and the latter needs *vivṛta* for its pronunciation. So, in a long *ṛ* there are two *vivṛta prayatnas* and two *īṣatśpṛṣṭa prayatnas.* It may be put down in this way.

'*ṛ* + *ṛ* > ə *r r* ə
>*vivṛta* + *īṣatśpṛṣṭa* + *īṣatśpṛṣṭa* + *vivṛta*

Kaiyata in his commentary points out that when the two *vivṛta* vowels of half a mora, preceding and succeeding the two *r*'s predominate they will be replaced by another long *vivṛta* vowel. As a result of it we get one long *ṝ*. But when the two *īṣatśpṛṣṭa* *ṛ* of one mora together become strong, the subsequent result is one nṛsiṁhātam *ṛ* of two morae.[10]

Similarly, the vowel *ḷ* is the combination of *l* and two vowel-elelents. The alphabetic sound *ḷ* takes *īṣatśpṛṣṭa* for its pronunciation and the two vowel elements take the efforts *vivṛta.* So, in a long which is written as *ṝ* as *ḷ* has no long form, there are two *vivṛta prayatnas* and two *īṣatśpṛṣṭa prayatnas.* It may be shown in the following way:

ḷ + ḷ
> ∂ //∂

> *vivṛta* + *īṣatspṛṣṭa* + *īṣatspṛṣṭa* + *vivṛta*

When the *vivṛta* vowels of half a mora together becomes strong, the subsequent result is one long *ḹ.* But where the two *l*'s of one mora together become prominent, we got one poculiar of two morae. Ordinarliy there is no writing device for this peculiar *ḷ.*

References

1. *repho' styṛkāre ca parasya cārdhe pūrve hrasr̄yāstu na vetarasmāt madhye saḥ* (RP xii 34).
2. *saṃspṛṣṭarephaṁṛvarnam* (AP i. 37).
3. *ṛkāraḷkārāvatha ṣaṣṭhā jihvāmulīyāḥ prathamaśca vargaḥ* (RP i. 41).
4. *Jihvāmūlīyānāṃ hanūmūlam* (AP i.20).
5. *ṛkkāu Jihvāmūle* (VP i.65).
   ḷlasitā dante (VP i.69).
6. *ṛḷvarṇamathaḥ sāvarṇyaṃ vācyam* (Vart. 150).
7. *ṛti savarṇe ḷ vā* (Vart 85).
8. *ḷti savarṇe ḷ vā* (Vart 85).
9. ∂ is an extra short vowel postulating in IE languages. It needs half, a mora for the pronunciation. By the modern philologists it is called Schwa.
11. *hotṛ ṛkāra iti sthite anena dvayoḥ ṛakārayoḥ sthāne ṛkāravi-lakṣaṇo nṛsiṃhavad dvayantarāmā ṛkāro rephadvayābhyān kaścid varṇo bhavati* (*Bālamanoramā Tīkā*, p. 87).
    This type of nṛsiṃhātamā ṛ is different from ordinary long ḷ. Accordingly a writing device in Devanagri script has been invented for this pecular ṛ.

15

SOME OBSERVATIONS ON VEDALAKṢAṆA: THE STUDY OF THE VEDAS IN THE PRĀTIŚĀKHYAS

MANJULA DEVI

The Prātiśākhyas are basically the treatises meant for the continuity of the accurate pronunciation in the recitation of hymns peculiar to a group of śākhās of a particular Veda. Anantabhaṭṭa, the noted commentator on the Vājasaneyi-prātiśākhya explains the term Prātiśākhya as follows– *śākhāyāṃ śākhāyāṃ prati pratiśākham, pratiśākhaṃ bhavanti prātiśākhyam.*[1] The Prātiśākhyas are often called the Pārṣada[2] which are the Upāṅgas, associated with the Śikṣā Vedāṅga. The term Pārṣada is a generic term applied to any work that belonged to a pariṣad. The term is explained by Durgācārya[3] in his commentary on the Nirukta to mean the treatises by which in a pariṣad (council of scholars) of one's own caraṇa, the peculiarities of accent, saṃhitā and the krama text, of pragṛhya vowels and separation of words are laid down as enjoyed for and restricted to certain śākhās (*svacaraṇapariṣadyeva yaiḥ pratiśākhāniyatam eva padāvagrahapragṛhyakramasaṃhitāsvaralakṣaṇam uchyate . . . tānīmāni pārṣadāni prātiśākhyānītyarthaḥ*). The term Lakṣaṇa is also used to designate the Prātiśākhyas.[4]

The *Ṛgvedaprātiśākhya* is the oldest of the Prātiśākhyas, belonging to the *Ṛgveda*. To the *Sāmaveda*, belong the *Ṛktantravyakaraṇa* and *Puṣpasūtra*. The *Vājasaneyiprātiśākhya* and the *Taittirīyaprātiśākhya* are the two Prātiśākhyas of the *Yajurveda*. The *Atharvaveda-prātiśākhya*, also called the

Śaunakīyacaturādhyāyikā belongs to the *Athamrvaveda.*

Uvaṭa has explained the need of the Prātiśākhyas in the following words:

śikṣā chandovyākaraṇaiḥ sāmānyenoktalakṣaṇam/
tadevamiha śākhāyāmiti śāstraprayojanam //[5]

i.e. the treatises on phonetics, the treatises on metre and Vedic grammar teach the general rules. But the Prātiśākhyas deal with the grammatical rules belonging to that particular śākhā only.

The study of the Vedas was enjoyed for the people belonging to the three higher castes for attaining the puruṣārthas—*iha hi dvijānāṃ vedābhyāsaḥ sakalapuruṣārthasiddheḥ kāraṇam iti vaidikaḥ siddhāntaḥ.*[6] It is specially enjoyed to a Brāhmaṇa who should study and understand the dharma and the Veda with six aṅgas without any purpose or reward—*bhāhmaṇena niṣkārаṇo dharmaḥ ṣadaṅgo vedo'dhyeyo jñeyaśca.*[7] The *Śatapathabrāhmaṇa* contains an eulogy to the Veda study under *svādhyāyo' dhyetavyah*[8] where it is stated that the study of the Veda is obligatory to all. The Upaniṣadic teacher instructs his pupils in his convocation address thus—*svādhyāyapravacanābhyāṃ na pramaditavyam,*[9] i.e. svādhyāya, the study of the Veda and pravacana, i.e. teaching it or daily repeating it. One should not be carried away only by observing them.

The study of the Veda was enjoined for all as the foremost duty because the sacrifices were performed by means of the Veda. That the Vedas are an indispensable aid to the performance of the sacrifices is asserted in the *Atharvavedaprātīśākhya* which states—*vedādhyanaṃ dharmaḥ . . . yajñatatirna pṛthag vedebhyaḥ.*[10] The sacrifices are the sure means to attain worldly and other worldly possessions—*yajñe punar lokāḥ pratiśṭhitāḥ.*[11] Śabarasvāmin states that the real purpose of the study of the Vedas is the knowledge about religious actions that it conveys and that from the mere memorizing of the Veda, no rewards are promised by those who know the lore of the sacrifices.[12] The Vedas should be studied in the traditional manner as handed down by those who understand the sacrifice.[13] The Vedic learning was transmitted orally which was the most effective method of teaching in ancient India. The pupil had to repeat what the teacher said exactly word for word, avoiding carefully the probable mistakes in pronunciation, annotation and in the mode of recitation. This was made absolutely for the preservation of the original text. The study of the Veda did not merely consist in learning the mantras by heart. The Nirukta condemns such person which states—*sthāṇurayaṃ bhārahāraḥ kilābhūdadhītya vedaṃ na vijānāti yo 'rtham/ yo' 'rthajña it sakalaṃ bhadram aśnute nākameti jñāna-vidhūtapāpmā//*[14] i.e. that man who having studied the Veda, does not know the meaning is indeed the bearer of a burden only, a branchless trunk. But he who knows the meaning, secures all happiness, with his sins being shaken off by knowledge, attains heaven. The *Vājasaneyiprātiśākhya* also states that spiritual merit is attained by the study and the teaching of the Veda, by hearing it from the teacher and knowing it letter by letter, syllable by syllable and word by word together with case-forms.[15]

The study of the Veda involves five things which are noted in the Dakṣasmṛti (i) comitting to memory the Veda, (ii) reflection over its meaning, (iii) keeping it fresh by repeating it again and again, (iv) japa i.e. inaudibly muttering by way of prayer, and (v) imparting it to its pupils:

vedasvīkaraṇaṃ pūrvaṃ vicāro'bhyasanaṃ japaḥ/
taddānaṃ caiva śiṣyebhyo vedābhyāso hi pañcadhā//[16]

The pivot of the whole education system was the teacher who was called an ācārya. Āpastamba holds that an ācārya is so called as the brahmacārin learns the dharma, i.e. the code of conduct from him—*yasmād dharmānācinoti sa ācāryaḥ.*[17]

Acquisition of knowledge was impossible without a teacher—*ācāryavān puruṣo veda*[18]—asserted the Vedic seer. The Taittirīyaprātiśākhya holds that one who knows very well the distinction of the pada and karma text, is versed in the succession of sounds, i.e. in the Saṃhitā text and distinctly knows the accents and moras, attains the perfection of a teacher—*pada-kramaviśeṣajño varṇakramavicakṣaṇaḥ/ svaramātrāvibhāgajño gacchedācāryasaṃsadam//*[19]

The teacher imparted the oral instructions to the pupils and it is enjoined that he should have control over his sense-organs while imparting the Vedic knowledge–*pārāyaṇaṃ vartayed* brahmacārī.[20]

The pupils should be devoted to the preceptor and to his studies which is enjoined in the *Ṛgvedaprātiśākhya*—*pārāyaṇaṃ vartayed brahmacārī guruḥ śiṣyebhyastadanuvratebhyaḥ.*[21] Uvaṭa has explained the term *anuvratebhyaḥ* in the present context as *gurāvadhyayane ca ye bhaktāśtebhyaḥ.*

While studying the Veda one must get oneself purified—prayataḥ.[22] He should wash his feet and perform ācamna, i.e. sipping water before going to the study of the Veda (*pādaśaucācamanādinā śuciradhīyītetyarthaḥ).*[23] There are several occasions where the sipping of water twice is necessary, one of the occasions being the study of the Vedas.[24] Haradatta on the *Āpastambadharmasūtra* (1.5.15.1) states that ācamana is a subsidiary matter in all religious acts.[25] The pupils should take food that is sweet and provided with ghee—*bhojanaṃ madhuraṃ snigdham.*[26] Uvaṭa has interpreted the term snigdha as ghṛtaprāya. The food enables a man to use all his faculties[27] and the purity of thoughts depends upon the purity of food[28]—*āhāraśuddhau sattvaśuddhiḥ.*

One should study the Vedas in a clean place (*śucau deśe*)—holds the *Vājasaneyiprātiśākhya.*[29] The *Gautamadha-rmasūtra* enjoins that one should not study the Vedas in a burial ground, at the extremity of a village, on a high road nor in an impure place—*śmaśānagrāmāntamahāpaṭhā-śauceṣu.*[30]

The *Āpastambadharmasūtra* also states that one should not study the Veda on a market place, or one may study the Veda on a high road, after having smeared a place with cowdung.[31]

The *Vājasaneyiprātiśākhya* opines that one should study the holy text in a way that it is not within hearing of a Śūdra or an outcast—*śūdrapatitayorasaṃśavaṃ svādhyāyo' dhyetavyaḥ.*[32] A Śūdra and an outcast, i.e. patita are same as the burial ground—*śmaśānavacchūdrapatitau.*[33]

As the study of the Veda is prohibited in a burial ground or in an area within the throw of a śamyā, therefore a Śūdra and a Patita are excluded from the study of the Veda—holds the *Āpastambadharmasūtra.*[34]

One should study the Vedas in the proper season, i.e. in agreeable period—*ṛtuṃ prāpya.*[35] Uvaṭa and Anantabhaṭṭa interpret the passage as follows—*hemantamṛtuṃ prāpya rātryāścaturthaprahare' dhīyīta.* Here the term ṛtuṃ may mean the proper time. The Dharmasūtras lay down some restrictive rules to be observed in respect to the time and place of the study of the Veda. As for example, the *Gautamadharmasūtra* states that one should not study the Vedas at midnight, in the twilight and while standing in water nor while rain falls—*niśāyāṃ sandhyodayeṣu, varṣati ca.*[36] The suitable period is therefore held by the two commentators for the study of the Veda as the season of Hemanta, comprising the months of margaśirṣa and Pauṣa where there is no rain, and the fourth prahara of the night, the period being the most pleasant and appropriate for studying and memorizing the Vedic texts. While studying the Veda, the pupil should place hiniself in convenient seat which is viewed in the *Vājasaneyiprātiśākhya.*[37]

The *Ṛgvedaprātiśākhya* holds that the pupil should sit to the right of the teacher if there is only one or two.[38] If, there are more pupils they should sit according to their own convenience.[39] The teacher should take his seat facing the east, the north or the north-east direction.[40] Having respectfully touched his feet (upasaṃgrahaṇa), the students invite the teacher saying—*adhīhi bhoḥ.*[41] The teacher then pronounces the auspicious syllable Om which is known as Praṇava. Om is to be recited in the beginning of the Vedic study—*Oṃkāraḥ svādhyāyādau.*[42] Gārgya Gopālayajvan in his *Vaidikābharaṇa* commentary on the Taittiriyaprātiśākhya derives the term Praṇava as follows: *praṇūyate prastūyate prārabhyate'nena veda iti praṇavaḥ.*[43] The syllable Om is the door of heaven for the teacher and the student as well; therefore, he should begin his lesson by pronucing it.[44] The *Ṛgvedaprātiśākhya* and the *Taittiriyaprātiśākhya* hold different views regarding the mode of utterance of the sacred syllable Om. The *Ṛgvedaprātiśākhya* states:

> *sa omiti prasvarati trimātraḥ prasvāra*
> *sthāne sa bhavatyudāttaḥ /*
> *caturmātro vārdhapūrvānudāttaḥ ṣaṇmātro*
> *vā bhavati dviḥsvaraḥ san//* [45]

While explaining the passage, Uvaṭa has stated very clearly that there are three views regarding the mode of utterance of Praṇava–*ime trayaḥ praṇavāḥ.* According to the first view, the word consists of three moras and is acute in proper scale—*sa oṃkāraśabdaśtrimātraḥ/ sthāne bhavati/ udāṭṭaḥ ca.* Uvaṭa again has stated—*kimidaṃ sthānamiti? upāṃśudhvānanimadopabdimanmandramadhyamatārāṇi sthānāni.* The *Taittiriyaprātiśākhya* explains–*sapta vācasthānāni bhavanti.*[46] The term sthāna is interpreted by Somayārya in his commentary to the relevant text thus–*yairvāk prayujyate yasmiṃśca tiṣṭhati tat sthānam/* i.e. it is called a sthāna whereby the voice is put to use and that wherein it stands. Upāṃśu is inaudible, which is without sound, without application of mind, but with effort, i.e. prayatna—*karaṇavadaśabdamamanaḥ prayogamupāṃśu.*[47] Dhvāna, i.e. murmur is inaudibleness of syllables and consonants—*akṣaravayañjanānāmanupalabdhirdhvānnaḥ.*[48] i.e. whisper is their audibleness *uplabdhirnimadaḥ.*[49]

Mandra, i.e. soft is the sound proceeding from chest, madhyama, i.e. middle is that sound proceeding from throat and tāra i.e. loud is that sound proceeding from head—*urasi mandram, kaṇṭhe madhyamam, śirasi tāram.*[50] According to the second view as laid down in the Ṛgvedaprātiśākhya, the syllable Om is pronounced with four moras with its first half as grave while the third view holds that it consists of six moras while twice accented.[51] The *Taittiriyaprātiśākhya* holds that o in Praṇava i.e. Om is to be uttered with two and a half moras–*okāraṃ tu praṇava eke'rdhatṛtiyamātraṃ brūvate.*[52] It is to be uttered with either one of acute, grave or circumflex which is held by Śaityāyana.[53]

According to Kauṇḍiṇya, it should be dhṛtaḥ pracayaḥ.[54] According to Plākṣi and Plākṣāyaṇa it is circumflex.[55] According to Vāmīki it is accute.[56] Some hold that with whatever tone the passage to be read at the very beginning of the study of the Veda, that tone is to be given to the utterance of Om.[57] The *Vājasaneyi Prātiśākhya* also holds that the syllable Om is entirely Udātta which contains three moras.[58] Thus, it is found that the opinions vary from school to school regarding the mode of utterance of the syllable Om which is obligatory to be pronounced at the beginning of the study. After the pronouncement of Om, the teachers begin the teaching of the Vedas to the pupils. He utters twice a word having only acute accent, a word without a consonant if not in the Kśaipra combination or a word used with iti in the Padapāṭha.[59] If the teacher utters two or more words, the first pupil repeats the first word and the others repeat the rest.[60] The teacher explains the grammatical rules such as the change of a final *m* to anusvāra (*paripannam),* the original form of a uṣma combination (*prākṛtamuṣma-bhāvam*), the dropping of a final *n* and its change to *r* or a uṣma (*nakārasya loparephoṣmabhāvam*), the absence of combination followed by *ṛ* (*ṛparam*), the combination of *r* (*rephasaṃdhi)* and hiatus (*vivṛti*).[61] The teacher recites only the first word if there is a compound and two words if they are without compounds.[62] The teacher recites the first praśna (a praśna consists of three *ṛks*) to the pupil on his right and the other students go around the teacher keeping him to the right. In this way, they all having learnt the praśnas, recited an adhyāya and at the end, they touched the feet of the teacher and departed.[64] They recited at the close of their study the stanza which was to be repeated everyday that is śatadhāramutsam.[65] They also recited the paridhānīya *ṛk* which goes as follows: *namo brahmaṇe namo'stvagnaye namaḥ pṛthivyai namaḥ oṣadhībhyah namo vāce namo vācaspataye namo viṣṇave mahate karomīti.*[66] The *Asvalāyanagrhyasūtra* holds *sa yāvanmanyeta tāvada-dhītyaitayā paridadhāti.*[67] i.e. the pupils having recited those texts as far as he thinks fit, finishes with the verse *namo brahmaṇe* etc.

These rules for teaching the Vedic texts are assigned to the Ṛgveda only as these are recorded in the Ṛgveda-prātiśākhya school.[68]

Thus, it can be deducted from what has been discussed above that in the ancient Indian education system, greatest importance was attached to handing down the Veda intact. Hence intense care was undertaken to preserve the proper accentuation of the Vedic texts. The teacher played the pivotal role in the whole process of imparting knowledge. The prime objective of acquiring the sacred knowledge was to know it properly which is conducive to the attainment of all kinds of prosperity and happiness. The *Vājasaneyiprātiśākhya* rightly observes—*jñāne/pauruṣyam/ svargyam/yaśasyam/āyuṣyam.*[69]

References

1. Introduction to the commentary (comm.) on the Vājasaneyi Prātiśākhyam
2. (a) Nirukta (Nir.) 1.17
   (b) śaunakaṃ ca viśeṣeṇa yenedaṃ pārṣadaṃ kṛtam. Viṣṇumitra in

his maṅgalācaraṇa of the Vargadvayavṛtti, Ṛgveda-prātiśākhyaṃ (Ṛg. Prā)

3. Durga on . . . padaprakṛtīni sarvacaraṇānāṃ pārṣadāni. Nir. 1.17
4. Vedādhyayanādanantaraṃ lakṣaṇajñānaṃ kuryāditi sāpekṣatvāt lakṣaṇasya, purvaṃ vedādhigame satyatha lakṣaṇaparīkṣāvasaraḥ. Somayārya on Tribhāṣyaratna comm. on T.Prā. 1.1.
5. Uvaṭa in his introduction to the comm. on Ṛg. Prā.
6. Viṣṇumitra on his vargadvayavṛtti on Ṛg Prā.
7. Quoted in Patañjali's Mahābhāṣya, Paśpaśāhnikaḥ
8. Ś.B. 11.5.7.1–9.
9. T.U., 1.11
10. AV. Prā. 14.101, 104
11. Ibid., 4.105.
12. Quoted by Medhātithi on Manu. 3.1
13. Yājñikairyathāsamāmnātam. Ibid., 103
14. Nirukta, 1.18
15. Vā. Prā., 8.43
16. Dakṣasmṛti, 2.34
17. Āp. Dh. S., 1.1.1.14
18. Chā. U. 6.14.2
19. (a) Tai, Prā., 24.6
    (b) Viṣṇumitra in his Vargadvayavṛtti on Ṛg. Prā., V.8
20. Ṛg Prā., 15.1
21. Ibid.
22. Vā. Prā. 1.20
23. Uvaṭa's comm., ibid
24. Āp. Dh. S., 1.5.15.1
25. Haradaṭṭa's comm. . . , ibid
26. Vā. Prā., 1.25
27. Chā. U., 7.9.1
28. Ibid., 7.26.2
29. Vā. Prā., 8.35
30. G.D.S., 2.7.18
31. Āp. Dh. S., 1.3.9.5
32. Vā Prā., 8.36
33. Āp. Dh. S., 1.3.9.9
34. Śūdrapatitasakāśe' pi śamyāprāsādādarvāṅ nādhyeyam. Haradatta, Ibid.
35. Vā. Prā., 1.23
36. G.D.S. 2.7.12, 13
37. Iṣṭam, Vā. Prā., 1.22
38. Ṛg Prā., 15.2
39. Ibid., 15.3
40. Ibid., 15.1

41. Ibid., 15.4
42. Vā. Prā., 1.16
43. Vaidikābharaṇa on Tai. Prā, 18.1
44. Ṛg Prā., 15.6
45. Ṛg. Prā., 15.5
46. Tai. Prā., 23.4
47. Ibid., 23.6
48. Ibid., 23.7
49. Ibdi., 23.8
50. Ibid., 23.10, 11, 12
51. Ṛg. Prā., 15.5
52. Tai Prā., 18.1
53. Ibid., 18.2
54. Ibid., 18.3
55. Ibid., 18.5
56. Ibid., 18.6
57. Ibid., 18.7
58. Vā, Prā., 2.51
59. Ṛg. Prā., 15.9
60. Ibid., 15.10
61. Ibid., 15.12
62. Ibid., 15.14
63. Ibid., 15.21
64. Ibid., 15.22
65. Ibid.,15.32 vide Uvaṭa, Ibid.
66. Vide, Uvaṭa, Ibid.
67. Āś Gṛ. S. 3.4.4.
68. Viṣṇumitra in his vargadvayavṛtti on Ṛg. Prā. V.7
69. V., Ibid.; Prā., Ibid., 8.37–41

16

NATURE OF VIVṚTTI IN ŚIKṢĀS AND PRĀTIŚĀKHYAS

Bhabani Prasad Bhattacharya

The ancillary Vedic texts usually called Vedaṅgas are six in number which go by the names of śikṣā (phonetics), kalpa (ritual or ceremonal), vyākaraṇa (grammar), nirukta (etymology), chandaḥ (metrics) and Jyotiṣa (astronomy). The Veda-lakṣaṇa texts, however denote Vedic texts on phonetics which include Śikṣās and Prātiśākhyas. In this connection let us look at the comment of Sāyaṇa on the word of 'śikṣā' which runs as follows–*śikṣante vedanayopadiśyante svaravarṇādayo yatrāsau śikṣā śikṣā vidyopādāne. śikṣate* which denotes works containing rules regarding the proper pronunciation of Vedic texts. At the beginning of the Taittirīya Upaniṣad I. I, we come across a detailed description of śikṣā (here it is spelt with a long 'i') which states—*śikṣāṃ vyākhyāsyāmaḥ. Varṇaḥ, svaraḥ, mātrā, valaṃ, sāma, santāna ityuktaḥ śīkṣādhyāyaḥ.* Here we find the subject matter of śikṣās. Varṇa which consists of varṇaḥ, svaraḥ, mātrā, valaṃ, sāma, and santāna. Varṇa means sounds which include both vowels and consonants By svara the three principal accents name udātta, anudātta and svarita are taken into account. Mātrā means quantity or the time taken in the pronunciation of short (*hrusva*), long (*dīrgha*) and probated (*pluta*) vowel. Vala denotes the sthāna (place of utterance) and prayatna (effort) in the pronunciation of sound. Sāma or sāmya refers to the correct pronunciation devoid of faults like Atidruta, ativilambita, nīti and etc.

The alphabetic sounds are characterised by qualities (*guṇaḥ*) and faults (*doṣaḥ*) in so far as their pronunciation is concurred. Their correct utterance is regarded as qualities while their incorrect utterance is rightly condemned as mistakes. Santāna means saṁhitā or euphonic combinatioṅ which generally goes by the name of sandhi.

In the light of the varied contents of śikṣā it will be interesting to look at the nature of vivṛtti which forms an important subject of discussion in the Śikṣās and the Prātiśākhyas (Prs.). Vivṛtti or hiatus is the interval or gap between two vowels. It is derived from Vivṛtti 'to fly in different directions' and means 'the opening of two vowels upon each other without blending, hiatus'. Hiatus means break or interruption in continuity, a break between adjacent vowels in the pronunciation of a word. When two vowels, due to euphonic combination (sandhi) or prakṛtibhāva, occur side by side, then in order to prevent their coalescence or merger for the sake of correct utterance, some kind of stopping is necessary. Such gap or interval goes by the name of Vivṛtti. In RP.II.3, Vivṛtti has been defined thus *svarāntaraṃ tu Vivṛttiḥ*. Uvaṭa, the commentator, says—'*asyāmeva saṃhitāyāṃ yat svarayorantaraṃ vakṣyati tadvṛttisaṃṣat syāt. nū itthā te pūrvathā ca* (RV.I.132.4), YŚ 94 says in this connection *dvayostu svarayormadhye sandhiryatra na dṛśyate. vivṛttistatra viñyeyā yā īśeti nidarśanam'*. Regarding the nature of hiatus. the commentary on Vyāsaśikṣā points out *'virāmaḥ tūṣṇīsbhāvaḥ kālaḥ syāt'* which defines it as a 'time of silence'. But this definition goes against the Indian theory of continuity of sounds so strongly maintained by Patañjali on Pañ I. 4.109 and other grammarians. In his Mahābhāṣya, we find '*paraḥ sannikarṣaḥ saṃhitā cedadrutāyāmasaṃhitam. paraḥ sannikarṣaḥ saṃhitā cedadrutāyām vṛttausaṃhitāsañā na prāpnoti. drutāyāmebo hi paraḥ sannikarṣo varṇānāṃ nādrutāyām.* There is also no proof to presume that the hiatus was accompanied by a glottal stop. By the hiatus then, the ancient grammarians may have meant a glide between one sound and another and this phenomenon is in a way confirmed by RP. ll. 4 which assigns only a quarter of a more (time of a svarabhakti) to the hiatus.

The syllabic quality of hiatus has been debated fiercely in the śikṣās and the Prs. Regarding its quality, different Prs. have expressed widely divergent views. According to TP, XXII. 13, pause for hiatus is of one morā, e.g. '*sa idhānaḥ, ta enam, tā asmat*'. RT.IV 35 prescribes only half a morā between the two adjacent vowels, whether they may be short or long. This view seems to be in consonance with RP. II 4 which prescribes half Vivṛtti. According to TP the pause for hiatus in the interior of a word is of half a morā '*pra-ugan*'. Inter word hiatus (hiatus in the same word simple for compund) or Antaḥpada vivṛtti also occurṣ in RP. II I3 where four such cases have been enumerated—*puraucatā titaunā praugaṃ nāmauktibhiḥ/ antaḥpadaṃ vivṛttayaḥ//* Though their duration has not been stated. However, in the Tribhāṣyaratna commentary on TP XXII B a couple of verses have been quoted which lay down four sub-divisions of hiatus and assign different qualities to them. Hiatus between a short and a long vowel is called Vātsānusṛti and it is of one morā in length, that between a long and a following short vowel is known as Vātsānusāriṇī and it is of the same length. Hiatus between two short vowels is called Pākavati and it consists of three quarters of a morā while that between two long vowels, goes by the name of pipilikā is of a quarter morā only.

In RP. II 4, the quality of Vivṛtti has been spoken of having optionally the same duration as svarabhakti. Tvaṭa, the celebrated commentator, however, explains in a different way. He says—'*tatrāyam vivṛttervibhāgastri . . . ubhayatohrasvā pādamātrākālā ṛbhubhyaḥ* (RV. IV. 33.1). *pratyu adarśi* (RV. VII.81.1). *ekatodīrghā ardhamātrākālā/ nū ithhā te* (RV. I.132.4). *yāno. . . .* (RV. IX.91.1)/ *ubhayatodīrghā pādonamātrākālā. tā īṃ vardhanti* (RV. I.155.3). *imā gāvaḥ sārameyā aichaḥ* (RV. X.I08.5). The above observation of Uvaṭa that Vivṛtti is of three-fold nature and is open to criticism. It should be noted in this connection that the so-called three divisions of Vivṛtti is nowhere recognized in the RP. It seems all the more probable that only two kind of svarabhaktis having been recognized in this Prātiśākhya (cf. I.33, I.35; VI 48, 49),Vivṛtti which is here said to have the same duration as svarabhakti should have the same two-fold division. Over and above, both the second and third varieties of Vivṛtti which are described by Uvaṭa as consisting of 1/2 (one half) and 3/4(three fourth) morā respectively are designated as long Vivṛtti in RP.II.79. In this connection let us look at the observation of Uvaṭa in his commentery on II. 79—*yato dīrghastato dīrghā vivṛttayaḥ, svarāntaṃ tu vivṛttiḥ (2/3) ityuktam tatra yata dīrghasvaro bhavati purastāt paścādubhayato vā tato dīrghā vivṛttayo veditavyā ghoṣā indo nṛsā asi* (RV. IX.2.10) *ya ānayat parāvataḥ* (RV. VI.45.1)/ *ta āpo . . . māmavantu* (RV. VII.49.1)

In the śikṣā works, however, a four-fold classification of Vivṛttis comes to our view. According to Yś 11 10, pipīlikā. pākavata, vatsānusāriṇī and vatsānusṛjitā (or vatsānusaṃśrita) are the four varieties of hiatus. The first variety arises when both the former and the latter vowels are long, the second variety occurs when both the vowels are short. When the preceding vowel is long and the succeeding vowel is short, the third variety comes in to being. In the fourth type the position is just the reverse i.e. the former is short and the latter long. Nāradīya Śikṣā II. 3.1-2 and Māṇdukī Śikṣā also express identical views in this connection.

We have already seen that when either of the vowels is long the Vivṛtti is called Dīrgha according to R.P. II. 79. Hence pipīlikā. vatsānusāriṇī and vatsānusṛjitā will all come under the ambit of Dīrgha Vivṛtti. The word 'Vivṛtti' makes its appearance in VP.VII. (*hrasvakaṇṭhyopakaṃ visarjanīyāntapadayutaṃ vivṛttyā*—A word ending in visarjanīya and preceded by a short guttural vowel., [i.e. *a*, if not rhotacised, (is intervened) by a hiatus (in parigraha)] where it is also used in the same sense as that of Śikṣās and other Prs. When there is a hiatus on each side of an intermediate vowel the hiatus is known as Dvisandhi Vivrtti acc to RP. II.80, e.g. *tasmā (a) adya samanā suktaṃ bhara* (RV. VIII.66.7) Uvaṭa makes the point clear *'madhyagatasvarasyobhayataḥ svarau yāsām vivṛttīnāṁ tā ubhayataḥ svarasvarāḥ.'*

Now a question arises regarding Uvaṭa's treatment of Vivṛtti (optionally) in RP. In RP. II.4 the learned commentator lays down three varieties of hiatus. But it goes against the Sūtrakāra who in his rule has stated that the duration of Vivṛtti resembles that a Svarabhakti, which has been divided into two classes namely dīrghatarā and hrasvatarā. So in consonance with the spirit of the rule, it should be of twofold. But Uvaṭa's interpretation in this context can be justified if we take the meaning of 'Vā' in the Sūtra into consideration. It may be possible that perhaps Uvaṭa bases his threefold division of Vivṛtti on the word 'Vā' (optionally) (*adhikavat*) in the rule. Here another observation of Uvaṭa deserves notice. He says—*'vivṛttiṣu pratyāderadarśnaṃ (14/59) iti doṣaṃ vakṣyati. Ataśchātyoṣṇavadvivṛttiriti saṁyaga vyākhyānaṃ na bhavati'*. The meaning of the above passage appears to be somewhat confusing to us. It might mean that, according to some authorities, just as there is a conformity between the decrease of chāyā (shadow) and the increase of uṣṇa (or *ātapa*) (heat), in the same way there is an agreement or correspondence between the decrease of the side-vowels and the increase of vivṛtti. But Uvaṭa is of the opinion that it is not true, as *pratyayāderadarśanaṁ* (XIV. 59) is recognized as a fault in pronunciation. According to the above rule, in hiatuses the initial letter of the following word disappeared as in *'yā aicchatha'* and *'ya auśijaḥ'*. The disappearance of diphthongs 'ai' and 'au' in the above two cases has been condemned as a mistake in its pronunciation. Here Uvaṭa's contention seems to be that otherwise *pratyayāderadarśanaṁ,* like *cāyāyā adarśanam* at the extreme point, ought to have been recognized as a fact and not as a fault. But, in view of the explicit rule *yato dīrghas tato dīrghā vivṛttayaḥ* (II.79) [when there is (at least) a long vowel, the hiutuses are long], doubt has been expressed about the accuracy of this suggested meaning mentioned above. Another plausible explanation can be offered in the following way—By the statement *chāyoṣṇavāda* etc. Uvaṭa here is referring to a view prevalent during that period which, on account of vā in the present sūtra, was suggested or held by some as an alternative to the view expressed by svarabhaktikāla. But all this is mere conjecture and I place the above statement of Uvaṭa to the bar of the academic world for a critical and unbiased view of the same.

Another interesting aspect of Vivṛtti should be taken into account before coming to an end. Sometimes the preceding vowel in a hiatus is nasalized. Thus the hiatus, which form *yacā* (sūtra 60) to one with its penultimate lengthened (sūtra 66) have been prescribed, have their penultimate nasalized. [*yacādayo yā vihitā vivṛttayaḥ plutogadhāntā anunāsiko-padhāḥ* (ṚP. II.67)] Uvaṭa says—*'ānunāsikyamupadhānāṃ vidhīyate'* (II.67). Pāṇini's rule *'āṅo' nunāsikaś candasi'* may be found handy in this connection. In the well-known Akṣasūkta (X.34), we come across a verse (X. 34.5) where in the third foot we find *nyuptāś ca vabhravo vācamakratanemīdeṣāṃ niṣkṛtaṃ jāriṇīva //* The preceding vowel 'a' in 'akrata' before 'e' has been nasalized. Here Dr. K.C. Chatterjee comments—'The vowel has been nasalized to avoid the hiatus.' Therefore, sometimes, nasalization has been assorted to in order to avoid the hiatus in an euphonic combination.

Let us now conclude the topic on the nature of Vivṛtti as revealed in the śikṣās and prātiśākhyas. In the foregoing pages we have discussed Vivṛtti or hiatus from various standpoints which include its salient feature, classification and its role in grammar, especially the śikṣās and the prātiśākhyas. The euphonic combination which goes by the name of sandhi, sandhāna and saṁhitā has in its wider scope includes Prakṛtibhāva and Vivṛtti. Though hiatus does not conform to the Indian theory of continuity of sounds strongly advocated by Patañjali and other grammarians. Vyāsaśikṣā's commentary explains Vivṛtti as *virāma* or *tūṣṇīmbhāva* (time of silence), *abasāna* or pause has also been defined as *virāma*' or pause here in the light of interpreting Vivṛtti as *virāma.* Whether *avasāna* and Vivṛtti are two different names of the same phenomenon or whether there is some distinguishing trait between the two phenomena it needs to be pondered upon. The problem presented by us appears somewhat puzzling before our eyes and it is for the assembled scholars to arrive at a reasonable solution at the earliest. Vivṛtti is an interesting phonetic phenomenon in śikṣās and prātiśākhyas and it requires further critical research from the standpoints of grammar and linguistics.

17

A REVISIT TO THE SPHOṬA THEORY IN RESPONSE TO QUERIES ON SPEECH PRODUCTION AND SPEECH RECEPTION

KARUNASINDHU DAS

The unique role of articulated speech (*vāc*) as a vehicle of communication among social human beings was eagerly noticed in India from a very early date of history. Invocation to gods and goddesses postulated as immanent beings behind everything in the universe was, therefore, performed verbally by incantation of *mantras,* though physical effort (*ceṣṭā*) of offering oblations and gesture (*iṅgita)* too had some part in propitiation. It is not without reason that the Nāṭyaśāstra of Bharata identified text (*pāṭha*), tune (*gīta*), movement and gesture (*abhinaya*) and aesthetic relish (*rasa*) as components of dramatic performance derived from the four Vedas. Bharata, for obvious reasons classified *abhinaya* (dramatic performance) into four viz. *kāyika* (physical), *āhārya* (augmented i.e. make-up, decoration of stage, light etc.), *sāttvika* (emotional) and *vācika* (verbal). To him, however, the last one is the predominant one over the rest for as he has properly ascertained, all others are comprehended in terms of *vāc.* Showing red eyes or a fist or shivering in the body conveys something to be understood verbally. Verily, as the *Vākyapadīya* states, nothing can be conceived without reference to *vāc.* It is the essence of the vast expanse of word and the world indeed.

Long before Bharata and even before Pāṇini, Yāska in his

Nirukta (Ch. 1) had offered a positive estimate of this efficacy of *vāc* in comparison with other tools of communication.[4] Concept of *vāc* in Vedic tradition, in fact, encompasses both physics and metaphysics of langugage. The *Devīsūkta,* otherwise called *Vāk-sūkta* (Ṛk. 10.125. 1–8), for example, admits origin of *vāc*[5] in the waters in deep ocean from where it is posited in the vast expanse of the universe by divine will.[6] It is called the conscious *(cikituṣī)* principle responsible for our sustenance and knowledge[7] and the abode for all though some might not be aware of the same.[8] Every being, human, superhuman or so, attains power, glory and merit out of it.[9] It pervades all regions,[10] spreads through all beings and goes even beyond them.[11] Its greatness lies in this that it blows like the wind.[12] It creates heaven and earth, and still transcends them.[13] A *Bṛhadāraṇyaka* passage[14] describes it as the holy cow granting favour through the four udders viz. *svāhākāra, vaṣaṭkāra, hantakāra* and *svadhākāra* towards gods, human beings and the departed souls. A verse in the *ṚK* itself went to the extent of identifying four levels of *vāc,* the first three being subtle ones of the fourth one alone of which human glottis can articulte.[15] Verily, *vāc* at all levels is really difficult to comprehend,[16] and the wise alone does succeed therein.[17]

This stratification of *vāc* took another turn in the *Māṇḍūkyopaniṣad* where four segments of the holy chant *OM* viz, a, u, m and the one beyond them are represented as four phases of Brahman in waking, sleep, deep sleep and byond that.[18] To *Chāndogya,* therefore, *OM* is the object of meditation.[19] Interestingly, the concept of *Oṅkāra-brahman* developed in due course into that of *śabdabrahman* and also distinction between *śabdabrahman* and *parabrahman* was emphasised in some quarters. While this relates *vāc* to the world in causal relationship, there was another move towards describing both name and frame, i.e. to say, the verbal and material worlds as imperfect manifestation of reality. The vast expanse of *vāc,* too, was taken notice of in right earnest so much so that a commentator on the relevant *Taittirīya* passage[20] compared it to the ceaseless flow of sound of an ocean and analysis of the same into intelligible components was devised as a step to comprehend the whole.

That the seeds prevalent therein sprouted and flourished subsequently can be duly testified in schools of *Vedāṅga,* poetics, and philosophy. It is no wonder that four out of the six *vedāṅgas* are addressed to various aspects of language study viz. phonetics and phonolology, metrics, morphology, and semantics. Yāska's *Nirukta,* for example, is used to two coinages viz, *vacana* and *śabda* for *vāc.* To him, too, it has two levels; the one which is perishable within a very few seconds of its articulation while the other is all-pervading and subtle as well at the same time, and hence capable of communicating among people.[21] The whole of the sciences of *Vyākaraṇa* and *Nirukta* is, in fact, addressed to explore the methods and nuances of *vāc* as a vehicle of communication. Poetics, including rhetoric and prosody, aims also at pace, tempo, music and beauty of figurative speech while schools of philosophy would concentrate, more or less, on *vāc* as a valid testimony to verbal cognition. To Bharata's *Nāṭyaśāstra,* again, *vāc* is meant for communicating to the audience by reciting the script of a drama for which he demands utmost attention of actors. Body language, make-up and the like in an enactment reveal, in fact, what a verbal expression has to say. This reminds one of the *Vp.* statement *arthapravṛttitattvānāṃ śabdā eva nibandhanam (Vp.* 1.13). As *Nś* envisages, it is *vāc* which constitutes and sustains śāstras, it excels all others in that respect and hence it may be safely called the cause of all of them.[24] That sounds produced from inanimate objects too can not be left aside for obvious reasons as noticed in Nyāya-Vaiśeṣika philosophy according to which any *śabda* is nothing but a physical property of *ākāśa,* an effect produced either out of conjunction or disjunction of two objects or so or from a previous sound.[25] For an elaborate classification of sounds in the above line one may refer to *Śabdārtharatna* (pp. 6–7) by Tārānātha Tarkavācaspati, a nineteenth century grammarian-philosoher of Bengal.[26] It comes out as follows:

śabda (sound) :

(1)	*abuddhihetu*	(2)	*buddhihetu*
	e.g. (1) rumbling sound of a cloud (produced in an inanimate object)	(2)	(caused by an animate being)
2a.	*svābhāvika* (natural)	2b.	*kālpanika* (artificial)
	a/ a. e.g. laugh, cry		
	b / a. *vādyādirūpa* (produced from drum) b /b. *gītirūpa* (song)		b / c. *varṇātmaka* (articulated phoneme)

Of course, a sound produced at its source and the one perceived at the hearer's end, in fact, are not the same. As early as in the second century BC. Patañjali's *Mahābhāṣya,* therefore, defined *śabda* from three different perspectives: first, it is that which when uttered by a speaker communicates something,[27] secondly, it is the sound from which something is usually comprehended by hearer,[28] and thirdly, it is an object of auditory perception, something posited in *ākāśa* though it is effulgently manifest by articulation, and conceived at the intellectual plane.[29] Distinction between initial sound and reverberation thereof was further clarified in the *Mbh* on P. 1.1.70 as one between *sphoṭa* and *dhvani.*[30] Then came identity of *r* in both *r* and *ṛ,* the type sound or the abstract sound image designated as *sphoṭa.*[31]

Now, use of *śabda* as a communicating vehicle *(arthaprayukte śabdaprayoge)* and concept of permanence thereof *(siddhe śabdārthasambandhe)* in both Kātyāyana's *Vārttika* and *Mbh* obviously lead to accepting two planes of *vāc* viz. the physical sound in either its grotesque subtle form and the image revealed thereby as the meaning bearing unit. This develops in due course into the *sphoṭa* theory of language in the Vp. verse viz. *dvāv upādānaśabdeṣu śabdau śabdavido viduḥ/ eko nimittaṁ sābdānām, aparo'rthe prayujyate* (Vp 1.44) Contribution of individual sounds coming out in sequence or revelation of *sphoṭa* is also taken notice of in Vp. 1.85. Verily, a combination of impressions left by the preceding sounds and the final sound itself may well play the catalytic agent in revealing a *sphoṭa.*[32]

As it occurs, Vp. has suggested some alternative ways to understand the relationship between *dhvani,* the revealer, the *sphoṭa,* the revealed. Both of them may either be grasped as non-different as a crystal in relation to redness in a red flower nearby (cf. *sphoṭarūpāvibhāgena dhvaner grahaṇam iṣyate*—Vp. 1.81). Or, a sound can be grasped exclusively in terms of revealing a *sphoṭa* (cf. *kaiścid dhvanir asaṁvedyaḥsvatantro'nyaiḥ prakalpitaḥ*—Vp. 1.81). Or, a sound may be perceived without the revealed, as flame is seen from a distance even if the light is far away.[33] The relationship may be noted also as one between a genre and an individual.[34] To Vp, the worlds of *nāman* and *rūpa,* i.e. to say, both verbal and material proliferations, are manifestations of *vāc.*[35]

The idea may be traced to the Vedic passage which propounds this world as but a form of the *Vairājapuruṣa* who is made up of nothing but the Vedas.[36] Admission of this intimate relationship between name and frame has got far-reaching implications in the realm of epistemology. As Bhartṛhari formulates, an object of knowledge is perceptible always in term of a name given thereto.[37] Cognition of meaning, therefore, entails the meaning-bearing as well. In other words, *śabda* offers itself too when it projects a meaning.[38] Verily a *śabda* never conveys a meaning without being itself a part of that meaning. Mere existence of *śabda* does not make any sense whatsoever.[39] Neither a speaker nor the hearer can afford to think of a communication without any reference to *śabda.*[40] Even articulation of a sound which is the end product of upward movement of the inner wind followed by placement of the tongue and its stroke or so at a particular place does not take place without an idea of *śabda*.[41] Every cognition, verbal or non-verbal, in fact, is infused with *śabda* and it always comes to light in the form of *vāc*.[42]

All this is in contradistinction to the proposition that *śabda* can be at best the cause of a cognition and nothing more than that. True, the conglomeration of causes rests in *vāc* (cf. *itikartavyatā loke sarvā śabdavyapāśrayā* Vp. 1.121), but the same is the case with an effect as well. This leads rightly to comparison of *śabda* to *tejas* which illumines others and is self-illuminating as well.[43] Concept of non-difference *(tādātmya)* between *śabda* and *artha* as it is propagated by philosopher-grammarians of the Pāṇinian school, justifies itself in this that one is posited in the other *(tasmād arthavidhāḥ sarvāḥ śabdamātrāsu niścitāḥ*—Vp 1.119).

Bhartṛhari, for obvious reasons, attends to both the holistic and analytic approaches to *vāc* prevalent among the intelligentsia. He propounds immutable *vāc* as the reality but still admits morphological analysis[44] as a facilitating device meant for beginners[45] since the latter, though unreal and untrue, may help one in arriving at truth.

Another area of linguistic deliberations where Vp. offers striking note of synthesis and reconciliation is treatment of standard and non-standard forms of language. A Vedic chant did not approve of any slipshod mistakes in articulation lest it spoils the magic power inherent therein and adversely affects the prospects of the reciter. Non-standard forms, however, were very much in use even among the learned in social communications.[47] And if Patañjali's enumeration of *varṇadoṣas* in the Mbh. paspaśā be any indicaiton, there were dialects, sociolects and idiolects with a plethora of phonetic and morphemic variations[48] in the language. So far as communication is concerned, this authority did not envisage any distinction between standard and non-standard forms (cf. *samānāyām arthāvagatau śabdena cāpaśabdena ca*–Mbh), though merit is assured in the former. The Mīmāṁsā on the other hand takes a different approach to this problem. Since human fault is made responsible for non-standard *(apabhraṁśa)* forms[49] it is the standard one that is accepted there as meaningful.[50] Kumārila even goes to the extent that truth and reality lie in standard forms only and that to speak of reality means maintaining the same in both form and content.[51] And the standard one is earmarked by the learned: *yam abhiyuktā upadiśanti eṣa eva sādhuriti.*—Śabara on J. 1.3.27.

True, some of the non-standard forms have been in vogue for long and some would like to assign some denotation thereto. But a mīmāṁsaka would never accept this position. He would even refuse to concede that a non-standard form may be secondarily significant by reminding one of the standard which is actually significant.[52]

Bhartṛhari however tends to admit that non-standard forms too are meaningful though not directly as it is in the case of synonyms but through reminding one of the standard one.[53] This holds good particularly for those who know *śabda* as well as the *apaśabda* variants thereof. It is like comprehending something from the indistinct utterance of a child. The hearer remembers thereby the proper form to grasp the meaning.[54]

However, for those who have acquaintance not with the standard form at all but with the non-standard only it is the latter alone that communicates[55] since no scope is left there for inferring the standard one from the other. It is not that there is any error involved in that understanding. Because no subsequent contradiction occurs to nullify the same.[56]

It obviously follows that the demarcation line between a *śabda* and an *apaśabda* can be drawn not in terms of semantic capability or otherwise but at the instance of a prescriptive vyākaraṇa.[57] Bhartṛhari notes that there are three divergent views in relationship between *śabda* and *apaśabda.* To some, standard words develop from the non-standard ones[58] while others suggest the reverse,[54] incapability of a speaker to pronounce correctly being the reason behind a faulty utterence. A third view visualizes independent existence of both and admits that either may fail to communicate if the other is intended.[60]

As for articualtion of individual sounds, there were several formulations in the *Śikṣā* and *Prātiśākhya* literatures. cf. *vāyuśarīrasamīraṇāt kaṇṭhorasoḥ sandhāne* (Taittirīya-prātiśākhya 2.2) which ascertained upward movement and stroke of the internal wind at the junction of *uras* and *kaṇṭha* for the purpose. As per *Pāṇinīyaśikṣā* 6.7,[61] on the other hand, action of *manas* and internal fire *(kāyāgni)* precedes that of the internal wind. The Vp. develops it further in a different way and records as many as three views in this respect in the verse viz. *vāyor aṇūnāṁ jñānasya śabdatvāpattir iṣyate* (Vp 1.107). Thus, it is either the wind within or the smallest particle of sound or knowledge of something in the process of externalisation that gives rise to an articulation. Vp. admits action of the internal wind but reminds one of the fact that this action is possible if only there is already an idea of *śabda (śabdabhāvanā)* at the intellectual plane of the speaker.[62]

Thus Bhartṛhari stands midway between tradition and innovations. His commitment to *trayī vāc* (cf. *trayyā vācaḥ paraṁ padam-* Vp. 1.158) and still reference to the subtlest one as *parā vag anapāyinī* have been duly construed and reconciled later on. Verily, contribution of the *pratyabhijñā* philosophy of Kashmir Śaivism to admitting *parā* and *paśyantī* as two different strata was gracefully accommodated by his followers in the grammar school. Besides, acceptance of *sphoṭa* as the bearer of meaning beyond the physical features of *vāc* is another interesting area of language study in Vp. It may be a really fascinating exercise to compare these levels of *vāc* with *deep structure* and *surface structure,* or, for that matter, *competence and performance* propounded in Noam Chomsky's scheme. Interestingly, an articulated *vāc* or its next subtle phase viz. *madhyamānāda* is held responsible for revelation of *sphoṭa* and hence the revealed one can never be conceived of without any reference to the articulated form. One deep-level structure, on the other hand, may come out with several surface structures and vice versa. As for competence and performance, the latter always falls short of the former. The problem was tackled in the Vp. in terms of a speaker's intention vis-a-vis his linguistic performance subsequently. To Vp. the *vāc* one articulates perfectly represents the mental image[63] in the intending speaker's mind. That it may not corroborate the actual state of things is however a different question[64] which grammarians do not bother about at all. Nor do they fight shy of propagating Bhartṛhari's theory of immutable *vāc* and efficacy of morpho-syntactical analysis thereof at the interpretation level. This, in fact, helps Vp. in meeting all possible ends at different perspectives.

As it occurs, ancient Indian tradition envisages *vāk, śabda* or *vākya* at two different planes. One is *indriyanitya* that is existent for a short while within the time-frame of a speaker's utterance and listener's audience. This is *dhvani.* The other pervades and persists in the intelligence of both speaker and listener and conveys the exact import. It is with those two planes in view that Bhartṛhari in his *Vākyapadiya* (Vp) observes:

dvā upādānaśabdeṣu śabdau śabdavido viduḥ.
eko nimittaṃ śabdānām aparo'rthe prayujyate.

(1.44)

Needless to say, each verbal cognition is sure to offer a communication within the framework of that verbal structure. And as Patañjali's analysis of the meaning of *gauḥ* shows, there are both transitory and non-transitory segments of meaning—the particular object, its properties and functions falling within the first category and genre to the second.

The initial verse of the Vp. viz. *anādinidhanaṁ brahma śabdatattvaṁ yadakṣaram/ vivartate'rthabhātivena prakriyā jagato yataḥ,* suggests that *sabdabrahman* has got a twofold manifestation in terms of *vāc* and *artha* and that the two are generally inseparable and non-different. A grammarian philosopher of Pāṇini's school would certainly prefer this genre of speech as meaningful and an ideational object as the meaning thereof to audible sounds and a material-object or so respectively for neither sound(s) nor a matter can survive beyond a very limited time-span. The grammarian theory of *sphoṭa* as the meaning-bearing item obviously leads to *bauddhārthavāda,* the theory of ideational object as the meaning of speech. It has got its root in Patañjali's *Mahabhāṣya* on at least six rules of Pāṇini. On *tad asyāsty asminn iti matup* (P 5.2.94), for example, the commentator observes that a meaning and its existence are invariably co-existent. As it comes out, by meaning is meant one which is existent in intelligence *(buddhisattāsamāviṣṭa)* be it in any expressions viz. *vṛkṣaḥ asti. vṛkṣaḥ nāsti. vṛkṣaḥ jāyate* and so on. If an external object viz. tree were denoted by the word viz. *vṛkṣa.* the subesquent verb viz. *asti* would be superfluous for a *padārtha* cannot be conceived of without existence. To state that a tree does not exist is therefore a self-contradiction. That 'a sprout comes out,' too is a tautology for what exits cannot be born once again. Such expressions as *vṛkṣah asti/ nāsti/ jāyate* are justified then, if only ideational existence at the intellectual plane is acceptable. So the expression viz. *vṛrkṣo nāsti* means that while idea of a tree exists at the intellectual plane, no such tree exists in reality. By *aṅkuro jāyate* is meant what exists in the intellectual plane now comes into being in reality. This justifies such expression as *śaśaśṛṅgaṁ nāsti, ākāśa-kusumaṁ nāsti* with this in view that a hare's horn or a flower in the sky is only ideational—it is totally absurd in terms of reality.

Of course, each meaning need not and does not tally with the real state of affairs. The case of mirage and aerial city of the celestial residents is cited as an instance to that effect in the *Mahābhṣya* on 4.1.3. It exists verily in the mind of a person and not as an external object. That it is perceived even then at times by some is due to superimposition of the mental state outside that. As Bhartṛhari observes—the idea of an external object is perceived here as the object itself. Grammarians toe the line of Yogācāra Buddhists in admitting that a preceding series of impressions would result in such ideas that occur as external objects (Vp 3.13.8). What a word means therefore may refer to external existence in terms of superimposition only.

In other words, what is conceived need not be existent really. To a grammarian of Pāṇinin's school, a word is meaningful simply because of its reference to an idea of an object or so. The words viz. *śaśaśṛṅga, ākāśakusuma, mṛgatṛṣṇikā* etc. are also thus meaningful substantives *(arthavat prātipadika)* declined according as they relate themselves to a verb or so in a sentence (cf. *rāhoḥ śiraḥ).* The Vp. does not mind even though a word means something absurd.[17] The question of semantic incompatibility does not cut ice here if syntax is all right. In Yoga terminology all this is *vikalpajñāna* which grammarians exemplify in the following verse: *eṣa bandhyāsuto yāti khapuṣpakṛtaśekharaḥ/ kūrmakṣīracaye snātaḥ śaśaśṛṅgadhanurdharaḥ* meaning, here goes the son of a barren woman, who has decorated his head with ethereal flowers, who took bath in the milk of a tortoise and who has taken up a bow made of hare's horn! Corroborating the above, a *Kūrmapurāṇa* verse states that the world we perceive exists within our mind only and not outside that (cf. *vipra, pṛthvyādi cittasthaṁ na bahiḥsthaṁ kadācana).*

Interestingly, a grammarian-philosopher of Pāṇini's school does not disapprove of the existence of the external world altogther. What he states is this that external world i.e, material objects cannot be denoted by word(s). It certainly distinguishes itself from both the *Yogācāra* viewpoint of momentary *vijñāna* and the *asatkhyāti* of *Śūnyavādins* on the one hand and *Nyāya-Vaiśeṣka* position of verbally cognising the material world on the other. Unlike *Yogācāra,* the Pāṇinian school admits a non-momentary cognizing agency and an external world as well. Besides, it does not accept the position of monistic Vedānta that this world is merely phenomenal owing its existence and sustenance to *ajñāna* which is supposed to cover the substratum par excellence viz. Brahman and superimpose the world thereupon by virtue of its *āvaraṇaśakti* and *vikṣepaśakti* respectively. While some of the Vedantins would like to make a distinction between the phenomenal world and an illusory snake on a rope, the Māṇḍūkya verse viz, *svapnamāye yathā dṛṣṭe gandharivanagaraṁ yathā* etc. and the *Vedāntasiddhāntamuktāvalī* by Prakaśānanda accept all but Brahman as merely illusory.[65] To the Vedāntin of this monistic order, every illusory object is a creation and manifestation of nescience. The grammarian would, however, refuse to subscribe to this view. Verily, how is it possible to create them without drawing upon their respective material causes? The Chāndogya statement viz. *vācārambhaṇaṁ vikāro nāmadheyaṁ mṛttiketyeva satyam* is cited in favour of this vyākaraṇa position to the effect that it suffices to accept ideational objects in verbal cognitions and not creation thereof. Verily, a potter at first visualizes a pot in his mind and then produces the earthen one. This is like painting something in mind's canvas and then drawing the same outside. Same is the case with ideational objects denoted by verbal expressions.

The Pāṇinian philosophy does not see eye to eye with other systems in respect of epistemology also. True, it follows in the footsteps of the Sāṁkhya and the Yoga systems and admits *cittavṛtti* (mental state) corresponding to the object of a cognition and thereby comes close to the Vedānta view of *viṣayākārā antaḥkaraṇavṛtti*. But a grammarian would never accept reflection of a meterial object in the *cittavṛtti* concerned. Because, an object in a dream never awaits any relation whatsoever to an external object. When a conchshell is taken for a piece of silver, it is the ideational piece of silver that is grasped as lying in front. In case of *surabhi candanam* too, the object of cognition can be nothing but ideational. Recollection of a piece of silver or fragrance of sandalwood experienced earlier playing *jñānalakṣaṇa sannikarṣa* does not sound fit for the purpose.

To Vyākaraṇa, this idea and the word denotative of the same are treated as non-different.[68] This has been evinced in the *Mahābhāṣya* in course of deliberations on what actaully the *śabda* is in a cognition relating to *gauḥ* or so. Verily, a word itself too is included in the meaning' of the same[69] so that it is a meaning and the meaningful as well like fire which is self-illuminating and illuminator of other objects too.[70] An object of verbal knowledge or for that matter, any knowledge is thus invariably interwoven with linguistic feature.[71] Bhartṛhari has rightly pointed out that every linguistic performance involves three viz., the linguistic element, speaker's knowledge and material object[72] referred to resembling the stoic formulation of a triangle of *seminon, lektōn* and *prāgma.*[73] Deliberations on causative verb forms envisaged in the *Mahābhāṣya* on *hetumati ca* (p. 3.1.26) contribute substantially to propagating that verbal cognition pertains to idea(s) only and not the material world at all. Thus, a description of the fall of Kaṁsa *(Kaṁsaṁ ghātayati)* at the hands of Kṛṣṇa in a poem or so would certainly mean *bauddhakaṁsasya bauddhakṛṣṇena bauddhahananam.* This is definitely preferable to admitting a secondary meaning of the sentence by taking recourse to the faculty of implication therein for the purpose. As Vp. clarifies:

śabdopahitarūpāṁstān buddher viśayatāṁ gatān/pratyakṣam iva kaṁsādin sādhanatvena manyate. buddhipravṛttirūpañca samāropyābhidhātṛbhiḥ/artheṣu śaktibhedānāṁ kriyate parikalpanā.(Vp 3.7.5-6).

Needless to say, it is not the objective state of affairs but speaker's intention that plays the vital role in any verbal communications. Bhartṛhari has rightly ascertained this speaker's intention *(vivakṣā)* in terms of a mental state *(buddhyavasthā)*. Thus the same object may be referred to as either agent or instrument or so with reference to an action: cf *knife* cuts his finger and he cut his finger with a *knife,* pierces with or from a bow *(dhanuṣaḥ vidhyati* and *dhanuṣā vidhyati)* and so on. Even one object or so may be referred to as many with a multidimensional approach viz. *ātmānam ātmanā vetsi* where *ātman* which is one in reality is taken for both object and instrument. As Bhartṛhari states: *sādhanavyavahāraśca buddhyavasthānibandhanaḥ.* (Vp 3.7.3). This has nothing to do with reality.[76] What is mentioned as *kartṛ* of an act is simply because the speaker intended on stating that way. So even if a cooking pot is simply the container *(ādhāra)* one may easily state: *sthāili pacati* (the cooking pot cooks), *sthāilyā pacati,* (cooks with the pot), *sthālyāṁ pacati (cooks* in the pot) etc. without any reference to reality.[75] A speaker may present something as different though it is not so. What is non-existent in reality may well be described as existent in a statement and vice versa *(sato 'vivakṣā*). True, a speaker's intention does not transgress the limits of popular usage. But it does not fall short of what is conceived in mind as *buddhyavasthā* either. It transpires therefore that neither *buddhyavasthā* not usage is bound to reflect the actual state of affairs. As Nāgeśa admits, if a verbal knowledge is corroborated in actual use to offer a *saṁvādipravṛtti,* i.e., to say, if what is meant by a verbal use is justified subsequently in actual use the knowledge is to be taken as valid. If, however, the words denote ideational objects only not to be corroborated in material terms, the cognition is invalid *(apramāṇa).* In other words, a verbal congnition cannot be relied on before it is put to test and justified in reality.

It is amazing to note that *Vyākaraṇa* which vows to bank totally on usage does not fight shy of accepting this queer position where a big question mark vitiates the very authenticity of each verbal cognition.

Evidently, the Pāṇinian school had to pass a long way for arriving at its finale. We had to wait till the eighteenth century AD for a comprehensive disquisition on *bauddhārthavāda* in

Nāgeśa's *Laghumañjūṣā.* Buddhist idealism, *Mimāṁsa* and *Nyāya* contributed thereto on the way not only by raising questions but also by making inroads at places in its theoretical formulations, at least, to some extent. A critical analysis of Ṭārānātha Tarkavācaspati's *Śabdārtharatna* (1851 AD) may reveal how the *Navyanyāya* realism could help in theorizing the ontological and epistemological pursuits of the neo-Pāṇinian grammarians.

Philosophy of non-Pāṇinian grammars is however more articulate in upholding objective realism. Commentaries on *Mugdhabodha, Saṁkṣiptasāra, Kātantra* and the like, for example, accept the proposition that what is meant by a word is not at all an idea externalized but an object in reality.[77] The problem of reference to *hare's horn (śaśa-viṣāṇa)* etc. obviously comes up for ready solution. Some of the *Kātantra* grammarians[78] would not mind admitting ideational existence of something beyond reality for the sake of the very few verbal expressions but it is nothing but an exception that proves the general rule. In response to Śrīpati's observation that a word may denote either an object or an idea,[79] Gopinātha, therefore, shows that while both *hare* and *horn* are real as separate entities, their relationship as the one between a part and the whole is no more than conceptual propounded with an eye to deceiving someone or so.[80] The Pāṇinian viewpoint of ideational word-meaning in each case of signification does not find favour with these grammarians.

Gopīnātha is equally critical of the *sphoṭa* theory of langugae. He has beautifully summarised the arguments put forward by propounders of *sphoṭa* and then repudiated them altogether. To a *sphoṭavādin,* individual sounds would manifest *varṇasphoṭa* which in turn would present *padasphoṭa,* the bearer of word-meaning which again would manifest *vākyasphoṭa,* the one responsible for conveying the sentence meaning.[81] As he argues *sphoṭa* is directly perceptible too. As we perceive a piece of cloth after perceiving individual threads, so also we can perceive *sphoṭa* after perception of individual sounds,[82] he observes. Gopīnatha, howerver, is not convinced by this argument. To him, *sphoṭa* is not at all perceptible. Besides, it is better to explain a word meaning as being conveyed by a word itself.[83] Thus even if an individual sound perishes instantly after articulation, each constituent sound of a word leaves an impression so that when the final sound is comprehended the accumulation of impression left by preceding sounds come forward and join in presenting the word as whole. This is what actually bears the word-meaning, he says.

As per the Pāṇinian tradition, relationship between an articulation and the objective world traverses a quadrangular path as follows:

articulation (1) → *sphoṭa*(2)
objective world (4) → ideational meaning (3)

The world, therefore, exists beyond the direct linguistic experience. Non-Pāṇinian grammars do not contribute to this view. They envisage a direct relationship between word and the world to the tune of the Naiyāyikas. Divergence of views among schools of Sanskrit grammar viz. Pāṇinian and non-Pāṇinian on speech production and speech reception is yet to be explored and studied in all details. Non-Pāṇinian grammars are seldom taken up for intensive study. The sooner we act and re-act, the better for realizing our finest intellectual culture.

References

1. *aṇganepathya-sattvāni vākyārthaṃ vyañjayanti hi Nāṭyaśāstra. . . .*
2. *na so' sti pratyayo loke yaḥ śabdānugamād ṛte* - Vp. 1.123.
3. *vāṅmayānīha śāstrāṇi vāṅniṣṭhāni tathaiva ca/tasmād vācaḥ paraṃ nāsti, vāg hi sarvasya kāraṇam.*
4. *vyāptimattvāt tu śabdasya, aṇiyastvācca śabdena saṃjñā-karanaṃ*

vyavahārārthaṃ loke.

5. *mama yonir apsv antaḥ samudre.* Ṛk 10.125.7.
6. *taṃ mā devā vyadadhuḥ purutrā bhūristhātrāṃ bhūry āveśayantim* Ṛk 10.125.3.
7. *mayā so annam atti yo vipaśyati. yaḥ prāṇiti, ya īṃ śṛṇoty uktam*—ibid. 10.125.4.
8. *amantavo māṃ ta upakṣiyanti*—ibid. 10.125.4.
9. *juṣṭaṃ devebhir uta mānuṣebhiḥ yaṃ kāmaye taṃ tam ugraṃ karomi, taṃ brahmāṇaṃ tam ṛṣiṃ taṃ sumedhām*—ibid., 10.125.5.
10. *ahaṃ dvyāvāpṛthivī āviveśa*—ibid. 10.125.6.
11. *tato vitiṣthe bhuvanāni viśvā tāmuṅ dvyāṁ varṣmopaspṛśāmi*—ibid 10.125.7.
12. *aham eva vāta iva pravāmī*—ibid. 10. 125.8.
13. *paro divā para ena pṛthivyaitāvati mahinā saṁ babhuva*— ibid. 10.125.8
14. *vācaṁdhenum upāsīta, tasyāścatvāraḥ stanāḥ. . . .*
    prāṇa ṛṣabho mana vatsaḥ—Bṛh. 5.8.1.
15. *catvāri vāk parimitā padāni. . . .*
    guhā trīṇi nihitā neṅgayanti, turīyaṁ vāco manuṣyā vadant—Ṛk 164.45
16. *uta tvaḥ śṛṇvan na śṛṇoty enām*—Ṛk 10.71.4.
17. *tāni vidur brāhmaṇā ye manīṣiṇaḥ*—Ṛk 1.164.45.
18. *jāgaritasthāno vaiśvānaro' (a) kāraḥ prathamā mātrā... svapnasthānas taijasa ukāro dvitīyā mātrā . . . suṣuptasthānaḥ prājño makāras tṛtyā mātrā... amātras caturtho . . . evam oṅkara ātmaiva*—Māṇḍūkya 9–12.
19. *OM ityetad akṣaram udgītham upāsita*—Chāndogya 1.1.1.
20. *vāg vai parācy avyākṛtāvadat . . . madhyato'vakramya vyākarot*—Ts. 6.4.7
21. *vyāptimattvāt tu śabdasya, aṇiyastvācca, śabdena saṁjñākaraṇaṁ vyavahārārthaṁ loke*—Nirutkta 1.
22. *vāci yatnas tu kartavyo nāṭyasyaiṣā tanuḥ smṛtā*—Nś 15.2.
23. *aṅganepathya-sattvāni vākyārthaṁ vyañjayanti hi* ibid.
24. *vāṅmayānīha śāstrāṇi vāṅniṣṭhāni tathaiva ca, tasmād vācaḥ paraṁ nāsti, vāg hi sarvasya kāraṇam*—Nś 15.
25. *ākāśasya tu vijñeyaḥ śabdo Vaiśeṣiko guṇaḥ*—Bp. 28.
26. *śabdo hi nāma pṛthivyadi-bhūta-catuṣṭaya-kriyājanyo'vakāśadeśotpanno dravyāśrito guṇaviseśaḥ*— p. 6.
27. *yenoccāritena sāsna-lāṅgula-kakuda-khura-viṣāṇinām sampratyayo bhavati, sa śabdaḥ*—Mbh. paspaśā.
28. *pratītapadārthako loke dhvaniḥ śabdah ity ucyate*—ibid.
29. *śrotropalabdhiḥ buddhinirgrāhyaḥ prayogenābhijvalitaḥ ākāśadeśaḥ śabdaḥ*—Mbh.
30. *sphoṭaḥ śabdaḥ dhvaniḥ śabdaguṇah*—Mbh on *taparas tatkālasya.* P. 1.1.70.
31 cf. the Mbh on *kṛpo ro laḥ;1* P. 8.2.18 : *ubhayataḥ sphoṭamātam nirdiśyate.*
32. *nādair āhitabījāyam antyena dhvaninā saha.*
    āvṛttaparipākāyām buddhau śabdo'vadhāryate—Vp. 1.85.

33. *dūrāt prabheva dīpasya*—Vp 1.104.
34. *anekavyaktyabhivyaṅgyā jātiḥ sphoṭa iti smṛtā*—Vp 1.93.
35. *śabdatatvaṁ yad akṣaram, vivartate'rthabhāvena prakriyā jagato yataḥ*—Vp. 1.1: also, *śabdasya pariṇāmo yam ity āmnāyavido viduḥ, chandobhya eva prathamam etad viśvaṁ vyavartata*—Vp 1.120.
36. *sa u evaiṣa ṛṅmayo yajurmayaḥ sāmamayo vairājaḥ puruṣaḥ puruṣo vai lokaḥ. puruṣo yajñaḥ, tasya ... tiśra āhutayaḥ tā eva . . . trayo jokāḥ.*
37. *arthayātayaḥ sarvāḥ śabdākṛtinibandhaṇḥ*—Vp. 1.15.
38. *artharupam tathā sabde svarupañca prakāśate*—Vp 1.50.
39. *viṣayatvam anāpannaiḥ śabdair nārthaḥ prakāśyate, na sattayaiva te 'rthānām agṛhītāḥ prakāśakāḥ*—Vp. 1.56.
40. *yathā prayoktuḥ prāg buddhiḥ śabdeṣveva pravartate/vyavasāyo grahītṛṇām evaṁ teṣveva jāyate*—Vp. 1.53 41.
41. *ādyaḥ karaṇavinyāsaḥ prāṇasyordhvaṁ samīraṇam/ sthānānām abhighātaśca na vinā śabdabhāvanām.*—Vp. 1.122.
42. *na so 'sti pratyao loke yaḥ śabdānugamād ṛte/ anuviddham iva jñānaṁ sarvaṁ śabdena bhāsate*—Vp. 1.123: *vāgrūpatā ced utkrāmed avabodhasya śāśvatī, na prakāśaḥ prakāśeta sā hi pratyavamarśinī*—Vp. 1.124.
43. *grāhyatvaṁ grāhakatvañca dve śaktī tejaso yathā, tathaiva sarvaśabdānām ete pṛthag avasthite*—Vp. 1.55.
44. *anvākhyeyāśca ye śabdā ye cāpi pratipādakāḥ*—Vp. 1.24.
45. *upāyāḥ śikṣamāṇānām bālānām apalāpanāḥ, asatye vartmani sthitvā tataḥ satyaṁ samīhate*—Vp. 2.238.
46. *mantro hīnaḥ svarato vaṇato vā mithyāprayukto na tam artham āha, sa v-gvajro yajamānaṁ hinasti.*
47. *yad vānaḥ tad vā naḥ iti prayoktavye yarvāṇaḥ tarvāṇaḥ. iti prayuñjate. yājñe punaḥ karmaṇi nāpabhāṣante*— Mbh. paspaśa.
48. *grastaṁ nirsatam avalambitaṁ nirhatam ambūkṛtaṁdhmātam atho vikampitam/saṁdaṣṭam ardhakaṁ drutaṁ . . . etāḥ svaradoṣabhāvanāḥ iti. ato 'nye vyañjanadoṣaḥ*—Mbh. paspaśā.
Also, *ekaikasya śabadasya bahavo 'pabhraṁśāḥ;*
tad yathā gaur ity asya śabdasya
gāvī, gonī, gotā, gopotalikā ity evamādayo 'pabhraṁśāḥ—ibid.
49. *śabde prayatnaniṣpatter aparādhasya bhāgitvam*—J. 1.3.25 whereupon Śabara comments: *aparādhāt gāvyādayo bhaveyuḥ* and Kumārila adds thereto the following: *ataścānaparādhena vyajyamāneṣu sādhutā, sāparādheṣv-asādhutvam.*
50. *anyāyascānekaśabdatvam*— J. 1.3.26 whereupon Śabara comments: *eko nāḍiḥ anye apabhraṁśāḥ.*
51. *yadvā satyatvam evedaṁ sādhutvam abhidhīyate . . ., arthasatyaṁ yathā vācyaṁ śabdesatyaṁ tathaiva hi, śabdānṛtam ca hātavyam arthānṛtavad eva naḥ.*
52. *apabhraṁśeṣu sādhutvaṁ tulyārthatvād yaducyate, lakṣaṇabhāvamārgeṇa tasyābhāvo'pi niścitaḥ.*

53. *te sādhuṣv anumānena pratyayotpattihetavaḥ, na śiṣṭair anugamyante paryanā iva sādhavaḥ tasmāt sākṣād avācakaḥ*—Vp 1.149. 150.
54. *ambāmbeti yathā bālaḥ sikṣamāṇah prabhāṣate, avyaktam tadvidāṁ tena vyakte bhavati niścayaḥ. evaṁ sādhau prayoktavye yo'pabhraṁśaḥ prayujyate. tena sādhuvyavahitaḥ kaścid artho 'bhidhīyate*—Vp. 1.151.152.
55. *pāramparyād apabhraṁśā viguṇeṣvabhidhātṛṣu, prasiddim āgatā yeṣu teṣāṁ sādhur avācakaḥ*—Vp. 153.
56. *apabhraṁśānām aśaktatve tato bodha eva na syāt . . . na ca śaktibhramāt tebhyo bodhaḥ bodhakatvasyābādhena tadgrahasya abhramatvāt*—Vbs. Also ef. *sādhutvajñānaṁ na śābde kāraṇaṁ, nāpyasādhujñānaṁ pratibandhakam*—Uddyota on p. 3.2.84.
57. *evañca yaḥ śabdo yatrārthe vyākaraṇe vyutpāditaḥ sa tatra sādhur iti paryavasitam*—ibid.
58. *daivī vāg vyatikīrṇeyam aśaktair abhidhātṛbhiḥ anityadarśināṁ tvasmin vāde buddhiviparyayaḥ*—Vp. 1.154.
59. *śabdaḥ saṁskārahino yo gaur iti prayuyukṣite*
tam apabhaṁam icchanti—Vp. 1.147.
60. *ubhayeṣām avicchedād anyaśaktivivakśayā. yo'nyaḥ prayujyate śabdo na so'rthasyābhidhāyakaḥ*—Vp. 1.155.
61. *manaḥ kāyāgnim āhanti, sa prerayati mārutam.*
mārutastūrasi caran mandraṁ janayati svaram.
62. *āmāyḥ karaṇavinyāsaḥ prāṇasyordhvaṁ samīraṇam. sthānnām abhighātaśca na vinā śabdabhāvanām*—Vp.
63. *sādhana-vyavahāraśca buddhyavasthānibandhanaḥ* (Vp. 3.7.3). Also cf. *nirūpite'rthe śabdaprayogād yathānirūpaṇaṁ sabdopapattiḥ*—Helārāja on Vp. 3.7.3.
64. *vivakṣāprāpitarūpabhedādhīnḥ . . . vāsta ve kāraka vyavahāre na ghaṭanām eti*—Helārāja on Vp. 3.7.90, and, *pūrvam arthaṁ vivakṣati tato buddhau tam arthaṁ nirūpayati, tatas tadbodhānuguṇaṁ śabdaṁ prayuṅkte*—Ambākartrī on—Vp. 3.7.3.
65. Paramārthasāra viz. *mṛgatṛṣṇāyām udakaṁ śuktau rajatam, bhujaṅgamo rajjvām, taimirikacandrayugavad bhrāntam akhilaṁ jagadrūpam.*
66. *anirvacanīyotpattivādaṁ nirākaroti . . . sṛṣṭivacanaṁ bhāktam. . . sāmagrīvyatirekācca anutpattiṁ vadatā śuktirajatādisthale'pi anutpattiḥ sūcitā*—*Laghumañjūṣā.*
67. *cetano hi nāmarūpe buddhau ālikhya ghṭa iti nāmnā kambugrīvādiniā rūpeṇa ca bāhyaṁ niṣpādayati*—ibid.
68. *ekasyaivārno bhedau śabdārthāvapṛthak kṛtau*—ibid.
69. *arthākāravṛttau jāyamānāyāṁ svkārasyāpi samarpaṇam*—ibid.
70. *grāhyatvaṁ grāhakavañca dve śaktī tejaso yathā, tathaiva sarvaśabdānām ete pṛthag avasthite*—Vp. 1.55
71. cf. *sāhacaryañca śabdānuviddhasyaivārthasyāvagamāt.*
72. *jñānaṁ prayoktur, bāhyo'rthaḥ, svrūpañca pratīyate, śabdair uccāritaḥ* etc.—Vp. 3.3.1.

73. cf. 'a word signifies a thought which, is turn, in related to an object.'—*History of Ancient Philosophy*—A.S. Bogomolov p. 282, Progress Publishers, 1985 Also. cf. 'three things are linked together: the thing signified, the thing signifying and the thing existing'. The thing signified is called lektōn. i.e., 'a thought represented by a linguistic sound or sign. It does not exist outside its form (sound and sign)' ibid., p. 283 (the existing—external real object).

74. *dharmair abhyuditaiḥ niyamo na tu vastuni, kartur dharmavivakṣāyāṁ śabdāt kartā pratīyate.* —Vp. 3.7.103.

75. *vāstave kārakavyavahāre na ghaṭnām eti*—Helārāja on Vp. 3.7.104.

76. *yatra cābhyantarārthasya bāhyārthena saṁvādaḥ sa śabdaḥ pramāṇam, visaṁvāde tv apramāṇam iti vyavasthā.*

77. (i) *śakti-lakṣaṇānyatrasambandhena jñeyamātaṁ vastu lyarthaḥ*—Rāma Tarkavāgiśa.

(ii) *idamādi-sarvanāma-prayogārthaṁ vastūcyate.*

tasyaiva viśeṣyatvena vivakṣitaṁ dravyam ucyate—Abhirāma on Saṁ, 5.43.

(iii) *abhidheyaṁ ghaṭapaṭādi arthaśabdavācyam . . . arthaśabdo'bhidheyaṁ vakti iti vānvayaḥ . . . arthaśabdena vṛttyupasthāpyārthasyoktatvātvāt. . . vastau tadvattvam*—*Kātantrapradīpa* by Puṇḍarīkākṣa Vidyāsāgara.

(iv) *pratīyamānaṁ vastumātram arthaḥ*—Ṭīkā on *Kātantra.*

78.(i) *dvividhā hi sattā—pāramārthikī prātitikī ca, tatrādyā vastusattā śaśaviṣāṇasya nāsti, tathāpi anyā abhidheyasattā astyeva*—Puṇḍarīkākṣa Vidyāsāgara in his *Kātantrapradīpa.*

(ii) artho hi divividhaḥ, paramārthasan, paramārthāsaṁśca śaśaviṣāṇādayastu paramārthāsantam iti. tāny ubhayāny api liṅgāni abhidhāyakatvāt—Gopīnātha on Śripati's rule viz. *dhātuḥ.*

(iii) artho hi dvividhaḥ pratipattihetuḥ. prayogahetuśca—Kavirāja.

79. *arthavad iti sato'sato vārthasyābhidhāyakam ucyate*—*Kātantra pariśiṣṭa on nama 1.*

80. *śaśo hi jātiviśiṣṭavyaktitayā arthavān, viṣāṇam api tathaiva, anayoścāvayavāvayavi vyavahāro sannapi vipralipsādinā vaktum pāryate iti.*

81. *varṇeṣvapi sphoṭah kalpyate, tena varṇasphoṭāt padasphoṭas tasmād arthapratipattiḥ, itthañca kramayaugapadyābhyām padebhyo vākyārthānupapattyā padasphoṭavyañjitād vā vākyasphoṭād vākyārthapratītiḥ*—Gopīnātha on *citivārthe, Kp, sandhi,* 106.

82. *pratyakṣena gṛhyate sphotaḥ taṭhāhi gaur ityatra buddhir upajāyate, . . . yathā tantvanubhavānantaram avayavī pratyakṣasiddhaḥ pataḥ. tadvat sakalavarṇānubhavānantaram anubhūyamānaḥ sphoṭaḥ pratyakẓasiddhaḥ eko'vayavī varṇābhivyaṅgya iti*—ibid.

83. *tad ayuktam, varṇavad apratibhāsamānatvāt, yadi sphoṭo'sthāyat tadā śabdavad upalambho'bhaviṣyat. arthapratiter anyathāsambhavācca*—ibid.

84. *pūrva-pūrva-varṇakṛtātiśyo'ntyavarṇen saha saṁgacchate, atiśayaśaca*

pūrva-pūrva-varṇānubhavajanita saṁskāraḥ, tathā cāntyavṛṇa-jñānasamaye smṛtijñāna viśiṣṭaṁ samūhajñānam utpadyate, antyavarṇagrahaṇakāle anubhūtavarṇajñānam anusandhānāt ataḥ śabdaṁ prati niyatavyūhaḥ kaścana sphoṭanāmākālpaniko'ṅgīkriyate—Ibid.

Abbreviations

Bṛh	— Bṛhadāraṇyakopaniṣad
Bp	— Bhāṣāpariccheda
Kp	— Kātantra-pariśiṣṭa
Mbh.	— Mahābhāṣya
Nś	— Nāṭyaśāstra
P	— Pāṇini
Ṛk	— Ṛk-saṁhitā
Sam.	— Saṁkṣipatasāra
Vbs	— Vyākaraṇa-bhūṣaṇa-sāra
Vp	— Vākyapadīya

18

AN INTRODUCTION TO THE NĀRADĪYA ŚIKṢĀ: AN ANCIENT INDIAN TEXT ON MUSIC

DIDHITI BISWAS

Nāradīya Śikṣā (NŚ) belongs to the Śikṣā branch of literature which occupies a very significant position among the six Vedāṅgas. It belongs to the *Sāmaveda* and is one of the most important texts for the appraisal of early Indian music. Besides this one, there are some more *śikṣās* belonging to the Sāmaveda e.g. Ṛktantra, Sāmatantra, Akṣaratantra and Puṣpasūtra. These texts deal with the technical sides of the Sāmaveda and *sāmagāna* and are quite indispensable for a *sāma*-singer. *Sāmagāna* is considered to be the source of Indian music and is held in high esteem by the modern musicologists too. However, it should be admitted that the *sāmagana* which has undergone many changes, has lost its true identity. And the music of today, through a process of evolution, both historical and cultural, has taken a new shape distancing itself from the *sāmagāna.* So, the books on the intricacies of the *sāmagāna* only, have also lost their importance to the modern musicologists.

NŚ holds a unique position in this context as it illustrates various aspects of Indian music, both sacred and profane. This text deals with the most intricate topics like pronunciation, *sandhi*, varieties of words according to the *svaras* or accent, *gātravīṇā* (the process of indicating of *samic* notes on the right palm) and others. At the same time this text does not miss the discourse on seven profane notes, their relative position in the orthodox sacred scale, *grāma, mūrchanā, śruti* and so on and these topics, no doubt, still maintain a living contact with the present day music. Thus this text commands a distinguished position in the history of musicology.

Like all the ancient Sanskrit texts NŚ also faces the problem of ascertaining its antiquity. The name Nārada is a very common one since the early Vedic age. In the Ṛgveda Nārada was known as a sage and some mantras were attributed to his credit. The epics and *Purāṇas* also mention one Nārada, son of Kāśyapa and a devotee of Lord Kṛṣṇa. This Nārada was known for his proficiency in playing *vīṇā* and also for his unusual talent in music. Moreover, we find three more texts Saṅgītamakaranda, Pañcamasārasaṃhitā, and Rāganirupana authored by Nārada.

All these Nāradas, no doubt, are different personalities. Among them the Ṛgvedic poet Nārada is the earliest one. It is indeed not possible to associate him with music in any manner if one studies the mantras he is considered to have composed. The Nārada of purāṇas and epics is a mythological character and his very existence has not been established beyond doubt. The other four Nāradas, the supposed authors of the four texts so far available, are considered to be the four different personalities by the scholars. Moreover, they belonged to different periods. The language and style of NŚ, especially its contents mark this book as the earliest of them. Though its exact period cannot be ascertained yet it can be placed safely before Bharata's Nāṭyaśāstra from the point of antiquity.

However, a survey of the content of the NŚ leads us to suggest that NŚ is not written by a single author in a particular period. And it contains in itself some earlier and some later portions. Some of its topics are recorded into the main body of the text in such a manner that at times they prove themselves irrelevant and at the same time they interrupt the continuity of the discussion of other topics. We can assume some of them as spurious and they can easily be detected from the different style of language and fashion of presentation. It has already been pointed out that the content of this text can be classified under two heads: (i) music both profane and sacred and allied subjects and (ii) pronunciation, accentuation, *sandhi* etc. as are generally found in other *śikṣā* texts also. These two subjects are broadly divided into two *prapāṭhakas* each of them being divided into eight *kaṇḍikās.*

The first *prapāṭhaka* records in general some topics related to music. e.g. the different types of *gaṇa* like *arcikā, gathikā, samika, svarāntara,* the importance of three primordial svaras and their varied applicatons in different Vedas, the *svaramaṇḍala,* the number of *mūrchanā, tāna,* the details of the Vedic and profane notes, a comparison between them, the rules of singing *sāmagāna,* the *gātravīṇā* and so on. The second *prapāṭhaka* mainly discusses some topics related to the recitation of the Sāmaveda, e.g. *udātta, anudātta, svarita, yama, kampasvara, padapāṭha, sandhi, svarabhakti* etc. These topics are no doubt very technical and are required to be studied by the students of Sāmaveda only. And obviously the students who are involved in the study of music only may not find adequate interest in this portion. However, the book ends with some behavioural rules for all the students in general.

The division of NŚ in two *prapāṭhakas* according to its two varieties of topics is not very well defined. It is observed that the deliberation on music comes to an abrupt end in the last but one stanza of the seventh *kaṇḍikā* of this *prapāṭhaka.* The last stanza of the seventh *kaṇḍikā* initiates the discourse on the *svaras, udātta, anudātta* and *svarita,* which are more closely associated with the recitation of the *mantras.* The eighth *kaṇḍikā,* the last one of this *prapāṭhaka* treats the *svarita* and introduces its seven varieties, which became the subject of the first *kaṇḍikā* of the following *prapāṭhaka.*

This text contains, in all probabilities some spurious or interpolated portions also. They can easily be detected from the different style of language and fashion of presentation also. Some of them are identified below:

- The discussion of *svaras* in the NŚ commences from I.2.15;16 and continues till the last verse of I.5. This discourse is occasionally interrupted by the insertion of the topic on the qualities of a singer (I.3) and the deliberation on the *grāmarāgas* along with the derivative meaning of *gāndharva* (I.4.5–12). These topics are absolutely irrelevant and inconsistent in the discourse of the musical notes. The insertion of the above mentioned topics indicates not only their later antiquity but also the incompetence and carelessness of the inserters.
- The third *kaṇḍikā* of the first *prapāṭhaka* that narrates the qualities of a singer is no doubt more close to the topic of the latter treatises. Moreover, it is composed in prose form quite betraying the style of the entire text of NŚ.
- The portion of the NŚ (I.4.5-11) containing the discussion of the *grāmarāga* is certainly a later interpolation. Because (i) The concept of *rāga* is a later development and it is discussed in details by Mataṅga in his text Bṛhaddeśī which belongs to a later period. *Rāgas* or *grāmarāgas* have not been treated by Bharata's Nāṭyaśāstra which is immediate posterior to the NŚ. It is really difficult to conceive that an important topic like *grāmarāga* being very much in existence before Bharata was not treated by him. So it can be suggested that this observation on *grāmarāgas* in NŚ, did not form an original part of the text and was included in the original book at a considerable later period. (ii) The reference to the notes *Kākali* and *Antara* (I.4.9) while describing the *Kauśikīrāga* reaffirms the interpolation

of this portion. NŚ was silent about these two notes during the detail discussion of the *svaras* or notes in the second *kaṇḍikā* of the first *prapāṭhaka.* But these two notes were well-known to the later texts and in all probabilities were made included in the NŚ later.

- The absence of the elucidation of the term *sarava* in NŚ is also an evidence of the later inclusion of the term. The text while describing the varieties of *gaṇa* describes the features of *arcika, gathika* and *sāmika* only without making any reference to the other three of them, i.e., *aurava, sarava* and *saṃpūrṇa.* So the authenticity of this portion becomes questionable and we think that this portion was incorporated in the main body at a period when the term *saravu* became popular and required no special illustration.
- The stanza I.4.9 shows the derivative meaning of *gāndharva,* the most popular form of pro-Vedic music. It is the only place where NŚ tried to indicate the scope of the *gāndharva* form of music in a very superficial way without any detailed deliberation on it. So, it gives rise to the authenticity this stanza.
- The three 'verses' of seventh *kaṇḍikā* of second *prapāṭhaka* (II.7.1, 2,16) are not metrical like the other verses but more like prose composition. Probably some original portions of NŚ were lost and they were substituted by some later writers with later ideas and thoughts.
- The concluding *kaṇḍikā* of NŚ (II.8) no doubt belongs to a later era. Its language indicates its lateness and the rules recorded in this part is applicable not only to the Sāmavedic students but all students in general.
- There are some verses where Nārada is glorified as an ancient teacher (I.7. 1 2). These portions are not certainly written by Nārada himself but was incorporated by some of his followers at a later period.

The observations, made above, indicate that the NŚ was originally authored by some Nārada, a musicologist anterior to Bharata but later on the text became interpolated and in a sense enriched too by the contributors of the later origin with concepts of advanced form of music.

Now, to gather an idea of the observations of Nārada and his method of deliberation let us select a topic taken up in the NŚ for elucidation. Considering the association of this treatise with music let us discuss in brief a topic on music taken up in the NŚ for deliberation. *Svara* forms the basis of any type of music and hence deserves priority in this discourse. In a long deliberation on the *svara* the NŚ exposed a great novelty as this text did not confine itself in the periphery of the Vedic music only but extended its observation on the profane music also. So not only the Vedic notes but the *laukika* notes also with all their distinctions are treated in the text with equal importance.

This treatise considers the cry of different animals and birds as the source of seven *laukika* notes (I.5.3-5). The peacock utters the *ṣaḍja*, the cow bellows the *ṛṣabha*, sheep and goat spell out the *gandhara*, *krauñca* bird speaks out the *madhyma* etc. NŚ, finds an intimate relation of the musical notes with the human body and indicates different parts of a body as the origin of the seven notes (I .5.5–6). The *ṣaḍja* arises from the throat, the *ṛṣabha* from the head, *gāndhāra* from the nose, *madhyma* from the chest and so on. However we are not sure whether the places of origin of the seven notes in the human body can claim really any scientific basis. It appears that the description carries an air of occultism in it.

NŚ (I.5.7-12) also specifies some human organs which help to produce the musical notes and thereby the etymology of their names is also suggested. The *ṣaḍja* is produced with the help of six (*ṣaṭ*) organs, nose, throat, chest, palate, tongue and teeth and hence it is so named. The sound of *ṛṣabha* resembles the roar of *ṛṣabha* (i.e., ox) and it is produced when the air of navel gets struck with the throat and head. The name *gāndhāra* is justified because it has got special association with nose as it carries the smell (*gandha*) and otherwise it is produced like the *ṛṣabha*. In this way the names of *madhyama* and *pañcama* are established. But the NŚ is silent about the rest two notes i.e., *dhaivata* and *niṣāda*. NŚ (I .7.1-2) shows the intimate relation of the human body with the Vedic *svaras*. According to this text the human organs, not only produce the musical notes they act as their residing place also. Vedic note *kruṣṭa* resides in the head, *prathama* in the forehead, *dvitīya* in between the two eye brows. *tṛtya* in the ears, *caturtha* in the throat, *mandra* in the tongue and *atisvārya* in the heart.

NŚ (I.4. 1–4) assigns to each of the *laukika svara* caste, colour and presiding deities. On another occasion the same text (I.5.13–14) names some deities or *ṛṣis* who contemplate on them. Thus the *ṣaḍja* is Brahmin by caste, green in complexion, and having Brahma as its presiding deity and the god Agni contemplates on this note. *Ṛṣabha* is *Kṣatriya* by caste and its complexion is like the colour of parrot, and Agni is its presiding deity. Brahman contemplates on this note.

However, it appears that two types of *saptaka* (music scales) were there during the time of Nārada, Vedic and *laukika*. The most important contribution of the NŚ is the comparison and equating of the Vedic and *laukika* musical notes in its own way (I.7.3–4). This treatise has taken the flute as representing the secular music and draws a correspondence between two progressions of *svaras* in the following way:

Notes of a flute (*laukika scale*)	*Sārma scale*
madhyama	*prathama*
gāndhāra	*dvitīya*
ṛṣabha	*tṛtīya*
ṣaḍja	*caturtha*

Notes of a flute (*laukika scale*)	*Sārma scale*
dhaivata	*pañcama*
niṣāda	*ṣaṣṭha*
pañcama	*saptama*

It shows that the scale was in the descending order and does not go in a straight way. And this inversion aroused considerable confusion among the scholars. M.S. Ramaswamy Iyer and others are in favour of inverse progression because this pogression is also confirmed by Nārada in the description of *samahasta anāmikāyaṃ ṣaḍjaṣtikaiṣṭhāyāṃ ca dhaivata/ tasyādhastāttu yo'nyaḥ syānniṣādaṃ tatra vinyaset//* (I.7.4) But Laksman Sankara Bhatta Dravida and others accept the straight progression as they find supprt from Triratnabhāṣya of TP (23.13): *teṣāṃ khalu saptayamānāṃ uttarottaradīptija pūrvāpūrvopalabdhiḥ syāt. tat kathaṃ atisaryadīptija mandropalabdhiḥ catarthat tṛtiyaḥ* etc. This progression is also maintained in Māṇḍukīśikṣā (8.14).

Another point is noted in this connection that is the confusion regarding the position of *kruṣṭa.* While singing the *Sāmans* the notes are indicated in different fingers by the singer. Now which finger is meant for which note is enumerated by the same text. The *kruṣṭa* is indicated by the tip of the thumb, the *parthama* is indicated by the lower phalanx of the same finger, *gāndhāra* by the index finger, *ṛṣabha* by the middle finger, the *ṣaḍja* by the ring finger, the *dhaivata* by the little finger and the *niṣāda* by the root of the same finger. This arrangement of notes start from the *kruṣṭa* that is *pañcama* of the non-Vedic scale. So the arrangement of notes runs like this: *pā mā ga re sā dhā ni* and differs from the original scale *mā gā re sā dhā ni pā.* In the original scale the highest and the first note is made equal to *madhyama* and the seventh or the lowest to the *pañcama.* But it is curious enough that *pañcama* is placed as the highest note in the arrangement of the musical hand. This arrangement of the notes is in keeping with their position in human body. The place of *kruṣṭa* is declared as head, that of the *prathama* is forehead and thus gradually in a descending way the place of *atisvārya* is assigned to heart. Moreover this note is also designated as *nīca* or low note.

From all these evidences it appears that all though *kruṣṭa* is designated by the seventh note, it should be taken as the starting note of the progression. *Kruṣṭa* is made equal to *pañcama* of the secular scale and is placed in the lowest scale but when it becomes the commencing note of the scale, it gets identified with the same *pañcama*, only the octave changes to a higher one. So far as the practical aspect of the scale is concerned it should run in the following way: *kruṣṭa, prathama, dvitīya, tṛtīya, caturtha, mandra, atisvārya.*

The Vedic notes according to the author of the NŚ (I.7.6–8) contain in them an enlivening effect on gods and creatures. The gods thrive on *kruṣṭa,* the men on *prathama,* the animals on *dvitiya* and so on. It is very curious to note that the idea, that music can exert a very good influence on worldly creatures which is viewed as modern concept was probably in knowledge of the early Indian musicologists also.

The NŚ, as pointed out before, is a treatise of the *sāmagāna* and also a path-finder of the ancient non-Vedic music. Sometimes it differs from the present concept of the term and occasionally presents the conjectures, we are not acquainted with, and hence difficult to understand and sometimes inexplicable too. But to trace the history of the Indian music it is a must read book. Moreover this text, while disseminating the theoretical aspect of the music, shows the sense of aesthetics along with the knowledge of anatomy, physics and acoustics in its own way. It is historically known that these subjects were not developed at that time in their true sense. But it can be suggested that the feature of this text along with other *śikṣā* and *prātiśākhya* literature can be really a subject of research for the scholars of those fields especially in the context of the study of the history of Indian science.

Bibliography

A Collection of śikṣās by Yājñvalkya and others, ed. by the pandits of Benaras Sanskrit College (1893) Benaras.

Bhise, Usha R. (ed.) (1986) *Nāradīyaśikṣā with the commentary of Bhaṭṭa Sobhakura.* Poona: BORI.

Biswas, Didhiti (translated with discussion) (2000) *Nāradīyaśikṣā* Calcutta (now Kọlkata); Papyrus.

Swami Prajnanananda (1973) *Historical Development of Indian Music.* Calcutta (now Kolkata): Firma KLM.

19

THE LAKṢANAGRANTHAS OF THE ATHARVAVEDA AND THEIR IMPORTANCE

TARAK NATH ADHIKARI

The Atharvaveda has come down to us in two recensions the *Śaunaka* and the *Paippalāda* though it is traditionally believed to have had nine recensions.[1] Again the Paippalāda recension is now established in a double-shaped character. The former one was discovered by Roth in 1875 from a single birchbark manuscript at the Library of Tübingen, Germany under the title *'The Atharvaved in Kashmir'*, which, in 1901 Bloomfiled and Garbe jointly published in the form of chromophotographic repro-duction. Its later edition was published.by L.C. Barret in Roman script between 1905–40. Its nāgarī reproduction was done by Raghuvira in between 1936–41. While the another Paippalāda was discovered by Durgamohan Bhattacharya in 1958–59 from Odisha. Professor Bhattacharya undertook editing the Oriyan Paippalāda tradition. It was later on taken up by his son Professor Dipak Bhattacharya. This *Paipapalāda* is bigger than the Śaunaka recension by nearly 2000 extra verses,[2] 3 volumes of it, upto 18 candas have been published from Asiatic Society Kolkata. Its complete edition also has been recently published from Odisa by one Pandit K. Upadhyay.

Anyway, *Śaunaka* tradition is more popular and retained by so called Sāyana commentary though commentary of a few *Kāṇḍas* has not come down to us so far.[3] The commentary itself is a big controversy. The subject matter of the AV itself is also a matter of controversy. But here, for obvious reason we shall not enter into these controversies. The purpose of this presentation is to draw attention to the Vedic scholars to the matter that the unsatisfactory nature of the so called Sāyaṇa commentary of the AV is not suffice to interpret the AV. At the same time I disagree to believe that the whole text of the AV is a socio-magico literature of low profile people. Here lies the importance of the *lakṣaṇagranthas* of the AV for textual criticism and content. We shall here try to highlight the *'Lakṣaṇagranthas,'* of the AV and their importance. lt is also to be stated that it is not possible to analyse all aspects of the *lakṣaṇa* texts, but shall try to highlight a few of those texts and their importance. Since they define the characteristics and describe the special features of Vedic texts,[4] Vijaypala observes in *'Kātyāyanīya Ṛksar-vānukramaṇi'* वेदाङ्गसमकालमेव वेदलक्षणग्रन्था अपि व्यरचन्त। तत्र प्रधानतो लक्षणानि द्विधा विभज्यन्ते प्रातिशाख्यानि चानुक्रमण्यश्चेति। The term lakṣaṇagrantha is not very clear. Sometimes it includes a few Vedāṇga texts and sometimes other than Vedāṇga texts of that particular saṁhitā. Aithal says that all these texts are known as 'Lakṣaṇagranthas.'

The enumeration of the *lakṣaṇagranthas* are first made in *caraṇavyūha.* According to this text, the Atharvaveda consists of five *lakṣaṇa* texts:— *Caturadhāyikā, Atharvaveda Prātiśākhya, Dantyoṣṭhavidhi, Pañcapaṭalikā* and *Bṛhatsarvāṇu-kramaṇī* लक्षणग्रन्था भवति। चतुरध्यायी, प्रातिशाख्यम्, पञ्चपटलिका, दन्त्योष्ठविधिः वृहत्सर्वाणुक्रमणी चेति। चरणव्यूह . . .)।

The AV is called *Pañcakcalpin,* which includes *Nakṣatrakalpa, Śāntikalpa, Saṃhitākalpa* and *Añgirā-kalpa.* This term *pañcakalpin* is notional as *Nakṣatrakalpa* is to be found in the first chapter of AV *paraśiṣṭa. Śāntikalpa* is also retained in the AV *parśiṣṭa* and *Kauśika Sūtra, Vaitānakalpa* is *Vaitāna Sūtra,* the Śrauta text and *Saṃhitāvidi* is the *Kauśika Sūtra,* while *Añgirākalpa* is retained in both *Kauśika*

Sūtra (6th Kāṇḍa) and AV *Pariśiṣṭa* Apart from these there are other *lakṣaṇa* texts like *Dantyoṣṭavidhi, Pañcapaṭalikā* and *Bṛhat sarvānukramaṇī* which serve specific pupose. We shall make a very short survey on the subject matter of these three texts. About *Caturadhyāikā* and AV *prātiśākhya,* we need not elaborate as these two texts chiefly discuss on the phonetic and other linguistic related matter of the AV, which are elaborately discussed by Whitney and Suryakant respectively. Other scholarly works are also undertaken by a number of scholars down the ages. It may be mentioned here only that Whitney made a mistake while editing *Caturadhyāyikā,* he equated it with *A Vprātiśākhya* (as the nomenclature or title suggests).

Apart from these two *lakṣaṇagranthas, Chaturadhyāyikā* and *Atharvaprātiśākhya,* there are a number of lakṣaṇagranthas which are mentioned in N.C.C. Descriptive catalogues of different Institutes. Following K.P. Aithal (*Vedalakṣaṇa Vedic Ancillary Literature)* and other Vedic scholars who worked on the Atharvaveda, I shall mention a few of them, which are important for the textual criticism though all of them are not mentioned in *Caranavyuha.*

(1) *Atharva Prāyaścittāni*—It is edited by J.V. Negelein in JAOS, XXXIII. (Pp. 71–144) and a German introduction along with mantra index was published by him in the next issue of JAOS. B.R. Modak has made a detailed survey on this text.[5]

(2) *Śāntikalpa*—It consists of two chapters. Both two chapters were edited by G.M. Bolling and published in JAOS, XXXI in 1913 and the 2nd chapter also in *'Transactions of the American Philological Association'* (Issue XXXV in 1904). But the edition of the second chapter is not satisfactory. It deals with various ceremonies to avert evil effects from various omens and portents referred in the AV Pariśiṣṭa.[6]

(3) *Dantyoṣṭhavidhi*—It is edited by Ram Gopal Shastri from Lahore in 1921 with a short Hindi introduction. It is a small treatise that deal with the articulation of ओत्वोष्टयोः समासे

वा 'ba' (ब) (a dantoaṣṭha letter according to Pāṇinian system) in The AV verses in different occasions. Total number of verses (12+11) = 23. The author is unknown. The letter 'ba,' whether it is a labial or dental. The problem is solved in this treatise e.g. if 'b' is followed by bḥ and not separated by avagraha (अनिङ्ग्ये), it is to be pronunciated as labial bringing two lips together. Examples are also given by 'bibhratiḥ' (Av. 3.14.3). while b with initial accent like *bāla* AV 1 35.3) *bāṇa* also have (labial) the same pronunciation according to *dantyoṣṭhavidhi*. For instance, one should lightly touch the upper part of the lower lip with the end of the upper teeth to produce the sound. One should not press the teeth harshly. It is compared excellently in the AV *Māṇḍūkī Śikṣa,* as tigress that carries her cubs, holding with teeth.[7]

Though the treatise is very small, but it is of high value as Vedic phoneticians were careful about the articulation even of a single letter like 'b' only. Again it is important because it gives a long list of words that bear the letter 'b', though some of which are not noticed in the present AV (Ś). (about 118 words I have counted). A few words like *'sambibam'* (Chap II) बद्धे बद्धानि तावां स्तेमघवन् महिमापो ते तन्वः शतम् उपोते बद्धेध /बद्धानि यदि वासि न्यर्बुदम्।। (AV 13/4/45) (Chap ll). Variant reading बुजे बुजः (Chap ll), but 'bājam' is found in AVs. 6.3, प्राबन्धायः, अधिबाले, तुछुब्दः तबुकः (Chap ll Maximum words occur in Chap II second unit (आकृति), *Kāṇḍas* XII-XVIII and in 3rd unit. This arrangement serves two purposes. Firstly it shows the nature of the *sūktas,* secondly the number of hymns in each division. Whitney's grand division slightly differ from Pañcapaṭalikā, particularly the 2nd and 3rd units. Modak considers the division of *Pañca* is more logical than Whitney, so far as the arrangement of the sūktas and anuvākas are concerned.[9]

The text is extremely useful for the arrangement of the *sūktas, anivākas,* verses of first 18 *Kāṇḍas* of the AV and extremely important for the textual criticism of the AV.

The book was first published from Lahore in 1920 by Bhagawaddatta with a Hindi translation and introduction. The book is rare and critical edition with notes and exegetical notes of this text is a dessideratum for present scholars.

Our special emphasis on the Atharvaveda *Pariśiṣṭa* is for more than one reason. This *Pariśiṣṭa* literature constitute, by far the most voluminus text among the *pariśiṣṭas* of the Vedic Literature. It has 72 chapters (*Pariśiṣṭas*). Actually the total number may be 79 in counting, as some of them are subdivided under one pariśiṣṭa. Such as 18 is subdivided 18a, 18b, 18c, Nineteen in 19a and 19b, No. 30 is divided into 30a and 30b, No 70, is again subdivided into 70a, 70b and 70c.

Weber first draws our attention to this literature and G.M. Bolling and Negelein under Bloomfield and Roth prepared its first edition into three parts into Roman script in 1909-10. They contemplated for a translation of the same but it could not be materialized. Mr. Ram Kumar Rai reproduced it in Nagari script without any extra notes from Chowkhamba Orientalia, Benaras in 1976. He also wished for a Hindi translation. That also could not materialized. Only a few chapters (57–63, parts of 64, 70 and 71) have been translated with notes by Miss Dina J. Kohlbrugge appeared in 1938. Gouda translated chapter 19, with notes. Lourens Pefer Van Dan Bosch in 1944 translated chapter 21–29, with notes as his Ph.D. Thesis. Myself once attempted for text reconstruction with introduction and exegetical notes in 1997–2001 as a UGC project on the basis of new mss not used by Bolling and Negelein. A few writings on it have been published by Weber, Negelein, Bolling, Fay, Hatfield, Goodwin and the present author. A highly valuable study of these pariśiṣṭas has been done by B.R. Modak in 1993. Yet a lot is left.

(a) First of all, a critical edition is a long dessideratum, Bolling and Negelein, though have given utmost effort, yet could not procure satisfactory reading. They themselves were not satistied with their edition.[10] They even could not procure readings at places, as mss are often corrupt.

(b) In spite of a few fragmented translation of a few chapters, no complete translation is so far available. As all the scholars, who worked on the AV and this AV Pariśiṣṭa have unhesitatingly felt the tremendous importance of it for the understanding of religion and philosophy of the AV.[11] No complete translation is done so far.

(c) A number of ancillary texts like *Nakṣatrakalpa, Śāntikalpa, Angirākalpa, Caraṇavyūha, Atḥarvana Nighaṇṭu,* etc appear in various chapters of the AV Pariśiṣṭa Thus, those who think to undertake to text-criticism of the ancillary literature of the AV, can get benefit from this text.[12]

(d) The magic, omens and portents, which are a part of the Avn religion can be understood better from the Pariśiṣṭas like 34–36, 50–72. *Varṇapaṭala* (Chap. 47) is a good supplement of phonetics. Thus, though the pariśiṣṭas have not been teachnically mentioned in the *lakṣaṇagrantha,* yet its importance is multifold. And it can be designated as *lakṣaṇa* text as well.

(e) No date has so far been ascertained. So scholars can work on the age of the this text along with its composers.

The *Pariśiṣṭas* are as their name suggests. 'addenda'/ appendices. Though, each and every Veda has one or more pariśiṣṭa, some of which are printed, some are in manuscript form and some only by name.[13] The AV Pariśiṣṭa is no doubt largest and a 'magnum opus'. Its subject matter is varied and a general classification has been given by Modak in his book.[14] It shows that the range goes from constellation to royal ceremony, from ritual to magic (so called), from phonetics to omens and portents. They are supplementary and complementary to the rites and rituals which are to be found in AV, but they are not always mentioned in the sūtra text. For instance, in the AV, there are hymns addressed to Night, (AV 5.5., 6.107; 19.47-50). (AV Pari 6 and 7). Performance of sacrifice requires various types of alters and the measurement of alters, kuṇḍa etc. are described in the AV Paris 24 and 25. The prātiśākhyas (two) of the AV do not supply the enumeration of alphabets and their articulation. This has been dealt in the Varṇapaṭala of the AV Pari. (AV Pari 47).

AV Pari has mentioned the names of a number of Ātharvaṇa priests like Bhargava, Śaunaka, Gautama, Paippalāda, Māhaki, Garga Ātreya, Kroṣṭuki, Paithīnasi, Sumantu, Usanas etc; who taught various practices.

Our ancient teachers and writers have taken materials from the AV Pari. Keśava in his *Paddhati*, Varāhamihira in his *Bṛhatsaṃhitā*, Hemadri in his '*caturvargacintāmaṇi*,' Sāyaṇa in his Commentary, drew materials from the AV Pari. Keśava refers as number of passeges in his *paddhati* ; for instance, araṇilakṣaṇa (from AV Pari 22), for dream, '*Svapnāddhyāya*' (AV Pari 68). Varāhamihira quotes from AV Pari 64, regarding *rāhucakra, ketucakcra, grahayuddha, sadyovṛṣṭi lakṣaṇa digdāhalakṣṇa* in his book. Sāyaṇa refers at least 55 places from AV Pari (Pūrvārdha) in his commentary of the AV. Hemadri refers AV Pariśiṣṭa to *Vratakhaṇḍa, dānakhaṇḍa,* etc in his *caturvargacintāmaṇi.* As the subject matter is diverse and huge, its inllucnce in later literature deserves attention. In spite of so much importance my suggestion is that, as these pariśiṣṭas belonged to a very late date and compiled by a number of ancient people, so the subject matter has been deeply influenccd by later literature like Purāṇa and Tantra. Thus one should be enough careful to put connection with the AV saṁhita. Otherwise, the interpretation of the AV, as somehow damaged at the hand of these free style interpreters may again get further interpolated.

We shall conclude with adding a few more information on the ancillary works of the AV that deserves to be mentioned. Weber mentioned of '*Ātharvaṇavidhāna*' in one of his writings. I have collected 'one' 'Atharvasaṃhitāvidhāna text published from Lal Bahadur Shastri Kendriya Vidyapith, New Delhi, published in 1988-89. It was written by one Kesava Deb Shastri. It may be a new text written for the purpose of application of the AV mantras following KS, VS and other ancillary literature. The subject matter as classified by Kauśika, has been exploited by the writer and rites are mentioned with Hindi notes. Verses of each *Kāṇḍa* and their applications are mentioned in the book. No special importance could be laid on this text as it only employs the rules of the sūtra texts. From the text it is not clear, whether Keshav Shastri himself composed the text.

A few manuscripts on Atharvanic texts were sent to Bloomfield by K.M. Chatfield, the then D.P.I. in 1882. The list is:

(1) आथर्वणवेदस्य अन्त्येष्टिकर्म
(2) आसुरीकल्प:
(3) समानय श्राद्धविधि:
(4) अथर्वतर्पणम्
(5) आथर्वणमिताक्षरा
(6) होमपद्धति:
(7) षोड़शोपचारपूजा (ब्रह्मवेदस्य)
(8) अनुष्ठानपद्धति: (कौशिकोक्तकर्मणाम्)

Beside one *Ānanda Saṃhitā* is mentioned by Caland, *Agastyasutra,* a magical text is recorded in the Catalogue of *Sanskrit Manuscripts, India Office* (No. 485[1])

Another important text on the AV is Atharvakautsavyākaraṇa. This text is actually a reproduction of two prātiśākhyas of the AV. But it contains an unpublished commentary by one Kṛṣṇadāsa. The commentary has six chapters viz (a) शास्त्रप्रशंसा, (b) स्थानप्रयत्नविवेक, (c) संज्ञा, (d) परिभाषा, (e) सन्धि; and (f) स्वरसाधन. The ms is in possession of VSM, Pune (No. 4179).[16]

Another small text is *Ātharvaṇarahasya* by Govinda Swamin. It is of 53 verses, dealing with AV Brāhmaṇas and AV-Upaniṣadas and it is spiritual in nature.

Rājābhiśekaprayoga is another unpublished text on royal ceremonices of the AV. Sri Srikanta Mondal, a research scholar is doing Ph.D. on it. It has 34 Folios. One copy has been procured from Asiatic Society. five copies of mss are kept in Saraswati Bhavan, Benaras, S.S. Viśvavidyalaya.

It is interesting to note that RV commentator Veñkaṭa Mādhava on RV. VIII 1, referred to a *'Paippalāda Brāhṃaṇa'* of which no catalogue gives any information. A small treatise on Ātharvaṇa medicine called 'Aṭharvavedacikitsā *Śāstra* was written by Priyaratna Arsha. The book is on Ayurveda based on the AV. The same author has written a book on Ātharvaṇa medical science. It is *'Atharvavedīya Mañtraśāstra,'* published from Hardwar in 1949.

A few more small texts on various aspects of the AV in manuscript form may be available if searched minutely. But I would conclude here with two remarks. It is a well known fact that text criticism work on the Atharvaveda has been neglected in comparison to that of the RV. Moreover maximum works have been done by classical western scholars. Participation of Indian scholars is comparatively low. As the subject matter of the AV is vast and heterogenons, so free style interpretation of the later dated texts of the AV have partly damaged its true character. It has been looked upon as a text of magical charms and spells. Thus in my opinion we shall be very careful while interpreting the AV on the basis of these ancillary texts that are written after a few centuries or millenia of the original text itself.

Books, Journals Consulted

1.	*Atharvaveda Saṃhitā*	:	Chowkhamba Sanskrit Pratisthan, Benaras, 2000
2.	*Atharvaveda Saṃhitā* (Trans) 2 Vols, W.D. Whitney	:	MLBD, Delhi, 1996 Rpt.
3.	*The Paippalāda Saṃhitā* of the Atharvaveda, vol-1	:	Dipak Bhattacharya. Asiatic Society, Kolkata, 1997
4.	*Atharvaveda Pariśiṣṭas* (3 parts)	:	G.V. Bolling and Nigelein, Leipzig, 1909–10
5.	–Do–	:	Ram Kumar Rai, Chowkhamba Orientalia, Varanasi, 1976
6.	Vedadalakṣaṇa Vedic Ancillary Literature (A Descriptive Bibliography)	:	K.P. Aithal, Indian Edn. MLBD, Delhi 1993
7.	*The Ancillary Literature* of the Atharvaveda	:	B.R. Modak, Rastriya Vedavidya Prathisthan, Delhi 1993
8.	Atharvasaṃhitā Vidhāna	:	Keshav Deb Shastri, Lal Bahadur Shastri Sanskrit Vidyapeeth, Delhi, 1988-89
9.	*Atharvavedīya Pañcapaṭalikā*	:	Bhagavatdatta, Lahore 1920
10.	–do– *Māṇḍūkiśikṣā*		–do– Lahore 1921
11.	–do– *Dantoṣṭhavidhi*	:	Ram Gopal Shastri, Lahore 1921
12.	–do– *Bṛhatsarvāṇukramaṇī*	:	–do– Lahore 1922
13.	*The Atharvaveda Parātiśākhya*	:	Surya Kant, Lahore 1939
14.	–do–	:	Viśvabandhu, Lahore 1923
15.	*The Vtharvaveda (Śaunaka)*	:	5 Vols, Viśvabandhu, VVRI, Hoshiarpur, 1960-64
16.	*Atharvaveda Pariśiṣṭa* (Chaps 21-29)	:	Doctoral thesis (unpub)
	(Trans & notes)	:	L.P. Van Den Bosch, 1978 (?)
17.	Atharvaveda Pariśiṣṭa (UGC Project) 5 chaps	:	T.N. Adhikari, 2000 (Text reconstruction) unpublished)
18.	*Gopatha Brāhmaṇa:* A critical study	:	T.N. Adhikari, Sanskrit Pustak Bhandar, Kolkata 1994
19.	–do– (Trans, Bengali)		T.N., Adhikri, SVS, R.B.U., Kolkata, 1999
20.	*Śaunakīya Caturadhyāyikā,* AV Prātisākhiya	:	MLBD, Delhi.

References

1. Patañjali, *Caraṇavyuha* (AV Pari 49.4.1), *Kātīya Pariśiṣṭa* Vācaśpattyam record nine recensions of the AV, of which some variation of titles are to be found. They are—*Paippalāda, Śaunaka, Cāraṇavidyā, Brahmavada, Tauda, Mauda, Devadarśa, Jājala* and *Vedasparśa.*

2. *Śaunkasaṃhitā* consists of about 730 ḥymns and bout 6000 verses, whereas the Kashmirian AVP records 825 hymns and 7192 verse and Oriyan AVP shows 923 hymns and 7899 verses. See AVP, Dipak Bhattacharya, edn. (P-XXII, Introduction). AVP Kashmir and AVP Oriya, mostly differ on arrangement of verses, and this is main reason of difference of counting.
3. So called Sāyaṇa commentary is missing in *Kāṇḍas* 5, 8 (partly), 9, 10–16, 20 (partly).
4. It is one type of Vedic ancillary texts as. Weber opined. (See forward of Aithals' *Vedalakṣaṇa* Catalogue). Aithal too subscribes the same view in his book referring *Tribhāsyaratna* commentary of Somācārya on Tait. Pri. and *Vaidākābharaṇa tīkā* of Gopālayajvā on the same text.
5. See Modak—*'The Ancillary Literature of the AV.,* pp. 89–108
6. AV Pari–Chapters 52, 54, 58–59, 64–65, 68–70, 72 deal with so many omens and portents, *'adbhūtani* and ceremonies to be performed to avert the evils.
7. यथा व्याघ्री हरेत् पुत्रान् दंष्ट्राभिर्न च पीड़येत्।
   भीता पतनभेदाभ्यां तद्वद् बर्गान् प्रयोजयेत्।। (*Māṇḍūki Śikṣā* 4.7)
8. See Modak, Ibid., pp. 169–74.
9. See Modak, "The division made by the *Pañcapatalikā* and sanctioned by the *Bṛhatsarvāṇukramaṇī* is more logical." Ibid., p. 155.
10. "We feel no hesitation in declaring that a perfect text of the Pariśiṣṭas is at present unattainble" "Introduction, AV Pari, Bolling and Negelein, p. II)
11. "The Atharvavedapariśiṣṭas constitute an invaluable record of ancient Atharvanic tradition, beliefs and practices," Modak, Ibid., p. 194. He also quotes Edgertion in this context, who thinks the complements and suppliments of the KS and VS are served excellently by *AV Pariśiṣṭas,* (Ibid., p. 194)
12. *Nakṣatrakalpa,* AV Pari—Chap. 1.
    Caraṇavyūha—AV Pari—Chap. 49.
    AV Nighaṇṭu—AV Pari—Chap. 48.
    AV Varṇapatala— AV Pari—Chap. 47.
    AV Prāyaścittāni—AV Pari—Chap. 52–72.
13. Ṛgveda—*Āśvalāyana Gṛhyapariśiṣṭa* (3 Chaps).
    Yajurveda (White) *Kātīyapariśiṣṭa* (18 Chaps) One *caraṇavyūha*
    Sāmaveda *Gobhila Gṛhyapariśiṣṭa* 2 Chaps Hillebrandt has mentioned 10 other parisiṣṭas which are not available in print. For names see, Modak—ibid., p. 191.
14. Modak—ibid., p. 191.
15. See Modak, ibid., of Introduction., p. 17.
16. For details see Aithal, *Vedalakṣaṇa,* p. 63.

20

NATURE OF ANUNĀSIKA : PHONETIC AND GRAMMATICAL SPECULATIONS

Parboty Chakraborty

In determining the position of nasal sounds of OIA language, ancient grammarians and phoneticians in India were far from unanimous. As a general feature, *Anusvāra* may be treated as the nasalization of a vowel, but the case is not always simple as it seems to be. In this connection, the term, *Anunāsika* also gives rise to some debatable issues, as both the cases of *Anusvāra* and *Anunāsika* may be taken as nasalization according to modern European scholars. But Pāṇini, a grammarian of Vedic and Classical Sanskrit, has made a difference clearly when he prescribes the sūtra, *anunāsikāt pro'nusvāraḥ* (Pāṇini 8/3/4). But *Anunāisika* is defined for those letters which are pronounced by the nose along with the mouth as described in *mukhanāsikāvacano' 'nunāsikaḥ* (p. 1/1/8). Here *Kāśikā* explains that Pāṇini mentions *mukha* (mouth) in his prescription in order to exclude *Anusvāra* from the scope of *Anunāsika* (cf *mukhagrahaṇaṃ kim anusvārasyaiva hi syāt*). From this, it is clear that *Anusvāra* is pronounced by the nose only. These two points have not been accepted wholly by the authorities of Śikṣās and Prātiśākhyas (Ś and Pr.) which will be discussed later. Interestingly, the followers of Pāṇini give the example of *Anunāsika* vowel where the vowels are nasalized not by *Anusvāra* but otherwise. It is not generally identifiable with an English technical term, rather it is popularly known by a symbol, called *candravindu* (ँ). So by Pāṇini's formulations for Vedic context, like *'āṅo' nunāsikaśchandasi'* (6/1/126), ā is used with nasal feature in *abhra ā apaḥ,* or in another case, *martyā*ँ*āviveśa.*

This may lead to some problems to a reader, because both the cases of anusvāra and anunāsika are specified 'nasalization of vowels' to the westem scholars. We may expect some solutions from Vedic scholars. Some alternative answers may be sought out from ancient Indian phonetic treatises too. In addition to the theoretical descriptions about all types of sounds in phonetic texts of India, some independent texts like Anunāsikalakṣaṇa and Anusvārā-lakṣaṇa (Ms. 56 and 57, mentioned in the *Vedalakṣaṇa* of K.P. Ithal) deserve special mention. Interestingly, in the text, *Anunāsikalakṣaṇa,* and in some other phonetic texts, both the cases of anusvāra and candravindu are exemplified as the cases of anunāsika. In this perspective, both are justified as nasalization.

Nasalization with anusvāra goes to its origin generally with m or n as suggested by Pāṇini (by *mo'nusvāraḥ, naścāpadāntasya jhali, samaḥ suṭi, kānāmreḍite, naścha-vyapraśān,* etc.) In Vedic phonetics, there may have more additional sources and the essential features of anusvāra, i.e. its nature, type, quality, style of pronouncing and the likes are elaborately discussed to determine its phonetic nature fruitfully. So these references should be taken in for consideration of thorough analysis.

On the question, viz. whether the anusvāra is a vowel or consonant, there are divergent opinions. Etymologically, it is treated like a vowel, i.e. svara in Tribhāsyaratna (*anu svaryate paścārdhe svaravaduccāryate ityanusvāraḥ*) in Taittirīya Prātiśākhya (TPŚ 1/1) (also in Yojuṣabhūṣaṇa in S. Varma's book, p. 153). According to the Ṛk-Prātiśākhya (ṚPŚ) this may be treated as a consonant or a vowel (*anusvāro vyañjanaṃ vā svaro vā.* ṚPŚ 1/5) Uvaṭa here clarifies that it possesses some features of a vowel, like shortness, longness, prolation, udātta-anudātta accents etc. But like a consonant, it has the qualities of ardhamātrā, saṃyoga etc. Interestingly, this perspective is not very strong, as it has been refuted in TP and in the commentaries of the ṚPŚ itself.

The rest of the vowels are designated as vyañjana by *sarvaṃ śeṣo vyañjanānyeva* (ṚPŚ 1/6), yet by mentioning the anusvāra as svaras or vyañjana, it is indicated that anusvāra has a separate identity differing from other vowels or consonants. Uvaṭa says . . . *tasmāt svaravyañjanātiriktamanyad varṇāntarametad ityeva jñāpanaparam*. But this sound is related to vowels more intimately than consonants in many respects—*pūrvasyānusvāravisarjanīyau* (ṚPŚ 1/24) declares that anusvāra is the part of its preceding vowel. Here anusvāra is mentioned in addition to consonants in *anusvāro vyañjanaṃ cākṣarāṅgam* (ṚPŚ 1/22). This is justified by the commentator—*avyañjanatvādanusvārasya grahaṇam* (TPŚ 21/6) also takes same way by *anusvāraḥ svarabhaktiśca*. *Śikṣāprakāśa* indicates that anusvāra is *āśrayasthānabhāgin* (5). So the sound to which anusvāra is attached to is the shelter of anusvāra. Likely, the Varṇapradīpikā Śikṣā also declares:

> *anusvāro visargaśca . . . navaite syuḥ parāśrayāḥ*/ 50
> *saṃyyogavāhā evaite nijasvaravivarjitāḥ*/
> *pūrvasyāṅgaṃ bhavantyete svara eteṣu pūrvavat* //51

So, anusvāra has no vowel element of itself. Siddheshwar Varma also commented that 'If Anusvāra was a pure nasalized vowel, . . . then even the question of its syllabic position could not arise' (p. 81. *Critical studies in the phonetic observation of Indian Grammarians*). In some cases anusvāra was regarded as independent syllable as observed in the Āraṇya Śikṣā of Kāṭhaka school (ibid., p. 82) According to the Pāriśikṣāṭīkā (as mentioned by Varma, p. 150), it has a deep and sweet sound like bells; i.e. sweet like the sounds of bells and deep like tiger's roar. On the other hand, pure nasalized sound is termed *rakta*, which proceeds from both the nostrils. It is exclaimed by the female persons of Surāṣṭra in uttering takrā̐. It is one of the cases of anunāsika as prescribed by Pāṇini in *mukhanāsikāvacano'nunāsikāḥ* (1/1/8). It is produced from both mouth and nostrils. So this differs from the anusvāra, as anusvāra is *nāsāmūlabhava*, but the anunāsika is not so (Varṇaratnapradīpikā Śikṣā–34). ṚPŚ and Atharva Prātiśākhya create ambiguity by using the terms nāsikya and anunāsika respectively for both the nasal consonants and the anusvāra.

Like grammar, phonetical texts also admit the origin of anusvāra as a substitution of *m* primarily followed by *r* or uṣmavarṇa s. This substitution is termed *paripanna* by old teachers as stated in the ṚPŚ (4/15). In these conditions anusvāra is replaced by other phonetic units in Vedic language. Thus, the changed form is found as डँ. ठँ. (symbols used in Śikṣā texts) as sarva ठँ. ṣaḍiti in Keśavī Śikṣā (in sūtra-style, 5).[1] It is to be pointed out here that for the symbol of ꣳ, the Vedic scholars designate it as grammar. In measuring duration, it is uttered as long after a short vowel, short after a long vowel and it becomes guru followed by a conjunct of consonants.[2]

Whether the anusvāra is hrasva or dīrgha, there is no uniform answer. To refute the scope of ardhamātrā; possessed by a consonant in general, TPŚ stated that it should be treated as a short vowel having the duration like *a*.[3] There are two types of anusvāra; viz ekamātrika and dvimātrika depending on saṃhitā, saṃyoga etc. according to Vaidikābharaṇa. It is echoed in Śikṣā texts too. Thus, Laghumādhyandinaśikṣā and the like mention three types of it.[4] They treat dīrgha and guru differently unlike grammarians. Suitable examples of three divisions are presented in *Yājñavalkya Śikṣā* (YŚ) (63, 65), *Laghvamoghā-nandinī Śikṣā* (LŚ) (15, 16), though the sign of ꣳ is used there. Thus, LŚ reads:

> *hrasvāt paro bhaved dīrgho haꣳsa iti nidarśanam*
> *dīrghāt paro bhavet hrasvo māṃsebhya iti darśanam*
> *gurau pare hyanusvāro gurureva hi sa smṛtaḥ*
> *siṃhyasīti tatra tāvadhakāre dirgha eva saḥ*
> *devānaṃ hṛdaye tadvat taskarāṇām yathā svake*

The *anusvāra* is of two *mātrā*-s if succeeded by *ṛ* or consonants.[5] But this becomes *hrasva* optionally caused by some cases as clarified by the YŚ (138–42).

Compared to this nature, there is another common substitution of *anusvāra* which has been noticed by our forefathers. Here *r* or *uṣmavarṇa* also should follow after that according to some scholars. Now in most of the *Śikṣā*-texts, the expression, *si* ꣳ *hyasi* is printed with this special mark. The *Prātiśākhyapradīpaśikṣā* describes the method and style of articulating this substitution of *anusvāra* (=ꣳ) in addition to defining its nature and type vividly.

Studying the prerequisites and instances concerning the change of *anusvāra*, one may have a question—whether ङ. and ꣳ are identical or not in utterance? Grammarians, though non-Pāṇinians specifically, are very explicit here and they have made formulations regarding ꣳ only. Here the *sārasvata* system is noteworthy.[6] Candrakāntatarkālaṃkāra, a Kātantra-grammarian of twentieth century, wrote a Vedic grammar named *Kātantrachandaḥprakriyā* on the basis of Kātantra system. He formulated and explained an aphorism, viz. *anusvāratsya rephosmaṇoḥ*.[7] He cited the instances like *oṣadha trāyasvaina svadhite maina* ꣳ *hiꣳsiḥ* (TS. 1/3/9), *parilikhita* ꣳ *rakṣaḥ* (TS. 1/2/5). But he observed that the followers of *Bahvṛca* and Atharvavedic schools prefer the simple *anusvāra* only.[8]

n is also sometimes changed into *anusvāra* first and then into ꣳ, as in *yasmi* ꣳ *ścandramā vibhāti* (TB. I/4/10). But there are other substitutes also for *n.* Sometimes it is elided and sometimes it is replaced by *r* depending on the preceding vowels of *n,* viz. *ā, ī, ū,* and followed by the semivowels, vowels etc. These changes also cause for nasalization of foregoing vowels with *candravindu* as suggested by the *Ṛk-prātiśākhya.*[9] This nasalization of a vowel originating from *n* is treated like *dīrghopadha-visarjanīya* followed by *carati, cakre, ca* etc. So there is an additional fricative sound as *s/ś/ṣ* for *uṣmabhāva* (cf. P. Sū. *naśchabyapraśān n> ru> : > s/ṣ/ś*). The example is *paśūn tāꣳscakre vāyavyā* (ṚPŚ. 4/75) like in *asmāꣳśca,* same result is also found in Uvaṭa's commentary. So some problem may arise to the resders (cf. ṚPŚ. 4/65–71).

With reference to the above three substitutes of *n,* the preceding vowel is prescribed to the nasalized (*anunāsika* in TPŚ.) but in presenting the examples, the sign of *anusvāra* is used; such as *agnīṃ rapsuṣadaḥ, saṃśitaṃ me brahma,* etc. But this style is not admitted in the Taittirīya school. So the next sūtra states: *naikeṣām* (TPŚ. 15/2). Here it is commented that the later view is more preferable than the former (*idameveṣṭanaṃ na pūrvam*). Consequently, avoiding *anunāsika, anusvāra* is strengthened in the formulation, viz. *tatastvanusvāraḥ* (15.3).[10]

Grammatical schools prefer here nasalization of the foregoing vowels of *n* for Vedic uses. Pāṇini's some formulations are: *ubhayatharkṣu* (P. 8/3/8), *diṛghādati samānapāde* (P. 8/3/3), *svatavān pāyan* (P. 8/3/7) etc. Candrakānta, the author of *Kātantrachandaḥprakriyā* formulated necessary aphorisms in this occasion. They are—*tasminnanusvārastasya chandogānām* (Sandhi—3/4), *anyatrāpi dṛśyate* (Sandhi–3/5), *anusvārapūrvāḥ śaṣaṣāḥ* (Sandhi—3/7). In the process of nasalization of vowels, a name is given by *Varṇaratnapradipīkā-śikṣā.* This is called *Upadhārañjana* as stated—

svarāṇāmānunāsikyam . . . .
upadhārañjanaṃ kuryāt svare vikaraṇe sati
lope prakṛtibhāve ca nopadhārañjanaṃ bhavet.[11]

In connection with the style of utterance of *anusvāra*, *nāsikā* (nostrials) is primarily accepted as the places of articulation according to the Sanskrit grammar. But differences of opinions in this case are recorded in Prātiśākhyas. As TPŚ says—*ekeṣāmanusvāra-svara-bhaktyośca*— (2/19). On this, Tribhāṣyaratna comments—*anusvāre hanvo-rupasaṁhāraḥ etadatnakeṣāṃ matam, anyeṣāṃ tu matam anusvārasyānunāsikamātratvaṃ.* But this last view is refuted by declaring—*taccintyam.* Those, who assure *hanupasaṃhāra* for *anusvāra,* admit it as *nāsikya* as recorded in *Tribhāśyaratna* (on TPŚ 2/19). To make harmony between these two opinions, Vyāḍi (or Vyāli) gives solution as expressed in ṚPŚ—*Vyālir nāsikyam anunāsikaṃ vā* (13/37). Here *nāsikya* refers to the style of uttering with nose only and *anunāsika* means uttering with both mouth and nose. In the instances, illustrated by Uvaṭa, *nāsikya* is exemplified in *tvaṃ rajendra* etc. but *anunāsikya* is in *havī ̐ ṣi,* which is actually nasalization of vowels with the mark of *candravindu.*

Concerning different degrees of prominence on nasality, views of three, individual teachers are found in TPŚ. According to Śaityayāna, nasalness is more prominent in the *anusvāra* and the last five plosives (17/1). But to Kauhaliputra, nasal quality should be equal in all the above cases (*samaṃ sarvatreti kauhaliputaḥ*–17/2). On the other hand, lesser degree of nasalness is required for *anusvāra* according to Bhāradvāja (*anuisvāre ṇviti bhāradvājaḥ* 17/3). But Sthavirakauṇḍinya specifies more acute or rapid nasalness for *anusvāra* originating from *m* or *n* (*pūrvāt pūrvāt uttorottaraṃ tībrataram.* The example is—*ye vā vanaspatīm ranu*). The consonantal part is additional element compared to a vowel (*vyañjanakālaś ca svarasyātrādhikaḥ*—17/5).

The actual view of the authorities of the TPŚ themselves

is revealed in—*anusvārottamā anunāsikāḥ* (2/30). *Vaidikābharaṇa* on it asserted that *anusvāra* is truly a consonant in its nature, according to this school. Those who stated that *anusvāra* is either a vowel or consonant, is not supported by Taittirīya school (actually it is in ṚPŚ). *Avusvāra* should be pronounced as half of *g* and its place of articulation is *nāsikā*; therefore, it is treated as *nāsikya*.[12]

According to PŚ, the sound of *anusvāra* will be like the sound produced from the musical instrument, *alāvuvīṇā*. This is applicable when *h, r, ś, ṣ, s* follow after *anusvāra*. But when followed by other consonants it is changed into corresponding nasal plosives (cf. *anusvārasya yayi parasavarṇaḥ* P. 8/4/58).[13]

Indian phonetical texts also immensely contribute in the area of nasalization with candravindu though sometimes clear distinction is not found regarding the nasal sound as *anusvāra*. Similar to Pāṇinian tradition, ṚPŚ accepts anunāsika produced from both the mouth and nose along with the varieties as nasal consonants, viz. *ṅ, ñ* etc. and with vowels like *māhā̐ mā spacanyāḥ* etc. This text defines these nasal sounds *rakta* as an adjective form of *raṅga* (ṚPŚ 1/36). It is compared to the rays of a pearl or colours of a red flower or water coloured by *lākṣārasa*.[14] Nasalization, therefore, signifies distinctly as an independent quality of letters or sounds. Thus when 'r' comes under elision or r*epha* or *uṣmabhāva* (ṚPŚ 4/68–74), then the preceding vowel of *n* is prescribed for nasalization (ṚPŚ 4/80). *Raṅga* has a deep and sweet sound, deep like the roar of a tiger (*vyāghrarutopama*), sweet like a sound of a bell (*ghaṇṭadhvanivat*), as described by S.Varma following Pāriśikśāṭīkā.

But nasalization (*anunāsika*) about consonants, especially semivowels is also very common in grammar and phonetical texts as it is used much in popular Sanskrit also. These nasal sounds are also treated as *rakta* (*antasthāḥ svesve ca pare'pi raktaḥ* ṚPŚ 6/19), found in '*yay̐, yay̐ sukham*' etc.

To explain the articulation of *raṅga*, a living instance is given in Pāṇini Śikṣā and other texts. The women of Surāṣṭra, while selling *takra*, they pronounce it as *takra* Ý. In such a way, vedic *raṅga*-s will be uttered.[15] In the utterance of *raṅga*, the preceding letter should not explicitely be articulated, the vowel will be long first and then nasalization will follow. Here the quantity of duration of *raṅga* is stated as having two *mātrā*-s of which one *mātrā* is in the heart, half is in the cerebral portion, half is in the nostril. The sound, rising from the heart, is polite and it is like the metal, named *kāṃsya* in its sound.[16] Two ends of a *ruṅga* will be equal, but the middle part is articulated with vibration.[17] Agreeing with these features, *Yājña-Śikṣā* adds—

dvimātro mātriko vāpī nāsāmūlaṃ samāśritaḥ/
ante prayujyate raṅgaḥ pañcamaiḥ sānunāsikaḥ //

In describing colours of sounds, the *Yājñā-Śikṣā* differentiates between *raṅga* and other nasal, sounds by—'raṅgaḥ śabalaḥ ānunāsikya iti nīlaḥ' (86). Modern thinkers opine for the same origin of the *anusvāra* and the *raṅga*, At the time when *anusvāra* was a pure nasalized vowel, it was represented by *raṅga*. But this may always not be justified from grammarians' point of view.

It has been mentioned earlier that Pāṇinians do not accept *anusvāra* and *anunāsika*, but nasal vowels with *candravindu* is *anunāsika*. Here *Tribhāṣyaratna*–commentary of Taittirīya Prātiśākhya (TPŚ) (1/1) makes difference with some reasons. According to it, *anusvāra* is a qualified sound as here duration is related; but anunāsika is a quality.[18] On the other hand, ṚPŚ and Atharva Prātiśkhya (APŚ) create ambiguity by using the forms, viz. *nāsikya* and anunāsika respectively for both the nasal consonants and the *anusvāra*.

From the above discussion, it may safely be stated that the accurate analysis of nasal sounds in Sanskrit, specially Vedic Sanskrit, deserves more in depth study considering ancient Indian traditional as well as linguistic view points. The syllabic status of *anusvāra* may be defined after a serious research on all types of phonetic discourses. Extended study on such an issue may help us to infer some dialects prevalent in pre-Vedic and Vedic times though the span of Vedic age is very long indeed.

Bibliography

1. (The) Aṣṭādhyāyī of Pāṇini : Trans. and Ed. Śrīśa Chandra Vasu, Vol. I and II, Delhi, M.L.B.D., 1988.
2. Kāśikā, Ed. Narayaṇa Miśra, Varanasi, 2000.
3. Kātantrachandaḥprakriyā of Candrakānta Tarkālaṅkāra, Kolkata.
4. Pāṇiniya-Śikṣa—ed. and trans., Manmohan Ghosh, Delhi, V.K. Publishing, House, 1991.
5. Vedalakṣaṇā.

References

1. cf. anusvārasaya ठँ. kāra ādeśaśchandasi smṛtaḥ/-keśavī śikṣā in verse-15 maḥ ꣳ kāra śaṣasaharepheṣu—sa . . . śivam. havīꣳṣyā/ svarāṣṭakaśikṣā 12. ठँ. Also svarabhaktipariśiṣṭaśikṣā 19 to 21.
2. hrasvād dīrgho dīrghād hrasvaḥ saṃyoge guruśca/ keśavī Śikṣā.
3. Anusvāraśca. TPŚ—1/34. On it Vaidikābharaṇa comments—anusvāro'kāreṇa tulyakālo bhavatītyarthaḥ. Śuci ꣳ ucayo dīdivāṃsam
4. hrasvo dīrgho guruśceti trividhaḥ parikirtitaḥ/ also, tasya traividhyamucyate . (Keśavaśikṣā—16).
5. anusvāro dvimātraḥ syād ṛvarṇa-vyañjanodaye/hrasvo vā yadi vā dīrgho yājñavalkya-Śikṣā—65.
6. ꣳ Chandasi. Anusvāraśchandasi ꣳ kāramāpad yate śa-ṣa sa-ha-repheṣu parathḥ catustri ꣳ śad. Vyañjanasandhi-sūtra—25. Sārasvata-vyākaraṇ.
7. sūtra-6 of the third section of sandhi in Kātantrachandaḥprakriyā.
8. bahṛcā ātharvaṇikāśca prāyo'nusvāram adhīyate—commented on the sūtra 3/6 of sandi.
9. ṚPŚ-4/48 e.g. pīvo annā̊ayi bhudhaḥ—In 4/49 *n* with penultimate ī/ū> r when followed by *hata, yoni, vacobhiḥ, yān* etc e.g. utparṇī̊

hatamurmyāṃ madantā, 4/70 raśmī riva yacchatam).

10. TPŚ 15/6 deals with different areas of anunāsika.
11. Varṇaratnapradīpikāśikaṣā 130-135.
12. anusvārottamā anunāsikāḥ, TPŚ 2/30. anusvāro vyañjanani vā svari veto paramatam. tannirāsārthamidamucyate. anusvāropyuttamaved vyañjanameva asmacchākhāyām, ardhagakāra-rūpatvā—TPŚ 2/49/52.
13. atavuviṇānirghoṣo,. dantya-mūya-svarānanu/ anusvāraṣtu kartavyo nityaṃ hroḥ śaṣaseṣu ca. Pāṇiniya Śikṣā-23
14. yādṛśī ratnavarṇābhā japāyāḥ kusume' thavā. tādṛśaṃ rañjayed varṇaṃ prānte nāsikhyamācaret. lākṣārasaṃ yathā toyaṃ nakārātaṁ padaṃ tathāsarvaraṅgaṃ vijānīyād—Yājñyavalkya Śikśā—216–18.
15. yathā souraṣṭtrikā nārR takra ityabhibhāṣte. evaṃ raṅgāḥ prayokatavyāḥ khe arā iva khedayā—Pāṇ. Śikṣā-26
16. nāsādutpadyate raṇgaḥ kāṃsyena samaniḥsavaraḥ. mṛduścaiva dvimātraḥsyād dṛṣṭimā iḍdeti nidarśanaṃ— Yājñya. Śikṣā—194
17. Pāṇ Śikṣā—27-30.
18. kālaviśeṣā śrayatvādasau dharmī, na tvanunāsika vaddharmaḥ Tribhāṣyaratna or TPŚ 1/1.

21

पारिशिक्षाया विश्लेषणात्मकः परिचयः

श्रीकृष्णः शर्मा

वैदिकवाङ्मये वेदाङ्गसाहित्यस्य मूर्धन्यं स्थानं विद्यते। वेदमन्त्राणां स्वरूपरक्षणाय, शुद्धसमुच्चारणाय, अर्थावबोधाय, यथाविधि विनियोगाय च यथासमयमाचार्यैः प्रणीतेषु शिक्षाव्याकरणनिरुक्तादिषु पट्सु वेदाङ्गेषु वेदपुरुषस्य घ्राणस्थानीयं शिक्षानामकं[1] वेदाङ्गम् अक्षुण्णं महत्त्वं धत्ते, यतो हि वर्णोच्चारणशिक्षां विना सुकुमारमतिरपि व्याकरणशास्त्रस्य अध्ययने नैव क्षमः सम्भवति। अपरञ्च, घ्राणस्य रूपरचना मुखस्य सौन्दर्यं सुतरां संवर्द्धयति-इति नास्ति तिरोहितं कस्यापि मतिमतः। मन्ये, एनामेव उपयोगितां प्रदर्शयितुं प्राचीनसाहित्ये शिक्षाशास्त्रस्य परिगणनं प्रथमे स्थाने समुपलभ्यते।[2]

भारतीयध्वनिशास्त्रिभिः ध्वनिशास्त्रीयतत्त्वनिरूपणपरा ये शिक्षाग्रन्थाः प्रणीतास्तेषां शृङ्खला सुतरां सुदीर्घा विद्यते। प्रख्यातो ध्वनिशास्त्री सिद्धेश्वरो वर्मा,[3] प्रतिपादयति यत् तेन पञ्चषष्टिः शिक्षाग्रन्थाः प्रत्यक्षीकृताः, तेषु पञ्चाशत् शिक्षाग्रन्थाश्च सम्यक्तया परिशीलिता इति। वेदानां विविधाः शाखा आश्रित्य तेन उपलब्धानां शिक्षाग्रन्थानां व्यवस्थितं वर्गीकरणं प्रस्तावितम्।

पारिशिक्षा

पारिशिक्षा कृष्णयजुर्वेदीयतैत्तिरीयशाखया सम्बद्धा वर्तते। इयं शिक्षा मद्रास-नगरीय-राजकीयहस्तलिखितग्रन्थागारे,[4] अथच तिरूवनन्तपुरस्थे केरल-विश्वविद्यालयीये प्राच्यशोधसंस्थाने[5] हस्तलिखितरूपा प्राप्यते। सर्व एव एते

हस्तलेखा ग्रन्थाक्षरलिखिताः सन्ति। एषु द्वयोः हस्तलेखयोः देवनागरीप्रतिलिपिः कुरुक्षेत्रविश्वविद्यालयस्य हस्तलिखितग्रन्थालये विद्यते।[6] पारिशिक्षायाः प्रकाशनं 1994 ई. वर्षे जर्मनीतोऽभवत् सम्पादकश्च विद्यते राल्फ स्टाटजेबक । महोदयः। पारिशिक्षाया इदं संस्करणम् एकमात्रं हस्तलिखितग्रन्थमाधृत्य प्रकाशितमिति सूचितं सम्पादकेन ग्रन्थान्ते (Summary भागे, पृ. 472-73)।

पारिशिक्षायाः प्रणेता

पारिशिक्षायाः प्रणेता कः ? इति जिज्ञासायां प्रथमं तावत् पारिशिक्षाया नामकरणमेव विचारणीयं वर्तते। किन्तु पारिशिक्षाया नामकरणमपि रहस्यमयमेव विद्यते। थ्योडर आफ्रेक्टमहोदयः[7] सम्भावयति यत् पारिशिक्षा वस्तुतः पाराशरी शिक्षा स्यादिति। किन्तु उभयोरपि शिक्षाग्रन्थयोः पारस्परिकपाठतुलनया इदं निश्चीयते यत् पारिशिक्षा पाराशरीशिक्षातो नितरां भिन्नास्ति। अत आफ्रेक्टमहोदयस्य उत्प्रेक्षा सर्वथा निरस्यते। अपि च, पाराशरीनामतः पारिरूपो ध्वन्यात्मको विकारो (विकाशो वा) सार्थको नैव प्रतीयते। अन्येषां शिक्षाग्रन्थानां नामकरणं विचारं विचारम् इदमेव अनुमीयते तदस्य ग्रन्थस्य प्रणेता पारिनामा कश्चिद् ध्वनिशास्त्री सम्भवेत्। तन्नाम आधृत्य एव अस्य ग्रन्थस्य 'परिशिक्षा' इति संज्ञा प्ररूढा। याज्ञवल्क्यशिक्षा, वासिष्ठी शिक्षा, पाराशरी शिक्षा, अमरेशी शिक्षा, गौतमी शिक्षा, लोमशी शिक्षा, केशवी शिक्षा, पाणिनीयशिक्षा-इत्यादिकं नामकरणं चात्रास्ति निदर्शनम्। अतः पारिनामको ध्वनिशास्त्री एवास्य प्रणेता स्यात्।

सिद्धेश्वरवर्मणो मतम्

डॉ. सिद्धेश्वरवर्मा भ्रान्तिवशात् शिक्षाकारं भाष्यकारं च एकमेव जनं स्वीचकार[8] स चास्ति रामसूनुः चक्रकविः। किन्तु कम्पनिर्णयप्रकरणस्य व्याख्यानसमाप्तौ निम्नाङ्किता शब्दावलिः तथ्यमिदं विस्फोरयति यद् याजुषभूषणभाष्यस्य प्रणेता मूलशिक्षाकारतो नितरां भिन्नो वर्तते-

"इति श्रीवस्तकुलतिलकश्रीरामसूनुविरचिते पारिशिक्षाव्याख्यानभूते वर्णक्रमपञ्चमुकुरायमाणे याजुषभूषणाख्ये कम्पनिर्णयः समाप्तः।। हरिः ओम्।[9]"

न केवलमेतावदेव, अपितु डॉ. सिद्धेश्वरो वर्मा याजुषभूषणभाष्ये समुद्धृतानि अन्यग्रन्थीयपद्यानि चापि मूलशिक्षापाठरूपेण परिगणयति। तद्यथा-

यः स्वयं राजते तं तु स्वरमाह पतञ्जलिः।
उपरिस्थायिना तेन व्यङ्ग्य व्यञ्जनमुच्यते।।

इत्येतत् पद्यं सिद्धेश्वरो वर्मा पारिशिक्षाया द्वादशं पद्यं मनुते। अत्रेदमवधेयं यत्- पद्यमिदं तिरुवनन्तपुरस्थे हस्तलिखिते मूलशिक्षाग्रन्थे नैव प्राप्यते, किन्तु तैत्तिरीयप्रातिशाख्यस्य कलिकात्तासंस्करणे त्रिभाष्यरत्ने (21.1) समुपलभ्यते। जर्मनीतः प्रकाशितायां पारिशक्षायामपि (पृ. 35) पद्यमिदं याजुषभूषणभाष्य एव प्राप्यते, न तु मूलशिक्षापाठे। पद्यमिदम् पारिशिक्षेतरग्रन्थस्यैव निश्चीयते।

भ्रान्त्याः कारणम्

भाष्यकारचक्रकविप्रणीतस्य याजुषभूषणभाष्यस्य सिताम्भोजनिष्ठम् इति मंगलाचरणानन्तरं द्वितीयपद्यस्य प्रस्तावनायाम् 'अथ इष्टदेवताप्रणामानन्तरं स्वगुरोः **वेदतल्लक्षणाद्यभिज्ञताप्रकाशनमुखेन वस्तुनिर्देशात्मकं मङ्गलमातनुते पदक्रमेति**' इत्यत्र 'आतनुते' इति प्रथमपुरुषस्य प्रयोगमभिलक्ष्यैव डॉ. वर्मा एतत्सम्भावयति यत् इमानि पद्यानि मूलशिक्षाया एव स्युरिति। किन्तु मूलशिक्षापाठस्तु भाष्यगतं—

"सतां मुदं सम्प्रति पारिशिक्षाव्याख्यानभूता हृदयङ्गमेयम्।
विलक्षणा याजुषभूषणाख्या कृतिर्मदीया वितनोतु कामम्।।"

इति चतुर्थस्थानीयं पद्यमतिक्रम्य एव पठ्यते। तथा हि-
अथ शीक्षाकारोक्तं मङ्गलश्लोकमाह-

प्रणिपत्य जगन्नाथं वासुदेवं सनातनम्।
गणाधिपं गिरां देवीं शिक्षां वक्ष्ये यथामति।। इति।

एवञ्च इतः पूर्वाणि चत्वारि प्रस्तावनासहितानि पद्यानि भाष्यकारस्यैव सन्ति न तु

शिक्षाकरस्येति निश्चयः। उत्तमपुरुषस्य स्थाने प्रथमपुरुषस्य प्रयोगो ग्रन्थकाराणां विशिष्टा शैली वर्तते। काव्यप्रकाश–साहित्यदर्पण–लघुशब्देन्दुशेखर–मुहुर्तचिन्तामणिप्रभृतिषु ग्रन्थेषु सर्वत्र प्रसंगप्रस्तावनासु प्रथमपुरुष एव प्रयुज्यते। अतो डॉ. वर्मणो भ्रान्तिर्निर्मूला एव ज्ञेया।

पारिशिक्षाया मङ्गलात्मकं पद्यमालक्ष्य इदमनुमीयते यदस्य प्रणेता वैष्णवमतावलम्बी आसीत्। स हि गणेशं सरस्वतीं चापि समाराध्यामास। तथाहि—

प्रणिपत्य जगन्नाथं वासुदेवं सनातनम्।
गणाधिपं गिरां शिक्षां वक्ष्ये यथामति।।

पारिशिक्षाया रचनाकालः

पारिशिक्षाया रचनाकालं निर्णेतुं काशकुशावलम्बन–न्यायेन विचार्यते। अस्मिन् सन्दर्भे तेत्तिरीयप्रातिशाख्यगतं गार्ग्यगोपालयज्वप्रणीतं वैदिकाभरणभाष्यं महत्त्वपूर्णां सामग्रीं प्रस्तौति। वैदिकाभरणप्रणेता गोपालयज्वा तैत्तिरीयप्रातिशाख्यस्य सूत्राणि व्याकुर्वन् पारिशिक्षायाः पद्यानि यथोपयोगं याजुषभूषणं च समुज्जहार। अतः पारिशिक्षाया रचनाकालं निश्चेतुं गोपालयज्वनः समयो निर्धार्यते।

जर्मनीतः प्रकाशितायाः पारिशिक्षायाः सम्पादकमनुसृत्य याजुषभूषणभाष्यं (कर्तृ) वैदिकाभरणभाष्यं (कर्म) त्रिभाष्यरत्नं (कर्म) चावलम्ब्य विरचितमस्ति।[10] मतमिदं विचारणीयं वर्तते, यतो हि पारिशिक्षायाः पद्यानि तदनु याजुषभूषणस्य पाठो वैदिकाभरणे समुपलभ्यते।

तैत्तिरीयप्रातिशाख्यस्य सम्पादकः कस्तूरिरंगाचार्य उल्लिखति यत् गार्ग्यगोपालयज्वना केदारभट्टप्रणीतस्य वृत्तरत्नाकरस्य ज्ञानदीपनाम्नी टीका प्रणीतासीत्। टीकेयम् आन्ध्राक्षरैः मद्रास–नगरीतः प्रकाशिता।[11] इतिहासकारैश्च वृत्तरत्नाकरस्य समयः दशमे शतके निर्धरितः।[12] एवञ्च इदमनुमीयते यद् गार्ग्यगोपालयज्वना "एकादशे शतके" ज्ञानदीपस्य वैदिकाभरणस्य च प्रणयनं कृतं भवेत्।

गार्ग्यगोपालजज्वनोऽपरसीमा चतुर्दशे शतके[13] प्रणीतां सिद्धन्तशिक्षामाश्रित्य निर्णेतुं शक्यते यत्र हि वैदिकाभरणस्य उद्धरणानि सम्प्राप्यन्ते। एवञ्च, वैदिकाभरणस्य (गार्ग्यगोपालयज्वनो वा) कालावधिः दशम–त्रयोदश–

शतकयोर्मध्ये निश्चीयते। एतदाधृत्य पारिशिक्षाया रचनाकालस्य अपरसीमा "दशमशतक" समीपवर्तिनी विद्यते।

पारिशिक्षा-रचनाकालस्य पूर्वसीमा तैत्तिरीयप्रातिशख्यगत-त्रिभाष्यरत्नस्य रचनाकालो भवितुमर्हति यत्र हि पारिशिक्षाया उल्लेखो नैव दृश्यते। किन्तु त्रिभाष्यरत्ने महाभारत-गरुडपुराण-देवीपुराण-विष्णुधर्मोत्तरपुराण-भविष्यत्पुराणादीनां पद्यानि प्राप्यन्ते। एतदाधृत्य तैत्तिरीयप्रातिशाख्यस्य सम्पादको राजेन्द्रलालमित्रोऽनुमिनोति यत् त्रिभाष्यरत्नस्य रचना ईश्वरीयेऽष्टमे शतकेऽभवत्।[14] एवञ्च, पारिशिक्षाया रचनाकालोऽष्टमदशमशताब्द्योर्मध्येऽनुमीयते।

पारिशिक्षायाः स्वरूपम्

पारिशिक्षा पद्यात्मकशैलीमनुसरति। पद्यानि प्रायः अनुष्टुब्वृत्तानुस्यूतानि सन्ति। यत्र तत्र उपजातिच्छन्दोऽपि प्रयुक्तम् अस्ति। सम्पूर्णेऽपि ग्रन्थे चत्वारिंशदुत्तरशतसंख्यानि पद्यानि वर्तन्ते।

पारिशिक्षाया विषयवस्तु

पारिशिक्षायां मङ्गलाचरणानन्तरं शास्त्रीयप्रतिज्ञा, वर्णसमाम्नायः, वर्णभेदः, वर्णक्रमः, वर्णधर्मः, शब्दोत्पत्तिः, वर्णानां स्थान-करण-प्रयत्न-देवतादयः, स्वरानुसारी हस्तचालनविधि, षड्जादिस्वराणां लक्षणम्, कम्पप्रचयस्वरयोर्विशिष्टं निरूपणम्, स्वरभक्तिः-इत्यादीनि प्रकरणानि सुव्यक्तं निरूपितानि सन्ति। अस्य शिक्षाग्रन्थस्य सारपूर्णा शब्दरचना अतीव मनोग्राहिणी विद्यते।[15] तद्यथा-

अथ शब्दोद्भवः, वायुशरीरकसमीरणात्।
कण्ठोरसोश्च सन्धाने तस्योत्पत्तिः प्रकीर्तिता।।
प्रातिश्रुत्कानि तस्यात्र भवन्त्येतानि पञ्च च।
उरःकण्ठशीर्षमुखं नासिकाया बिलद्वयम्।।16।।

पारिशिक्षा, 24, 25, 26

अत्रायं सारो यत् शब्दं प्रयोक्तुमना वक्ता स्वकीयं मनो नियुङ्क्ते, तथाभूतं मनः शरीरवर्तिनं जाठरमग्निर्मभिहन्ति। ततश्च जाठरोऽग्निः मूलाधरवर्तिनं वायुं प्रेरयति। तथारूपः प्रेर्यमाणो वायुः मूलाधाराद् ऊर्ध्वमागच्छन् कण्ठोरसोर्मध्ये शब्दम् उत्पादयति। ततश्च सोऽव्यक्तः शब्दः उरः-कण्ठशीर्षमुखनासिकादिषु

प्रविभज्यमानो वर्णत्वमेति। अत्र मुखपदेन तालुदन्तोष्ठादीनामपि परामर्शः।

पारिशिक्षायाष्टीका याजुषभूषणम्

पारिशिक्षाया विषयवस्तु स्पष्टयितुं याजुषभूषण-नाम्नी टीका परममुपादेया विद्यते। गद्यात्मकस्य अस्य व्याख्यानस्य प्रारम्भे पद्यचतुष्टयं प्राप्यते। तत्रत्यं तृतीयं पद्यमालक्ष्य याजुषभूषणस्य प्रणेता चक्रनामा विद्वान् निश्चीयते। चक्रस्य पितुरभिधानं 'राम' इत्यासीत्। स एव चक्रस्य विद्यागुरुरप्यासीत्।[17] रामो वेदपाठस्य विविधप्रणालीनां विशेषज्ञ आसीत्। स्वजनकस्य (रामस्य) पाण्डित्यमनुरुध्यैव चक्रस्य 'रामसूनु' इति पैतृकं नामान्तरमपि प्ररूढमासीत्। सोऽयं चक्रनामा विद्वान् वत्सगोत्रीय आसीत्।[18] अनेन ईश्वीय एकादशे द्वादशे वा शतके अस्य याजुषभूषणस्य प्रणयनं कृतं भवेदिति प्रतिपादितं पारिशिक्षारचनाकाल-विचारणावसरे पूर्वमेव।

याजुषभूषणस्य मङ्गलपद्ये हयग्रीवस्य वन्दनं कृतं चक्रेण।[19] अनेन ज्ञायते यदयं विद्वान् वैष्णवं मतमवलम्बते स्म। तैत्तिरीयशाखायाः सर्वेऽपि शिक्षाग्रन्थाः केवलं दक्षिणभारत एव समुपलभ्यन्ते,[20] इति कृत्वा याजुषभूषणकारोऽपि दाक्षिणात्यो भवेदिति। किं बहुना, अस्य ग्रन्थस्य हस्तलिखितग्रन्था अपि दक्षिणभारत एव सुलभा नान्यत्र।

याजुषभूषणस्य प्रतिपादनशैली नितरां सुगमा सुबोधा चास्ति। टीकाकारो मूलशिक्षायाः पद्यानि शब्दशो ब्याचष्टे। वर्णाक्षरस्वर-व्यञ्जनान्तस्थोष्मोपसर्ग-जिह्वामूलीय-प्रभृतयः पारिभाषिकाः शब्दा व्युत्पत्तिपरकं व्याख्यानमश्रित्य व्याकृताः। तथाहि—

वर्णः

वर्ण्यन्ते व्यक्तं ध्वन्यन्त इति वर्णाः, अकारादयः। (पृ. 3)

अक्षरम्

न क्षरन्तीत्यक्षराणि, क्षरणमन्याङ्गतया चलनं तदभावात्। (पृ. ४)

स्वरः

स्वयं राजन्ते नान्येन व्यज्यन्त इति स्वराः (पृ. 6)

अन्तस्थाः

जिह्वामध्यप्रभृतीनां करणानाम् अन्तैर्जन्यत्वादन्तस्था इत्याख्या। (पृ. 7-8)

ऊष्मा

ऊष्माख्या बाह्यप्रयत्नयोगादूष्माण इत्याख्या। (पृ. 8)

उपसर्गः

गतितया कर्मप्रवचनीयतया पदान्तरैः (उप) संसृज्यन्त इत्युपसर्गाः। (प. 9-10)

विसर्गः

वायोर्विसर्जनेन जन्यत्वाद् विसर्जनीयः। (पृ. 10)

अनुस्वरः

अनुस्वर्यते पश्चार्धे स्वरवदुच्चार्यते इत्यनुस्वारः। (पृ. 10)

स्थालीपुलाकन्यायेन प्रदर्शितां शब्दावलिमक्षिलक्ष्यीकृत्य याजुषभूषणस्य सरलशैली स्पष्टमेव सुगमा विद्यते। याजुषभूषणस्य एषा शब्दरचना वैदिकाभरणादिषु भाष्येषु शब्दश उद्धृता दृश्यते।

एवञ्च, याजुषशिक्षाग्रन्थेषु पारिशिक्षायाः तदीयभाष्ययाजुषभूषणस्य च महनीयं स्थानं विद्यते।

टिप्पण

1. छन्दः पादौ तु वेदस्य हस्तौ कल्पोऽथ पठ्यते।
ज्योतिषामयनं चक्षुर्निरुक्तं श्रोत्रमुच्यते।।
शिक्षा घ्राणं तु वेदस्य मुखं व्याकरणं स्मृतम्।

पाणिनीय-शिक्षा, 41-42

2. तत्रापरा ऋग्वेदो यजुर्वेदः सामवेदोऽथर्ववेदः शिक्षा कल्पो व्याकरणं निरुक्तं छन्दो ज्योतिषमिति।। मुण्डकोपनिषद्, 1.1.5
अथांगानि। तत्र देबलः-शिक्षा-व्याकरण-निरूक्त-छन्दः-कल्प-ज्योतिषमिति।
वीरमित्रोदयः, परिभाषाप्रकरणम्, पृ० 20

3. प्राचीन भारतीय वैयाकरणों के ध्वन्यात्मक विचारों का विश्लेषणात्मक अध्ययन, पृ० 36
4. पाण्डुलिपिक्रमसंख्या, 924, 925, 15925
5. पाण्डुलिपिक्रमसंख्या, 2087
6. पाण्डुलिपिक्रमसंख्या, 50730 तथा 19655
7. केटेलागस केटेलोग्रम प्रथमो भागः पृ. 335
8. प्राचीन भारतीय वैयाकरणों के ध्वन्यात्मक विचारों का विश्लेषणात्मक अध्ययन, पृ. 57
9. तुलना–

   सतां मुदं सम्प्रति पारिशिक्षाव्याख्यातभूता हृदयङ्गमेयम्।
   विलक्षणं याजुषभूषणाख्या कृतिर्मदीया वितनोतु कामम्, ।।

   याजुषभूषणस्य प्रस्तावनापद्यम्, 4
10. द्र., Pāriśikṣā und Sarvasa-Mataśikṣā, p. 473 (Summary)
11. तैत्तिरीय-प्रातिशाख्यस्य भूमिका, पृ. 18
12. हेमचन्द्रः (1088-1172 ई.) छन्देऽनुशासने केदारभट्टमालोचयति। त्रिविक्रमो भट्टः (1100 ई.) वृत्तरनाकरे टीकां प्रणिनाय। एतदाधृत्य कुन्दनलाल शर्मा निजग्रन्थे 'वेदाङ्ग,' (पृ. 84, 500) वृत्तरत्नाकरस्य समयं 1000 ई. वर्षं निश्चिनोति।
13. प्राचीन भारतीय वैयाकरणों के ध्वन्यात्मक . . . पृष्ठ 54
14. तैत्तिरीयप्रातिशाख्यस्य प्राक्कथनम्, पृष्ठ 6
15. तुलना–

   तैत्तिरीयप्रातिशाख्ये–अथ शब्दोत्पत्तिः ।। 2.1 ।। वायुशरीरसमीरणात् कण्ठोरसोः सन्धाने ।। 2.2 ।। त्रिभाष्यरत्नम् . . . वायुश्च शरीरञ्च वायुशरीरे तयोः समीकरणं तस्मात्। . . . अत्रेत्थं समासः, राजदन्तादित्वाच्छरीरशब्दस्य परनिपातः। शरीरे वायुः, वायुशीरं, तस्य समीरणं तस्मात्। अस्मिन् मते वायोः समीरकर्तृत्वमेव न तु कर्मत्वम्।
16. तनयो विनयोज्जवलस्य तस्य प्रथितो वैदिकवावदूकसिंहः।
   कृपया महतां स चक्रनामा ह्यपि वर्णक्रमलक्षणं करोति।। याजुषभूषणमं 3
17. स मे विजयतेतरां प्रथितरामनामा गुरुः ।। तदेव, 2
18. इति श्रीवस्तकुलतिलकश्रीरामसुनुविरचिते . . . याजुषभूषणाख्ये कम्पनिर्णयस्समाप्तः ।।
19. सिताम्भोजनिष्ठं रथाङ्गाब्जमुद्राः तथा पुस्तकं तं कराब्जैर्दधानम्।
   प्रणभ्याश्ववक्त्रं त्वहं पञ्चवर्णक्रमाणां निदानं प्रवक्ष्ये प्रबन्धम्।।
20. प्राचीन भारतीय वैयाकरणों के ध्वन्यात्मक विचारों . . . पृष्ट 46

सहायकग्रन्थसूची

1. Catalogus Catalogorum (Theodor Aufrecht) Franz Steiner Verlag GMBH, 1962.
2. तैत्तिरीयप्रातिशाख्यम् त्रिभाष्यरत्नसहितम्, सं० राजेन्द्र लाल मित्र, एशियाटिक सोसायटी, बंगाल, कलकत्ता, 1871 ई०।
3. तैत्तिरीयप्रातिशाख्यम् त्रिभाष्यरत्न-वैदिकभरणभाष्यसहितम-, सं० आर. शाम शास्त्री, मोतीलाल बनारसीदास, दिल्ली, 1985 ई.।
4. पाणिनीयशिक्षा सं० मनोमोहन घोष, कलकत्ता विश्वविद्यालय, कलकत्ता, 1938 ई०।
5. पारिशिक्षा (हस्तलिखिता) Acc. Nos. Madras 924, 925, 15925, Trivandrum 2087, Kurukshetra 50730 (K). 19655 (M).
6. Pāriśikṣā Und Sarvasa-Mataśīkṣā Von, Ralf Stautzebach, Franz Steiner Verlag, 1994.
7. प्राचीन भारतीय वैयाकरणों के ध्वन्यात्मक विचारों का विवेचनात्मक अध्ययनः विद्धेश्वरवर्मा, हरियाणा साहित्य अकादमी, चण्डीगढ़, 1985 ई०।
8. मुण्डकोपनिषद् (उपनिषत्संग्रहः) जगदीश लाल शास्त्री, मोतीलाल बनारसीदास, दिल्ली, 1980 ई०।
9. वीरमित्रोदयः (श्रीमित्रमिश्र), चौखम्बा संस्कृत बुक डिपो, बनारस, 1909 ई०।
10. वेदांग (कुन्दन लाल शर्मा), विश्वेश्वरानन्द वैदिक शोध संस्थान, होशियारपुर, 1983 ई०।

22

ACCENT IN THE ṚK PRĀTIŚĀKHYA: A STUDY

INDRANI KAR

All the four vedas (Ṛk, Sāma, Yajur, Atharva) are divided into the two parts—*mantra* and its *brahmāṇa.* The mantra part is of metric composition and it contains mainly praise for the deities (*stuti*). This part is well-known as Saṁhitā. On the other hand, the Brāhmaṇa part deals with the application of the mantras. In the opinion of some scholars, mantra is the theory part of the veda and Brāhmaṇa is the practical part of the same veda. It is well-known fact that the mantras were preserved through *guru-śiṣya-paramparā.* Gradually, this system of learning broke the barrier of geographical territory and gave birth to new generation of *guru-śiṣya-paramparā* or tradition. As a result, we find that the pronunciation and arrangement of the mantras are changed in the course of time. Even we find differences in opinion regarding the usage of each mantra. The paramparās differ from each other on pronunciation, arrangement, usage and other things related to a mantra. Here from arises the concept of *śākhā,* Each *sampradāya* or group of the *guru-śiṣya* tradition is known as *śākhā* or branch or recension. But here we should remember that the vedic *śākhās* are not a part of a veda, as we see in a tree, they represent the concerned veda entirely. So in this way we may get different arrangements or usage of the mantras but the mantras are, as a whole, the same.

The treatise that deals with the phonetic intricacies pertaining to each *śākhā* of the saṁhitās, is known as

Prātiśākhya. It is derived as *śākhāyāṃ śākhāyāṃ prātiśākhaṃ, prātiśākhaṃ bhavam–prātiśākhyam.* Or *śākhyāṃ śākhyaṃ pratipratiśākhyam, pratiśākhya + aṇ (adhikṛtya kṛte granthe—* Pa IV, 3, 87) = *Prātiśākhyaṃ.*

A Prātiśākhya is a phonetic text as it deals with the phonetic part of the vedic verses or words, such as, alphabetical system, their pronunciation, method of articulation etc. It is a kind of grammatical text pertaining to each *śākhā* of the *saṃhitās.* Its contents are very close to that of śikśās. Chronological appearance of these two types of text, i.e. *prātiśākhya* and *śikṣa,* vary. Yet according to Siddheswar Verma (*Critical Studies in the Phonetic Observation of Indian Grammarians,* Delhi, 1961), the Prātiśākhyas are very earlier than the *śikṣas.* According to him, date of the *prātiśākhyas* more or less fifth century BC. Some of the *śikṣās* also belong almost to the same time but later than the *prātiśākhyas.* Of course, there are many *śikṣās* which were written much later than that date.

As we get many *śikṣās* or recensions of each veda, it is obvious the numbers of *prātiśākhyas* connected to each veda will be numerous. But practically the case is different. Perhaps most of them are lost in due course of time just as we do not get all recensions of the vedas. Those who were prevalent at a later date are found. Such is the case, we think, with the *prātiśākhyas.*

However a list of *prātiśākhyas* that are known today is given below:—

Ṛgveda	Sāmaveda	Yajurveda	Atharvaveda
1. *Ṛk Prātiśākhya*	2. Sāma *Prātiśākhya* 3. *Puṣpasūtra* 4. *Pañcavidha-suṛra* 5. *Ṛktantra*	6. Taittirīya *Prātiśākhya* (Black) 7. Vājasaneya *Prātiśkhya* (White)	8. Atharvaveda *Prātiśākhya*

The present paper will attempt to focus on the accent

system of the ṛk Prātiśākhya (=RP). For the proper understanding of the subject, the contents of the RP will be discussed first and then its accent system will be elaborated.

Traditionally we believe that the author of RP is Śaunaka, whose disciple was Āśvalayana. It is available both in *sutra*-form and in metrical form. Scholars opine that the *sutra*-form was the earlier version, the metrical form is of later date. The RP consists of 18 *paṭalas* or chapters. The chapters are designated here as *paṭalas.* At the very beginning we get *vargadvaya* starting with *parāvare brahmaṇi* etc. Here we get eight verses and a special alphabetical order which help us to understand the sūtras of the first *paṭala* in continuation. But we do not get the commentary of Uvaṭa for this *vargadvaya.* Instead we get Viṣṇumitra's commentary on this. Though some scholars hold the view that this *vargadvaya* is not the part of the RP, but the content of *vargadvaya* emphasizes on the fact without this some sūtras of the lst *paṭala* will lose their significance and hence we have to accept it as the part of RP.

The first *paṭala,* known as *paribhāṣā paṭala,* deals with *maṅgalācaraṇa,* subject matter, alphabetical order, classification of alphabets (*samānākṣarādi*), place of articulation, technical terms (*nāmnyādi saṃjñā*). Subject matter of the second *paṭala* is *svarasandhi.* It elaborated *anvakṣara* (*anuloma-pratiloma*), *vivṛtti, praśliṣṭasandhi, kṣaiprasandhi* etc. *Svara* or accent is the concern of the third *paṭala* of RP *udātta, anudātta, Svarita* etc. are discussed along with *sandhisvara, pracayasvara, parigrahasvara, avagrahasvara* and others. The subject matter of this *paṭala,* the main focus point of this paper, will be elaborated later. The fourth *paṭala* has *vyañjanasandhi* as its subject. The topics that are dealt here are *avaśaṅgamasandhi, vaśaṅgamasandhi, paripātana-sandi, antaḥpātasandhi* and so on. The fifth *paṭala* of the RP has discussed ṇatvavidhi and ṣatvavidhi. whereas the sixth *paṭala* is known as Dviruktaprakaraṇa. It emphasises on dvirvacana. abhinidhānam, svarabhakti etc. Next three *paṭalas*, i.e. seventh, eighth, ninth, have their subject matters as plutībhāva, antaḥpadapluti, padāvayavapluti respectively.

The tenth and eleventh *paṭalas* of the RP have kramavidhi as their subject matters. In the tenth, the kramavidhis are told, whereas in the eleventh the causes (hetu) of kramavidhi are stated. The twelfth *paṭala* again deals with the alphabets. But this time *varṇasaṃyoga* is discussed along with *padavibhāga*. Accent is also discussed with reference to these topics. The thirteenth *paṭala* is known as Śikṣā *paṭala*. Here the places of articulation of the sounds are determined in detail. Even the discussion on the morās (*mātrā*) is found here in connection with the pronunciation of sounds. Next chapter, i.e., the fourteenth *paṭala* discusses *varṇoccāraṇadoṣāḥ*, faults in pronunciation, which is very much essential for a phonetic text, *Pārāyaṇa* is the focus of the fifteenth *paṭala* of the RP. How to teach or how to learn the vedas are depicted here. The entire process of reciting the Vedas is taught here. It is essential for the teacher, as well as, for the learner of the veda. The next three *paṭalas*, the sixteenth, seventeenth and eighteenth *paṭalas*, have discussion on *chandaḥ* (metre). Principal metres, their varieties, *pragāthās* are dealt with in these chapters along with same accentual discussion. As in the modern conception *chandah* (metre) and also punctuation (*yati cinha*) belong to the phonetics, so in the RP and also in some other texts the inclusion of metre is quite significant in those days. As metre gives us the value of *svara* and also its *mātrā*, *chandaḥ* must be included as a part of phonetics and in the chapter of *chandaḥ* the question of *virāma*, *yati cinha* etc. are discussed. It also serves the purpose of punctuation for recitation. So in the RP, the inclusion of the chapter of *chandaḥ* is justified even in the modern conception of the subject. Now let us concentrate on the main focus point of this presentation—accent or *svara*. Accent is a phonetic phenomenon as it deals with the pronunciation of the vedic verses and hence the RP has an elaborate discussion on this topic. The third chapter, though known as *svara paṭala,* there are other chapters too where we get some rules related to *svara.* For example, Chapter, Xll, XV, XVII bear some pertinent rules for accent.

A vedic word is always accented. What sort of emphasis has to be given on a syllable (akṣara) that determines the accent of that particular syllable. Accent, as told by RP, is primarily of three types:

(1) Udātta or the acute
(2) Anudātta or the grave
(3) Svarita or the circumflex

udāttaścānudāttaśca svaritaśca trayas svarāḥ/
āyāmaviśrambhākṣepaistu ucyante 'kṣarāśrayāḥ// RP. III.1

The acute and the grave accents are uttered by stretching (*āyāma*) and relaxing (*viśrambha*) of the body or the vocal muscles. The circumflex is uttered by carrying across (*ākṣepa*) of the body or the vocal muscles. Uvaṭa says (RP II.1)—

āyāmo nāma vāyunimittamūrddhagamanaṃ gātrāṇām/ tena ya ucyate sa udāttaḥ/viśrambho nāma adhogamanaṃ gāṭrānāṃ vāyunimittam/ tena ya ucyate so'nudāttaḥ/ ākṣepo nāma tiryaggamanaṃ gātrānāṃ vāyunimittam/ tena ya ucyate sa svaritaḥ/

Pāṇini says in this context of Udātta etc. as–*uccairudāttaḥ, nīcairanudāttaḥ, samāhāraḥsvaritaḥ* (Pā. 1.2.29-31). Every sound has its own place of articulation, such as. velar, palate etc. This place of articulation has various parts of its own. The Udātta is uttered from the higher part of this place of articulation, the Anudātta is from the lower part and the Svarita is from the combination of these two parts. This combination nature of Svarita is stated in the RP thus—*ekākṣarasamāveśe pūrvayoḥ svaritaḥ svaraḥ/ tasyodāttatarodāttādardhamātrādhīneva vā* RP. III.2.

It is not pure like the acute or grave. When the acute is

combined with the following grave in a single syllable, the resultant is a circumflex. The former part and later part of this accent is uttered in different pitch. The first half is uttred in a note higher than the acute, though originally if is an acute (RP. III.2). The remaining portion is uttered in the same pitch as an acute, though actually it is grave —

anudāttaḥ paraḥ śeṣah sa udāttaśrutirna cet/
uddāttaṃ vocyate kiñchit svaritaṃ vākṣaraṃ padam// RP. lll.3.

The *svarita* needs special attention as it has not only a striking feature, but also different varieties according to their nature. The varieties found in the RP are seven in number as shown below:

(i) *Ajātya* (dependent)—It is the common type of circumflex that is totally dependant on an acute immediately preceding it. We have already discussed this one in the name of *svarita.* e.g. *hotā.*

(ii) *Jātya* (independent) — We know that an *anudātta* when preceeding by a *udātta,* becomes *svarita.* This is dependent or *ajātya svarita* known to all. But when not preceded by an *anudātta,* a *svarita* stands *svarita* of its own is called *Jātya* or independent circumflex. There is no condition of preceding or following. *udāttapūrvaṃ svaritamanudāttaṃ pade kṣaram/ ato'nyat svaritaṃ svaraṃ/jātyamācakṣate pade //* RP. III.4. e.g. kva, kavyā etc.

(iii) *Abhinihita* (absorbed)—When an acute or *udātta* e or o is followed by a grave or *anudātta,* the resultant is circumflex, e.g. *te + avardhanta = te'vardhanta.* It is a reflected in the RP in this way—*ikārayosca praśleṣe kṣaiprābhinihiteṣu ca/ udāttapūrvarūpeṣu śākalasyaiva-mācaret//* RP. III.7.

(iv) *Kṣaipra* (hastened)—When an acute or *udātta* i or u is followed by a grave or *anudātta* vowel. The resultant becomes a circumflex or *svarita,* e.g. *nu + indra =*

nvindra. It is reflected in the verse RP III.7 as quoted earlier.

(v) *Pṛśliṣṭa* (contracted)—This is not a regular outcome of all *praśliṣṭa sandhi.* When an acute or *udātta* i, is followed by a grave or *anudātta* i, the resultant becomes a circumflex or *svarita,* e.g. *sruci* + *iva* = *srucīva.* The RP. III.7 has stated this one also. It is to be remembered here that according to Māṇḍūkeya, all resultant of the *Praśliṣṭa sandhi* should be circumflex.

(vi) *Tairovyañjana* (intervened by consonant)—When preceded by an acute or udātta and not followed by an acute (udatta) or a circumflex (svarita), and intervened by one or more consonants (vyañjana), a grave (anudātta) is changed into a circumflex (svarita), e.g., agnim/ īle = agnim īle/ the RP says—*udāttapūrvaṃ niyataṃ vivṛttya vyañjanena vā/ svaryate'-ntarhitaṃ na cedudāttasvaritodayam//* RP. III.9.

(vii) *Vaivṛtta* (intevened by hiatus)—When preceded by an acute (udātta) and not followed by an acute (udātta) or a circumflex (svarita) and intervened by a hiatus, a grave vowel is changed into a circumflex (svarita), e.g. yaḥ + indra = ya indra, where the grave i (i) becomes a circumflex vaivṛtta because of the preceding hiatus or pause. This hiatus is due to the sandhi, so this circumflex is regarded to be a variety of sandhija circumflex. This variety is stated under the verse quoted earlier, i.e. RP. III.9.

The RP records all the names that were mentioned in the previous paragraphs—

vaivṛttatairovyañjanau kṣaiprābhinihitau ca tān/
praśliṣṭañca yathāsandhi svarānācakṣate pṛthak// RP III.10

It is clearly mentioned in this verse that this five types of circumflex (*svarita*), i.e., vaivṛtta, *tairovyañjana, kṣaipra, abhinihita* and *praśliṣṭa,* are the results of *sandhi*—so they can be called sandhija circumflex. So we may classify these varieties of svarita this way—

svarita or circumflex

- *Ajātya* (dependent) (RP III. 2.3)
- *Jātya* (independent) (RP. III. 4)
- *Sandhija* (Semi-dependent)
  - Abhinihita (RP III.7)
  - kṣaipra (RP. III.7)
  - Praśliṣṭa (RP III.7)
  - Tairo-vjāñjana (RP III.9)
  - Vaivṛtta (RP III. 9)

The discussion on primary three accents then leads us to two other accents, though they are not original ones, but variations of grave and circumflex respectively. They are —

4. *Pracaya* or the accumulated
5. *Kampasvara*

The accumulated accent or *pracaya* is introduced in the RP in the following manner—

svaritādanudāttānāṃ pareṣāṃ pracayasvaraḥ / udāttaśrutitāṃ yāntyekaṃ dve vā bahūni vā// RP. III.12.

The graves (*anudātta*) that follow a circumflex (*svarita*) become *pracayas* or accumulated. Whatever may be the number of grave, one or two or more, all become *pracayas.* Their utterance will be same with that of the *udātta,* e.g. *agnimīle purohitam; nāstyābhyām* etc.

Some teachers utter the last few syllables or only the last syllable of these *pracayas* as grave. This is stated in the RP. Thus *kecit tvekamanekaṃ vā niyacchantyantato'kṣaram / ā vā śeṣānniyuktantūdāttasvaritodayam//* RP III. 12

For example, *ardavda vrata pramati rvaśiṣṭaḥ*/Here *ti* is

grave, prior to that all are accumulated. But if there is an acute or circumflex just after an accumulated, it always becomes grave, not pracaya. As the RP says *niyamaṃ kāraṇādeke pracayasvaradharmavat.* RP III. 13, we have to accept this grave as conditional.

In Aṣṭādhyāyī, for the graves following a circumflex the name *pracaya* is not found. But there ekaśruti (or monotony) is prescribed as their accent—*svaritāt saṃhitāyām anudāttānām* (Pā. 1.2.39) it has new term *sannatara* for the pracaya which is according to the RP. (III. 13) is grave—*udāttasvaritaparasyasannataraḥ/* (Pā 1.2.40)

The last one the kampasvara is a variation of circumflex. This terminology is not used in the RP, but it is of a common usage. When a circumflex of jātya or abhinihita or praśliṣṭa or kṣaipra origin followed by an acute or other circumflex, that previous circumflexis uttered with a vibration of the tone—*jātyo'bhinihitaścaiva kṣaipraḥ praśliṣṭa eva ca/ ete svarāḥ prakampante yatro ca svaritodayāḥ//* RP III.19

e.g., *jātya-kvā 3 bhīśavaḥ; abbinihita-divo 3sme; kṣaipra-apsva 1 ntaḥ; praśleṣa-abhi3dam/*

The above discussion was on the accent and their variations. The RP has far fetched the discussion with how to utter svara properly, accentuation in specified cases (eg. *upasarga, om* etc.), unaccented feet and so on. At the same time *Pada* text is also discussed with reference to the *saṃhitā* text and its accent. For *Pada* text, there is also discussion on accent of *avagraha, parigraha.* Double accented compound words.

Last, but not the least, a discussion on 'Faults of accents', is very much needed. Accent must be articulated without any doubt (*asandigdha*). No indistinctness should take place (*avikṛṣṭa*). Tremor should be avoided while uttering (*akampita*). The circumflex should not be carried too far (*nātinirhana*) and the first 2 *svaras* should not be dragged too far (*nātivivartana*). The RP states it thus—

asandigdhān svarān bruyādavikṛṣtānakampitān/
svaritaṃ nātinirhanyāt pūrvau pūrvau nātivivartayet //
RP III.8.

To sum up the discussion made above I may say that this is a study of accents as found in the RP but not a critical one. It has ample scope for further study on a comparison basis with other Prātiśākhyas, as well as with Pāṇinian grammar and others. My attempt is to elicit opinion from scholars to throw light on the proper understanding of the accent system of the RP.

23

VEDALAKṢAṆA—HOW DOES IT ESTABLISH THE MAGNANIMITY OF THE SĀMAVEDA

BHASKARNATH BHATTACHARYYA

The word *Vedalakṣaṇa* (*VL*) means the ancillary Vedic texts as opined by the contemporary Vedic scholars, like the orientalists as they defined it as the *aṅga-granthas*, which almost always help to explicate or to find out the exact import and corollary of the Vedic *mantras* and finally to differentiate the particular meaning and temperament of a particular *mantra* of a particular branch of the Veda consumed from another one. Actually *VL* is a methodological compound word consisting of two immediate parts *Veda* and *Lakṣaṇa*. The word Veda indicates here the collection of the *mantras* and the *brāhmaṇas* both (*mantrabrāhmaṇayor vedanāmadheyam–Apastamba*). The word *lakṣaṇa* is a technical term in the Vedic tradition of metaphysics. So the compound word *VL* stands for a text which would help the reader to come over the ambiguity of any *mantra* of each branch of the Vedas from another one (*vedasya vedānāṁ vā lakṣaṇam* by 6th ending Tatpuruṣa compound). So, if the definition of the word *lakṣaṇa* concentrates to differentiate one from another then it befits with the exact purpose and objective of a *śikṣā* or a *Prātiśākhya* text in the domain of the Vedic literature. The connotation of the words śikṣā or *Prātiśākhya* deals with that most important discipline of articulation or pronunciation of a particular *mantra* of a specific recension of a particular Veda traditionally. Indian tradition has had the four types of method of teaching and propagating the same to the predecessor. They are to receive the *śāstras* from own teacher (*adhīti*), to understand the meaning of the same lines received from the teacher (*bodhaḥ*), to perform the same in his own life (*ācaraṇam*) and lastly to preach over (*pracāraṇam*) the same to the disciples of next generation. In case of the four Vedas these very four methods of teaching are adopted like all other *śāstras* or disciplines in the Indian tradition of knowledge. In the *śikṣā* texts six apparatus of this discipline are discussed as *varṇa, svara, mātrā, valam, sāma* and *santāna*. All these six apparatus are seen to be applied in the foresaid methods of teaching and preaching for the propagation and preservation of the Vedas. Here the word Veda represents the four Vedas—Ṛk, Sāma, Yaju and Atharva. Particularly the *Lakṣaṇa* is a technical term which envisages the idea and area of *Śikṣā* and *Prātiśākhya*, called as ancillary Vedic texts under discussion. According to the grammatical connotation the word *Lakṣaṇa* means that which defines an object undoubtedly from another—*lakṣyate jñāyate anena iti lakṣna*. In the definition of the word *lakṣaṇa* our tradition says more that *lakṣaṇa* narrates the immediate interior difference between two things avoiding the three essential components for a definition i.e. too narrowness (*avyāpti*), too wideness (*ativyāpti*) and absurdity (*asambhava*)—*avyāptyativyāptyasambhavadoṣa-trayarahitattve sati itaretaravyāvartakattvaṃ lakśaṇattvam*. So this is how a *Prātiśākhya* becomes an ancillary text determining the interior difference between two Vedas or two branches of a same Veda—*pratiśākhāyāṃ bhava iti prātiśākhya*. In the *Śikṣā* texts there are mainly six points to discuss—*varṇaḥ, svaraḥ, mātrā, valam, sāma, santāna* on which the characteristic of a Veda or a particular branch of a Veda totally depends on. All the branches of the four Vedas deal with these six summits annotated in the *Śikṣā* which are also seen to be narrated in the different *Prātiśākhyas*. Therefore, it is very much impossible and impracticable to determine the spirit, uniqueness and the magnanimity of a particular Veda without the help of an ancillary text or *Prātiśākhya* of that Veda concerned.

It is well known that the Vedas and concomitant literature constitute the horizon against which Indian culture and civilization developed and got nourished. Vedas are one of the earliest records of man's bravado and belief, ideas and values, hopes and aspirations, his profound quest and attempts to get answers to those undying inquisitions. Vedas are the repertoire of ancient Indian thought in its various manifestations. Out of the four Vedas, Sāmaveda occupies a very special place. We have an axiom in the *Vibhūti-yoga* of the *Śrīmadbhagavadgītā* which claimed that the Sāmaveda is most favourite to Lord Kṛṣṇa among the four Vedas *vedānāṃ sāmavedo'smi* (10/22). Here Lord identifies himself with Sāmaveda. implying the salience of Sāmaveda. In terms of volume, Sāmaveda is the shortest one consisting only of 1875 *mantras*. Out of these, majority of *mantras* are taken from Ṛgveda. Sāmaveda can be viewed as a collection of *mantras* that are meant to be sung in a sacrificial site. All the four Vedas have their *mantras* and *brāhmaṇas* and the *mantras* of all the Vedas are in the form of *Ṛk* known as *prakṛti*, being chanted with three main *swaras—udātta, anudātta* and *svarita*, except the Sāmaveda. The eightfold dissection of this *prakṛtipāṭha* are known as *vikṛtipāha*. They are *śikhā, mālā, jaṭā, rekhā* etc. chanted also in three same scales like *prakṛtipāṭha*. The *mantra* section of the Sāmaveda is divided into *ārcika* and *gāthika* or *gāna* known as *prakṛti* in the tradition. Then the *ārcika* can be subdivided into *pūrvārcika* and *uttarārcika*. Both the *pūrvārcika* and *uttarārcika* are known as *gāna* section of this Veda breaks up into *prakṛti* and *ūha* or *vikṛti*. *Prakṛti* part chanted inside the village is known as *grāmageya* and *āraṇyageya* was the name of the part chanted in a forest, outside the village. *Grāmageya* portion of *Pūrvārcika* of the Sāmaveda is known as *prakṛti* and *ūhagāna* as *vikṛti* collected in the *uttarārcika.* Likewise, the *āraṇyageya* part of *pūrvārcika* is referred as *prakṛti* of *rahasyagāna* or *ūhyagāna* known as *vikṛti. Pūrvārcika* is also referred to as *Chanda ārcika.* In these two parts we find several *mantras* addressed to Agni, Indra, Pavamāna Soma etc. These addresses are known as *stotra* in the sacrificial society. *Stotra* is also a technical term means to praise the qualities of a particular deity through music—*pragīta guṇiniṣṭhaguṇā bhidhānaṃ stotram.* Actually the most important and prominent feature of the Sāmaveda lies here. In the other Vedas praises to sacrificial deities are also available, but they are simply chanted continuously in three *svaras* or tones. But in the Sāmaveda there are *seven svaras* or notes used regularly at the time of chanting beside those previous three tones. They are–*prathama, dvitīya, tṛtīya, caturtha, mandra, kruṣṭa and atisvāryya.* The priests of the Sāmaveda still use these seven notes traditionally to make their oblation more attractive, attention-grabbing and ear enjoying. It is known to everybody that any presentation presented through music becomes more attracting and more admirable to all. An axiom of *Śrīmadbhāgavatam* may be remembered here—oh Nārada I do reside there, where my devotees sing—*mad bhaktā yatra gāyanti tatra tiṣṭhāmi nārada.* Beside this another unanimous rule is there in the field of Indian Epistemology that anything would be acepted when it is used more—*prādhānyena vyapadeśā bhavanti.* So in the Sāmaveda there are seven notes or svaras—*prathama, dvitīya, tṛtīya, caturtha, mandra, kruṣṭa* and *atisvāryya* more when the others have only three or four regular notes used in all the Vedas. It can be said undoubtedly that variety makes a thing important and attractive. In the case of the Sāmaveda that has also become a most important and attractive to each and everyone among the all Vedas for multicolored application of *svaras* or musical notes. So this is how through which Sāmavedins became famous also using frequently the seven notes to glorify their importance and establish the magnanimity of this Veda than the others.

For example an important *Śikṣā* text of Nārada deals with the subject matter of articulation and tidbits of pronunciation of the Sāmaveda which also claims this Veda as the best one. Nārada opined here that the tunes used nowadays in the Indian classical music *ṣaḍja, ṛṣabha, gāndhāra, madhyama, pañcama, dhaivata* and *niṣḍa* (i.e. *sa, ri, ga, ma, pa, dha, ni*) are all came out accordingly from the tunes used by the samavedins like *caturtha, tṛtīya, dvitīya, prathama, kṛuṣṭa,* and *atisvārya.*

yat sāmagānāṃ prathamaḥ sa veṇor madhyamaḥ svaraḥ/
yo dviṭījaḥ sa gāndhāras tṛtīyas tu risbhaḥ smṛtaḥ//
chaturthaḥ ṣaḍja ityāhuḥ pañcamo dhaivato bhavet/
ṣaṣṭho niṣādo vijñeyaḥ saptamaḥ pañcamaḥ smṛtaḥ//
NS. 5..1–2

Though the *seven* svaras used in the Sāmaveda *prakṛtipātha* are very much present in those *udātta, anudātta* and *svarita svaras* practised in *prakṛtipātha* of other tradition but it is too difficult to locate them distinctly even by a scholar also. All of these technical terms and methodological topics have been discussed and annotated by the then composers of different *śikṣā* texts and *prātiśākhyakāras* meticulously had established the originality and magnanimity of the Sāmaveda.

(with the assistance of Indira Dutta Gupta and Ishita Chakraborty, Project Assistants, School of Vedic Sudies, Rabindra Bharati University. Kolkata-700 050).

24

EUPHONIC COMBINATION IN THE ṚK-PRĀTIŚĀKHYA: A BRIEF STUDY

SOMA BASU*

The Vedalakṣaṇa texts, a highly interesting field of traditional Indian learning, are of multifaceted importance. Towards the end of the Vedic period there were three branches of linguistic study, phonetics (Śikṣā), etymology (Nirukta) and grammar (Vyākaraṇa), but their oldest systematical works have not survived as observed by Gonda. Grammar was linked up with the ritual duties of the priests. Phonetics was the basis or the other two branches namely, Nirukta and Vyākaraṇa. The significance of studying Indian grammatical traditions lies mainly in the history of the study which begins with the Śikṣā and Prātiśākhya. They contain instructions on pronunciation, intonation, euphonic changes of sounds in word combinations, elongation of vowels etc. The holistic manner of recitation of the Saṃhitās is not itself actual works of grammar still they deal with subjects which belong to grammar. They bear the testimony of the fact that the texts of the Saṃhitās have been preserved without any change throughout all these centuries since the time of the Prātiśākhyas, the Ṛgveda Prātiśākhya

*Jointly written by Smt. Srabanti Sarkar, Sri Kashinath Nanddi, PhD. scholars and Smt. Sanjukta Ghosh Smt. Ranu Ghosh, Project Assistants, School of Vedicd Studies.

(RPŚ) being the oldest text book of Vedic phonetics. The Vedic Saṃhitās are the work of phoneticians or grammarians as we get the mantras in a complete grammatically analytic form.

Great care was taken to preserve the proper accentuation of the Vedic texts. Sanskrit is the mother of most of the Indian languages. The breadth of outlook of the Vedic sages, our ancestors, was truly remarkable. In the *Atharvaveda* there is realization that the earth bears people speaking various languages differing according to the region. There is a well-known story how *Tvaṣṭṛ* repeating the words 'indrasatrur vardhasva' in wrong accents caused the fire to be extinguished instead of inflaming it against Indra as he intended. The legend is narrated in the Taittiriya Saṁhita 2.4.12.1 and the Satapatha Brahmana 1.6.3.8. *Tvaṣṭṛtr* wanted to pronounce the word 'indraśatruḥ' (meaning 'destroyer of Indra') as a Tatpuruṣa compound (in which the last syllable of the compound has the udātta accent), while he actually pronounced the word as a Bahuvrihi (meaning 'whose killer would be Inḍra,' in which case the first word of the compound has the udāttu accent (as in 'indraśatrurḥ'). (Vide. Pāṇini 6.I.223 and 6.2.1).(Kane, P.V., *History of Dharmaśāstra*, vol. III, pt. I, p. 347)

brahmaṇena niṣkāraṇaṃ ṣaḍaṅgo vedo'dhyeyo jñeś ca—the Veda has to be studied along with its six ancillary texts. The lakṣaṇa granthas or texts which define the characteristics and describe the special features of Vedic texts are generally termed Veda-lakṣaṇa. They are of ancillary nature and generally classified under Vedāṅga, a few of them more precisely under the Śikṣā. Such texts are not only interesting from the point of view of the preservation of Vedic texts but are also very instructive for an understanding of the various devices or methods of learning that were exclusively developed for this purpose and also for knowledge of the various aspects of the history of the transmission of Vedic texts. To attain the goal of perfect preservation of the sacred texts, a sound knowledge of pronunciation techniques is required. To name a few works on them: Akṣaralakṣaṇa-paribhāṣā, Ṛgveda-pada ratna, Atharva-kautsa-vyākaraṇā etc.

Maximum importance has to be attached to the first of the four categories of the Veda lakṣaṇa texts which are as follows—

(1) works on Vedic phonetics, phonology and grammar, the first branch of linguistics to attain independent status; examples are the Prātiśākhyas and the Śikṣās which deal with such topics as the alphabet (varṇa-samāmnāya). organs of articulation, etc (sthāna, karaṇa, prayatna), correct pronunciation (uccāraṇa), euphonic combination (sandhi), proper accentuation (*svara*), etc.;
(2) works on Anukramaṇis such as Sarvānukramaṇis, Bṛhaddevatā (indices of the Seers, Deities and metres);
(3) works containing lists of words having peculiar characteristics in the Vedic texts; and
(4) works dealing mainly with modes of recitation

Tradition of oral transmission from teacher to pupil, from early times to the present day is most important, since it is the only method recognized as authentic and authoritative so far as the preservation of the sacred texts is concerned. Attempting for preservation of the sacred texts in a strictly oral tradition, not only the words but also their correct articulation led to an inquiry into the production of the sounds of speech.

Śikṣā and Prātiśākhya are the two main categories that constitute the sources of Indian phonetics. Śikṣā dealing with the science of phonetics of the Vedas, occupies a very important position in the Lakṣaṇa for facilitating easy learning and memorization. Some peculiar but very useful devices have been applied from time immemorial which is now practised even today by following traditional system of education. Śikṣā texts deal with besides place of utterance of sounds, rules for correct articulation etc. word-isolate system called padapāṭha ascribed to Śākalya. The phonetic teaching necessary for Vedic studies is embodied in the Prātiśākhya which actually is based on early Śikṣā tradition as may be found in the Brāhmṇas and Āraṇyakas. As a matter of fact, both act as an aid to analytical study of Vedic recensions.

About the Prātiśākhya, i.e., the oral traditions J.Gonda in Vedic Literature vol. I, p. I7 states—

"The safeguards of Vedic texts are the Prātiśākhyas which were composed for the purpose of exhibiting—in oral instruction—all the changes necessary for constituting the Saṃhitā-text on the basis of the Padapāṭha."

They are practical aphoristic handbooks compiled in every Vedic School dealing with correct pronunciation of Veda mantras on the whole of greater interest of various topics i.e., Sandhi, qualities, accentuation etc.

The Prātiśākhyas are technical works on Vedic studies. Different Prātiśākhyas affiliated to each branch of each of the Vedas have been composed by the different Sūtrakāras like Śaunaka, Kātyāyana, Puṣpaṇi, Śākaṭāyana and so on commented upon by such great grammarians as Uvaṭa, Anantabhaṭṭa, and Ajātaśatru etc.

Prātiśākhyas though very old from thousand point of its composition may be designated as grammar in its embryonic stage. They had already been known to Yāska, the author of Nirukta—padaprakṛtiḥ saṁhitā padaprabhṛtīni sarvacaraṇ-ānāṃ. . . .

Prātiśākhyas are in turn much older than Yāska himself. All existing Prātiśākhyas in their present forms are later than Pāṇini.

Prātiśākhyas are aids in understanding the ancient Indian tradition on phonetics and phonology as well as methods of preserving the sacred texts.

ṚV 10.71 reveals the busy analytic minds of Ṛgvedic poets in the creative process of poetry:—

saktum iva titaunā punanto yatra dhirā manasā vācam akrata /
atrā sakhāyaḥ sakhyāni jānate bhadraiṣāṃ lakṣmīr nihitādhi vāci //
(*ṚV* 10.7I.2)

To preserve these Saṃhitās which became a pressing need with the texts from generation to generation became the first and foremost aid. Without oral instruction the leaving of the Vedas was condemned as brahmasteya:

brahma yastvananujñātamadhīyānādavāpnuāt/
sa brahmasteyasaṃyukto narakaṃ pratipadyate //
(Manusaṃhitā 2.116)

The Saṃhitā text has disjointed words as its prakṛti—'saṃhitā padaprakṛtiḥ padāntān padādibhiḥ sandadhed iti yat sā/kālāvyavāyena etc . . . (RPŚ 2.1). lt is called Saṃhitā because while combining the finals of words to the initials of words, it proceeds without any interval of time. padāntādisv eva vikāraśāstram pade dṛṣṭeṣu vacanāt pratīyāt . . . (RPŚ 2.2). In the Vajasaneyī Prātiśākhya (VPŚ) the rule 'padāntapadādyoh sandhiḥ' (3.3) says the same i.e. sandhi occurs between last syllable of the first word and the first syllable of the last word. Also it has been told in the RPŚ that one should make the euphonic combinations according to the succession of words—ānupūrvyena sandhīn (2.2), the VPŚ has to say —'*na parakālaḥ pūrvakāle punaḥ*' (3.4)

The uniqueness of the Ṛgveda Prātiśākhya is being noted in a very brief style, followed by a brief note on a few of the varieties of Sandhis along with mentioning their counterparts as found in other Prātiśākhyas.

What is unique in Ṛgveda Pratiśakhya (RPŚ)?

The uniqueness lies in the fact that this Prātiśākhya is singularly free from the use of such terms as ghu, sim, gha etc. as appearing from the point of view of technical terms, as are commonly found in works like the Aṣṭadhyāyī or Vājasaneyī Prātiśākhya. In other words, it never tries to explain the meaning of such common suffixes as—kāra in 'a-kāra' etc., or-ipha in repha or of words like apṛktā, upadhā etc., whose meaning is clear of itself. It is also to be noticed here that at the same time there are several technical terms used in the Prātiśākhya whose meaning is not understandable without the aid of the commentary, to mention a few of such terms padya, vigraha, vikrama, vicchheda, parigraha, samaya etc.

Unlike other works where technical terms are defined in itself which are used in the body of that particular work, this Prātiśākhya contains many technical terms which though defined are never used again in it, mention may be made of a number of Sandhis (euphonic combination). The fault of pronunciation bears a great historical value many of which can be taken as indicative of particular tendencies of the speakers contemporary with the author, tendencies which have effected corresponding phonetic changes in contemporary Prākṛt.

There are several phenomena of euphonic combination (Sandhi) found in the Prātiśākhyas. They are four in number according to the commentary of Uvaṭācārya's commentary '*dvayoḥ dvayor vyañjanayoḥ vyañjana-svarayoḥ svara-vyañjanayor iti.*' Amongst a large number of sandhis found in the Rk-Prātiśākhya such as yama, krama, abhinidhāna, svarabhakti, bhugna; sāmavaśa or prosodial lengthening, praślista, kṣaipra and many more, we are interested in briefly dealing with the last four.

Bhugna—When the two vowels i.e., 'a' and 'ā', which arise from labials i.e., 'o' and 'au,' are followed by a non-labial vowel, there is an insertion of 'v' which is technically called 'bhugna'.

Sāmavaśa or prosodial lengthening —The term Sāmavaśa-sandhiḥ occurring in the Ṛgveda-Prātiśākhya means lengthening of a short vowel before the following consonant. This is also known as 'pluti'. Its main purpose is to make up the metrical deficiencies in the Vedic Mantras where the 'orthographic quality is different from the metrical (phonetic) one.

The cases may be divided in the cases such as lengthening in (a) simple words and (b) compound words, giving further sub-headlines as lengthening (i) in the final syllable (ii) in the initial syllable (iii) in the medial syllable. Such cases are shown with illustrations —

Through this treatment of Sāmavaśa Sandhi of Vedic cadence of Vedic mantras can be understood and appreciated according to Śaunaka and Śākalya.

Praśliṣṭa or contracted sandhi —

Kṣaipra or hastened sandhi—A non-guttural monophthong is changed into its semi-vowel—*samānākṣaram antaḥsthāṃ svām akanṭhyam svarodayaṃ* (RPŚ 2.21). The *Taittiriya Prātiśākhya* 10.14 *ivarṇākārau. savakārau.*

The Aṣṭādhyāyī sūtra—iko yaṇ aci (6.1.77)

The Taittiriya Prātiśākhya

Almost every phenomenon of Sandhi is called by a technical name and it is noteworthy to mention that several of these are never again used in the text. By every phenomenon I mean the classification of Sandhis as according to the author of the Ṛk-Prātiśākhya which is as follows:—

- euphonic combination of a vowel and a following consonant (*paṭala* II).
- euphonic combination of a consonant and a following vowel (*paṭala* II)
- euphonic combination of a vowel followed by a vowel *paṭala* II)
- euphonic combination of a consonant followed by a a consonant (*paṭala* IV)
- cerebralization or nati (*paṭala* V)

— treatment of conjunct consonants or karma, abhinidhāna, yama, and svarabhakti (*paṭala* VI)
— prosodial lenghthening or samavasa sandhi (*paṭala* VII-IX)

When the words esaḥ, syaḥ, sah, or vowels precede and a consonant follows these 'combinations' according to the succession of syllables are in the 1 natural order (anvakṣara-sandhayaḥ anulomāḥ).

25

PHONETIC STUDIES IN ANCIENT INDIA

SATYA RANJAN BANERJEE

The analysis of a language in the form of grammar can be done from the various points of view. The analysis could be Descriptive (or Synchronic), Historical (or Diachronic), Comparative (or Panchronic) and Philosophical (or Psychological).

Generally the analysis of a language is done either descriptically or synchronically from the point of view of time. This point of view of a language may be looked upon for a long time, or particular stage of its development. The glaring instances are A.A. Macdonell's *Vedic Grammar* (Strassburg, 1900) or W.D. Whitney's *Sanskrit Grammar* (1890 edn.). In these two grammar books, generally the phonology and morphology portions of a grammar are described.

When the study of a language is done historically—showing different forms of a language at different stages of its development, it is Historical or Diachronic study. The very good example of this type of grammar is Edward Vernon Arnold's "Sketch of the Historical Grammar of the Ṛgveda and Atharvavedas," JAOS, (vol. 18, 1897, pp. 203-351). *Altindische Grammatik* of Jacob Wackernagel in several parts is another example of this type. Whitney's *Sanskrit Grammar* can also be cited for this category, though basically it is descriptive.

The Comparative or Panchronic Grammar compares different aspects of a grammar (including vocabularies) with its other cognate languages belonging to the same family. Because of this comparative study, there arose a new subject known as "Comparative Philology". A good example of this type of grammar is Karl Brugmann's *Grundriss der vergleichenden Grammatik der indogermanischen Sprachen*, Strassburg, 1886–1900.

The study of a language can be made philosophically or psychologically also. This study is made on a different level. It is the philosophy or psychology of a language that is very prominent in this category. Bhartṛhari's (650/51 AD) *Vākyapadīya* (in three parts) is the first attempt in India to philosophise the Sanskrit grammatical terms. He has described every topic of a grammar philosophically. In Europe, Thomas of Erfurt's (1324 AD) *Grammatica Speculativa* was famous for this system of psychological grammar. In modern times Otto Jesperson's *The Philosophy of Grammar* (London, 1924) deals with the philosophical aspects of grammatical categories. *The Philosophy of Sanskrit Grammar* (Calcutta University, 1930) by Prabhat Chandra Chakraborty is the philosophical study of Sanskrit grammar.

To be very frank, a full knowledge of a language in all its aspects can only be possible when scholar really studies the grammar of a language from all these four points of view.

Whether Descriptive or Historical, and Comparative or Philosophical, the grammatical study is made from five points of view. These five parts of a grammar are—Phonology, Morphology Syntax, Semantics and Etymology.

In Phonology, the sound system of a language is analysed. How many sounds of a language are found, what are their pronunciation, how they are produced or articulated, their place of utterance, the behaviour of sound changes, accent, ablaut, euphonic combination and so on. Any type of sound analysis is described in phonology. As a result, there are subjects like phonetics, phonemics and generative phonology.

In Morphology, anything concerning a word is described. When the amalgamation or combination of some sounds gives a good sense and people use it in a society, it is called a word. In a morphological domain, there are mainly three parts. These parts are—Formation of words, Parts of speech and Grammatical categories.

The formation of a word is made by various means, such as, by suffixes (*kṛt, taddhita, uṇādi)*, by the process of *samāsa* (compound), by feminine suffixes, by analogy, metathesis, metanalysis, popular etymology, by means of Blends, by Contamination, by Hybrid formation, by means of Clipped words and so on. Words thus formed are divided into eight parts of speech known as noun, adjective, pronoun, verb, adverb, preposition, conjunction and interjection.

In a dictionary, all these words known as different parts of speech are found. This is mainly the vocabulary of a language. The third part of morphology is the Grammatical Categories, which mean the basic nature of all parts of speech. As soon as a noun is uttered its basic features are also included, such as, number, gender, case, case-terminations and declension. Apart from these, noun also includes genus and species, abstract and concrete and sundry other aspects.

In addition to the characteristic feature of noun, adjective has three more features such as, formation of adjective, Degrees of Comparison (Possessive, Comparative and Superlative) and numerals (both ordinals and cardinals).

The Pronoun discusses the division of pronoun, pronominal adjectives and adverbs, and the basic Deictic nature of pronoun.

The verb has many features. It discusses about root, person, number, voice, tense, mood, augment, reduplication, *vikaraṇa* (aspects), verbal stem system, personal termination and conjugation. It also discusses infinitive, participle, and gerund. It also discusses Passive, Causative, Denominative, Desiderative and Frequency or Intensive.

The Adverb discusses its formation and nature, its comparison and classification based on meanmg.

The Preposition, Conjunction and Interjection describe their various divisions and their nature.

The Syntax states the order of words in a sentence, how order of words is set up in a sentence. Though languages are different, there is an order of the placement of words in a language. This is discussed in the syntax portion.

The Semantics discusses the nature of meaning of words. It discusses various kinds of meaning, such as, *vācyārtha, lakṣyārtha, vyaṅgārtha,* the elevation and denomination of meaning, ornaments, defects and so on.

The etymology discusses the original meaning of a word with derivation. By etymological process, we often get the original meaning of a word.

Coming back to the Prātiśakhyas, which deal with Phonetics, it is one of the greatest contributions of the ancient Indian minds.

Phonetics is one of the greatest contributions of ancient Indian minds. More than 2500 years ago from today, grammatical literature occupied the full and detailed discussions of phonetic for the proper pronunciation and correct representation of sounds. Actually what we get about the Sanskrit sound systems is from the Prātiśaāhyas and Śikṣās of ancient treatises. Prātiśākhyas as the name indicates, is a text book of each Saṁhitā, i.e. each Saṁhita has a text book on phonetics, and hence the name Prātiśākhyas. Each Saṁhitā has different text books, and the contents of each are practically the same except a few variations which depend either on a *śākhā* or recension of a Saṁhitā. The Prātiśākhyas, in general, "contain instruction upon the pronunciation, the accentuation, the euphonic alterations of the sounds in the composition of words and in the initial and final sound of words in the sentence, upon the lengthening of vowels, in short upon the whole mantra of the recitation of the Saṁhita". (Winternitz, *History of Indian*

Literature, University of Calcutta, 1930. vol 1, 283f).

Each Saṁhitā has a Prātiśākhya. To the Ṛgveda we have Ṛgveda Prātiśākhyas (Max Müller,1856–69); to the Yajurveda we have Taittirīya-prātiśākhya (Whitney, JAOS, IX, 1871); and the Vājasaneyī-prātiśākhya (Weber, *Indische Studien,* IV, 1854); to the Atharvaveda, we have Atharva-prātiśākhya (Śaunakīya Caturādhyāyika) (Whitney, JAOS, VII,1862); also Atharva-prātiśākhya ed. by Suryakanta Sastri (1939) and by Visva Bandhu Sastri, (part -1 1923); to the Sāmaveda we have four texts: Sāma-prātiśākhya (ed. by Satyavrata Samasrami, Uṣā,1890; Puṣpasūtra (ed. by R. Simon,1909); Pañcavidha Sūtra (ed. by R. Simon,1913); Ṛktantra (ed. by Suryakanta Sastri, 1933) and also by A.C. Burnell in 1879.

Apart from Prātiśākhyas, the Śiksās are also equally important for Phonetic texts. Each Saṁhitā has also some Śikṣās. As the Śikṣās are many, I only mention a few important ones. Apart from the Pāṇīniya śikṣā, we have—'Āpiśali-śikṣā', 'Bhāradvāja-śikṣā', 'Kauhali-śikṣā', 'Saiśirīya-śikṣā' 'Sarvasammata-śikṣā', 'Vyāsa-śikṣā', 'Nārada-śikṣā,' 'Lomasī-śikṣā', 'Gautamī-śikṣā,' 'Māṇḍukī-śikṣā,' 'Yajñavalkya-śikṣā', and so on. On the study of the śikṣās, see F. Kielhorn, Indian Antiquary, vol V, 1876. A full study of the Śikṣās is brilliantly done by Siddheśvar Varma in his *Critical Studies in the Phonetic Observations of Indian Grammarians,* Royal Asiatic Society, London, 1929. *Phonetics in Ancient India,* London, 1953 is a good contribution of the present day.

However all the Prātiśākhyas and Śikṣās are exceptionally important for the development of Sanskrit sound system and their method and manner of pronunciation. Apart from this, they are important in some other sense also. I, therefore, conclude by quoting Winternitz who says—"These works are of two fold importance: firstly for the history of grammatical study in India, which, as far as we know, commences with these Prātiśākhyas. Though they are not actually grammatical works themselves, they treat of subjects pertaining to grammar, and the quotations from so many grammarians prove that the study of grammar was already flourishing at their time. Secondly, they are still more important because they are pledges of the fact that the texts of the Saṁhitās as we have them today, have remained unaltered through all the centuries since the time of the Prātiśākhyas. Thus the rules of the Ṛgveda-Prātiśākhya take for granted that, at the period of the latter, the Ṛgveda-Saṁhitā was not only firmly established in its division into ten Maṇḍalas, but that even the order of the hymns in each Maṇḍala, was the same as it is now. Indeed, the minute rules of Śaunaka leave no doubt that, at the period of the latter, the text of the Ṛgveda-Saṁhita read, word for word and syllable for syllable, almost exactly as we find it at the present day in our printed edition." *(HIL,* vol I, pp 284-85).

After this preliminary discussion about the ancient Indian phonetics, I now give some of the examples of the Prātiśākhyas where they describe some of the topics of phonetics.

Let us take the sound system of Sanskrit as described by the Prātiṣākhyas.

From the description of the Prātiśākhyas we know how many sounds are enumerated. In normal parlance, all the accepted Sanskrit sound systems are enumerated. Besides these, some unusual sounds in Sanskrit, perhaps found in Vedic literature, are also described. In normal parlance, the following sound-systems are accepted:

(1) Vowels: *a, ā, i, ī, ū, ṛ, ṝ, ḷ, ḹ, e, ai, o, au.*
(2) Consonants: *k, kh, g, gh, n; c, ch, j, jh, ñ; ṭ, ṭh, ḍ, ḍh, ṇ; t, th, d, dh, n; p, ph, b, bh, m; y, r, l, v, ś, ṣ, s, h (kṣ)*

Normally all these sound-systems are used in both Vedic and classical Sanskrit. But about *kṣ* there is a controversy. In most of the Prātiśākhyas this sound is not recognised as it is a combination of two sounds. But Puruṣottama (12 century

AD) has accepted this sound *(ka-kārādi kṣa-kārāntāḥ varṇamālā prākīrtitaḥ)*. In modern Indo-Aryan languages, in some of the languages, *kṣ* is included in their alphabetic system; in some, it is not accepted. As *kṣ* has a different symbol some have accepted it, while others do not. Thus far, the sound-systems are stereotyped and straightforward. But difficulty arises about some sounds. In different Prātiṣākhyas some unknown sounds are described. These are in general—

χ, θ, δh, ϕ, bh

These are the second and the fourth letters of a *varga*. These sounds are basically spirantised, i.e. are pronounced with more air together with something like hissing sound. That is why they are represented by the Greek symbols. As Sanskrit has not developed any special sign for that they are gradually lost or merged with their Sanskrit counterpart. Some of the sounds may occur in the *Śatapatha Brāhmaṇa*, but they are not recognizable. We can infer this because of the nature of other sounds. In the *Śatapatha Brāhmaṇa*, *y* and *v* are regarded of three kinds as *guru*, *laghu* and *īṣat pṛṣṭa* (light). *Guru* is represented by doubling the sound as *yy*, while *laghu* is simple, while the light *y* is symbolized by the end of a word. That is why, in the Middle Indo-Aryan (=MIA) stage: this intervocalic *y* is elided and that is why, Hemacandra (1088-1172 AD) has a *sūtra* where intervocalic *k-g-c-j, t-d-p-y-v* are elided in Prakrit *(k-g-c-j-t-d-p-y-vāṃ prāyoḥ luk*-1.177). In Albert Weber's edition of ŚB, this is represented by these symbols. In MIA some of the indeclinables are doubled initially. For example, *iva* becomes *vva* (cf. Hemacandra, *miva-piva-viva-vva-ya-via ivārthe vā*—2,182), similarly, *jjeva* (Māhārṣṭri) and *yyeva* in Magadhī. Some of the OIA peculiarities are found in MIA.

In case of the enumeration of the Sanskrit alphabetic system, they have a peculiar way of saying it. Some are straightforward, and some are not. For example, in the Ṛk-prātiśākhya, in their *vṛttis,* it is enumerated in a simple way. While in the Sāma-prātiśākhya *iti* is added to every single sound, e.g. *a iti, ā iti* and so on. In the case of consonants, they are *kiti, khiti, giti* and so on. In the Taittirīya and Atharva-Prātiśākhyas, they are straightforward and even though some peculiar sounds like χ, θ, δh, ϕ, bh are mentioned. In the *Pāṇinīya-śikṣā,* there is a reference of 63 or 64 sounds in Sanskrit. These are 21 vowels and 25 *sparśavarṇa* and 8 *antaḥstha* and *uṣma varṇas,* 4 *yama varṇas, anusvāra* and *visarga, k* and *p* and *ḷ pluta.* (21 + 25 + 8 + 4 + 5 = 63) and ँ *(candravindu)* included and in all 64 letters. Later on, *pluta svara* is counted separately as different vowels, though *pluta svara* has no signs but sometimes is represented by the numeral 3 (as *a3, ā3* etc.) or by the horizontal lines after the letter (as *a, ā* etc.). Thus this is the picture of Sanskrit alphabet.

Every sound-system has some characteristics. These characteristics are considered in case of vowels such as, mora of vowels, whether heavy or light, vowels have the quality of considering acute, grave and circumference accents, vowels can have the qualities of nasals and non-nasals, vowels could be *saṃvṛta* (close) and *vivṛta* (open), cardinal qualities of vowels and so on. In a similar way, consonants are diversely classified as *aghoṣa* (unvoiced) and *ghoṣa* (voiced) while again is divided into *alpaprāṇa* (unaspirated) and *mahāprāṇa* (aspirated). And in these categories we get *sparśas* (plosives), *antaḥstha* (semi-vowels), *śis-dhvani* (sibilants) and aspirates *(h),* and then *anusvāra, visarga* and *candravindu.* Sometimes grammarians considered some more sounds as—*k, kh, p* and *ph* and four *yama-varṇas.* Besides this, in Vedic we find *ḷ* and *lh.*

Consonants are marked with *halanta,* but as *halanta* consonants are difficult to pronounce, a vowel is inserted in it for easy pronunciation *(hakārādiṣu a-kāra uccāraṇārtha*—Bhaṭṭoji Dīkṣita).

After giving emphasis on the arrangement of sound-system, the Prātiśākhyas have described the manner of pronunciation. How the sounds or *varṇas* are pronounced: How the manner of articulation is described at the time of uttering a sound: What is the position of tongue at that time and so on. Some examples will illustrate the case in point. Take, for example, the manner of pronunciation of *a*—sound.

The first letter of the alphabetic system is *a*. The place of utterance is throat *(kaṇṭha) (a-ku-ha-visarjanīyānāṃ kaṇṭha*—Bhaṭṭoji Dīkṣita). That is why, *a* is regarded as a *kaṇṭya varṇa.*

According to the Prātiśākhya, the correct pronunciation of *a* is *hrasva* (short) *ā* and not ə (a) as is pronounced in Bengali and in some other languages. Grammatically *a* is open *(vivṛta),* spreading the mouth *a* is pronounced. However, *a* has two pronunciations: *saṃvṛta* (contracted one) and *vivṛta* (open) with one symbol. Apart from Prātiśākhya, Pāṇini (fourth century BC) has recorded these two types of pronunciation by his sūtra—*a a* (8.4.68) which Bhaṭṭoji Dīkṣita has explained as debaring. *vivṛta a* is also pronounced *saṃvṛta (vivṛtam anudya saṃvṛto'nena vidhīyate).* Grammatically, the two *a*'s are not homogenous *(sāvarṇya)* as their manner of utterance is not the same with *vivṛta.* That is why in *sandhi* we have euphonic combination with *a+a/ā* by the sūtra *akaḥ savarṇe dīrghaḥ* (6.1.10). As the symbol is one, it is very difficult to understand which one is *saṃvṛta a.*

To this question, the answer is simple. Where there is no *sandhi* with *a* + *a* one is to be considered as *saṃvṛta,* such as, *bhava + anti = bhavanti; nara +am= naram* and so on. That is why, in these two cases Pāṇini has to make two sūtras for the formation of these two words and similar other words. In this way it is accepted that *a* has two types of pronunciation.

Then the manner of articulation of *a* is given. It is said that when *a* is pronounced the position of tongue is laid down lying and at the back it approaches towards the soft palate and when the air is coming out by the side of the tongue, the sound *a* is pronounced. As the air comes from the throat *(kaṇṭha)* it is known as *kaṇṭhya varṇa*. In this way, all the sounds of the Sanskrit alphabetic system are described.

But all the Prātiśākhyas do not maintain the same type of pronunciation of all sounds. Their place of pronunciation is not the same. For example, take the case of *ṛ*.

The Treatment of Ṛ in Old Indo-Aryan

The treatment of the Indo-European (= IE) *ṛ* (as also Indo-Iranian (= IIr *ṛ*) in Old Indo-Aryan (= OIA) and Middle Indo-Aryan (= MIA) is manifold. This IE *ṛ* is fully preserved in OIA as *ṛ* and it becomes ə rə in Avestan and *ar (ra)* in Old Persian (= OP). In MIA it is changed into different vowels, such as, *a, i, u* preceded or followed by *r*. The reason why *ṛ* is changed into difficult vowels accompanied or preceded by *ṛ* is difficult to ascertain. But it is a normal guess that the change of *ṛ* into different vowels is generally determined by the influence of the consonants which stand in the vicinity of the original *ṛ*. The usual change of *ṛ* is *a (r)* or *ṛa*, and the sibilants or palatals change it into *i (r)* or *ri* and the labials to *u(r)* or *ru*. This fact can partly be substantiated by a comparative study of the Iranian and Indian materials as preserved in the phonetic treatises of India. The present study reveals the fact that some amount of reason can be traced on the basis of pronunciation of *ṛ* as prevalent in the time of the dissemination of the Indo-Iranian people as a branch of Indo-European.

The pronunciation of *ṛ* as recorded in different phonetic texts might play a prominent part in the transformation of the sound into MIA. It is a fact worth noting that in the Prātiśākhyas and in some Śikṣās the cerebral pronunciation of *ṛ* is not recorded. "The earliest available record of the cerebral pronunciation of *ṛ* and *r* may be noticed in the

Varṇa-Sūtra of Candragomin *(mūrdhā ṛ-ṭu-ra-ṣāṇām,* no. 6), the lower limit of whose date, according to Leibich, was the seventh century AD. It is possible that the later grammarians of the Pāṇinian school and some of the Śikṣās borrowed this opinion from Candragomin, whose work exercised considerable influence on the later development of Indian grammatical literature." Bhaṭṭoji Dīkṣita (1630 AD ?) on Pāṇini's *tulyāsyaprayatnaṃ savarṇam* (1.19), records that *ṛ* is cerebral *(ṛ-ṭu-ṛa-ṣāṇāṃ mūrdhāḥ)*. However, the pronunciation of *ṛ* as recorded in the phonetic texts is tabulated thus:

Velar *jihvāmūlīya*	Al veolar	Cerebral
RP. *ṛkāra - ḷkārāvatha ṣaṣṭha ūṣmā jihvāmūlīyaḥ* (1.18) AP. *Jihvāmūlīyānāṃ hanumūlam* (1.20) a comm. under it. cf. also VP.I. 65,69, RKT.4.	TP. *upasaṃ hṛta + are ca jihvāgram ṛkāra-r-kāra-ḷ-kāreṣū-barsveṣū prasamharati* (II.18) *barsva* ="the high places behind the row of teeth."	PS. *syur mūrdhanyā ṛ-ṭu-ra-ṣāḥ* (17) *cf.* Candragomin quoted above

From this it appears that *ṛ* was a velar *(jihvāmaūlīya)* sound in RP,VP, AP and RKT, i.e., its place of origin is the root of the tongue, while TP describes it as an alveolar or post-dental, i.e., the tongue touches the gum above the upper teeth, whereas in PŚ and Sanskrit grammar it is a cerebral sound.

The velar quality of *ṛ* might be responsible for its change into *a* which is also a velar sound, as is also corroborated by the evidence of Avestan əɾə and OP (Old Persian). *ar* side by side with *ur.* As the *r* quality is not lost altogether in Avestan and OP., its development into *ar* or *ra* is quite obvious. This is evident in the Aśokan, Niyā or Kharoṣṭhī Prakrit in the Western part of India, where *r* is preserved.

The velar pronunciation of *ṛ* seems to be the oldest, and

therefore this oldest tendency of *ṛ* is to transform *ṛ* into *a* through *ar* or *ra* as the place of utterance is the same. This tendency first started in the Iranian and was preserved in the Ṛgveda. For example, in the ṚV we find *vikṛta* and *vikaṭa, vṛta* and *vaṭa, bhṛta* and *bhaṭa, nṛt* and *naṭa* used side by side. In Iranian also the change of *ṛ* to *ar.* ə ɒ is quite frequent, e.g. Av. *ap r nāyu* 'boy', Phl. *apurnāyak,* N.P. *barnā, burnā;* Av. *k* ərə *ma* 'warm', Phl. *karm,* NP. *kirm;* Av. *sarə ta* 'cold', Phl. *sart,* N.P. *sard.* This change of *ṛ* > *a* occurs in almost all stages of MIA. For instance, OIA. *mṛta* > Aś. *maṭa,* Pā. *maṭa;* Pkt. *maa;* OIA. *mṛga* > *Aś. maga* (G), Pā. *maga,* Pkt. *maa;* OIA. *apakṛṣta* > Aś. *apakaṭha,* Pkt. *apakaṭṭha;* OIA. *prakṛta* > Niyā, *pragata* Pā. *pagata,* Pkt. *paaa/payaa;* OIA. *ṛṇaheta* > Niyā *anahetu;* OIA. *kṛta* > Pā. *kata,* Pkt. *kaa/kaya;* OIA *gṛha* > Pā. *gaha,* Pkt. *gaha – vai;* OIA. *ghṛta* > Pā. *ghata,* Pkt. *ghaa;* OI A. *mṛtyu* > Pā. Pkt. *maccu;* OIA. *satkṛta* > Pkt. *sakkaya.*

The alveolar quality of *ṛ* as given by TP might have influenced its change into *i* also accompanied or preceded by *r.* For example, OIA. *kṛta* > Aś *kiṭa* (M); OIA. *mṛga* > Aś. *mriga* (M) *miga* (Dī); OIA. *kṛtya* > Niyā *kica;* OIA. *kṛta* > Niyā *kida;* OIA. *ṛṇa* > Pā *iṇa,* Pkt. *iṇa/riṇa;* OIA *ṛṣi* > Pā. Pkt. *isi;* OIA. *tṛṇa* > Pā. Pkt. *tiṇa,* also *taṇa* in Pkt. The change of *ṛ* to *i* occurs also in the Iranian dialects, e.g., OIA. *tṛṣṇā* > Av. *traŠna* 'thirst', Phl. *tiŠn,* NP. *tiŠ;* Av. *ar Ša* 'bear', Phi. NP. *xirs,* Kurd. *vire, hirs;* Av. *g ərə pta* 'seized', NP. *giriftah,* Bai. *gipta.*

In Niyā Prakrit the regular treatment of *ṛ* is *ri.* Sometimes the written form is found as *ṛ* or *ṛr* though perhaps the actual pronunciation would be *ri;* e.g., OIA. *kṛta*> Niyā. *Krita,* OIA. *Kṛṣṭi* > Niyā *krisati,* OIA. *ghṛta* > NP. *ghrida,* OIA. *gṛhastha* > Niyā. grihasta, OIA. *dṛḍha* > NP. *driṭha,* OIA *pṛcchati* > Niyā, *prichati.* In Pāli also *ṛ* becomes *ri* as also in Pkt; e.g., OIA *ṛte* > Pā. *rite,* Pkt. *nie;* OIA. *ṛddhi* > Pkt. *riddhi.*

Apart from the fact that the influence of the neighbouring labial sound often changes *ṛ* to *u* also accompanied by *r,* the evidence of the Prātiśākhyas is not strong enough to record its pronunciation with a labial sound which is preserved in some NIA languages, such as Oriya. Marāṭhi, and even in some south Indian languages. But we have evidence by which we can say that the combination of *ṛ* + *t* is often changed to *u* in the Western region; e.g., OIA. *ṛtu* > Pkt. *uu,* in Mahārāṣṭrī. The change of *ṛ* to *u* is also one of the earliest phenomena which is found in OP. as well as in ṚV., e.g., √*kṛ* > OIA. 2nd imp. *kuru* (as if from **kṛnu),* OIA. *kṛṇoti* > Pkt. *kuṇai.* This change of *r* to *u* is not due to the immediate association of a labial consonant. But, on the contrary, instances are available where the same word is found with *u* and other vowel as well. Historically *u* is the general tendency in Aśokan and in later inscriptions, such as, Gandhara and Niyā in the North-Western Prakrits. For example, OIA. *vṛkṣa* > Aś *vracha* (G), Pkt. *vaccha, rukkha.* Grammatically, though *rukkha* is derived from *vṛkṣa,* it can really be derived from *rukṣa* which has become *rukkha* in Pkt. and Pāli and its modern Indian cognates are Old Beng. *rukh,* Ur. *rūkha,* Mar. *rūkh,* Simh. *ruk, rik,* Gyp. *ruk.* Other examples are OIA. *mṛta* > As. *muṭa;* OIA *mṛga* > Aś. *mruga;* OIA. *vṛddha* > Aś. *vuddha.*

The evidences of Niyā, Pāli and Pkt. show that the development or *ṛ* into *u* is very regular; e.g., OIA. *bhṛti* > Niyā. *hudi,* OIA. *prabhṛta* > Niyā. *prahuda;* OIA. *ṛtu* > Pā. *utu,* Pkt. *uu* (M), *udu* (Ś); OIA. *ṛṣabha* > Pā. *usabha,* Pkt. *usaha, vusaha;* OIA. *vṛddha* > Pā. *vuddha,* Pkt. *vuḍḍha.* In Iranian dialects this tendency is also noticed, e.g., Av. *kə rə naoiti* 'makes', Paz. *kunon,* NP. *kunad,* Gil. *kudan,* also *kardan,* OIA. *akṛṇavam* 'I did' > O.P. *akunavam,* OIA. *akṛṇot* > OP. *akunaus* (cf. Av. *kərəta* 'done'); Av. *vərəoka* 'kidney', Phl. *gurtak,* NP. *gurdah,* Bal. *guttiy.* Both in Niyā and Pāli *ṛ* is developed into *ru,* e.g., OIA. *pṛcchati* > Niyā. *pruchati;* OIA. *mṛduka* > Niyā. *mruduka;* OIA *pṛṣṭheṣu* > Nīyā. *pruthesu.* In Pāli OIA *bṛṃhayati* becomes *brūheti.*

Though instances are available where *ṛ* is changed to *e,* this is very rare both in OIA and MIA, and also in Iranian; e.g., OIA *gṛha* > *geha* (both in OIA and MIA), Old Hindi *geha,* Mar. *geh,* Sirph *gē, geya.* OIA *gṛhya* > Pkt. *gejjha* (also in Aś). The Aś *dekhati* (cf. OIA. *prekśate)* presupposes **dṛkṣyati* in the sense of *drakṣyati.* OIA *bṛhatphala* > Pā. *Beha-pphala.*

Ar. *Var ša* 'forest' > Phi *vešak,* NP. *bešah.*

The change of *ṛ* to *o* is extremely rare, except one or two instances it is seldom found, e.g, OIA. *mṛṣa* > Pkt. *mosā, mŭsā,* Pā. *musā,* so also OIA. *mṛṣāvādin* > Pkt. *mosāvāa, mūsāvāa,* Pā. *musāvādi(n).*

It is to be noted that though *ṛ* is altogether lost in MIA,.its retention in Apabhraṃśa may be regarded as a sort of Sanskritization, which began at the time of Apabhraṃśa and perpetuated at the emergence of NIA dialects. For example, OIA *tṛṇa* > Ap. *tṛṇu, taṇu, tiṇu,* OIA *sukṛta* > Ap. *sukṛdu, sukidu.*

The above survey, at least, tells us that pronunciation of *ṛ* was not uniform throughout the age. This fact is also corroborated by the evidences of the *Prātiśākhyas* and *Śikṣās* which have recorded the different types of pronunciation of *ṛ* as were current in ancient times. The change of *ṛ* into *a, i, u* accompanied by *r* shows the type of pronunciation of *ṛ*. In some areas, *r* was pronounced with all *a*-colouring vowel, and in some with *i*-or *u*-colouring. In all cases it is accompanied by *r*. These different types of pronunciation are nothing but dialectal, and as a result they have developed accordingly even in OIA and also in MIA. This still holds good in the NIA. dialects.

Let us take the case of r (Was it dental in Sanskrit?)

The place of origin of *r*[1] is stated as teeth *or* teeth-ridge (alveolar) in different Prātiśākhyas and not cerebral *(mūrdhaṇya)*. They are tabulated thus:

RP. (1.19.20)	Roots of the teeth or teeth ridge	
VP. (1.68)	Roots of the teeth	Cf. also
AP.+ comm. (1.28+comm.)	Roots of the teeth or a point close to the teeth	Yājña Ś
TP. (II.41)	Dental, i.e. the middle of the front of the tongue touches a point close to the teeth.	Cf. also Vyāsa Ś XXIV.13.14
RKT. (8)	The teeth, or the roots of the teeth	
PŚ, APŚ, CarŚ.	Cerebral	
Candragomin (seventh century AD)	Cerebral	*mūrdhā ṛ-ṭu-raṣāṇām* (*ṣu* 6)

From the above tabular from, it can be said that the pronunciation of *r* as recorded in the Prātiśākhyas was dental or alveolar or to a point close to the teeth and not Cerebral The cerebral pronunciation of *r* came later. It is found in the *Pāṇinīya Śikṣā* (PŚ) and Cadragomin (seventh century AD): though the exact geographical place for PŚ is not available, it is guessed that the PŚ was composed in the eastern India or in an area connected with the eastern languages (cf. Siddheswar Varma, p. 9.). "Apart from the documents mentioned above, the treatment of the development of *r* + *t* in the Middle Indo-Aryan also tells us the twofold pronunciation of *r* in ancient India. It is seen that the development of *r* + *t* in MIA is twofold. In one group, mainly in the West, *r* + *t* is changed into dental, i.e. assimilated into *t t,* e.g. Skt. *vartate* > West Aśokan *vattati,* Sindhi *wartana wartaṇu?* where as in the other group, generally in the Eastern *r* + *t* became cerebral i.e., assimilated into cerebral *ṭ ṭ,* e.g. Skt. *vartate* > East Aśokan *vaṭṭati,* Sinhalese *vatānu,*

Behārī, Beng. *vaṭe* "he is !"[2]

The origin of *r* also tells the same story in the Indo-European. The Indo-European *r* and *l* an dental, as there is no Cerebral sound in IE language. In Greek and Latin and other cognate European languages, there is no cerebral sound. Even in prehistoric Indo-Iranian this IE *r* and *l* became *r* as is seen in Avestan and Old Persian. Even in prehistoric time, Sanskrit *l* was introduced secondarily for some Indo-Iranian *r,* e.g., IE **reudh- > Skt. rudhira*(red), Goth. *raūdus,* * *roudh-* > Old ChSl. *rudu,* Russ. *ruda* (ore) **rudh*—Gk. ερευθαζ, ερυθραζ (redden), Lat. *rūbidus, ruber,* Goth. *raups* , OE. *read* Eng. *red*

From the same IE * *rudh* or **rudha,* Sanskrit has *loha* (**ludha*), meant first 'reddish', and then reddish things, such as, copper, metal, iron etc. and similarly also *lohita* and *rohita* meant first 'ruddy'. And in a similar way IE *l* is represented by *r* in Sanskrit. For example,

IE * *leuqe *louqe* > Skt. *roca* (shining), *roci-s* ('ray of light') and

IE * *leuqe tai* > Skt. *rocate,* and so on. On the other hand,

Skt. *loka* < IE * *louqo,* 'world' (originally meant 'light of space').

This is to say, from the same root the development of *r* and *l* is found side by side.

IE * *leuqe* - : * *louq*-(shine)

where *l* > *r*	where *l* remains
roca (< * *leque)*	*loka* (< * *louqo-*)
rucis (< * *leuqis)*	*lokate* (< * *Louqotai)*
rocate (< * *Louqetai)*	*locate* (< * *Louqetai)*
	Lokana (seeing)
	Locana (illumination, the eye)

It appears from the above that IE *l* or *r* could interchange as both *r* or *l* in Sanskrit, though historically the occurrence of *l* is quite rare in the Ṛgveda, while that of *r* is very much common. And in this respect, the Ṛgveda is very much close to Indo-Iranian which had developed only one phoneme *r* for both *r* and *l.*

In the early part of the Ṛgveda *l* is a very rare occurrence, while in the later portions of the Ṛgveda, *l* is more frequent (say nearly eight times) than the older parts. As a result, the interchanges between *r* and *l* started in the Ṛgveda; e.g., *alaṅkāra* vs *araṅkāra, alaṅkṛta* vs *araṅkṛta.* It is interesting to note that in the AV *l* is seen many times more frequent than the RV. This tendency of the AV shows that as the Aryans moved towards the east, the frequency of *l* went on increasing and this is what is preserved in Māgadhī Prakrit, a Prakrit dialect in the eastern part of India where *r* is replaced by *l*. In the light of the above explanation, the interchange of *r* and *l* in the well-known passage of the ŚB— *te' surā he 'laya he' laya iti parābabhūvuḥ*—may be interpreted thus:

(i) "In a passage often repeated in the Brāhmaṇas it is said that the Asuras suffered defeat at the hands of the gods because they mispronounced the word *arayaḥ* as *alayaḥ*. This would suggest that in the later Vedic age, when the word *asura* had lost its original meaning and became a general term of opprobrium, the propensity of the easterners to pronounce *l* for *r* was noticed and frowned upon by the orthodox Aryans." Or,

(ii) "It may mean that the Asuras referred to were none but those of the incoming Aryans who, being of a particular group with its particular phonetic laws, not only retained the IE *l*, but also made it the representative of IE *r*. In short, the behaviour of *l* and *r* in the Ṛgveda suggests as clearly that the invading Aryans were not quite homogeneous in speech as the increase of *l* at the expense of *r* suggests increasing eastern influence on the Vedic language" (Vedic Age, 1951, p. 335). As a result we have two roots from one original root; e.g.,

(i)	*dar* and *dal* < *dṛ*	(vii)	*pru* (ṚV)	: *plu*
(ii)	*rūp* (ṚV) *lūp* (AV)	(viii)	*puru*	: *pulu*
(iii)	*rap* (ṚV) *lap* (AV)	(ix)	√*mruc*	: √*mluc*
(iv)	*rambh* and *lambh*	(x)	√*prus*	: √*plus*
(v)	*car* and *cal*	(xi)	*caram*	: *calaṃ*
(vi)	*ruc* and *luc*	(xii)	*sahamura*	: *sahamula*
		(xiii)	*jargur*	: *jargul*

This tendency is found as a dialectal variation as well:

Udicya [North-Western] Early Vedic	Prācya *(madhya)* [Midland and eastern] Late and post Vedic
pravate	*plavate*
raghu	*laghu*
rambhate	*lambhate*
rihanti	*lihanti*
roman	*loman*
rohita	*lohita*
śrīra, śrila	*Ślīla*

Though the ṚV has a general tendency for *r*, the MS has a general preference for *l* over *r*. The AB has a number of case of *r* (*uruka, bahura*) for more usual *l (uluka, bahula)*. In the Gṛyasūtras and Dharmasūtras this tendency continued; e.g.,

graspa 'tuft of grass' (PG. I.15.4): *glaspa* (AG. I.14.4)
pleṅgha (ApDh. I.11, 31.16) for *preṅgha* 'swing'.
jvar : *jval* (Kathāsarit. 5.118.122)

Though at a later time the frequency of occurrence of *l* increased and replaced some ṚV *r* in some words, it never competed with *r* in general.

As regards the choice between *r* and *l*, no definite rule can be ascertained in Sanskrit. Apparently it can be interpreted that the retention of *r* and *l* in Sanskrit is a matter of dialectal admixture, and it is also found that in one of the dialects of Middle Indo-Aryan, i.e., in Magadhi, the *r* is replaced by *l*. And so in Sanskrit we can say that some dialects have changed Indo-Iranian *r* into *l* either totally or under certain conditions not yet known to us. In fact, it can be said that in Sanskrit the existence of *r* and *l* side by side represents dialectal variations (hence the dictum *ra-layor abhedaḥ*).

Even the Fortunatov's Law is not fully operative with regard to *r* and *l*. The Fortunatov's Law says that in the combinations of Indo-European *l* and a following dental or *s*, the *l* disappeared and the following dental is cerebralized, whereas the Indo-European *r* under similar circumstances remains unchanged. Though this rule was accepted by many, but some scholars believed that the cerebralization of dental are due to Prakrit influence. Examples are:

l + dental > cerebralized	*r* + dental > remains unchanged
**paltos* > Skt. *paṭas*, OSl, *platīno*,	**qérto* > Skt. *kartāmi* (Epic),
Rus. *polotnó*,	Cl. Skt. *kṛntāmi*,
Skt. *paṭa-lam*,	Lith. *kertu*.
Gk. πε϶λτη, Icl. *Feld*	**u̯értō* > Skt. *vartāmi*, (Epic),
**paltus* > Skt. *paṭus*	*Varte*, Lat. *vertō*,
cf. Gk. *Platus*	Goth. *watra l*,
**bhāls > Skt. bhāṣṭe, bhaṣati,* (bricks),	*-rs* > Skt. *varś*,
Lith. balsas,	Gk. *ersē*
Icl. *bjalla*, Eng. bell	
-lth >Skt. *jaṭhara*,	
Goth. *kilthei*	

Though Fortunatov's Law is quite operative in many cases, there are exceptions where this law is not operative, a least, it is seen when IE *l* + dental developed into *r* + dental (or *r* + *t*) the law is not operative; *e.g.*, *jartu* side by side with *jaṭhara*, and this is connected with Gothic *kilthei*. Similarly, the IE *l* + dental did not disappear in Gk. *lélson* which is connected with Sanskrit *kar ṣu*. Some more exceptions are also noticed:

Skt. *kāṭa-s* (mat)	kartana (spinning)
	cf. Gk καpr*os*
Skt. *kaṭús* (sharp)	**kartus (cf.* Lith. *kartus)*
Skt. *naṭa-s* (dancer, actor)	*nartakas* (dancer)
	nṛtyāmi (I dance)
Skt. *bhaṭa-s* (soldier)	*bhṛtas* (hired)
	cf. Gk θε'ρω

Besides these, there are cases where the original dentals were cerebralized, which are explained as nothing but the influence of Prakrit; e.g.,

Skt. *aṭāmi* (I roam) Vedic *atāmi*
bhṇāmi (I speak) Vedic *bhānāmi*

From the above discussions, it appears that there has always been an interchange between *r* and *l*. This interchange is possible, apart from dialectal differences, where the place of utterance and the manner of pronunciation are the same. *l* is dental, and therefore we can assume that *r* was also dental in the primitive IE stage and also in the Proto-Indo-Aryan stage. This tendency is reflected in the Vedic Sanskrit and also in the Middle Indo-Aryan, particularly in Prakrit. That is why the treatment of *r* + *l* has a twofold function. In one group, mainly in the Western, *r* + *t* > *tt* (assimilated) and in the other mainly in the Eastern, *r* + *t* > *ṭṭ* (cerebralized). This twofold function of *r* + *t* is clearly noticed in Prakrit. In one group, as recorded by Hemacandra (1088-1172 AD) in his Prakrit grammar, under the *dhūrtādi*-class (II.30), *r* + *t* is assimilated as *tt,* e.g., *dhūrta* > *dhutta, kīrti* > *kitti; vārtā* > *vattā, āvartana* > *āvattaṇa, kārtika* > *kāttia, kartari* > *kattarī, mūrti* > *mūrta* > *mutta, muhūrta* > *muhutta.* In the other group *r* + *t* becomes ṭṭ (cerebralized probably under the influence of the cerebral sound *r),* e.g., *pravartate* > *payaṭṭai, vartula* > *vaṭṭula, nṛtyati*> *naṭṭai, kāivarta* > *kevaṭṭa* and so on. Even the cases of *r*+ *d* > *ḍḍ* are cerebralized, e.g., *kaparda* > *kavaḍḍa, gardabha* > *gaḍḍaha.* This difference in the treatment of *r* + *t* may be explained from the point of view of the pronunciation of *r.* When *r* was dental in a particular area, there was a case of simple assimilation, as *kīrti* > *kitti* above. But gradually when the pronunciation of *r* was changed into cerebral, the combination of *r* + *t* became cerebralized, as *vartate* > *vaṭṭai* above.

It is difficult to ascertain the place where *r* was dental

and the exact time of this change of pronunciation into cerebral. The fact that Kātyāyana (250 BC) has made a Vārtika like *ṛ-ḷ-varṇayor mithaḥ sāvarṇyaṃ vācyam* (under Pā I.1.9), shows that he, at least, noticed this difference and prescribed it as a grammatical rule by making them homogeneous. Pāṇini (4th century BC) has a sūtra *ato l-rāntasya* (VII.2.2) which states that "a is lengthened *(vṛddhi)* when it is followed immediately by the final *r* or *l* of a root in the *s*-aorist of active voice *(parasmaipada)*." For example, *kṣar* > *a-kṣār-īt, jval* > *a-jvāl-īt*. This treatment of roots ending in *r* or *l* may be due to the fact that they are homogeneous by nature. By the time PŚ was composed *r* became a cerebral sound *(syur mūrdhanyā-ṛ-ṭu-ra-ṣāḥ)* and by the time of Candragomin seventh century AD) *r* became completely cerebralized as he has a sūtra—*mūrdhā ṛ-ṭu-ra-ṣāṇām* [Sū No. 6].

From all these facts mentioned above we are actuated to conclude that *r* was dental in Sanskrit, at least, in the primitive Indo-Aryan stage (as reflected in the earlier evidences), and in course of time it became cerebral, and hence the interchanges between *r* and *l*, and the dictum *ra-layor abhedhaḥ*.

Let us take the case of semi-vowel (Antaḥsthaḥ)

Antaḥsthaḥ, a term applied to the semi-vowels *ya, ra, la, va* being between or in the midst; a standing between vowels and consonants and being formed by a slight contact of the vocal organs *(īśatspṛṣṭam antaḥsthānām)*; or they stand between *sparśa (ka-ma)* letters and *uṣman (śa, ṣa, sa, ha)*.

Antar tiṣṭhatīti antaḥsthaḥ—Sounds which are in between *(antar)* plosives and sibilants are semi vowels or semi-consonants. Both the names are possible although the semi-vowel is more prominent than the other.

It is not a definition of either *antaḥstha varṇa* or semi-vowel but it is the positional reference of the consonantal positions. Sometimes when the definition could not be given generally, the positional reference is mentioned. The same happens also in Greek and Latin alphabets. As for example, in Greek, normally the third letter, i.e. *ga, da* and *ba* are regarded as 'messon' (meaning middle sound) because in Greek and Latin alphabet *k,* g, *ng (ṇ)* are in the third position of the alphabetic systems. So it is also a positional description.

Description of the sound

The semi-vowels are according to Sanskrit alphabet *y, r, l, v, y* is generally pronounced as *ia,* so in *ia* originally it is a mixture of two sounds in pronunciation but when that sound is *saṃprasāraṇa* (weak grade) it is *i* only, that means, *a* is dropped in the pronunciation. So the *i* is regarded as consonant because it is included in the consonant system but actually it is a sort of a vowel and that is why its name is a semi-vowel. The Americans consider it as a semi-consonant also because it belongs to the consonantal system.

Conclusion

The study of all the Prātiśākhyas will reveal the fact that the descriptions of all the sounds are not the same in all the Prātiśākhyas. If the Prātiśākhyas are not composed at a particular time, rather at different times, then it is true to say that they have recorded the different pronunciation of the sound-system as was current at that time. This helps to understand the growth and development of the sound-systems. Another important feature is the manner of articulation. The description of the tongue at the time of uttering the sounds—what is the position of the tongue, when the sound is produced? In so remote antiquity, this is the Prātiśākhya, which describes this procedure which is the subject of modern Phonetics. The other parts of the phonetics, such as accent, ablaut, *sandhi* and some phonetic variations like Anaptysis, Metathesis etc. are straightforward. In fine, I can say that a comprehensive and comparative study of all the Prātiśākhyas is a *sine qua non,* so that we can understand the growth and development of all the sound-systems of Old Indo-Aryan.

References

1 Taken from my article published in the Bulletin of the Department of Comparative Philology and Linguistics, vol. X, 1987.

2. Inverted portion is from my previous article. In all the places inverted portion is from the said article.

S. Varma, *Critical Studies in the Phonetic Observations of Indian Grammarians,* London, 1929 (also reprinted by Munshiram Manohar Lal Publishers, Delhi, 1961, p. 8).

26

SANDHIKĀRIKĀ: AN UNPUBLISHED LAKṢAṆA TEXT

Nabanarayan Bandyopadhyay

The Vedas are to be studied along with its six ancillary texts (. . . *ṣaḍaṅgo vedo'dhyeyo jñeyaśca*). The Lakṣaṇa-granthas or texts which define the characteristics and describe the special features of Vedic texts are generally termed Veda-lakṣaṇa, especially found in the South Indian Vedic tradition. They are of ancillary nature and generally classified under Vedāṅga, a few of them more precisely under the śikṣā and Pratiśākhya (*prātiśākhyaṃ nāma lakṣaṇam praṇīyate*— Gopālayajvan in *Tribhāṣyaratna*). The Veda-lakṣaṇas or 'nomenclative grammatical works' according to Suryakanta, a highly interesting field of Vedic grammar, are of multifaceted importance. Such texts are not only interesting from the point of view of the preservation of Vedic texts but are also very instructive for an understanding of the various devices or methods of learning that were exclusively developed for this purpose and also for knowledge of the various aspects of the history of the transmission of Vedic texts, grammar and linguistics. To attain the goal of perfect preservation of the sacred texts, a sound knowledge of pronunciation techniques is required. To name a few works on them: *Akṣaralakṣaṇaparibhāṣā, Ṛgveda-pada-ratna, Atharva-kautsa-vyākaraṇa, Sāmasaptalakṣaṇa,* etc. can be highly considered.

Out of the four categories of the Veda-lakṣaṇa texts which

are as follows:

(1) works on Vedic phonetics, phonology and grammar, the first branch of linguistics to attain independent status,
(2) works on Anukramaṇī-s,
(3) works containing lists of words having peculiar characteristics in the Vedic texts, and
(4) works dealing mainly with modes of recitation.

Maximum importance has to be attached to the first category.

Tradition of oral transmission—from teacher to pupil, from early times to the present day, is most important, since it is the only method recognized as authentic and authoritative so far as the preservation of the sacred texts is concerned. Attempting for preservation of the sacred texts in a strictly oral tradition, not only the words but also their correct articulation led to an inquiry into the production of the sounds of speech. Towards the end of the Vedic period there were three branches of linguistic study, phonetics (śikṣā), etymology (nirukta) and grammar (vyākaraṇa) but as observed by Jan Gonda, their oldest systematical works have not survived the hazards of oral tradition. Grammar was linked with the ritual duties of the priests who developed it. Phonetics were the basis for the other two branches : as a matter of fact, phonetics and phonology are taken for granted by all authorities of etymology and grammar.

Śikṣā and Pratiśakhya are the two main categories that constitute the sources of Indian phonetics. Śikṣā, dealing with the science of phonetics of the Vedas, occupies a very important position in the Lakṣaṇas for facilitating easy learning and memorization. Some peculiar but very useful devices have been applied from time immemorial which are now practiced even today by following traditional system of education. Śikṣā texts deal with besides place of utterance of sounds, rules for correct articulation, etc., word-isolate system called padapāṭha ascribed to Śākalya. The phonetic teaching necessary for Vedic studies is embodied in the Prātiśākhya which actually is based on early Śikṣā tradition as may be found in the Brāhmaṇas and Āraṇyakas. As a matter of fact, both act as an aid to analytical study of Vedic recensions.

Importance of the study of the Lakṣaṇa texts

Suryakanta in the preface of the *Laghuṛktantrasaṃgraha and Sāmasaptalakṣaṇa* opined,

> "In the introduction to my Atharva-Prātiśakhya I proposed the twofold development of Prātiśakhya and suggested an early origin for the nomenclative grammatical literature. This literature, though very vast in extent and potential in its bearing on the history of early Vedic grammar, has not yet been even critically treated either in Europe or India." (p. 3).

So we understand that the methodological and didactic aspect of Vedic phonetic and grammatical tradition is yet to be thoroughly and systematically investigated in modern Vedic scholarship and research. A recent study reveals that there are about 200 Śikṣā-like (out of 1619 entries in Aithal's book) treatises which have not so far received that amount of serious attention of the scholars which they deserved. Very few of them have come out only in the form of popular editions, not in critically edited shape.

Although the importance of the *padapāṭha* i.e. word-for-word-recitation, has been recognized, we know that it has neither been systematically studied or researched upon, nor there is a proper edition as it is recited by traditional pundits. Fortunately enough, some facts have been observed by the traditional reciters and also carefully recorded in the manuscript copies of the *padapāṭha.*

Since these are not yet been noticed by modern editors, there is ample scope for a reverification of an important genre of literature dealing with the ancient science of Vedic phonetics. We do hope with the search and corresponding analysis of manuscript materials a great amount of knowledge-system reposed in Vedalakṣaṇa texts might come to light and even might prove helpful in breathing fresh life in the systems of recitation of many Śākhā-Saṃhitās facing extinction.

In view of the importance of this vast material for the study of Vedic texts and the unsatisfactory, meagre amount of work done so far, an attempt involving search of hitherto undiscovered and/or unexplored manuscripts and their subsequent serious analysis with deliberations on and critical analysis of the theme proposed, might be made to enable ourselves to benefit by uncovering the knowledge of the Vedic texts in modern as well as traditional manner.

Though several general as well as particular studies and dissertations have been made on the Prātiśākhya and the Śikṣā keeping their comparative and historical perspective in mind, yet there is a dearth of publication of critically edited Vedalakṣaṇa texts on the basis of extant manuscripts. The fact that literary manuals generally tend to neglect these works or passing remarks given even by the most recent histories of literature the bare fact remains very evident that these texts or works seem to have failed to attract the attention of modern scholars. A large number of texts belonging to this genre of literature are still lying unknown to us as shown in the monumental descriptive bibliography of works of Vedic Ancillary literature titled *Veda-Lakṣaṇa* prepared by K. P. Aithal in 1991, where a categorical list of Lakṣaṇa texts is given furnishing the title of the mostly unpublished/less known texts awaiting to be critically edited. He himself proposed to edit the following unpublished śikṣā texts (see Introduction, p. 20):

Amoghānandinī-śikṣā, Ātreya-śikṣā, Āraṇya-(ka-)śikṣā Savyākhyā, Kālanirṇaya-śikṣā Savyākhyā, Kauśiki-śikṣā, Cārāyaṇīya-śikṣā, Pāriśikṣā Savyākhyā, Yohi-prāpti(-śikṣā), Lakṣmīkānta-śikṣā, Laugākṣi-śikṣā, Varṇakrama-śikṣā, Vāsiṣṭhi-śikṣā(1), Vāsiṣṭhi-śikṣā(2), Śaṃbhu-śikṣā, Sarva-saṃmata-śikṣā Savyākhyā, Siddḥānta-śikṣā Savyākhyā, Svara-vyañjana-śikṣā, śikṣā-samuccaya.

In the mean time, some of the texts from the above list have already been published or waiting for publication, for example, Kālanirṇaya-śikṣā, Pāriśikṣā Savyākhyā, Sarva-saṃmata-śikṣā, Yohi-prāpti(-śikṣā), etc. The author of this paper has undertaken the editing of the Kauśiki-śikṣā (see his paper, "Phonetic Observation in the Kausikasiksa", 2010).

After the publication of this volume by Aithal, a plethora of manuscripts of this type of texts has also been discovered through huge survey done by National Mission for Manuscripts. The following important printed texts just before or after the publication of *Veda-Lakṣaṇa* by Aithal may be referred to for the interested scholars:

1. *Svaramañjarī of Śrī Narasiṃhasūri*, ed., G.V. Devasthali, BORI, Poona, 1985.
2. *Cāturjñānam of Śrī Rāvaṇa* (with the comm. 'Vaidika'), ed. Śrī Janārdana Pāṇḍeya, Sampurnanand Sanskrit University, Varanasi, 1992.
3. *Śaunakaśikṣā*: (Text with com. of K.N.M.Divakaran Namboothiri); *Tāṇṭam, Bahvṛcahastalakṣaṇadīpikā*, K.V. Vasudevan; *Vedavikṛtivivaraṇa*, P.M.Damodaran Namboothirippad; *Sūktaślokāḥ* (with comm. of Kompamkulam Vishnu Namboothiri); *Trisandhā*, K.P. Krishnan Bhattathiripad; *Vedapāṭhanādhyāya-saṅgraha, Sarvānukramaṇī-padyavivaraṇa*, K.P. Krishnan Bhattathiripad; *Sarvānukramaṇīvyākhyā*, Akkithan Narayana Namboothiri; *Nānābhedaprakaśinī*, K.M. Vasudevan Namboothiri; In: *Preservation Techniques of the Ṛgveda Chanting of Kerala*, ed., C.M. Neelakandhan & K.A. Ravindran, Vedic Studies, Sree Sankaracharya University of Sanskrit, Kalady, Kerala, 2010.
4. *Veda-Padapātha-carcā* by K.V. Abhyankar, *Upalekha-sūtram of Bhāradvāja-Bṛhaspati*, ed. by him with

explanation, BORI, Poona, 1974.

5. *Gāyatravidhānasūtra of Shuṅga* (with an anonymous comm.), ed. B.R. Sharma, Vishveshvaranand Institute, Hoshiarpur, 1971.
6. *Mātrālakṣaṇa* (with trans., exp., notes, etc.), Wayne Howard, IGNCA, New Delhi, in association with MLBD, 1988.
7. Atharvavedīyā Pañcapaṭalikā (with Hindi trans.), ed., Bhagawaddatta, Meharchand Lachhmandas Publications, New Delhi, 1920, 1985 (reprt).
8. *Charaṇavyūhasūtra* (with comm. of Mahidāsa), ed., Umesh Chandra Sharma, Viveka Publications, Aligarh.
9. *Bhāṣikasūtra of Maharṣi Kātyāyana* (with comm. Mahāsvāmin and Anantabhaṭṭa), ed., B.B. Chaubey, VVBIS & IS, Hoshiarpur, 1975.
10. *Vedavikṛtilakṣaṇa*-Saṃgraha, comp. and ed., K.V. Abhyankar and G.V. Devasthali, BORI, 1978.
11. *Ṛgvidhāna*, trans. and ed., M. Bala Krishna Reddy, pub. M. Suman Kumari, Puttaparthy, Andhra Pradesh, 2011.
12. *Yajurvidhānasūtra of Kāgtyāyana* (with comm. Sādhanā), ed., Rameshchandra Dash Sharma, Manyata Prakashan, New Delhi, 2004.
13. *Śukla-Yajurvidhānasūtra with comm. by Kālanātha*, ed., K.P. Annashastri, Chaukhamba Vidyabhavan, Varanasi, 2001 (reprt).
14. *Vedic Tantrism, A Study of Ṛgvidhāna of Śaunaka* (with text and trans.), ed., M.S. Bhat, MLBD, Delhi,1987.
15. *Pratihārasūtra with vṛtti by Varadarāja*, ed., B.R. Sharma, Kendriya Sanskrit Vidyapeetha, Tirupati, 1973.
16. *Pañcavidhasūtra and Mātrālakṣaṇa* (with comm.), ed., B.R. Sharma, Kendriya Sanskrit Vidyapeetha, Tirupati, 1970.
17. *Lakṣaṇacandrikā*, (a comm. on the Tait. Prāti by Mahīdeva Rāmachandra Gadre), ed., Nirmala Ravindra Kulkarni, Bharatiya Kala Prakashan, Delhi, 2004.

18. *Taittirīya Prātiśākhya* (with comm. of Māhiṣeya and Hindi explanation by Sushil Kumar Pathak), ed., Jamuna Pathak, Choukhamba Skt. Series Off., Varanasi, 2007 (Sankrit).
19. *Ṛgveda-Prātiśākhya* (with Bengali trans. and exp.), Amar Kumar Chattopadhyay, Sanskrit Pustak Bhandar, 2008 (I-V, X, XVI-XVIII, Paṭalas, 2007).
20. *Kauṇḍinya Śikṣā*, ed. P.S. Ramachandradu, Sanskrit Academy, Osmania University, Hyderabad, 1980.
21. *Puṣpasūtra*, 2 vols.,(with trans. by G.H. Tarlekar), IGNCA and MLBD, 2001.
22. *Pāṇinīya Śikṣā* (with Bengali trans.), ed., Pradip Kumar Ghosh, Anveshan Prakashani, Kolkata, 1394 (BS).
23. *Nāradīya Śikṣā* (with Bengali comm.), ed., Pradip Kumar Ghosh, Research Institute of Indian Musicology, 2010.
24. *Śikṣā Śāstra of Pāṇini* (with Sans. and Hindi comm. of Udayanācārya), Ramlal Kapur Trust, Revali, Sonipat, 2008.
25. *Akṣaratantra* (with vṛtti), ed., Shri Krishan Sharma, Nirmal Book Agency, Kurukshetra, 2010.
26. Yajñavalkyaśikṣā (with Sans.& Hindi comm.), Naresh Jha, Chaukhamba Surabharati Prakashan, 2010.
27. *Atharvavedīyā Māṇḍukīśikṣā*, ed., Bhagawaddatta, Meharchand Lachhmandas Publications, New Delhi, revised 2009.
28. *Śaunakīya Ṛgvedaprātiśākhya* (I-IV & XVI Paṭalas), ed., Taraknath Adhikari, Sanskrit Book Depot, Kolkata, 2009.
29. *Nāradīyaśikśā* (with Sanskrit comm by Shivraja Ācārya Kauṇḍinyāyaya, Chowkhamba Vidyabhavan, Varanasi, 2008.
30. *Śikṣā-Mahābhāṣya* (Pāṇīni & Āpiśali Śikṣā), ed. Gayatri Devi, Chaitrarshi, Bahvrich, UP, 1985.
31. *Pāṇinīyaśikṣā* (with Sans. com. & Hindi trans.), ed., Balakrishna Sharma & Shrinivas Rath, Kalidasa

Academy, Ujjain, 2050 (VS).

32. *Kauṇḍinyāyana-Śikṣā* (with comm.), Shivraja Ācārya Kauṇḍinyāyana Chaukhamba Vidyabhavan, Varanasi, 2009.

33. *Śaunakīya Caturādhyāyikā: A Prātiśākhya of the Śaunakīya Atharvaveda with the commentaries Caturādhyāyībhāṣya, Bhārgava-Bhāskara-Vṛtti and Pañcasandhi,* ed. Madhav Deshpande, Harvard Univ. Press, 1997.

The valuable information gathered so far may be utilized for the purpose of editing, study and research. This is very unfortunate that this is the most neglected field and if it is not done now, there is always the fear of leaving the job undone for ever.

Steps undertaken for the Study

In view of the above reasons, the School of Vedic Studies, Rabindra Bharati University, Kolkata, organized a national seminar on " Vedalakṣaṇa texts: Search and Analysis" under the auspices of National Mission for Manuscripts, IGNCA, New Delhi and had undertaken a major research project on 'The Ancillary Texts on Vedic Phonetics'.

Unpublished Texts and Sandhikārikā

As a part of this project, I selected an unpublished text entitled Sandhikārikā along with a gloss (*svopajña vṛtti*) for editing, based on a single manuscript (G 6173) available in the Asiatic Society, Kolkata. The name of the author is probably Gaṇeśa-datta as noted in the front folio. It is a work on Sandhi (euphonic combination) in 31 verses with author's own commentary called Dīpa-Kalikā. The examples of Sandhi have been given mainly from the Vājasaneyi-Saṃhiṭā of the Śukla Yajurveda. It is a complete text (containing 40 folios) written in Devanāgari script of the nineteenth century, and the material is handmade paper.

The condition of the manuscript is fair (size 15.5 × 7 cm).

Beginning of the text with commentary:

vande gaṇeśacaraṇadvandvaṃ vidyaikasādhanam/
siddhibuddhipradātāraṃ bhaktasarvārthasādhanam//
sarasvatīṃ gurūṃścaiva yājñavalkyādikān munīn/
vande sandhikārikāyāṃ vyākhyāṃ kurve yathāmati//
(fol.1b):

iha khalu vyākaraṇaśāstreṣu mandādhikāriṇāṃ vaidikānāṃ sugamasandhijñānārthaṃ sandhikārikām ārabhate/tatra maṅgalapūrvakaṃ prathamaślokaḥ (fol.2a)

First śloka of the text:

natvā śrigaṇanāthasya caraṇaṃ vedavarṇitam/
bālāṇāṃ sukhabodhārthaṃ kurve'haṃ sandhikārikām//
(fols. 2a-2b)

End of the text:

imāṃ sandhikārikāṃ ca vicārantīha vaidikāḥ/
sandhijñānaṃ bhavet teṣāṃ śighram eva tu niścitam//
(fol. 39a)

End of the comm:

iti ślokasyāsyārthasya spaṣṭārthaṃ //6// (fol. 39a)

Colophon

iti śrīgaṇeśadattasandhikārikā di[di]*pakalikā samāptaṃ/* [ptā]/
śubhaṃ. bhavatu// (fol.39b)

Other Texts on Sandhi

There is also a text 'Sandhikārikā' referred to in the descriptive catalogue of the Sanskrit Manuscripts in the Tanjore Maharaja Serfoj's Saraswati Mahal Library, Tanjore, but no details are available and another text Sandhiprakaraṇa on the Sandhi of Vedic words in Malayalam with Sanskrit quotations (See TCD 30-E). Other type of works on Sandhi is Sandhi-gāṇa-pada-gāna and Sandhyuccāraṇa-lakṣaṇa (see Aithal, entries 1362 and 1364 respectively).

Concept of Sandhi

Actually speaking, the concept of Saṃhitā and Sandhi goes back to very early period. We know that there are two modes of Vedic recitation–Prakṛti and Vikṛti. To the former mode belong the Saṃhita, Pada and Kramapāṭhas–*nirbhuja, pratṛṇṇa* and *ubhayam antareṇa* respectively, according to the Aitareya Āraṇyaka (III.1.3):

yaddhi sandhiṃ vivartayati tannirbhujasya rūpam, etc.

This is repeated in the Ṛk-Prātiśākhya:

sandher vivartanaṃ nirbhujaṃ vadanti śauddhākṣaroccāraṇaṃ ca pratṛṇṇam etc.

Without proper knowledge of Sandhi (also called morphophonetics in linguistics), Saṃhitāpāṭha cannot be pursued. But it is difficult to comprehend the rules of Sandhi at places. Various Pṛātiśakhyas and Vyākaraṇas throw light on these rules. Still writing of the texts of ancillary character was felt necessary for easy understanding and memorization of the rules in verse-form by the students of the Vedas.

Some Definitions

At the outset of the commentary some well-known definitions about the alphabets have been given:

tatra akāra-ākāra ityādi aṃ aḥ ityantāḥ ṣoḍaśasvarāḥ/
eṣāṃ madhye viśeṣaḥ// e ai o au iti sandhyakṣarasaṃjñā//
tataḥ kakārādikṣkāraparyantaṃ vyañjanasaṃjñā.

Then the definitions viz, sparśa, antaḥstha, uṣman, etc. have been mentioned.

The second kārikā runs thus:

akārākārayoḥ sandhir vyatyayo dīrghatāṃ ca na/
ikāre etvam āpnoti ukāre otvam eva ca//

a/ā + *a/ā* = *ā* (Pāṇinisūtra (Pā)-*akaḥ savarṇe dīrghaḥ*); e.g. *pra* + *arpayatu* = *prārpayatu.* This type of sandhi is lengthening (*Dīrghīkaraṇa*), but *a/ā* + *i* = *e;* e.g. *ā* + *idaṃ* = *edaṃ* etc.; *a/ā* + *u* = *o* (*Guṇīkaraṇa–ādguṇaḥ* Pā. 6.1.87). The system of discussing euphonic combination systematically starts with *a, i, u, ṛ, l, e, ai, o, au,* etc. (e.g. *a/ā* + *a/ā,a/ā* + *i/ ī, a/.ā* + *u/ū, a/ā* + *ṛ/ḷ, a/ā* + *e/ai,a/ā* + *o/au, aṃ* + *k, kh* etc., *aḥ* + *k, kh* etc.). As per treatment of the topics concerned we find all kinds of linguistic features like Vowelization, Devocalization (*Aghoṣīkaraṇa*), Vocalization (*Ghoṣīkaraṇa*), Aspiration (*Mahāpṛāṇikaraṇa*), Nasalization, Assimilation, Palatalization, Cerebralization, Progressive Assimilation, Regressive Assimilation, De-assibilation, Assibilation (*uṣmīkaraṇa*), Dissimilation, Shortening, Augmentation/ Intrusion, Elision, Doubling, Ceasura, etc. We may recall the famous line of Vājasaneyi-Prātiśākhya: *svarasaṃskārayoś-chandasi niyamaḥ.* Here all those operations relate to *saṃskāra.*

Few Extracts from the Text

It will not be out of place if we quote some kārikās from the text. Regarding *Yaṇ* and *Pragṛhya sandhi* it has been said:

ikāro yatvam āpnoti akārādi svare pare /
pragṛhyavarjam ikāre pare ced dīrghatām iyāt// 5// (fols 8b–9a)
ekāraukārayoścaiva akāre paraṭaḥ sthite /
lopayeti saṃhitāyāṃ kvacin netīha vai sphuṭam // 8// (fol. 11b) (e.g. *te'vantu*) (Here is a case of *abhinidhāna*).
yaralaveṣu savarṇatvaṃ sānunāsikatāṃ ca vai /
śaṣasaharakāreṣu guṃkāratvaṃ yājuḥṣu ca //12//(fol.15b)

In some cases where Vedic examples are not available some *laukika* examples have been given; e.g.

vācaḥ khalati laukikodāharaṇam/ tathaiva // vājaśca . . . yaste kasya //laukikaṃ// kvacin naivetyasyodāharaṇaṃ / (fol. 20a).

Some other comments read—*sarvatrodāharaṇābhāvāt yāni kānicitlikhyate/* (22b). Some variations according to Mādhyandina or Kāṇva have also been noted: *saḥ/ imā/ semā/ mādhyandinīyānām udāharaṇam/ saḥ auṣadhīḥ// sauṣadhīḥ* (22b–23a). Examples may be sought from other sources: *sarvatodāharaṇābhāvād anyatrānusandheyaṃ* (25a). Special treatment in Kāṇvaśākḥā–*yatra ḍakārasya ḷakāraḥ/ dvitvekṣare pare tu neti/ kāṇvaśākhiṇāṃ tvayaṃ viśeṣāṃ// nātvitareṣāṃ kvacinyaśakhināṃ tu anusvāraṃ guṃ? kāra na bha(va)ti(tī) ślokārthaḥ// . . . dvitvapare tu vīdvaṅgaḥ/* (fol. 32b–33a) Regarding doubling it has been analysed:

rephahakārābhyāṃ pare vyañjanaḥ dvirbhāratvaṃ prāpnoti / nanu uttaravākye nāsmin dvibḥāvatvam / siddhe sati kimartham uktaḥ rephahakāraparam iti cet tatrāha pūrvavākyasya vyañjanaparatvaṃ// aparavākyasya tu sparśaparatvam/ ataḥ rephahakārau sparśo'pi vyañjanāntabhāvān naiva doṣaḥ// etc. (fols 33b–34a)

Some kārikās have been taken from Yājñavalkya Śikṣā or any earlier source, such as definition of *Svarabhakti* (Yāj. Śikṣā, 13)

kāriṇī kurviṇī cai(va) hariṇī hāriṇī tatḥā/
tavaddhaṃsapaḍā nāma pañcaitā svarabhaktayaḥ //
kariṇī rahayor yoge kurviṇī lahakārayoḥ /
hariṇī raśayor yoge hāriṇī laśakāarayoḥ //
yā tu haṃsāḍūḍā nāma sā tu rephaṣakārayoḥ // etc. (fol. 38a)

Conclusion

Though the text is probably of late origin and the personal history and date of the author Ganeśa-datta are unknown, the importance of the text is not the less for learning basic features of Vedic euphonic combination. If the text with the gloss is critically edited on the basis of the available manuscripts, it will be of much help to the student of Vedic grammar. It has aptly been stated in the Ṛk-prātiśākhya:

padakramavibhāgajño varṇakramavicakṣaṇaḥ /
svaramātrāviśeṣajño gacched ācāryasampadam//

Bibliography

Bandyopadhyay, Nabanarayan. 2010. "Phonetic Observation in the Kauśikaśikā," *Studies on the Śikṣās and the Prātiśākhyas*, ed. Bhagyalata Pataskar, Adarsha Sanskrit Shodha Samstha (Vaidik Samshodhana Mandala), Pune.

Chattopadhyay, Amarkumar, ed., 2008. *Ṛgveda-Prātiśākhya* (with Bengali trans. and exp. I–V, X, XVI–XVIII Paṭalas). Kolkata: Sanskrit Pustak Bhandar.

Deshpande, G.T., 2011. *Pre-Paṇinian Grammar.* Mumbai: Popular Prakashan Pvt. Ltd.

Deshpande, Madhav, ed. 1997. *Śaunakiya Caturādhyāyika: A Pratiśakhya of the Śaunakīya Atharvaveda: with the commentaries Caturādhyāyībhāṣya, Bhārgava-Bhāskara-Vṛtti and Pañcasandhi.* Harvard Oriental Series, 52. Cambridge, Mass: Harvard University Press.

Deshpande, Madhav, 2002. *Recitational Permutations of the Śaunakīya Atharvaveda: Critically ed. with an introduction.* Harvard Oriental Series, 61. Cambridge, Mass.: Harvard Univ. Press.

Dwivedi, K.D. 1980. *Bhāṣāvijñāna evam Bhāṣāśāstra.* Varanasi: Vishvavidyalay Prakashan.

Gonda, Jan. 1975. *Vedic Literature*: (Saṃhitās and Brāhmaṇas). A History of Indian Literature Series, Vol 1, Fasc 1. Wiesbaden: Otto Harassowitz.

Parameswara Aithal, Kota, comp. 1991. *Veda-Lakṣaṇa: A descriptive Bibliography = Vedic ancillary literature.* Stuttgart:

Steiner.

Rangacharya, K. and Shama Sastry, R., ed. 1985. *Taittirīya Prātiśākhya* with *Tribhāṣyaratna* of Somayārya and *Vaidikābharaṇa* of Gargya Goppāla-yajvan. Delhi: Motilal Banarsidass. (Reprint of Mysore Government Oriental Library Series 33, 1906).

Sarma, Kundanlal. 1983. *Vedāṅga: Vaidik Vāṅmay ka Bṛhad Itihāsa.* Hoshiarpur: Vishvesvaranand Vedic Research Institute.

Sastri, C. Sankararama, ed. 1994. *Aṣṭādhyāyī Sūtrapāṭha.* Delhi: Sharada Publishing House.

Scharfe, Hartmut. 1977. *Grammatical Literature.* Wiesbaden: Otto Harassowitz. (A History of Indian Literature, vol. V, fasc 2).

Shastri, Jagadishlal, ed. 1978. *Vājasaneyi-Mādhyandīna-Śukla-Yajurveda-Saṁhitā* (with commentaries of Uvaṭa and Mahīdhara and appendices including Yajñavalkyaśikṣā). Deihi/Patna/Varanasi: Motilal Banarsidass. (Reprint: 1971).

Shastri, Haraprasad. 1923. *A Descriptive Catalogue of Sanskrit Manuscripts in the Government Collection* under the care of the Asiatic Society of Bengal. Vol II: Vedic Manuscripts. Calcutta: The Asiatic Society.

Suryakanta, ed. 1942. *Laghuṛktantrasaṃgraha and Sāmasaptalakṣaṇa.* Lahore: Mehar Chand Lacchman Das.

Tripathi, Rama Prasada, ed. 1989. *Śikṣāsaṃgraha of Yājñavalkya and Others.* Varanasi: Sampurnanand Sanskrt University.

Varma, Siddheshwar. 1961. *Critical Studies in the Phonetic Observations of Indian Grammarians.* Delhi: Munshiram Manoharlal. (Reprint: London: Royal Asiatic Society, 1929).